Clinical Handbook of Co-existing Mental Health and Drug and Alcohol Problems

Co-existing mental health and drug and alcohol problems occur frequently in primary care and clinical settings. Despite this, health professionals rarely receive training in how to detect, assess and formulate interventions for co-existing problems, and few clinical guidelines exist.

This handbook provides an exciting and highly useful addition to this area. Leading clinicians from the UK, the US and Australia provide practical descriptions of assessments and interventions for co-existing problems. These will enable professionals working with co-existing problems to understand best practice and ensure that people with co-existing problems receive optimal treatment. A range of overarching approaches are covered, including:

- working within a cognitive behavioural framework;
- provision of consultation-liaison services, training and supervision;
- individual, group and family interventions; and
- working with rurally isolated populations.

The contributors also provide detailed descriptions of assessments and treatments for a range of disorders when accompanied by drug and alcohol problems, including anxiety, depression, schizophrenia, bipolar disorder and learning difficulties.

The *Clinical Handbook of Co-existing Mental Health and Drug and Alcohol Problems* will enhance clinicians' confidence in working with people with co-existing problems. It will prove a valuable resource for psychologists, psychiatrists, counsellors, social workers and all those working in both primary and secondary care health settings.

Amanda Baker is Associate Professor at the Centre for Mental Health Studies, University of Newcastle, New South Wales, Australia.

Richard Velleman is Professor of Mental Health Research at the University of Bath, UK, and Director of the Mental Health Research & Development Unit, Avon and Wiltshire Mental Health Partnership NHS Trust, UK.

Clinical Handbook of Co-existing Mental Health and Drug and Alcohol Problems

Edited by Amanda Baker and Richard Velleman

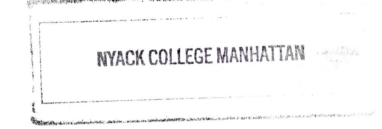

Routledge
Taylor & Francis Group

LONDON AND NEW YORK

First published 2007
by Routledge
27 Church Road, Hove, East Sussex BN3 2FA

Simultaneously published in the USA and Canada
by Routledge
270 Madison Avenue, New York, NY 10016

*Routledge is an imprint of the Taylor & Francis Group,
an informa business*

Typeset in Times by
RefineCatch Limited, Bungay, Suffolk
Printed and bound in Great Britain by
MPG Books Ltd., Bodmin, Cornwall
Paperback cover design by Design Deluxe

This publication has been produced with paper manufactured to
strict environmental standards and with pulp derived from
sustainable forests.

British Library Cataloguing-in-Publication Data
A catalogue record for this book is available from the British Library

Library of Congress Cataloging-in-Publication Data
Clinical handbook of co-existing mental health and drug and alcohol
    problems / edited by Amanda Baker & Richard Velleman.
        p.; cm.
Includes bibliographical references and index.
ISBN13: 978–1–58391–775–6 (hbk)
ISBN10: 1–58391–775–6 (hbk)
ISBN13: 978–1–58391–776–3 (pbk)
ISBN10: 1–58391–776–4 (pbk)
    1. Mental illness—Treatment—Handbooks, manuals, etc. 2.
Substance abuse—Treatment—Handbooks, manuals, etc. I. Baker,
Amanda. II. Velleman, Richard.
    [DNLM: 1. Mental Disorders—complications. 2. Delivery of
Health Care—methods. 3. Mental Disorders—diagnosis. 4. Mental
Disorders—therapy. 5. Substance-Related Disorders—
complications. WM 140 C6407 2006]
    RC480.5C5537 2006
    616.86′0651—dc22

                                                  2006012771

ISBN: 978-1-58391-775-6 (hbk)
ISBN: 978-1-58391-776-3 (pbk)

Contents

SECTION 4
Training, supervision and future directions

Contributors

Mohammed Abou-Saleh: MPhil, PhD, FRCPsych; Professor of Psychiatry and Honorary Consultant in Addiction Psychiatry, Department of Mental Health, St George's and South West Thames Mental Health Trust, UK.

Mohammed was previously Professor and Chairman of the Department of Psychiatry and Behavioural Sciences, Faculty of Medicine and Health Sciences, United Arab Emirates University, and a reader in psychiatry at the University of Liverpool. His research interests include biological psychiatry, dual diagnosis, addiction prevention and psychopharmacology.

Rory Allott: ClinPsyD; Clinical Psychologist, Pennine Care NHS Trust, UK.

Rory has wide research interests including drug prevention and intervention. He has used MI and CBT in a range of health settings, including inpatient, community health and diabetes services. He currently provides integrated motivational interviewing and cognitive behaviour therapy with psychosis and substance misuse.

Andrew Baillie: MPsych (Clin), PhD; Clinical Psychologist, Psychology Department, Macquarie University, Australia.

Andrew is a clinical psychologist whose major research interest is in the treatment of anxiety disorders. He was previously at the National Drug and Alcohol Research Centre, Sydney, in a research capacity.

Amanda Baker: BA (Hons), MPsychol, PhD; Associate Professor, Centre for Mental Health Studies, University of Newcastle, Australia.

Amanda is a clinical psychologist who has practised in mental health and drug and alcohol settings in the UK and Australia for over 20 years. In 2003 Amanda commenced a five-year NHMRC Career Development Award to develop evidence-based practice and trials among people with co-existing mental health and drug and alcohol problems.

Christine Barrowclough: PhD; Professor of Clinical Psychology, School of Psychological Sciences, University of Manchester, UK.

Christine has over 20 years of clinical and research experience in psychological treatments for psychosis. In the past 10 years, along with colleagues in Manchester, she has developed and published work describing the evaluation of specialized approaches for working with people with psychosis and comorbid substance misuse.

Gabrielle Barter: DClinPsy; Clinical Psychologist, Tees, Esk and Wear Valleys NHS Trust, UK.

Gabbie has worked as a research psychologist in the drugs field and clinically with adults with learning disabilities in community and secure forensic settings. She has completed further training in forensic behavioural science and psychotherapy.

Roger Bloor: MD, MPsyMed, FRCPsych; Senior Lecturer in Addiction Psychiatry, Keele University Medical School, UK.

A former Royal Air Force psychiatrist, Roger returned to the NHS 20 years ago as a consultant with special responsibility for drugs and alcohol. In addition to his academic post, he is Medical Director of an NHS Trust.

Sandra Bucci: BSc (Psych) (Hons); BSc (Exercise Science); D PsycholClin; Clinical Psychologist, Psychological Assistance Service, Hunter New England Health Service, Australia.

Sandra is a clinical psychologist working in an early intervention team for young people at ultra high risk of psychosis (PAS). She previously worked in research evaluating cognitive behavioural techniques among people with psychosis and alcohol and other drug problems at the Centre for Mental Health Studies, University of Newcastle.

Vaughan J. Carr: MB, BS, MD, FRCPC, FRANZCP; Professor of Psychiatry, University of Newcastle, Australia; Director, Centre for Mental Health Studies, Newcastle, Australia; Scientific Director, Neuroscience Institute of Schizophrenia and Allied Disorders, Sydney, Australia.

Vaughan is a psychiatrist who has conducted research into schizophrenia and early psychosis, depression, posttraumatic stress, psychiatry in general practice, dual diagnosis, mental health economics and service evaluation.

Jennifer S. Coelho: BSc, MA; PhD; Post-Doctoral Fellow, Faculty of Psychology, Maastricht University, The Netherlands.

Jennifer completed her graduate training in Psychology at the University of Toronto, specializing in Eating and its Disorders. She completed part of her clinical training at the Peter Beaumont Centre for Eating Disorders (Sydney, Australia), and has also worked in the Eating Disorders Program at Toronto General Hospital.

Jennifer M. Connolly: BSc (Hons); School of Medicine, University of Queensland, Australia.

Jennifer Connolly obtained a BSc (Hons) from the University of Queensland in 1998 and has since worked on numerous comorbidity projects while completing her PhD on affect recognition in schizophrenia. Her other research interests include body image and body shape preferences.

Alex Copello: BSc, MSc, PhD; Clinical Director, Substance Misuse Services, Birmingham and Solihull Mental Health Trust, UK; Senior Lecturer, University of Birmingham, UK.

Alex is a consultant clinical psychologist and, in addition to the positions above, is Director of the Birmingham and Solihull Mental Health Trust Applied Addiction Research and Development Programme.

Sarah Corfe: MBChB, MRCPsych; Psychiatry Trainee, St George's Hospital Medical School, UK.

Sarah qualified from Birmingham University in 1993 and is a psychiatry trainee on the St George's training scheme in London. As part of her training she has undertaken both clinical and research work in the field of eating disorders.

Ilana Crome: MD, FRCPsych; Professor of Addiction Psychiatry and Academic Director of Psychiatry, Keele University Medical School, UK.

Ilana has been involved in the field of addiction for 20 years. She is Lead Clinician and Consultant in Addiction for the Young People's Service of North Staffordshire Combined Healthcare NHS Trust. She has played an active role in service development, research, training and policy domains, has published widely and lectures extensively.

Ellen M. Crouse: PhD; Postdoctoral fellow, Neuropsychology Laboratory, Department of Psychiatry, Dartmouth Medical School, USA.

As a graduate student, Ellen was extensively trained in DBT for borderline personality disorder. Currently, she is researching biological markers in neurodegenerative disorders with Dr Andy Saykin at Dartmouth.

Keith M. Drake: New Hampshire-Dartmouth Psychiatric Research Centre, USA.

Keith is an undergraduate studying psychology and biology at Connecticut College. He has aided in research into the treatment of PTSD and social phobia in substance use populations through Dartmouth Medical School. He is pursuing a career in psychology.

Paul Earnshaw: MSc; Mental Health Social Worker and Cognitive Behavioural Therapist, Bolton, Salford and Trafford Mental Health NHS Trust, UK.

Trained in motivational interviewing, Paul is a member of the Motivational Interviewing Network of Trainers. He has research interests and experience in assertive outreach, risk assessment and approved social work.

Mike Fitzsimmons: Cognitive Behaviour Nurse Therapist, Lancashire Care Trust, UK.

Mike has worked in a number of clinical settings, particularly community mental health with a special interest in homelessness. He is currently working as a therapist on the MIDAS trial.

Emma Godfrey: BSc (Hons), MSc; Trainee Clinical Psychologist.

Emma is currently training as a clinical psychologist. She worked as a research psychologist with the COMPASS Programme and was involved in the evaluation of the integrated treatment approaches in assertive outreach and the consultation-liaison service.

Hermine L. Graham: BSc (Hons) Psych, ClinPsyD; Consultant Clinical Psychologist, Birmingham and Solihull Mental Health NHS Trust (BSMHT), UK; Lecturer in Clinical Psychology, School of Psychology, University of Birmingham, UK.

Hermine worked as Head of the COMPASS Programme from its inception in 1998 until 2003. She developed and evaluated this innovative programme. Her clinical and research interests include the role of cognitive therapy and cognitive processes in problem substance use in people with psychosis.

Gillian Haddock: PhD; Professor of Clinical Psychology, School of Psychological Sciences, University of Manchester, UK.

Gillian holds honorary consultant clinical psychologist appointments in Mental Health Trusts in the north-west of England. Her particular interest is in the development and evaluation of psychological treatments for psychosis.

Leanne Hides: BBehSc (Hons), PhD (Clin); Clinical Research Coordinator, Substance Use Research and Recovery Focused (SURRF) Program, ORYGEN Research Centre, University of Melbourne, Australia.

Leanne Hides is a clinical psychologist with expertise in the assessment and treatment of co-occurring mental health and substance use disorders. Her PhD examined the relationship between substance use and psychosis in young people and she has continued developing her research interests in the assessment, formulation and treatment of co-occurring substance use and mental health disorders.

David J. Kavanagh: PhD; Professor, School of Medicine, University of Queensland, Australia.

David has a PhD in psychology from Stanford. He primarily researches the nature and treatment of addictive and mental disorders, especially where they occur together.

Frances J. Kay-Lambkin: BSc (Psych) Hons; PhD; Researcher, Centre for Mental Health Studies, University of Newcastle, Australia.

Frances is a registered psychologist who completed her PhD on developing and disseminating integrated treatments for depression and co-existing alcohol/other drug use problems. She has presented many workshops and training courses on mental health treatments and assessments, with a particular focus on comorbid mental health and alcohol/other drug use problems.

Brian Kelly: BMed, FRANZCP, FAChPM, PhD; Professor of Psychiatry and Director, Centre for Rural and Remote Mental Health, University of Newcastle, Australia.

Brian is a psychiatrist with a clinical and research interest in the mental health problems within the general health care system, and is currently leading the development of a program of rural mental health research, education and service development for rural and remote areas in New South Wales.

J. Hubert Lacey: MD, MPhil, FRCPsych, DipObst; Clinical Director, Eating Disorders Service, St George's Hospital Medical School, UK.

The St George's Eating Disorders Service, of which Hubert is Clinical Director, is the largest in the UK. Hubert is also lead clinician of the Yorkshire Centre for Eating Disorders. After gaining his personal chair, he was made Chairman of the Department of Psychiatry at St George's, University of London. He established the European Council on Eating Disorders. His particular interests are clinical treatment, nutritional aspects of fertility and comorbid variants of eating disorders.

Terry J. Lewin: BCom (Psych Hons); Research Manager, Hunter New England Mental Health, Australia.

Terry is a psychologist who has specialized in research project management in the mental health field for over 20 years. He has been associated with many externally funded research projects and has published widely.

Ian Lowens: Consultant Clinical Psychologist, IMPACT, Salford, UK.

Ian works in an early intervention team in Salford. He has a special interest in combining motivation interviewing and cognitive therapy approaches.

Dan I. Lubman: BSc (Hons), MB ChB, PhD, FAChAM, FRANZCP; Senior Lecturer and Consultant Psychiatrist, SURRF Program, ORYGEN Research Centre, University of Melbourne, Australia.

Dan Lubman leads a clinical research team focused on investigating substance use and comorbidity in youth. He is involved in a number of pharmacological and psychological treatment trials, as well as an innovative cross-sectoral clinical program addressing comorbidity in young people.

Mark P. McGovern: PhD; Associate Professor, Department of Psychiatry, Dartmouth Medical School, USA; New Hampshire-Dartmouth Psychiatric Research Centre, USA.

Mark specializes in the treatment of substance use and co-occurring disorders. He has published widely in addiction treatment research and recently received a career development award from the National Institute on Drug Abuse.

Kim T. Mueser: PhD; Professor, Departments of Psychiatry and Community and Family Medicine, Dartmouth Medical School, USA; New Hampshire-Dartmouth Psychiatric Research Centre, USA.

Kim is a licensed clinical psychologist. His clinical and research interests include the psychosocial treatment of severe mental illnesses, co-existing mental health and drug and alcohol problems and posttraumatic stress disorder. He has published extensively and given numerous lectures and workshops on psychiatric rehabilitation.

Sarah Nothard: ClinPsyD; Therapist, Manchester Mental Health and Social Care Trust, UK.

Sarah's research and clinical interests involve working with people with psychosis and, in particular, the concept of recovery. She has worked in an early intervention trial, rehabilitation settings and a community mental health team.

Steven C. Pierce: PsyD; Associate Director of Psychology, Capitol Region Mental Health Centre, Department of Mental Health and Addictions Services, Hartford, CT, USA.

Steve took up his position in 1993 and developed a dual diagnosis group treatment program. He currently implements the integrated dual diagnosis treatment (IDDT) model on the Co-occurring Disorders Unit at CRMHC, and has conducted multiple trainings on the IDDT model.

Claudia Sannibale: MPsych (Clin), PhD, MAPS; Research Fellow, National Drug and Alcohol Research Centre, University of New South Wales, Australia; Senior Clinical Psychologist, Drug Health Services, Royal Prince Alfred Hospital, Sydney, Australia.

Claudia is a clinical psychologist with over 20 years of clinical experience. She has worked predominantly in alcohol and other drug services and, to a lesser extent, in mental health services. Her main area of interest is treatment of alcohol dependence and co-existing mental health problems, especially in women.

Gina Smith: RMN, RGN, MSc; Consultant Nurse, Family Interventions for Psychosis, Avon and Wiltshire Mental Health Partnership NHS Trust, UK; Clinical Director of Studies, Postgraduate Programme in Mental Health Practice, University of Bath, UK.

Gina has a long-standing interest in helping families cope with severe mental disorder, but her efforts to incorporate this into routine practice were met by the usual barriers until 1998 when she undertook a project to try to operationalize family interventions. This achieved its aim and subsequently won an NHS Beacon award.

Christopher Thornton: BSc (Hons) MClinPsy; Consultant Clinical Psychologist, Peter Beumont Centre for Eating Disorders, Sydney, Australia; School of Psychology, University of Sydney, Australia.

Chris is a consultant clinical psychologist to the Peter Beumont Centre for Eating Disorders in Sydney and a clinical associate with the Department of Psychology, University of Sydney, Australia.

Derek Tobin: BSc (Hons); Clinical Nurse Specialist and COMPASS Programme Team Manager, Birmingham and Solihull Mental Health Trust, UK.

Derek's background is in community mental health nursing. He has been involved in facilitating the implementation and evaluation of integrated treatment in assertive outreach team settings, including the provision of regular supervision.

Stephen W. Touyz: BSc (Hons), PhD; Co-director, Peter Beumont Centre for Eating Disorders, Sydney, Australia; Professor of Clinical Psychology and Honorary Professor of Psychological Medicine, School of Psychology, University of Sydney, Australia.

In addition to the posts above, Stephen is a consultant to the Adult Eating Program at Westmead Hospital, Sydney, Australia.

Richard Velleman: BSc, MSc, PhD, FBPS, FRSS; Professor of Mental Health Research, University of Bath, UK; Director, Mental Health R&D Unit (joint unit of the Avon and Wiltshire Mental Health Partnership NHS Trust and the University of Bath), UK.

Richard is a clinical psychologist who has founded statutory addictions services, helped develop the Families and Psychosis Service within AWP, worked as an NHS Trust board director, undertaken many externally-funded research projects and published very widely on a range of mental health topics, especially related to the impact of addiction on families.

Emma Whicher: BA, MB, BS, MA, MRCPsych; Consultant Psychiatrist in Addictions, St George's and South West Thames Mental Health Trust, UK.

Emma is a Consultant for both community and inpatient addiction services in South West London. She graduated in Natural Sciences from Cambridge University and trained in clinical medicine at St Mary's Hospital Medical School. Her further psychiatry training was undertaken at Leeds Community Mental Health Trust and South West Thames and St George's Mental Health NHS Trust.

Foreword

Wayne Hall and Michael Farrell

Co-existing mental health and drug and alcohol problems are very common among people who seek help for either type of problem. Indeed, co-existing problems are so common in people requesting assistance from mental health and drug and alcohol treatment facilities that we should probably assume that those presenting with either probably have both, until proven otherwise. Despite this, clients with both kinds of problems have been poorly diagnosed and treated. The physical and cultural separation of mental health and drug and alcohol services in most developed countries means that staff working in either of these service areas have not been well trained to recognize, assess and treat clients with problems traditionally dealt with by the other. This book makes a strong case for ensuring that anyone working in modern health services has the skills to screen for, detect and provide brief interventions for co-existing mental health and substance-related disorders.

This book has a number of commendable features. First, it considers co-existing mental health and drug and alcohol problems more broadly than a traditional view of 'dual diagnosis' would suggest. Drug and alcohol problems in persons with psychoses are a pressing and serious problem for the affected individuals, their families and mental health services. But the editors have appropriately interpreted their task more broadly to include co-existing anxiety, affective, personality, learning and eating disorders and so on. The contributing authors have also argued that symptoms of anxiety and affective disorders that do not meet diagnostic criteria for disorders should also be assessed and dealt with.

Second, the book sets out important implications of co-existing mental health and alcohol and drug problems for treatment. The detailed reviews of particular patterns of co-existing disorders reveal that people with these complex problems generally have a poorer treatment response and poorer prognosis, and suffer greater distress and disability, than those who do not. The contributing authors make powerful cases for improving our ability to help individuals and families affected by co-existing mental health and substance use problems.

Third, the editors have pulled together a veritable 'who's who' of the fields of substance use and mental health from many parts of the world to provide a global overview of these topics as they are manifested in differently organized health care systems. This book has also helpfully covered areas, such as learning disability, that all too frequently get left out.

Fourth, the authors provide sensible advice on how to improve care for persons with co-existing mental health and alcohol and other drug problems. The prevalence and extent of co-existing problems are generally much better documented than the effectiveness and cost-effectiveness of different ways of responding to the challenge that they present for treatment. The authors, while acknowledging the limitations of the existing evidence base on treatment effectiveness, nonetheless make clear that this does not justify inaction. As the editors argue, the default response of doing nothing is unacceptable from both an ethical and a practical point of view. It condemns individuals to ineffective treatment and the prolongation of disability while overwhelming treatment facilities with clients who repeatedly cycle through services, with a consequent negative effect on staff morale.

Creating super-speciality treatment centres for 'dual diagnosis' disorders is an expensive option with virtually no evidence of effectiveness. These facilities may improve the treatment of the minority of clients who can be treated in them, although this remains to be demonstrated. But they represent a costly and resource-intensive approach that even well-resourced countries in the developed world cannot afford. The opportunity cost of providing these services is likely to be at the expense of treating many more people with co-existing problems at a much lower cost.

Good clinical outcome and health services research is clearly needed to decide how best to respond to co-existing mental health and drug and alcohol problems. In the interim, we would be wise to adopt the approach advocated in this book by:

- improving the skills of practitioners in mental health and alcohol and drug services in screening for, detecting and assessing the most common co-existing problems that they are likely to encounter in routine practice;
- training staff in the use of psychological interventions that are supported by evidence from controlled clinical trials, such as brief interventions, motivational enhancement, cognitive behavioural treatment and family and group interventions; and
- delivering these in a stepped care approach that uses assessment and brief interventions as the first-line interventions, reserving more intensive types of interventions for those clients who do not respond to first-line care.

The chapters on the treatment of alcohol and drug problems also address the fact that staff in mental health and other health services are often sceptical (if not pessimistic) about the effectiveness of treatment for alcohol and drug dependence. As the evidence reviewed in this book makes clear, treatment for substance dependence does produce substantial improvements in many clients. There is a need to replicate these results in generic mental health settings to convince staff in these facilities that they have a role to play in addressing alcohol and other drug problems in their clients.

If the messages of this book about assessment and treatment are heeded, and the treatment outcome and health services research that the authors recommend is undertaken, then the quality of treatment provided for co-existing disorders will be substantially improved. This outcome would be welcomed by people with co-existing mental health and drug and alcohol problems, their families, and all staff involved in the delivery of mental health and alcohol and drug treatment.

Wayne Hall

Professor of Public Health Policy
School of Population Health
University of Queensland
St Lucia
Australia

Michael Farrell

Reader in Addiction Psychiatry
National Addiction Centre
Institute of Psychiatry
King's College London
London
UK

Preface

Co-existing mental health and drug and alcohol problems are so common that, in clinical settings, a large proportion of presentations can be assumed to have such problems. Despite this, clinical services are separated along mental health and drug and alcohol lines and clinicians have rarely been trained in how to detect, assess and formulate interventions for co-existing problems. Consequently, people with co-existing mental health and drug and alcohol problems often do not receive optimal treatment, and are sometimes turned away from one type of service until the other service can 'fix' the other problem.

We argue that treating co-existing mental health and drug and alcohol problems is core business for mental health and drug and alcohol services, yet there are few clinical guides to assist staff. This book provides practical descriptions of assessments and interventions for co-existing problems, with a view to enhancing motivation, confidence and competence to do so. It combines clinical wisdom, practice-based evidence and brief reviews of the existing evidence base for different combinations of co-existing mental health and drug and alcohol problems.

There are four sections with a total of 20 chapters, each written by leading clinicians in the United Kingdom, the United States and Australia. The first section consists of two chapters and provides an overview of the clinical imperative facing mental health and drug and alcohol staff and the clinical prelude to intervention. The five chapters in the second section refer to the general processes important in working with people with co-existing mental health and drug and alcohol problems: preparation for change; working within a cognitive-behavioural framework; family interventions; working with people in groups; and provision of a consultation-liaison service. The chapters in this section will inform clinicians sufficiently for them to use the material flexibly within their clinical work and services. The content in section three follows a similar format to that of David H. Barlow's *Clinical Handbook of Psychological Disorders* (2nd edition, Guilford Press, New York, 1993), which we have found to be of immense clinical utility. These chapters briefly review the evidence base for treatment, describe the context of therapy in terms of significant therapist and client variables, provide a detailed description of intervention and follow this with a case study. Useful clinical resources are also listed in these chapters. This section describes how to adapt approaches to co-existing disorders among specific sub-groups of people (young people, rurally isolated populations, people who are homeless), and provides detailed descriptions of treatment for anxiety, depression, schizophrenia, bipolar disorder, eating disorders, personality disorders and learning difficulties when accompanied by drug and alcohol problems. The final section covers training and supervision – vitally important aspects of providing good quality interventions and services for co-existing problems.

A note on terminology. We have used the rather clumsy term 'co-existing mental health and drug and alcohol problems' throughout the text (as opposed to 'dual diagnosis' or 'co-morbidity') because, as we explain later, we take a symptom-focused and largely psychological view of such problems. In addition, 'dual diagnosis' can be taken to imply the fulfilment of two sets of diagnostic criteria, whereas many people experience more than two co-existing problems without necessarily meeting formal diagnostic criteria for all of them at the same time. We have used the term 'client' rather than 'patient' as we are not adopting a medical viewpoint in this book; we have not used the term 'consumers' as this is an aspirational statement: we might aspire to a situation where people with co-existing problems can pick and chose their mental health services as if they were consumers or customers, but this is not true (yet!). Similarly, we have used the term 'disorder' rather than 'illness' when describing mental health problems, reflecting our psychological approach. We have used the term 'drug and alcohol problems' in the title of this book and have tended to use it ourselves in chapters written by us, but have not imposed the use of this term upon chapter authors. As is the case with mental health problems, there is no assumption in this book that people should fulfil formal diagnostic criteria for abuse or dependence in order for their drug and alcohol use to be considered potentially problematic. We have also used the European and Australian terminology of substance or drug 'misuse' as opposed to 'abuse' (some people 'abuse' – as in inflict pain on – animate objects such as children, partners or animals, whereas people 'misuse' inanimate objects such as substances). Although we recognize that the term 'drug and alcohol problems' does not reflect the high prevalence of tobacco smoking among people with co-existing problems, we have asked chapter authors to consider the role of smoking among their client groups.

We have used English spelling and hope this does not offend our readers from the United States too much! We have also sought to minimize references to non-generalizable aspects of the individual health care systems in various countries.

We feel particularly privileged to have assembled such outstanding contributors to this book and have very much enjoyed working together and with the chapter authors to make the book come together. On our parts, we feel we have contributed our expertise from having worked clinically, academically and managerially in services attended by people with co-existing mental health and drug and alcohol problems. We hope that both new and experienced clinicians find this book useful as the need to assess and treat co-existing problems becomes increasingly recognized.

Amanda Baker and Richard Velleman, September 2005

Acknowledgements

Thanks to the Avon and Wiltshire Mental Health Partnership NHS Trust and the University of Bath for providing support and encouragement over many years for my work, and for providing a brief academic 'home' on two occasions for Amanda Baker when she took two short sabbatical periods in Bath, where the ideas for this book were developed (first visit) and some of the draft chapters were edited (second visit). Thanks also to my colleagues within the Mental Health Research and Development Unit at the University of Bath for their ongoing interest and support, and to my friend and mentor Professor Jim Orford at the University of Birmingham, for half a lifetime's encouragement, stimulation and friendship.

RV, September 2005

Thanks to the University of Newcastle for granting sabbatical leave and thus providing the opportunity to work with Richard Velleman on this book. Thanks also to my colleagues at the Centre for Mental Health Studies, University of Newcastle, particularly Professor Vaughan Carr, Dr Frances Kay-Lambkin and Terry Lewin, who have worked with me to develop our research into the treatment for co-existing mental health and drug and alcohol problems. I am grateful to the staff and clients of mental health, drug and alcohol and numerous other services who have assisted us in our work. I very much appreciate the contribution of Louise Thornton in the preparation of this manuscript.

AB, September 2005

Co-existing mental health and drug and alcohol problems

Steps towards better treatment

Amanda Baker, Frances J. Kay-Lambkin and Terry J. Lewin

KEY POINTS

1   Co-existing mental health and drug and alcohol problems are very common in clinical practice.
2   The experience of clients with co-existing problems is likened to a huge dysfunctional traffic roundabout.
3   Screening, assessing and intervening with clients with co-existing problems must become core business for health practitioners and health services; skill in this area needs to be a fundamental capability of practitioners working within both specialist mental health *and* drug and alcohol services.
4   There are no clear indications for a 'best treatment'.
5   There are indications that assessment and brief interventions are useful for some people with co-existing problems.
6   The high prevalence of co-existing problems and evidence for the utility of briefer interventions for some people implies that a 'stepped' model of care may be useful.

INTRODUCTION

As we show later, co-existing mental health and drug and alcohol problems (hereafter referred to as co-existing problems) are extremely common. There are four possible options for the treatment of these co-existing problems: (i) the creation of treatment 'super centres' to which (all) people with co-existing problems should be referred; (ii) identification of and intervention for drug and alcohol problems by mental health services; (iii) identification of and intervention for mental health problems by drug and alcohol services; or (iv) we do nothing (Manns 2003).

The last of these options has tended to be a common (but thus far ineffective) response from mental health and drug and alcohol services, and this chapter discusses some of the consequences of this approach. Doing nothing is understandable, given that mental health and drug and alcohol services have usually been run separately, health workers have generally been trained to be responsive to client presentations rather than to identify problems opportunistically, and busy clinics within mental health and drug and alcohol settings often require people to fit into existing programs and do not have the flexibility to assess for co-existing problems and tailor treatments accordingly (Baker and Hambridge 2002). Consequently, people with co-existing problems often report difficulty navigating their way through the available treatment services, sometimes falling between the cracks of the existing systems, or being shuttled from one service to another while issues of primary versus secondary aetiology or diagnosis are clarified.

We believe that doing nothing for co-existing problems is an understandable yet unacceptable approach, given the distress and confusion that such an approach engenders, and given the growing evidence base for treatments for co-existing problems, briefly reviewed later in this chapter.

So, what of the remaining three options for treatment of co-existing problems? Hall and Farrell (1997) have pointed out that the creation of a psychiatric super-specialty dealing with co-existing problems, with treatment conducted in super centres, is likely to be a very expensive approach and its effectiveness remains to be demonstrated. They suggest that options (ii) and (iii) represent better alternatives. This involves mental health and drug and alcohol clinicians screening, assessing and intervening for co-existing problems within their respective treatment settings and the development of better links between services, with clients presenting with more established problems being referred for specialist treatment. Havassy et al. (2004) found few differences between groups of clients with co-existing problems from mental health and drug and alcohol treatment settings, suggesting that treatment providers should be prepared to provide interventions for both mental health and drug and alcohol problems. How best do we progress this approach? In this chapter, we propose a new model for screening, assessing and treating co-existing problems that will hopefully empower primary care, mental health, drug and alcohol and specialist clinicians to offer services flexibly and more effectively, with acknowledgement of each other's essential roles.

This chapter provides a context for the rest of this book by outlining some key features of co-existing problems that need to be considered before intervening, defining the nature of co-existing problems, describing the current experience of clients and clinicians, briefly reviewing the evidence base and proposing a new model of treatment delivery for co-existing problems. The chapter is based largely upon an article by the authors (Kay-Lambkin et al. 2004), and also draws upon two recent papers by Baker and Dawe (2005) and Kavanagh et al. (2003).

KEY FEATURES OF CO-EXISTING MENTAL HEALTH AND DRUG AND ALCOHOL PROBLEMS AND THEIR IMPLICATIONS FOR INTERVENTION

Kavanagh *et al.* (2003) have delineated several key features of co-existing problems that have fundamental implications for treatment. These include the high frequency of co-existing disorders, higher rates of co-existing problems in more intensive treatment settings, poorer physical and psychiatric outcomes among those with co-existing rather than single problems, the high functional impact of drug and alcohol use in psychosis, relationships of mutual influence rather than a clear causal pathway, inadequate service provision related to insufficient detection of co-existing problems and exclusion policies, and the possible need for different intervention strategies for different subgroups. The implications of each of these for a new intervention model are discussed below.

High frequency of co-existing problems

Of particular importance in developing a new intervention model is the high frequency of co-existing problems. The first large-scale epidemiological study to collect information on co-existing problems in the community was the United States Epidemiological Catchment Area (ECA) study of the National Institute of Mental Health (NIMH) (Regier *et al.* 1990). Over 20,000 interviews were conducted among community and institutional populations by five university research teams between 1980 and 1984. Among people with any lifetime mental disorder (other than a substance use disorder), over a quarter (29 per cent) had a lifetime history of one or more substance use disorders: 22 per cent had an alcohol use disorder and 15 per cent had another drug use disorder. Conversely, among individuals with a lifetime alcohol use disorder, 37 per cent had at least one other (non-substance use) mental disorder, and 53 per cent of those with a lifetime drug use disorder had at least one mental disorder other than alcohol use disorder. Of individuals with a lifetime history of alcohol disorder, 45 per cent had a co-existing mental or other drug disorder, and 72 per cent of those with any drug disorder had a co-existing mental or alcohol disorder.

The highest rates of alcohol or other drug use disorders were found among people with antisocial personality disorder (84 per cent), followed by bipolar disorder (61 per cent), schizophrenia (47 per cent), affective disorders (32 per cent) and anxiety disorders (24 per cent). Since the lifetime prevalence of affective and anxiety disorders is greater in the community (8 per cent and 15 per cent respectively) than antisocial personality disorder (3 per cent) and schizophrenia (2 per cent), their contribution to the total prevalence of co-existing problems is much greater. The most prevalent co-existing mental disorders among people with an alcohol disorder were: anxiety disorders (19 per cent), antisocial personality disorders (14 per cent), affective disorders (13 per cent) and schizophrenia (4 per cent). The most prevalent mental disorders among those with any drug use disorder were: anxiety disorders (28 per cent), affective disorders (26 per cent), antisocial personality disorder (18 per cent) and schizophrenia (7 per cent) (Regier *et al.* 1990).

The implication of this very large number of people in the community with common mental health and drug and alcohol problems is that relatively inexpensive, highly accessible interventions that focus on the high prevalence problems of anxiety, depression, and the use of nicotine, alcohol and cannabis are needed (Kavanagh *et al.* 2003). This chapter outlines how primary care and brief interventions have a major role to play in working towards better treatment of co-existing problems. In Chapter 3, David Kavanagh and Jennifer Connolly present brief motivational approaches that can be adapted to primary care settings.

Higher rates of co-existing problems in more intensive treatment settings

In the ECA study, the odds of finding a substance use disorder in those in specialist mental health disorder treatment settings were about double those of finding a substance use disorder in the non-treated population with mental disorders. Further, the odds of finding a mental disorder among those in specialty treatment for alcohol disorders and other drug disorders were 3.8 and 4.2 respectively (Regier *et al.* 1990). This is because individuals with multiple disorders have greater incentives to seek treatment and are found more often in treatment settings (Berkson 1946).

The implications are that interventions for co-existing problems should be the core business of health services, and skill in their delivery needs to be a fundamental capability of practitioners working within specialist mental health and drug and alcohol services (Kavanagh *et al.* 2003). The model of treatment in this chapter allows for both brief, primary care level interventions, most appropriate to people with high prevalence, low severity problems (e.g. depression and alcohol problems), and more intensive interventions, more appropriate for people with high severity, low prevalence presentations (e.g. schizophrenia and cannabis use). Chapter 4, on cognitive-behaviour therapy (CBT), outlines some general principles underlying the development of a case formulation specific to co-existing problems and possible CBT interventions, and subsequent chapters offer suggestions for specific mental health problems accompanied by drug and alcohol problems. Staff within specialist mental health and drug and alcohol services could and should consult with primary care staff (see Chapter 7 on consultation-liaison) and offer training (see Chapter 18 on training).

Poorer physical and psychiatric outcomes among those with co-existing rather than single problems

Since the ECA study, three national surveys have been undertaken to establish the prevalence of co-existing substance use and mental disorders, in the US (Kessler *et al.* 1994, 1996), the UK (Jenkins *et al.* 1997) and Australia (Henderson *et al.* 2000). All have reported similar high rates of co-existing problems (Andrews *et al.* 2001). Andrews *et al.* (2001) have reported that co-existing problems are associated with greater disability and service use. Only half of those with co-existing problems had consulted services and of those who had not, over half reported they did not need treatment. General practitioners (GPs) were the principal caregivers, either alone or in consultation with another health professional. Andrews *et al.* (2001) concluded that there should be a focus on better knowledge regarding mental health and drug and alcohol use among clients and on improving the clinical competence of practitioners. Kavanagh *et al.* (2003) recommended that interventions should address multiple problems and employ strategies to enhance engagement and retention in treatment (see Chapter 3).

High functional impact of drug and alcohol use in psychosis

The Australian National Survey of Mental Health and Well Being (NSM-HWB) provided estimates of the population-level association between psychotic symptoms and substance use (Degenhardt and Hall 2001). The majority of people who screened positively for psychosis were daily tobacco smokers and around one-quarter reported daily alcohol use and at least weekly cannabis use (Degenhardt and Hall 2001). Dependence among alcohol and cannabis users was significantly more likely among cases of psychosis than non-cases (Degenhardt and Hall 2001). There are several implications for interventions among persons at risk of psychotic illness: the mental health risks of problematical substance use needs to be more widely disseminated; more attention should be given to the physical health risks of heavy or problematical substance use (including smoking-related diseases, cognitive impairment, liver damage, cardiovascular disease, contraindications with antipsychotic medications, lowered treatment compliance, increased housing instability and homelessness); and all treatments among persons with psychotic symptoms need to address potential problematical substance abuse (Degenhardt and Hall 2001). In a UK comparison of surveys from a national household sample, a sample of institutional residents with psychiatric disorders and a national sample of the homeless population, substance-related disorders were much higher in the homeless sample than the other two samples (Farrell *et al.* 2003). As such, service planning also needs to consider different subsections of the population, such as homeless people (Farrell *et al.* 2003; see also Chapter 10 on homelessness and co-existing problems, Chapter 13 on treatment of schizophrenia and drug and alcohol problems and Chapter 14 on treatment of bipolar disorder and drug and alcohol problems).

Relationships of mutual influence rather than a clear causal pathway

Treatment services and providers tend not to be sensitive to the severity and consequences of co-existing problems among their clients, and tend to consider one problem secondary to another (Havassy *et al.* 2004). However, co-existing problems often appear to be in a relationship of mutual influence rather than falling neatly into primary versus secondary categories, and the relationship between disorders may change over time (Kavanagh *et al.* 2003; Mueser *et al.* 1993). For example, depression may trigger alcohol use at some times and the reverse may occur at others (Hodgkins *et al.* 1999). In addition, focusing on finding the primary disorder can result in treatment providers and clients becoming confused about optimal treatment, resulting in suspension of treatment plans until diagnostic clarity is reached (Westermeyer *et al.* 2003). It follows that a specific case formulation and treatment plan addressing factors maintaining co-existing problems should be developed (see Chapter 4). Treatment may, but not necessarily, involve attempting resolution of one problem before another, or may involve addressing co-existing problems simultaneously, depending on the case formulation.

Inadequate service provision related to insufficient detection of co-existing problems and exclusion policies

It was noted above that doing nothing to treat co-existing problems has been a dominant approach to service delivery. Efforts to detect co-existing problems and to offer interventions have been hampered by the separation of mental health services and drug and alcohol services. An evidence base for treatment has been slow to accumulate because the co-existence of mental health and drug and alcohol problems usually leads to exclusion from studies conducting research into either single disorder. Implications for the inclusion of people with co-existing problems in future research are discussed in Chapter 20.

Possible need for different intervention strategies for different subgroups

Kavanagh *et al.* (2003) point out that a relationship of mutual influence between mental health and drug and alcohol problems may suggest that integrated treatment would be best. However, they also point out that while the (sparse) available evidence among people with psychosis and drug and alcohol problems is supportive of an integrated approach, whether this is also the case among people with anxiety or depression and co-existing drug and alcohol problems is unclear. They suggest that different intervention strategies may be necessary in different subgroups (Kavanagh *et al.* 2003), an idea which the proposed model in this chapter highlights. In at least a proportion of people, mental health and co-existing drug and alcohol problems may be unrelated (Hall 1996), with the co-occurrence simply representing the co-probability of two otherwise unrelated disorders. Although integrated interventions may also be effective with this group, interventions for separate problems delivered by different clinicians, either sequentially or in parallel, may also be feasible.

Subsequent chapters of this book address these fundamental treatment issues for co-existing problems. A stage-based approach is adopted throughout, beginning with brief interventions which may be applied at a primary care level and less intensive clinical (e.g. group) interventions, leading up to innovative specialist interventions for different combinations of mental health and alcohol and other drug problems. Training and supervision are addressed in Section 4 of this volume in Chapters 18 and 19, as the workforce needs to develop confidence and competence in this challenging area.

WHAT CO-EXISTING MENTAL HEALTH AND DRUG AND ALCOHOL PROBLEMS ARE WE TALKING ABOUT?

Co-existing problems may meet criteria for diagnoses according to classifications such as the *Diagnostic and Statistical Manual of Mental Disorders, Fourth Edition* (DSM-IV; APA 2000). However, conditions do not necessarily need to meet DSM-IV criteria in order for co-existing problems to be present, and for these multiple presenting conditions to impact significantly on client functioning across many domains. Thus, in this book, co-existing mental health and drug and alcohol problems refer primarily to co-existing problems which may or may not meet formal diagnostic criteria for mental health disorder, or drug or alcohol misuse or dependence.

THE TREATMENT ROUNDABOUT AND A STEPPED CARE APPROACH

There is a pressing need to develop a model of treatment for co-existing problems that is relevant to the unique and complex experiences of people with co-existing problems and that clinicians can use to guide their assessment and treatment plans (Brady *et al.* 1996). Kay-Lambkin *et al.* (2004) have proposed the traffic roundabout as a useful metaphor for describing the decision-making and treatment-seeking processes of people with co-existing problems when attempting change. For clients, attempting to access treatment may seem rather like being caught in traffic gridlocked on an enormous, multi-laned, busy roundabout, with many possible exits to consider yet with few road signs to direct the traffic. In addition, the roundabout metaphor can be used to describe alternative treatment approaches among people with co-existing mental health and drug and alcohol problems. Previously, we have proposed that a stepped care approach to treatment provides a useful framework (Baker and Dawe 2005; Kay-Lambkin *et al.* 2004) that may help to clear the gridlock and provide a flexible treatment pathway for more people with co-existing problems. For example, a stepped care approach could be viewed as a series of smaller, interconnected roundabouts, with simplified decisions and more orderly progression (through assessments and interventions).

A stepped care approach acknowledges client and service provider experiences, provides a flexible framework relevant to health professionals performing a variety of functions (e.g. screening, assessment, treatment and follow-up), is commensurate with different levels of training, qualifications, experience and abilities and different settings (e.g. primary care or specialist), and is flexible enough to meet the needs of individuals with various combinations of problems of varying severity. A stepped care approach facilitates the entry of a large number of people into treatment who would otherwise not have had access (Scogin *et al.* 2003). By offering assessment and then low-cost, simple and the least intrusive interventions as a first step, treatment resources, such as clinician time, are maximised, and such interventions may be sufficient for many people. Indeed, assessment and regular monitoring may be all that is necessary to trigger a process of change, a finding that has been well established in the treatment of hazardous and harmful drinking (Heather and Tebbutt 1989). However, it is unlikely that such an approach will be effective for more complex presentations (Baker and Dawe 2005).

A stepped care approach involves screening and assessment followed by the application of a series of tiered interventions to clients, with less intensive treatments being offered as a first step, and more intensive, targeted treatments being made available contingent on the client response to the previous tier of treatment (Baker and Dawe 2005). That is, clients receive the simplest, least intensive treatment first, and then proceed to more intensive or different treatment programs as necessary (Schippers *et al.* 2002). Stepped care approaches to treatment have been applied to mental health and drug and alcohol problems separately, including depression (Scogin *et al.* 2003), anxiety (Baillie and Rapee 2004), alcohol problems (Sobell and Sobell 2000), smoking (Smith *et al.* 2001) and in the treatment of heroin dependence with methadone maintenance (King *et al.* 2002).

When considering the use of a stepped care approach, four domains need to be evaluated: severity of drug and alcohol problems; severity of mental health problems; social support; and treatment history (Schippers *et al.* 2002). Baker and Dawe (2005) have also suggested that consideration of the developmental trajectory involved for individuals, in relation to the order of emergence of their presenting problems, needs some consideration (i.e. whether mental health symptoms were present prior to or following initiation of regular alcohol/other drug use). In addition, adequate resources, reasonable organisation, alignment of efforts with multiple stakeholders, education and ongoing staff supervision, service audits and regular feedback are needed (Schippers *et al.* 2002).

Sobell and Sobell (2000) have described the stepped care approach as a means of linking evidence-based treatments together in an organised, sequential fashion. They suggest the following three components as the basic framework by which clinicians could implement a stepped care approach to treatment with their clients:

1   competent screening/assessment, considering risk factors such as suicidality, risk of harm to others, intoxication, possible drug or alcohol withdrawal effects, accommodation requirements and mental health and physical problems (for which stepped care guidelines can be used);
2   brief outpatient intervention, with progress closely monitored; and
3   if response to treatment is unsatisfactory, increase the intensity of treatment, or change the focus of treatment altogether.

Baker and Dawe (2005) have recommended formalising the Sobells' structured stepped care approach to co-existing problems, with systematic monitoring and decision-making regarding when to step up or discontinue treatment in place at each step. Given evidence that assessment and regular monitoring can trigger behaviour change (Heather and Tebbutt 1989), a proportion of people may benefit sufficiently from competent screening and assessment. Following further monitoring, brief or more intensive interventions could be offered depending on the results of screening and/or assessment. Thus, clients do not always progress from Step 1 to Step 2 then to Step 3, but may step up or down according to needs indicated by regular monitoring over time. Information regarding the degree of severity of problems in the domains of mental health and drug and alcohol use could be used to inform the approach to treatment (together with information regarding social support, treatment history and developmental trajectory). People may require different intensities of treatment depending on the severity of problems. However, regular monitoring should be in place to assess early gains that may be sufficient for some people to exit treatment before intensive interventions are offered. Figure 1.1 illustrates how different combinations of treatment may be appropriate. The three columns in Figure 1.1 (mild, moderate and severe) summarise the client characteristics that should influence the choice of treatment pathways. Each column describes a prototypical client and possible

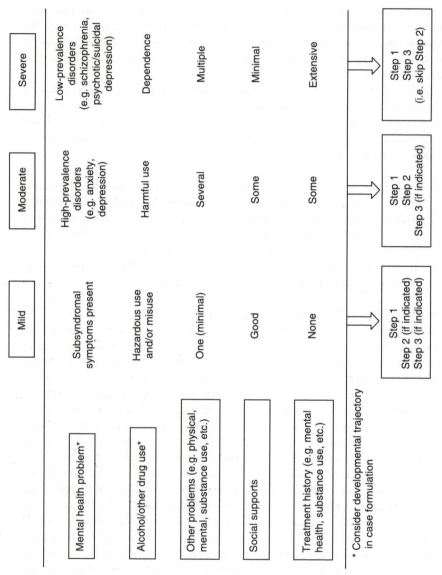

	Mild	Moderate	Severe
Mental health problem*	Subsyndromal symptoms present	High-prevalence disorders (e.g. anxiety, depression)	Low-prevalence disorders (e.g. schizophrenia, psychotic/suicidal depression)
Alcohol/other drug use*	Hazardous use and/or misuse	Harmful use	Dependence
Other problems (e.g. physical, mental, substance use, etc.)	One (minimal)	Several	Multiple
Social supports	Good	Some	Minimal
Treatment history (e.g. mental health, substance use, etc.)	None	Some	Extensive
	Step 1 Step 2 (if indicated) Step 3 (if indicated)	Step 1 Step 2 Step 3 (if indicated)	Step 1 Step 3 (i.e. skip Step 2)

* Consider developmental trajectory in case formulation

Figure 1.1 Examples of different pathways to treatment using a stepped care model based on increasing problem severity and/or distress.

stepped intervention. However, as detailed below, clients with co-existing mental health and alcohol/other drug use problems may not fit neatly into these pathways.

A person presenting to a mental health service for management of schizophrenia would score on the grid as having a severe mental health problem and, if drinking at a hazardous level as indicated by a brief screening instrument such as the Alcohol Use Disorder Identification Test (AUDIT) (Saunders *et al.* 1993), may score in the mild to moderate range for alcohol use. If the individual had good social support and no or very little previous treatment for excessive drinking, the mental health practitioner may consider offering a brief intervention for hazardous drinking (Martino *et al.* 2000). If, on the other hand, the client had minimal social support (and/or social support was primarily via other problem drinkers) and/or previous unsuccessful brief interventions for alcohol consumption, the mental health practitioner may offer a more intensive intervention aimed at increasing social supports and reducing drinking (e.g. Copello *et al.* 2002). Alternatively, if assessment revealed that drinking had been exacerbated by distress associated with auditory hallucinations resistant to medication, medication review and an intervention including CBT strategies for hallucinations, reducing drinking and enhancing coping strategies other than drinking may be appropriate. If the same client is managed by their GP, screening and brief intervention for alcohol consumption would be appropriate, followed by more intensive or different intervention by the GP or referral to a mental health or drug and alcohol service, if necessary. More detailed assessment would inform the treatment approach for the client, with ongoing monitoring indicating response to treatment and maintenance of change during follow-up. Although severity of dependence on drugs and/or alcohol and severity of mental health problem are important considerations, client progress and functioning would guide the stepped care treatment plan, rather than any predetermined set of symptoms or characteristics (see Chapter 4 for a more detailed discussion about the relationship between stepped care and severity and type of problem).

Although the concept of stepped care may be common in clinical practice, integral to the stepped care approach is regular, thorough assessment and monitoring of the client. Assessment and monitoring should not be limited to diagnostic instruments, but should incorporate estimates of occupational functioning, social/relationship functioning, quality of life issues and so on, whether measured formally with validated scales or informally in discussions with the client (Davison 2000). This is particularly important for people with co-existing problems, given that they will often present with many subsyndromal issues that may affect their response to the treatments being offered.

We now turn to a brief overview of the developing evidence base for treatment of co-existing problems. Different psychological treatments for specific combinations of mental health and drug and alcohol problems are reviewed in more detail in Sections 2 and 3 of this book. The following broad review provides a context for the chapters that follow. Although pharmacological treatment approaches are not reviewed in this book, the psychological treatments covered are complementary to pharmacological approaches and are commonly delivered within a multidisciplinary framework.

SOME EVIDENCE IN SUPPORT OF A STEPPED CARE APPROACH TO CO-EXISTING MENTAL HEALTH AND DRUG AND ALCOHOL PROBLEMS

There is a growing evidence base for the efficacy of assessment and monitoring, and brief and more intensive interventions (Steps 1, 2 and 3 above) among people with co-existing problems. However, no studies have evaluated the efficacy of a structured stepped care approach in which people are monitored for response in mental health and drug and alcohol domains and interventions are stepped up or down accordingly.

Screening and assessment as minimal intervention (Step 1)

As in the alcohol literature (Heather and Tebbutt 1989), a robust and fascinating finding has been that benefits are seen in research participants with co-existing problems who receive control treatments, or no treatment apart from completing a thorough assessment and receiving regular scheduled follow-up appointments (e.g. Baker *et al.* 2002b, 2005; Hulse and Tait 2003; Lehman *et al.* 1998). Screening and assessment for co-existing problems could be regarded as forms of minimal intervention. This is important because, rather than placing treatment for co-existing problems in the 'too hard' basket, evidence is emerging that similar mechanisms may sometimes underlie change in drug and alcohol use among people with co-existing mental health problems and those without such problems. It has been suggested that among the active ingredients of minimal interventions are the provision of formal feedback, presented in a style that is commensurate with the person's stage of change for drug and alcohol use, and a positive interpersonal style (i.e. non-confrontational, empathic, flexible, non-authoritarian, etc.) (Zweben and Zuckoff 2002). It may also be that level of treatment acceptance or readiness to accept help may be a contributing factor to whether or not clients make changes to their life circumstances. Certainly, for these people, minimal interventions may be helpful. This is encouraging, given that primary care as well as specialist clinicians can deliver such interventions.

Brief interventions (Step 2)

Brief motivational interventions based on the work of Miller and Rollnick (2002) are reviewed in Chapter 3. They have been applied in inpatient and outpatient contexts among people with co-existing psychosis and major depression and drug and alcohol problems, and by practitioners with little formal psychological training. Collectively, this suggests that, if shown to be effective, brief motivational interventions could be used by many treatment providers within the context of usual treatment, in medical, public health, mental health and/or drug and alcohol settings with large numbers of people with co-existing problems.

In a recent review of treatments for people with severe mental illnesses, Drake *et al.* (2004) suggested that brief interventions may represent an important new development in the field of co-existing problems and that there may be a subset of individuals for whom a brief intervention is all that is needed. Motivational interviewing may be particularly effective for people with co-existing problems in increasing treatment engagement and adherence (Handmaker *et al.* 2002). Brief motivational interventions have shown effectiveness in improving engagement with and adherence to treatment at psychiatric outpatient services among clients with depression and cocaine dependence (Daley *et al.* 1998) and among psychiatric inpatients with co-existing substance misuse or dependence (Martino *et al.* 2000; Swanson *et al.* 1999). On the other hand, Baker and colleagues (2002a, 2002b) reported that a brief motivational intervention among psychiatric inpatients was not associated with increased outpatient attendance at a specialist service for people with co-existing problems. However, they did report a trend for participants who received the motivational interview to report a clinically significant, short-term reduction in polydrug use. Hulse and Tait (2003) reported a similar initial (12-month) advantage of motivational interviewing among psychiatric inpatients with alcohol problems (not dependence) but in the longer term (five years) those who received assessment only reduced their drinking just as much. Kavanagh and colleagues (2004) reported that a motivational intervention was associated with less substance use at six months among inpatients with a psychotic illness compared with standard care. Thus, there is accumulating evidence for the effectiveness of brief interventions, at least among some people with co-existing problems.

More intensive interventions (Step 3)

Evidence is emerging that for some people with co-existing problems, more intensive interventions are required to produce improvements in their symptoms, general level of functioning and levels of substance use. In determining the optimal treatment approach for people with co-existing problems, researchers have suggested that longer, more intensive treatment programs should integrate strategies addressing both mental health and drug and alcohol problems within the same treatment program, preferably delivered by one clinician (Drake *et al.* 1998; Mueser *et al.* 2003). Indeed, researchers are beginning to apply treatment strategies that have shown benefits for people presenting with either a mental health or drug and alcohol problem to people with co-existing problems. For example, CBT has the best-documented efficacy of the non-pharmacological approaches to the treatment of depression (APA 2000) and has also been used effectively among people with alcohol (Shand *et al.* 2003), cannabis (Copeland *et al.* 2001) and amphetamine use (Baker *et al.* 2005), as well as psychotic disorders (Kopeloxicz and Liberman 1998) and anxiety disorders (Andrews *et al.* 2003). Consequently, researchers are beginning to evaluate the effectiveness of CBT among people with co-existing problems. Overall, the results for drug and alcohol use have tended to be modest and the evidence for a focus on co-existing disorders versus single disorders mixed.

The small number of studies conducted among people with co-existing problems to date is reviewed in more detail in Chapter 4 on CBT. Two randomised controlled trials of CBT conducted among people with psychosis (Baker *et al.* 2005; Barrowclough *et al.* 2001; Haddock *et al.* 2003) reported high levels of dependence among their samples, modest short-term benefits of CBT for substance use compared to control conditions and improvements in general functioning compared to control conditions. Bachmann *et al.* (1997) reported that a four-stage integrated intervention that included both individual and group-based treatments resulted in a moderate decrease in positive symptoms of psychosis over the 12-month follow-up period, but no change in negative symptoms or levels of drug use. A controlled trial of alcohol treatment with adjunctive treatment for social anxiety (Randall *et al.* 2001) was not found to be more effective than alcohol treatment alone, while adjunctive CBT for depression (Brown *et al.* 1997) was more effective for both depression and drinking.

Clearly, more research is required to develop evidence-based, validated interventions, including the practical application of stepped care approaches. Given that the nature of co-existing problems is complex, it is likely that a range of intervention strategies will need to be applied in order to assist such clients in meeting their goals (Kavanagh *et al.* 2003). Moreover, an intervention suitable for one individual with co-existing problems may not necessarily be the optimal intervention for another (Kavanagh *et al.* 2003).

According to Baker *et al.* (2005), around 51–60 per cent of regular amphetamine users will still be using above a threshold requiring intervention after a brief outpatient intervention (Step 2). Of these, between 16 per cent and 23 per cent will be experiencing above-threshold levels of depression in addition to continuing to use amphetamines at harmful levels. For these non-responders, a Step 3 intervention is indicated, which is more intensive than the treatment approaches applied at previous steps. Step 3 approaches may need to be delivered by more experienced clinicians, specialising in the target areas of need for the client.

Step 3 interventions could include pharmacotherapy and longer programs of psychological treatment. If co-existing issues are not resolved at this step, then an integrated approach to treatment could be adopted, incorporating both mental health and drug and alcohol use approaches simultaneously, with the same clinician (or team of clinicians) delivering all components of the treatment (Mueser *et al.* 2003). Once clients have received the Step 3 intervention, they may require further treatment steps, or receive regular scheduled follow-ups to enhance relapse prevention or early response to relapse.

CONCLUSION

Co-existing problems are commonly encountered in clinical settings, regardless of the service in which clinicians operate (e.g. mental health services, drug and alcohol services, general medical settings etc.). Epidemiological surveys reveal that the rates of co-existing problems are high and increasing. Yet the complexity of presentations among people with co-existing problems, coupled with the exclusion of this population from many mental health- and/ or drug- and alcohol-focused research programs, leaves clinicians uncertain as to the most appropriate model or approach to intervention for this group. We suggest that the roundabout is a useful metaphor for describing the treatment experiences of people with co-existing problems.

The lack of a comprehensive model of intervention for co-existing problems may lead to poorer treatment outcomes and increased utilisation of services. The model of stepped interventions for people with co-existing problems may provide the framework required to guide clinician decision-making and treatment planning for this population. This book is organised so that the reader may step up care from brief interventions in Chapter 3, through group interventions in Chapter 6, to specialised treatments for specific co-existing conditions in Chapters 8–17.

KEY RESOURCES

Screening and diagnostic instruments for people with co-existing mental health and alcohol/other drug use problems

Dawe, S., Loxton, N. J., Hides, L., Kavanagh, D. and Mattick, R. P., *Review of Diagnostic Screening Instruments for Alcohol and Other Drug Use and Other Psychiatric Disorders*. Canberra: Commonwealth of Australia, 2002. Available at http://www.nationaldrugstrategy.gov.au/publications/monographs.htm (accessed 8 August 2005).

Epidemiology, prevention and treatment of co-existing mental health and alcohol/other drug use problems

Teesson, M. and Proudfoot, J., *Comorbid Mental Disorders and Substance Use Disorders*. Canberra: Commonwealth of Australia, 2003. Available at http://www.nationaldrugstrategy.gov.au/publications/monographs.htm (accessed 8 August 2005).

Cognitive behavioural intervention for regular amphetamine users

Baker, A., Kay-Lambkin, F., Lee, N. K., Claire, M. & Jenner, L., *A Brief Cognitive Behavioural Intervention for Regular Amphetamine Users*. Canberra: Australian Government Department of Health and Ageing, 2003. Available at http://www.nationaldrugstrategy.gov.au/publications/illicit.htm (accessed 8 August 2005).

REFERENCES

American Psychiatric Association (APA), *Diagnostic and Statistical Manual of Mental Disorders*, Fourth Edition. Washington: APA, 2000.

Andrews, G., Creamer, M., Crino, R., Hunt, C., Lampe, L. and Page, A., *The Treatment of Anxiety Disorders Second Edition. Clinician Guides and Patient Manuals*. Port Melbourne: Cambridge University Press, 2003.

Andrews, G., Henderson, S. and Hall, W., 'Prevalence, comorbidity, disability and service utilisation', *British Journal of Psychiatry*, *178*, 145–53, 2001.

Bachmann, K. M., Moggi, F., Hirsbrummer, H.-P., Donati, R. and Brodbeck, J., 'An integrated treatment program for dually diagnosed patients', *Psychiatric Services*, *48*, 314–16, 1997.

Baillie, A. J. and Rapee, R. M., 'Predicting who benefits from psychoeducation and self-help for panic attacks', *Behavior Research and Therapy*, *42*, 513–27, 2004.

Baker, A. and Dawe, S., 'Amphetamine use and co-occurring psychological disorders: A review of the literature and implications for treatment', *Australian Psychologist*, *40*, 87–94, 2005.

Baker, A. and Hambridge, J., 'Motivational interviewing: Enhancing engagement in treatment for mental health problems', *Behaviour Change*, *19*, 138–45, 2002.

Baker, A., Lee, N. K., Claire, M., Lewin, T. J., Grant, T., Pohlman, S. *et al.*, 'Brief cognitive behavioural interventions for regular amphetamine users: A step in the right direction', *Addiction*, *100*, 367–78, 2005.

Baker, A., Lewin, T., Reichler, H., Clancy, C., Carr, V., Garrett, R. *et al.*, 'Motivational interviewing among psychiatric in-patients with substance use disorders', *Acta Psychiatrica Scandinavica*, *106*, 233–40, 2002a.

Baker, A., Lewin, T., Reichler, H., Clancy, R., Carr, V., Garrett, R. *et al.*, 'Evaluation of a motivational interview for substance use with psychiatric inpatient services', *Addiction*, 97, 1329–37, 2002b.

Barrowclough, C., Haddock, G., Tarrier, N., Lewis, S., Moring, J., O'Brien, R. *et al.*, 'Randomized controlled trial of cognitive behavioural therapy plus motivational intervention for schizophrenia and substance use', *American Journal of Psychiatry*, 158, 1706–13, 2001.

Berkson, J., 'Limitations of the application of four-fold tables to hospital data', *Biometric Bulletin*, 2, 47–53, 1946.

Brady, S., Hiam, C. M., Saemann, R., Humbert, L., Fleming, M. Z. and Dawkins-Brickhouse, K., 'Dual diagnosis: A treatment model for substance abuse and major mental illness', *Community Mental Health Journal*, 32, 573–8, 1996.

Brown, R. A., Evans, M., Miller, I. W., Burgess, E. S. and Mueller, T. I., 'Cognitive-behavioral treatment for depression in alcoholism', *Journal of Consulting and Clinical Psychology*, 65, 715–26, 1997.

Copeland, J., Swift, W., Roffman, R. and Stephens, R., 'A randomized controlled trial of brief cognitive-behavioral interventions for cannabis use disorder', *Journal of Substance Abuse Treatment*, 21, 55–64, 2001.

Copello, A., Orford, J., Hodgson, R., Tober, G. and Barrett, C., 'Social behaviour and network therapy: Basic principles and early experiences', *Addictive Behaviors*, 27, 345–66, 2002.

Daley, D. C., Salloum, I. M., Zuckoff, A., Kirisci, L. and Thase, M. E., 'Increasing treatment adherence among outpatients with depression and cocaine dependence: Results of a pilot study', *American Journal of Psychiatry*, 155, 1611–13, 1998.

Davison, G. C., 'Stepped-care: Doing more with less?' *Journal of Consulting and Clinical Psychology*, 68, 580–5, 2000.

Degenhardt, L. and Hall, W., 'The association between psychosis and problematical drug use among Australian adults: Findings from the National Survey of Mental Health and Well-being', *Psychological Medicine*, 31, 659–68, 2001.

Drake, R. E., Mercer-McFadden, C., Mueser, K. T., McHugo, G. J. and Bond, G. R., 'Review of integrated mental health and substance abuse treatment for patients with dual disorders', *Schizophrenia Bulletin*, 24, 589–608, 1998.

Drake, R., Mueser, K. T., Brunette, M. and McHugo, G. J., 'A review of treatments for people with severe mental illnesses and co-occuring substance use disorders', *Psychiatric Rehabilitation Journal*, 27, 360–74, 2004.

Farrell, M., Howes, S., Taylor, C., Lewis, G., Jenkins, R., Bebbington, P. *et al.*, 'Substance misuse and psychiatric comorbidity: An overview of the OPCS National Psychiatric Comorbidity Survey', *International Review of Psychiatry*, 15, 43–9, 2003.

Haddock, G., Barrowclough, C., Tarrier, N., Moring, J., O'Brien, R., Schofield, N. *et al.*, 'Randomised controlled trial of cognitive-behaviour therapy and motivational intervention for schizophrenia and substance use: 18 month, carer and economic outcomes', *British Journal of Psychiatry*, 183, 418–26, 2003.

Hall, W., 'What have population surveys revealed about substance use disorders and their comorbidity with other mental disorders?' *Drug and Alcohol Review*, 15, 157–70, 1996.

Hall, W. and Farrell, M., 'Co-morbidity of mental disorders and substance misusers', *British Journal of Psychiatry*, 171, 484–5, 1997.

Handmaker, N., Packard, M. and Conforti, K., 'Motivational interviewing in the treatment of dual disorders', in Miller, W. R. and Rollnick, S., eds, *Motivational Interviewing: Preparing People for Change, 2nd ed*, pp. 362–76. New York: Guilford Press, 2002.

Havassy, B. E., Alvidrez, J. and Owen, K. K., 'Comparisons of patients with comorbid psychiatric and substance use disorders: Implications for treatment and service delivery', *American Journal of Psychiatry, 161*, 139–47, 2004.

Heather, N. and Tebbutt, J., *The Effectiveness of Treatment for Drug and Alcohol Problems: An Overview*. Canberra: Australian Government Publishing Service, 1989.

Henderson, S., Andrews, G. and Hall, W., 'Australia's mental health: An overview of the general population survey', *Australian and New Zealand Journal of Psychiatry, 34*, 197–205, 2000.

Hodgkins, D. C., el-Guebaly, N., Armstrong, S. and Durfour, M., 'Implications of depression on outcome from alcohol dependence: A three-year prospective follow-up', *Alcoholism: Clinical and Experimental Research, 23*, 151–7, 1999.

Hulse, G. K. and Tait, R. J., 'Five-year outcomes of a brief alcohol intervention for adult in-patients with psychiatric disorders', *Addiction, 98*, 1061–8, 2003.

Jenkins, R., Lewis, G., Bebbington, P., Brugha, T., Farrell, M., Gill, B. and Meltzer, H., 'The national psychiatric morbidity surveys of Great Britain: Initial findings from the household survey', *Psychological Medicine, 27*, 765–74, 1997.

Kavanagh, D., Mueser, K. T. and Baker, A., 'Management of comorbidity', in Teesson, M. and Proudfoot, H., eds, *Comorbid Mental Disorders and Substance Use Disorders: Epidemiology, Prevention and Treatment*, pp. 78–120. Canberra: Commonwealth of Australia, 2003.

Kavanagh, D., Young, R., White, A., Saunders, J. B., Wallis, J., Shockley, N. *et al.*, 'A brief motivational intervention for substance misuse in recent-onset psychosis', *Drug and Alcohol Review, 23*, 151–5, 2004.

Kay-Lambkin, F. J., Baker, A. and Lewin, T. J., 'The "comorbidity roundabout": A framework to guide assessment and intervention strategies and engineer change among people with co-morbid problems', *Drug and Alcohol Review, 23*, 407–24, 2004.

Kessler, R. C., McGonagle, K. A., Zhao, S., Nelson, C. B., Hughes, M., Eshleman, S. *et al.*, 'Lifetime and 12-month prevalence of DSM-III-R psychiatric disorders in the United States: Results of the national comorbidity survey', *Archives of General Psychiatry, 51*, 8–19, 1994.

Kessler, R. C., Nelson, C. B., McGonagle, K. A., Edlund, M. J., Frank, R. G. and Leaf, P. J., 'The epidemiology of co-occurring addictive and mental disorders: Implications for prevention and service utilisation', *American Journal of Orthopsychiatry, 66*, 17–31, 1996.

King, V. L., Stoller, K. B., Hayes, M., Umbricht, A., Currens, M., Kidorf, M. S. *et al.*, 'A multicentre randomised evaluation of methadone medical maintenance', *Drug and Alcohol Dependence, 65*, 137–48, 2002.

Kopeloxicz, A. and Liberman, R. P., 'Psychosocial treatments for schizophrenia', in Nathan, P. E. and Gorman, J. M., eds, *A Guide to Treatments that Work*, pp. 190–211. New York: Oxford University Press, 1998.

Lehman, C. L., Brown, T. A. and Barlow, D. H., 'Effects of cognitive-behavioral treatment for panic disorder with agoraphobia on concurrent alcohol abuse', *Behavior Therapy, 29*, 423–33, 1998.

Manns, L., 'Comorbidity: Why does it matter?' in Teesson, M. and Proudfoot, H., eds, *Comorbid Mental Disorders and Substance Use Disorders: Epidemiology, Prevention and Treatment*, pp. 143–6. Canberra: Commonwealth of Australia, 2003.

Martino, S., Carroll, J. M., O'Malley, S. S. and Rounsaville, B. J., 'Motivational interviewing with psychiatrically ill substance abusing patients', *American Journal on the Addictions*, *9*, 88–91, 2000.

Miller, W. R. and Rollnick, S., *Motivational Interviewing: Preparing People for Change*, *2nd ed.* New York: Guilford Press, 2002.

Mueser, K. T., Drake, R. and Wallach, M. A., 'Dual diagnosis: A review of etiological theories', *Addictive Behaviors*, *23*, 717–34, 1993.

Mueser, K. T., Noordsy, D. L., Drake, R. and Fox, L. W., *Integrated Treatment for Dual Disorders: A Guide to Effective Practice*. New York: Guilford Press, 2003.

Randall, C. L., Thomas, S. and Thevos, A. K., 'Concurrent alcoholism and social anxiety disorder: A first step toward developing effective treatments', *Alcoholism: Clinical and Experimental Research*, *25*, 210–20, 2001.

Regier, D. A., Farmer, M. F., Rae, D. S., Locke, B. Z., Keith, S. J., Judd, L. L. and Goodwin, F. K., 'Comorbidity of mental disorders with alcohol and other drug abuse: Results from the Epidemiologic Catchment Area (ECA) study', *The Journal of the American Medical Association*, *264*, 2511–18, 1990.

Saunders, J., Aasland, O. G., Babor, T. F., de la Fuente, J. R. and Grant, M., 'Development of the Alcohol Use Disorder Identification Test (AUDIT): WHO collaborative project on early detection of persons with harmful alcohol consumption – ii', *Addiction*, *88*, 791–804, 1993.

Schippers, G. M., Schramade, M. and Walburg, J. A., 'Reforming Dutch substance abuse treatment services', *Addictive Behaviors*, *27*, 995–1007, 2002.

Scogin, F. R., Hanson, A. and Welsh, D., 'Self-administered treatment in stepped-care models of depression treatment', *Journal of Clinical Psychology*, *9*, 341–9, 2003.

Shand, F. L., Gates, J., Fawcett, J. and Mattick, R. P., *The Treatment of Alcohol Problems: A Review of the Evidence*. Canberra: Australian Commonwealth Department of Health and Ageing, 2003.

Smith, S. S., Jorenby, D. E., Piasecki, T. M., Baker, T. B., Fiore, M. C., Anderson, J. E. *et al.*, 'Strike while the iron is hot: Can stepped-care treatments resurrect relapsing smokers?' *Journal of Consulting and Clinical Psychology*, *69*, 429–39, 2001.

Sobell, M. B. and Sobell, L. C., 'Stepped-care as a heuristic approach to the treatment of alcohol problems', *Journal of Consulting and Clinical Psychology*, *68*, 573–79, 2000.

Swanson, A. J., Pantalon, M. V. and Cohen, K. R., 'Motivational interviewing and treatment adherence among psychiatric and dually diagnosed patients', *Journal of Nervous and Mental Disease*, *187*, 630–5, 1999.

Westermeyer, J., Weiss, R. D. and Ziedonis, D., *Integrated Treatment for Mood and Substance Disorders*. London: Johns Hopkins University Press, 2003.

Zweben, A. and Zuckoff, A., 'Motivational interviewing and treatment adherence', in Miller, W. R. and Rollnick, S., eds, *Motivational Interviewing: Preparing People for Change, 2nd ed*, pp. 299–319. New York: Guilford Press, 2002.

Chapter 2

Co-existing problems
From conceptualization to case formulation

Richard Velleman

KEY POINTS

1   There is a growing awareness within both mental health and substance misuse services of the importance of co-existing problems. Clients with these co-existing problems impact upon a wide range of professionals, and often present major challenges due to their complex needs.

2   In this book we have used a broad and inclusive definition of co-existing problems, and have deliberately not used medicalized terminology such as dual diagnosis or co-morbidity.

3   Although many people suffer from co-existing mental health and substance use problems, many will not present themselves to health professionals. A wide range of professionals need to develop skills in detecting these problems, via a raised awareness of such co-existing problems and via routine screening.

4   All services need to develop routine screening and, where substance misuse or mental health difficulties are identified, the nature and severity of those problems and their associated risks should be assessed. Good routine screening and risk assessment procedures will involve a mixture of self-report methods, laboratory tests, and information from collateral data sources (other agencies, and family and friends).

5   Assessment of substance misuse needs to form an integral part of standard assessment procedures for mental health problems, and vice versa.

6   Assessment of the relationship between substance misuse and mental health problems should be longitudinal and open to revision. Because such co-existing problems are likely to be complex, it is probable that an assessing clinician will need to liaise and/or collaborate with other professionals and agencies in order to complete a comprehensive assessment, and to develop and implement effective interventions.

7   Assessments will utilize clinical interviews, standardized assessments, and family and other non-substance-misusing social networks, and will be used towards a collaborative case formulation with the client.

INTRODUCTION

Chapter 1 has shown how highly prevalent the co-existence of these problems is, with very large numbers of people in the community experiencing both common mental health and drug and alcohol problems. This chapter will look at what is meant in this book by 'co-existing problems', and will discuss detection, presentation, and assessment – all as a route into the remainder of the book, where there are detailed examinations of the process of working with people with such co-existing problems, and then a discussion of a wide variety of treatment issues specific to various populations.

THE GROWING AWARENESS AND IMPORTANCE OF CO-EXISTING PROBLEMS

The concept of co-existing problems (sometimes called dual diagnosis or co-morbid problems: see below) with mental health and substance use has gained prominence in the last few decades, for a number of reasons (Abou-Saleh 2004; Crawford and Crome 2001; O'Brien *et al.* 2004). These include the increasing availability and accessibility of alcohol and illicit drugs within the community, the deinstitutionalization of people with severe mental health problems, and the increasing expectations that agencies will address co-existing problems, despite deficits in staff training and organizational constraints limiting the interface between services.

Clients with co-existing problems impact upon the range of professionals working within mental health services and alcohol and drug services, and a variety of agencies in the statutory and non-statutory sectors. Clients with co-existing problems often present the social rehabilitation service network with a major challenge, as their individual needs in medico-psycho-social terms, and their collective needs in organizational terms, are both complex and highly demanding. Further, in economic terms, this group have significantly higher overall healthcare costs than those with either substance use or mental health problems alone (Hoff and Rosenheck 1998, 1999).

Because many of these clients will have lost touch with (or been discharged from) specialist medical, psychiatric and addiction services, they often pose particular difficulties for those in the non-statutory sector and in primary care, who often feel they are having to cope 'as best as they can'. This creates a paradox: the services within which the staff are meant to have higher levels of skill in dealing with complex problems have tended to discharge or lose contact with these clients, and hence the 'safety net' services where staff often have lower levels of training are the ones that have primarily to deal with these complex problems.

In summary, then, co-existing problems with substance use and one or more of a range of mental health issues (anxiety, depression, schizophrenia, bipolar disorder, etc.) are highly prevalent, often begin in youth, and place an immense burden on individuals, families, and society. Because of their seriousness, and the fact that many services do not deal adequately or appropriately with them, co-existing problems are associated with underachievement or failure for affected individuals across many domains, including academia, employment, relationships, social life, and health; they are also associated with greater involvement with the criminal justice system, failed treatment attempts, poverty, and homelessness. Finally, the risk of suicide is high for persons with co-existing mental health and substance use problems.

WHAT IS MEANT BY 'CO-EXISTING MENTAL HEALTH AND DRUG AND ALCOHOL PROBLEMS'?

As presented in Chapter 1, within this book 'co-existing mental health and drug and alcohol problems' refer to situations where people have problems related both to their use of substances (from hazardous through to harmful use and/or dependence) *and* to their mental health (from problematic symptoms through to highly prevalent conditions such as depression and anxiety, and to the low prevalence disorders such as psychosis). Substance use in this book may refer to alcohol, tobacco, illicit drugs, and/or misuse of prescribed or over-the-counter medications.

Our definition is a broad and inclusive one, and this is deliberate. For us there are many reasons for using such a broad, inclusive approach. This is an area where there are many debates about terminology, and underlying these are issues of professional power and control. One common term used to describe similar territory is 'dual diagnosis', referring broadly to the concurrent existence in an individual of two psychiatric diagnoses: a substance use disorder and one or more psychiatric disorders. We have not used this term within this book for a number of reasons:

- The term implies a medicalized viewpoint (diagnosis has historically been under the control of medically trained professionals), and this is not our perspective.
- Dual diagnosis focuses on the 'diagnosis' aspect, and yet for us the issue is the problems these people have (i.e. both separate sets of problems, and also situations where the two sets of problems may have a multiplicative effect), not whether any individual has the necessary symptoms in the correct patterns to receive two different psychiatric diagnoses.
- Mental disorder and substance misuse are different types of problem, each with its own continuum of severity from mild to severe. At what point does an individual cross a threshold with each of these problems so that he/she can be considered as having a 'dual diagnosis'? These thresholds will be partly determined by 'existing beliefs about the benefit

of therapeutic input, what constitutes harmful substance misuse, and what is meant by mental disorder' (Banerjee *et al.* 2002: 2).

- A diagnostic approach brings with it a focus on 'primary diagnosis'. As discussed in Chapter 1, this is unhelpful, especially as it is often not clear which is the underlying problem, and usually by the time someone is referred into specialist services, both problems are of sufficient magnitude as to need help. Alternatively, the services involved may try to split the problems in order to deal with both in parallel, but the problems are likely to be intertwined within the individual.

- It is also the case that staff's decision whether the primary diagnosis is 'substance misuse' or 'mental illness' will often depend on the knowledge and experience of the assessor, and the method of assessment. Furthermore, it is also likely (given clinicians' lack of training and knowledge about the other problems which they have not specialized in) that staff from mental health services may be more likely to attribute presenting problems to substance use and vice versa, so shifting responsibility for the case from themselves to the other service.

- The term is inexact: it could apply to any two diagnoses, not only the ones we are referring to in this book. Indeed, 'dual diagnosis' has been applied over recent years to a number of different groups of people with two co-existing conditions such as personality disorder and mental health problems or learning disability and mental disorder.

- The term has a 'fixed' quality (one's symptoms make a pattern which is diagnosable or not), but in reality people's substance misuse and mental health problems usually vary over time. For example:

  — People may vary the type and amount of substances they use (e.g. they may stay clear of opiates or cocaine but use alcohol or cannabis occasionally).
  — They may react differently to the same substance depending on its quality, their environment, their mood or state of mind, and their general health.
  — Their mental health problems may fluctuate (e.g. they may have episodes where their problems are very pronounced followed by long periods of stability).
  — Their vulnerability may fluctuate (e.g. a person may be especially vulnerable to using alcohol during periods of paranoia, or of mania; Hawkins and Gilburt 2004).

- The term also implies that the person has only the two sets of problems, one concerned with substance use and the other with their mental health symptoms. In reality, people given the label 'dual diagnosis' typically have complex needs rather than two distinct problems. The focus on substance misuse and mental health problems may mean that other areas of concern are missed such as a history of childhood sexual abuse, housing issues, or child protection issues. As one service user quoted by Hawkins and Gilburt (2004: 2) said: 'Dual diagnosis is a label they give you, but even at my most buoyant I think I've got more than two problems.'

- The label 'dual diagnosis' implies that there is a homogenous group of clients with similar problems. In reality, people with co-existing problems are a very mixed group.

A final reason why we favour looking at problems as opposed to diagnoses is that, even if the term 'diagnosis' was acceptable, the relationship between problems and diagnosis may be unclear within this population. There may be many instances where a co-existing psychiatric disorder (or even the medication being taken to help control psychiatric symptoms) may mean that any given amount of alcohol or of a drug might have a different or far greater effect than it might on other people. Similarly, there may be many instances where the use of alcohol or a drug may cause mental health problems to occur, some of which may be short-lived, others of which may trigger chronic and severe mental health problems (e.g. psychosis).

The UK Department of Health *Dual Diagnosis Good Practice Guide* (2002: 7) describes a simple set of four possible relationships:

- A primary psychiatric illness precipitates or leads to substance misuse.
- Use of substances makes the mental health problem worse or alters its course.
- Intoxication and/or substance dependence leads to psychological symptoms.
- Substance misuse and/or withdrawal leads to psychiatric symptoms or illnesses.

Another term which is widely used is 'co-morbidity', but again this puts the emphasis on the 'morbid' processes and diagnostic categories, and not on a simple delineation of the range and extent of the problems which someone's mental health difficulties or substance use behaviours are causing them. Other terms which have been used to describe this population include mentally ill chemical abuser (MICA), chemically addicted mentally ill (CAMI), and co-occurring addictive and mental disorders (COAMD). Our position, then, is that 'co-existing mental health and substance use problems' is an extremely heterogeneous category, and as such the broadest and most inclusive definition is the most helpful. Given this heterogeneity, the emphasis needs to be on individualized assessment (see below) and formulation (see Chapter 4).

DETECTION AND ASSESSMENT

How do we help people to detect co-existing problems?

Many people with co-existing mental health and substance use problems present in contexts other than healthcare (especially and increasingly within the criminal justice system, but also within a range of social care settings relating to housing, relationships, family problems, etc.). In addition, often they do not recognize that they have such co-existing difficulties. They are often initially recognized as having problems by others, such as managers in the workplace, partners, and families, who may then refer them on to agencies. How can workers within such agencies detect these problems?

There are two answers to this. The first is that workers in these social care systems need to raise their awareness of both of these problems, and be alert to the high probability of people with co-existing problems presenting themselves at their agencies. This is especially the case in all agencies working within the criminal justice system (police, courts, prison, etc.) and in all agencies working with homelessness and housing (see Chapter 10 for a more detailed discussion on this). Banerjee *et al.* (2002) list some highly useful indicators which should alert clinicians that co-existing problems might be an issue. First, there are general demographic pointers. As Mueser *et al.* (1992) pointed out, the more of these factors that are present, the higher our 'index of suspicion' should be that there may be co-existing problems: young age, male, family history of substance misuse, homelessness, disruptive behaviour, poor family relationships, repeated hospitalizations, and legal difficulties. Then there are statements or observations that may warrant further investigation:

- Drug use blocks out unpleasant thoughts, memories, or feelings.
- Drug use helps alleviate symptoms of mental health problems.
- Drug use helps cancel or balance out unwanted side-effects of medication.
- Individual appears 'low in mood' for long periods of time in the absence of obvious stressors.
- Frequent mood swings from 'high' to 'low' in the absence of a diagnosis of bipolar disorder.
- Individual no longer appears to enjoy activities that they once found enjoyable or has lost contact with friends and peers.
- Appears over-suspicious and/or discloses strange thoughts or speech patterns.
- Recent weight gain or loss of more than 15 per cent of body weight (Banerjee *et al.* 2002).

The second way to assist detection is via more routine screening. Co-existing problems are now becoming so common that most helping but non-health agencies need to be very aware of this as a probability and hence should routinely screen for both of these problems (especially agencies working within the criminal justice system and with homelessness). Good routine screening will involve a mixture of self-report methods, laboratory tests, and data from collateral sources (other agencies, and family and friends).

Because many people are reluctant to discuss their substance use or their mental health difficulties with others, empathic interviews are usually the best way to obtain information. People's reluctance is understandable: they realize that if they reveal their substance use issues within a criminal justice context, or either of these issues (mental health or substance use) within a housing context, they are likely to have a poor outcome from the interaction. Interviewers (and agencies) need to be aware of this and need to develop policies and procedures such that it is in people's best interests to be open and honest about their problems.

When undertaking a screening interview, it is good to begin with general questions about use of legal substances such as alcohol and tobacco, and of prescribed medications, thus opening up the subject area in a non-threatening manner. Gradually, the interviewer can ask about the other substances which clients use (including over-the-counter medications and illicit drugs). Some clients have difficulty remembering or may suffer cognitive impairment; having a pre-typed list of all substances which can be shown to them can be very helpful, and also means that the interviewer does not have to run laboriously through (or remember themselves) each likely substance (Banerjee *et al.* 2002). Similarly, it is good to begin with general questions about mental health, asking about their worries or concerns (as opposed to 'anxiety') and periods of feeling low or down (as opposed to 'depression') before moving on to ask about any other symptoms which emerge during the interview.

As well as using screening interviews, it can also sometimes be useful to use brief screening self-completion questionnaires, although all of these may also be interviewer-administered too (if, say, someone has reading or concentration difficulties). Although there has been criticism of the use of self-report measures with people with mental health problems (e.g. Atkinson *et al.* 1997), it is still the case that this is one of the most effective methods of obtaining relevant information.

Rapid scales to gauge initially the extent of any alcohol or other drug use and dependence are best, given that screening assessments are best if they are undertaken speedily.

Rapid scales for alcohol misuse problems include:

• the Fast Alcohol Screening Test (FAST; Hodgson *et al.* 2002), a four-item questionnaire which is seen as less intrusive by staff and clients than the CAGE;
• the Cut down, Annoyed, Guilty, Eye-opener Questionnaire (CAGE; Rydon *et al.* 1992);

- the Alcohol Use Disorders Identification Test (AUDIT; Saunders *et al.* 1993), a 10-item measure of harmful or problematic drinking where a score of eight or more indicates a strong likelihood of hazardous/harmful alcohol consumption).

Rapid scales for either drug or alcohol problems include:

- the Severity of Dependence Scale (SDS; Gossop *et al.* 1995, 1997), where a total score is calculated for all five questions in the scale, and a score of five or more is usually considered indicative of problem substance use);
- the Dartmouth Assessment of Life Instrument (DALI), a general screening tool for drug and alcohol use that has been specifically tested for use with people with severe mental disorders (Rosenberg *et al.* 1998);
- the Alcohol, Smoking, and Substance Involvement Screening Test (ASSIST; WHO ASSIST Working Group 2002), an eight-item screen for alcohol and substance use;
- the 10-item Drug Abuse Screening Test (DAST-10; Skinner 1982), a self-report instrument specifically designed to screen for drug and alcohol problems which can be employed among people with severe and enduring mental disorders;
- the 28-item Drug Abuse Screening Test (Staley and el-Guebaly 1990) which has also been tested with a psychiatric patient population; and
- the Cannabis Use Disorders Identification Test (CUDIT; Adamson and Sellman 2003).

All clients should be screened for smoking and the Fagerstrom Test for Nicotine Dependence may be useful (Heatherton *et al.* 1991).
   Rapid scales for mental health problems include:

- the Manchester Short Assessment of Quality of Life (MANSA; Priebe *et al.* 1999), a 25-item measure of quality of life, derived as a short form of the Lancashire Quality of Life Profile;
- the Kessler Psychological Distress Scale (K10; Kessler *et al.* 2002), a 10-item measure of psychological distress which take about two minutes to complete, and is a good proxy for whether the person is likely to have a mental disorder; and
- the Social Functioning Scale (SFS; Birchwood *et al.* 1990), a relatively brief, objectively scored self-report measure that assesses symptoms and functioning by addressing multiple facets of community adjustment, including social engagement and withdrawal, interpersonal behaviour, prosocial activities, recreation, independence, and employment or occupation.

Agencies can also employ mechanical and laboratory tests to screen for substance use (e.g. a breathalyser for recent alcohol use, and urine, blood, or hair tests for screening of recent or longer-term drug use). Caution needs to be used with such tests. First, they can serve to reduce trust between agencies and clients, and reduce the chances of engagement. Second, the best these tests can do is inform agencies about *use* of drugs, not about problems. As stated at the start of this chapter, the focus for professionals in screening, assessing, and intervening with co-existing problems needs to be on working with the problem component, not the use.

As part of screening, it is important to undertake a risk assessment related to the possibilities of suicide, overdose, blood-borne virus infection, aggression, and violence. The assessment of degree of risk will be based on a variety of factors: the severity of the substance misuse, including the combination of substances used, which is known to be related to the risk of overdose and/or suicide; and an exploration of the possible association between substance misuse and increased risk of aggressive or anti-social behaviour.

It is also the case that certain groups of individuals warrant specific attention (Department of Health 2002), including the following.

Young people

Substance misuse is a major contributory factor in the development of mental health problems in the young. For example, early onset of substance misuse is linked with higher rates of major depressive disorders and it is estimated that a third of young people committing suicide are intoxicated with alcohol at the time of death (see Chapter 8 in this volume).

Homeless people

Studies have identified high levels of concurrent substance misuse and mental health problems among groups of homeless people and rough sleepers. Homelessness almost trebles a young person's chance of developing a mental health problem. Assertive outreach to these groups and in-reach to hostels are necessary (see Chapter 10 in this volume).

Offenders

Both mental health problems and substance misuse play a major role in youth offending, and their combination, together with low adherence to medication, may lead to a higher risk of violence among adults with severe mental health problems. These factors will necessitate partnerships with the criminal justice system and in-reach to detained offenders or suspects. Prisoners have high levels of mental disorder and substance misuse so a close working relationship between prisons, their substance misuse services, and community substance misuse and mental health services is vital.

Women

Significant differences between men and women have been found in terms of patterns of substance misuse and mental health problems:

- Women who misuse substances are significantly more likely than other women or men to have experienced sexual, physical, and/or emotional abuse as children.
- Substance misuse lifestyles can impact on women's sexual health and establish a pattern of re-victimization.
- Women are more likely to present at mental health or primary care services for psychological difficulties than for any associated substance misuse problem.
- Women therefore tend to access alcohol and drug services later than men, and this may explain their more severe presentation.
- Women may have children, or want children, and this can deter them from contact with statutory services for fear of their children being removed.

The complexity and severity of need among women with co-existing problems requires the development of tailored services that are both attractive to women and relevant to their needs. In the UK, a women's mental health strategy addressing some of these issues has been developed (Department of Health 2003).

Indigenous and culturally and linguistically diverse communities

Although definitive studies of the influence of culture and ethnicity upon individuals with co-existing problems have yet to be conducted, it is known that severe mental health problems and substance misuse present differently across cultures and ethnic groups. For example, ethnicity is associated with poor access to services, and with different meanings and values attributed to drugs and alcohol. Service provision must therefore be congruent with and sensitive to the needs of each cultural group.

How do we help people assess? Specialized assessment after detection

Once it is clear that someone may have co-existing problems, they will need to undergo more thorough assessment. Each chapter in the remainder of this book looks at specific recommended assessments, depending on the pattern of co-existing problems experienced. This section will therefore make some common points, and outline a few of the most useful assessment tools.

General principles

- Given the nature of the client group, a good assessment may take an extended period of time to complete. This is especially the case with difficult-to-engage clients, in order to assess fully their complex needs.
- Because substance misuse can itself generate psychological and psychiatric symptoms, and people can self-medicate using alcohol or drugs to help deal with their mental health symptoms and problems, assessment of this relationship should be longitudinal and open to revision.
- Collaboration and extensive liaison with a wide range of agencies is vital to the overall process, and ultimately to successful intervention and outcomes for service users.

Clinical interview

We need to ensure that an assessment of both a client's substance use and problems, and their mental health difficulties, is highly client-centred. This means that we need to start by adopting a 'problems' approach (Velleman 2001) which tries to clarify the range of problems which a person has/can reveal at this stage, and then helps the client prioritize them as targets to be worked on – that is, clarifying with the client what their problems are, and which problems they wish to work on. Assessing co-exisiting problems with substance use and mental health requires careful and empathic interviewing (Velleman 2001).

Assessment of these areas will probably need to cover a wide range of domains, and will need to examine both wants and needs. Domains will include mental health issues and symptoms, and substance use and misuse (covering alcohol, tobacco, and a range of other drugs). Assessment must focus on what the client's goals and aspirations are. As always, the task is to ensure engagement is retained and enhanced, while at the same time conducting a comprehensive assessment, and thus developing a clear formulation of the person's presenting concerns. It is well established that a well-conducted assessment can increase engagement in treatment and be a therapeutic intervention in itself; at the same time, too formal an approach, or too long a session with someone whose concentration is impaired, can be very counterproductive. Good clinical judgement is required!

It is important that we obtain good developmental histories of both conditions, and clarify how they have overlapped in time. I have usually found it beneficial to do this pictorially with a client, using a 'lifetime timeline'. I adopt a life-history approach to assessment, although this can be problematic when clients are very disorganized or have a very unclear recollection of past events. In this life-history approach I assist the client in mapping relevant information from their past onto a lifetime timeline which includes their major life events and the onset and development of their substance use/misuse and their mental health problems and symptoms (including in both domains details of any periods of no or reduced problem, and antecedent and consequential events related to these).

It is also vital to clarify the current frequency, intensity, and duration of both sets of problems. We should examine a number of factors: the client's use of both alcohol and other drugs; their experience of their mental health problems and symptoms; their drinking and drug-taking behaviour; the effects of the use of alcohol and other drugs; the client's thinking concerning their mental health problems and symptoms (expectations, values, definition of the problem, understanding of its cause); their thinking in relation to their alcohol and drug use (again, their expectations, values, definition of the problem, understanding of its cause); and the context (family, employment, social) within which the client has been experiencing their mental health problems, and has been drinking and using other drugs.

The best method of looking at current problems is to ask clients to monitor their drinking and/or substance use, and their mental health problems and symptoms, over the following week or two, in a systematic fashion, collecting information relating to each set of difficulties about how often (e.g. both how often they experience their symptoms, and how often they consume substances), how much (i.e. how severe the symptoms are, and how much is consumed), when, where, and with whom. This can form a good introduction to the idea of self-monitoring; it is useful to suggest that ongoing and recorded self-monitoring of both substance use and problematic mental health symptoms is maintained.

If this prospective assessment is problematic (because of the need for a more immediate assessment, or due to the client's problems in undertaking homework tasks or difficulties in concentration), then another useful technique may be to utilize a more recent version of the timeline approach outlined above, where a retrospective assessment is undertaken of the much more recent past. This is known as the 'timeline follow-back' interviewing technique (Sobell and Sobell 1992), and involves asking individuals to reconstruct their mental health problems or their drug use/drinking behaviour over a specified interval – the past week or two, or sometimes longer (some studies have reported collecting this information in relation to substance use over the whole of the previous three months).

The twin aims of the assessment are: (i) to develop a comprehensible formulation of how a client's problems in different domains developed and are being maintained (see Chapter 4 for an in-depth discussion of formulation); and (ii) to assist clients in deciding which problem areas to work on and, of these, what is a sensible prioritization of the order with which they should be tackled (always bearing in mind that it is likely that more than one problem area will need to be tackled simultaneously).

It is also extremely positive in both substance misuse and mental health work (and hence in work with both sets of problem) to utilize family and other non-substance-misusing social networks (e.g. Chapter 5 of this volume; Copello *et al.* 2005; Pharoah *et al.* 2003), both as part of the assessment process and hence as collateral sources of information, and as part of a social-context focussed treatment approach which enables the work undertaken within therapeutic sessions to be more easily generalized into clients' outside lives.

Questionnaires and assessment tools

A range of validated assessment instruments to enhance clinical techniques are available: see Dawe *et al.* (2002) for a review of the available screening and diagnostic instruments for people with co-existing mental health and alcohol/other drug use problems. Assessments should examine alcohol and drug use and problems in the past as well as in the present, including nicotine. Among the most useful instruments are the following.

1   Alcohol and drug problems

   i   The Clinicians' Rating Scale for Alcohol Use (CAUS) and Drug Use (CDUS) (Drake *et al.* 1996) is based on DSM-IV diagnostic criteria for substance-related disorders and has been reliably used to classify the severity of substance use among people with severe mental health problems.
   ii The Substance Abuse Treatment Scale (SATS; also a clinician rating) seeks to assess the stage of treatment and the extent to which clients are engaged in discussing their substance use or receiving substance abuse treatment (Drake *et al.* 1996).
   iii The Readiness to Change Questionnaire – Treatment Version (Heather *et al.* 1999) is a 15-item measure for assessing motivational readiness to change alcohol use behaviour and is based on the 'stages of change' model. It allocates drinkers to one of three stages: pre-contemplation, contemplation, and action. There are also versions of this scale which have been adapted for use with other drugs, although the adapted versions have not been subject to the same stringent reliability and validity tests as the original version. Another similar scale is the Stages of Change Readiness and Treatment Eagerness Scale (SOCRATES; Miller and Tonigan 1996), which also measures readiness to change.
   iv The Chemical Use, Abuse, and Dependence Scale (CUAD; Appleby *et al.* 1996) is reliable in assessing severity of drug and alcohol problems in people with severe mental disorder.
   v   The Opiate Treatment Index (OTI; Darke *et al.* 1991) is a structured interview, measuring six behavioural domains: drug use, HIV risk-taking behaviour, social functioning, criminality, health status, and psychological functioning. The OTI in its complete form takes

20–30 minutes to complete. In some studies, only selected components of the instrument have been administered. The drug use questions allow the calculation of a quantity/frequency estimate (Q score), through the addition of consumption amounts on the two previous days of opiate use and dividing this value by the time intervals between days.

vi   The Addiction Severity Index (ASI; McLellan *et al.* 1980) looks at the use of a range of substances over the previous 30 days. Adequate psychometric properties for use with clients with co-existing problems have been published (Hodgkins *et al.* 1999; Zanis *et al.* 1997).

vii   The Leeds Dependence Questionnaire (LDQ; Raistrick *et al.* 1994) is a 10-item questionnaire used to measure psychological dependence across a wide range of substances. It is often completed for the client's most frequently used substance, although it can be completed as appropriate for each relevant one.

2   Mental health problems

i   The Psychiatric Research Interview for Substance and Mental Disorders (PRISM), based on DSM-IV (APA 1994), has been used extensively in studies of co-existing severe mental disorder and drug and alcohol problems and has been found to have good reliability in diagnosing primary depression, psychosis, and bipolar affective disorder in clients with co-existing drug and alcohol problems (Hasin *et al.* 1996).

ii   The Global Assessment of Functioning Scale (GAF; APA 1994: 32) is a measure that assesses the individual's overall functioning on a rating scale that ranges from 0 to 100.

iii   The Quality of Life Scale (QLS; Heinrichs *et al.* 1984) provides an 'external assessment' of QOL based on client self-report and on the interviewer's assessment of their current life circumstances. This is a 21-item scale based on a semi-structured interview designed to assess deficit (as opposed to positive) symptoms. Factor analysis has shown fundamentally the same structure for men and women.

iv   If it is thought that there may be a severe mental health problem (one of the psychoses) then other assessment ratings can be used. The Positive and Negative Syndrome Scale (PANSS; Kay *et al.* 1987) is a 30-item measure of client symptomatology which provides balanced representation of positive and negative symptoms and gauges their relationship to one another and to global psychological difficulties. It comprises four scales measuring positive and negative syndromes, their differential, and general severity of the mental health difficulties. In studies of people diagnosed with schizophrenia, the four scales have been found to be normally distributed, with support for their reliability and stability. There is also the Psychiatric Assessment

Scale (PAS; also known as the KGV; Krawiecka *et al.* 1977; revised by Lancashire 1994), a semi-structured interview tool that is very useful for discovering the detailed phenomenology of psychosis. Other measures specifically of psychotic symptomatology include the Beliefs About Voices Questionnaire (BAVQ; Chadwick and Birchwood 1995) and the Cognitive Assessment of Voice Interview Schedule (CAVIS; Chadwick *et al.* 1996).

3   Medication compliance: The Drugs Attitude Inventory (DAI; Hogan *et al.* 1983) is a self-report scale shown to be highly predictive of compliance.

CONCLUSION

In this chapter I have looked at many of the issues which lie at the heart of how co-existing problems are conceptualized, and at how they are detected and assessed. There are many debates about the appropriateness of various ways of describing people with co-existing problems with their mental health and their substance use. In this book we have used a broad and inclusive definition of co-existing problems, and have deliberately not used medicalized terminology such as 'dual diagnosis' or 'co-morbidity'.

Partly because clients with these co-existing problems impact upon a wide range of professionals, and often present major challenges due to their complex needs, there is a growing awareness within both the mental health and substance misuse fields of the importance of co-existing problems. However, often the complex and interrelated nature of these clients' problems is not detected.

Although many people suffer from co-existing mental health and substance use problems, many will not present themselves to health professionals. A wide range of professionals need to develop skills in detecting these problems: detection will be increased via raised awareness of such co-existing problems, and via routine screening and risk assessment. Within more specialized services, the assessment of substance misuse needs to form an integral part of standard assessment procedures for mental health problems, and vice versa.

Assessment of such complex problems is rarely a speedy task: given the nature of the client group, a good assessment may take an extended period of time to complete, and the assessment of the relationship between substance misuse and mental health problems should be longitudinal and open to revision. Because such co-existing problems often extend beyond the competencies of any one professional group, it is vital to have high levels of collaboration and extensive liaison with a wide range of agencies, as well as with clients' families and other non-substance-misusing social networks.

Having undertaken a fuller assessment, the next stages are case formulation (see Chapter 4) and then intervention.

KEY RESOURCES

Banerjee, S., Clancy, C. and Crome, I., *Co-existing Problems of Mental Disorder and Substance Misuse (Dual Diagnosis): An Information Manual.* London: Royal College of Psychiatrists Research Unit, 2002. Available at http://www.rcpsych.ac.uk/cru/complete/ddippracmanual.pdf (accessed 19 August 2005).

Crawford, V. and Crome, I., *Co-existing Problems of Mental Health and Substance Misuse ('Dual Diagnosis'): A Review of Relevant Literature.* London: Royal College of Psychiatrists Research Unit, 2001. Available at http://www.rcpsych.ac.uk/cru/complete/literature%20review.pdf (accessed 19 August 2005).

Dawe, S., Lowton, N., Hides, L., Kavanagh, D. and Mattick, R., *Review of Diagnostic Screening Instruments for Alcohol and Other Drug Use and Other Psychiatric Disorders, Monograph 48,* 2nd ed. Canberra: Commonwealth Department of Health and Ageing, 2002. Available at http://www.health.gov.au/internet/wcms/publishing.nsf/content/health-pubhlth-publicat-document-mono48-cnt.htm/$file/mono48.pdf (accessed 19 August 2005).

Department of Health, *Dual Diagnosis Good Practice Guide.* London: HMSO, 2002. Available at http://www.dh.gov.uk/assetroot/04/06/04/35/04060435.pdf (accessed 19 August 2005).

Department of Health, *Mainstreaming Gender and Women's Mental Health: Implementation Guidance.* London: Department of Health, 2003. Available at http://www.dh.gov.uk/assetroot/04/07/20/69/04072069.pdf (accessed 19 August 2005).

Department of Health, *Women's Mental Health Strategy.* London: Department of Health, 2003. Available at http://www.dh.gov.uk/policyandguidance/healthandsocialcaretopics/mentalhealth/mentalhealtharticle/fs/en?content_id=4002408&chk=opsonr (accessed 19 August 2005).

Hawkins, C. & Gilburt, H., *Dual Diagnosis Toolkit: Mental Health and Substance Misuse.* London: Rethink and Turning Point, 2004. Available at http://www.rethink.org/dualdiagnosis/ (accessed 19 August 2005).

Kendall, T., Worrall, A., Banerjee, S., Clancy, C., Mears, A., Burns, P. and Quaye, S., *Dual Diagnosis Information Project.* London: Royal College of Psychiatrists Research Unit, 2004. Available at http://www.rcpsych.ac.uk/cru/complete/ddip.htm (accessed 19 August 2005).

Mears, A., Clancy, C., Banerjee, S., Crome, I. and Agbo-Quaye, S., *Co-existing Problems of Mental Disorder and Substance Misuse ('Dual Diagnosis'): A Training Needs Analysis.* London: Royal College of Psychiatrists Research Unit, 2001. Available at http://www.rcpsych.ac.uk/cru/complete/training%20needs%20analysis.pdf (accessed 19 August 2005).

Teesson, M. and Proudfoot, H., *Comorbid Mental Disorders and Substance Use Disorders: Epidemiology, Prevention and Treatment.* Canberra: Commonwealth Department of Health and Ageing, 2003. Available at http://www.health.gov.au/internet/wcms/publishing.nsf/content/health-pubhlth-publicat-documentmono_comorbid-cnt.htm/$file/mono_comorbid.pdf (accessed 19 August 2005).

REFERENCES

Abou-Saleh, M. T., 'Dual diagnosis of substance misuse and psychiatric disorders: A U.S.–U.K. perspective', *Acta Neuropsychiatrica*, *16*, 1–2, 2004.

Adamson, S. and Sellman, J., 'A prototype screening instrument for cannabis use disorder: The Cannabis Use Disorders Identification Test (CUDIT) in an alcohol dependent clinical sample', *Drug and Alcohol Review*, *22*, 309–15, 2003.

American Psychiatric Association (APA), *Diagnostic and Statistical Manual of Mental Disorders*, 4th ed. Washington: APA, 1994.

Appleby, K., Dyson, V., Altman, E., McGovern, M. and Luchins, D., 'Utility of the Chemical Use, Abuse and Dependence Scale in screening patients with severe mental illness', *Psychiatric Services*, *47*, 647–9, 1996.

Atkinson, M., Zubin, S. and Chuang, H., 'Characterising quality of life among patients with chronic mental illness: A critical examination of the self-report methodology', *American Journal of Psychiatry*, *154*, 99–105, 1997.

Banerjee, S., Clancy, C. and Crome, I., *Co-existing Problems of Mental Disorder and Substance Misuse (Dual Diagnosis)*. London: Royal College of Psychiatrists Research Unit, 2002.

Birchwood, M., Smith, J., Cochrane, R., Wetton, S. and Copestake, S., 'The Social Functioning Scale. The development and validation of a new scale of social adjustment for use in family intervention programmes with schizophrenic patients', *British Journal of Psychiatry*, *157*, 853–9, 1990.

Chadwick, P. and Birchwood, M. J., 'The omnipotence of voices II: The Beliefs About Voices Questionnaire', *British Journal of Psychiatry*, *166*, 773–6, 1995.

Chadwick, P., Birchwood, M. and Trower, P., *Cognitive Therapy for Delusions, Voices and Paranoia*. Chichester: John Wiley, 1996.

Copello, A., Velleman, R. and Templeton, L., 'Family interventions in the treatment of alcohol and drug problems', *Drug and Alcohol Review*, *24*, 369–85, 2005.

Crawford, V. and Crome, I., *Co-existing Problems of Mental Health and Substance Misuse (Dual Diagnosis): A Review of Relevant Literature*. London: Royal College of Psychiatrists Research Unit, 2001.

Darke, S., Ward, J., Hall, W., Heather, N. and Wodak, A., *The Opiate Treatment Index (OTI) Researcher's Manual. National Drug and Alcohol Research Centre Technical Report Number 11*. Sydney: National Drug and Alcohol Research Centre, 1991.

Dawe, S., Loxton, N. J., Hides, L., Kavanagh, D. and Mattick, R. P., *Review of Diagnostic Screening Instruments for Alcohol and Other Drug Use and Other Psychiatric Disorders, Monograph 48*, 2nd ed. Canberra: Commonwealth Department of Health and Ageing, 2002.

Department of Health, *Dual Diagnosis Good Practice Guide*. London: HMSO, 2002.

Department of Health, *Mainstreaming Gender and Women's Mental Health: Implementation Guidance*. London: Department of Health, 2003.

Drake, R., Mueser, K. T. and McHugo, G. J., 'Clinician rating scales: Alcohol Use Scale (AUS), Drug Use Scale (DUS) and Substance Abuse Treatment Scale (SATS)', in Sederer, L. and Dickey, B., eds, *Outcomes Assessment in Clinical Practice*, pp. 113–16. Baltimore: Williams and Wilkins, 1996.

Gossop, M., Best, D., Marsden, J. and Strang, J., 'Test–retest reliability of the Severity of Dependence Scale', *Addiction*, *92*, 353, 1997.

Gossop, M., Darke, S., Griffiths, P., Hando, J., Powis, B., Hall, W. and Strang, J.,

'The Severity of Dependence Scale (SDS): Psychometric properties of the SDS in English and Australian samples of heroin, cocaine and amphetamine users', *Addiction*, *90*, 607–14, 1995.

Hasin, D., Trautman, K., Miele, G., Samet, S., Smith, M. and Endicott, J., 'Psychiatric Research Interview for Substance Misuse and Mental Disorders (PRISM): Reliability for substance abusers', *American Journal of Psychiatry*, *153*, 1195–201, 1996.

Hawkins, C. and Gilburt, H., *Dual Diagnosis Toolkit: Mental Health and Substance Misuse*. London: Rethink and Turning Point, 2004.

Heather, N., Luce, A., Peck, D., Dumbar, B. and James, I., 'Development of a treatment version of the Readiness to Change Questionnaire', *Addiction Research and Theory*, *7*, 63–83, 1999.

Heatherton, T. F., Kozlowski, L. T., Frecker, R. C. and Fagerstrom, K. O., 'The Fagerstrom test for nicotine dependence: A revision of the Fagerstrom Tolerance Questionnaire', *British Journal of Addiction*, *86*, 1119–27, 1991.

Heinrichs, D., Hanlon, E. and Carpenter, W., 'The Quality of Life Scale: An instrument for rating the schizophrenic deficit syndrome', *Schizophrenia Bulletin*, *10*, 388–98, 1984.

Hodgkins, D. C., el-Guebaly, N., Armstrong, S. and Durfour, M., 'Implications of depression on outcome from alcohol dependence: A three-year prospective follow-up', *Alcoholism: Clinical and Experimental Research*, *23*, 151–7, 1999.

Hodgson, R., Alwyn, T., John, B., Thom, E. and Smith, A., 'The FAST (Fast Alcohol Screening Test)', *Alcohol and Alcoholism*, *37*, 61–66, 2002.

Hoff, R. and Rosenheck, R., 'Long-term patterns of service use and cost among patients with both psychiatric and substance abuse disorders', *Medical Care*, *36*, 835–43, 1998.

Hoff, R. and Rosenheck, R., 'The cost of treating substance abuse patients with and without comorbid psychiatric disorders', *Psychiatric Services*, *50*, 1309–15, 1999.

Hogan, T., Awad, A. and Eastwood, R., 'A self-report scale predictive of drug compliance in schizophrenics: Reliability and discriminative validity', *Psychological Medicine*, *13*, 177–83, 1983.

Kay, S., Fiszbein, A. and Opler, L., 'The Positive And Negative Syndrome Scale (PANSS) for schizophrenia', *Schizophrenia Bulletin*, *13*, 261–76, 1987.

Kessler, R., Andrews, G., Colpe, L., Hiripi, E., Mroczek, D., Normand, S. *et al.*, 'Short screening scales to monitor population prevalences and trends in non-specific psychological distress', *Psychological Medicine*, *32*, 959–76, 2002.

Krawiecka, M., Goldberg, D. and Vaughan, M., 'A standardised psychiatric assessment scale for rating chronic psychotic patients', *Acta Psychiatrica Scandinavica*, *55*, 209–308, 1977.

Lancashire, S., *Revised Version of KGV Scale*. Manchester: University of Manchester (Department of Nursing, Psychiatry and Behavioural Sciences), 1994.

McLellan, A., Luborsky, L., Woody, G. E. and O'Brian, C., 'An improved diagnostic evaluation instrument for substance abuse patients: The Addiction Severity Index', *Journal of Nervous and Mental Disease*, *168*, 26–33, 1980.

Miller, W. and Tonigan, J., 'Assessing drinkers' motivation for change: The Stages of Change Readiness and Treatment Eagerness Scale (SOCRATES)', *Psychology of Addictive Behaviours*, *10*, 81–9, 1996.

Mueser, K. T., Yarnold, P. and Bellack, A. S., 'Diagnostic and demographic correlates of substance abuse in schizophrenia and major affective disorder', *Acta Psychiatrica Scandinavica*, *85*, 48–55, 1992.

O'Brien, C., Charney, D., Lewis, L., Cornish, J. W., Post, R. M., Woody, G. E. *et al.*, 'Priority actions to improve the care of persons with co-occurring substance abuse and other mental disorders: A call to action', *Biological Psychiatry*, *56*, 703–13, 2004.

Pharoah, F., Rathbone, J., Mari, J. and Streiner, D., *Family Intervention for Schizophrenia (Cochrane Review)*. The Cochrane Library Issue 2. Oxford: Update Software, 2003.

Priebe, S., Huxley, P., Knight, S. and Evans, S., 'Application and results of the Manchester Short Assessment of quality of life (MANSA)', *International Journal of Social Psychiatry*, *45*, 7–12, 1999.

Raistrick, D., Bradshaw, J., Tober, G., Weiner, J., Allison, J. and Healey, C., 'Development of the Leeds Dependence Questionnaire (LDQ): A questionnaire to measure alcohol and opiate dependence in the context of a treatment evaluation package', *Addiction*, *89*, 563–72, 1994.

Rosenberg, S. D., Drake, R., Wolford, G. L., Mueser, K. T., Oxman, T. E., Vidaver, R. M. *et al.*, 'Dartmouth Assessment of Lifestyle Instrument (DALI): A substance use disorder screen for people with severe mental illness', *American Journal of Psychiatry*, *155*, 232–8, 1998.

Rydon, P., Redman, S., Sanon-Fisher, R. W. and Reid, A. L., 'Detection of alcohol-related problems in general practice', *Journal of Studies in Alcohol*, *50*, 197–202, 1992.

Saunders, J., Aasland, O. G., Babor, T. F., de la Fuente, J. R. and Grant, M., 'Development of the Alcohol Use Disorder Identification Test (AUDIT): WHO collaborative project on early detection of persons with harmful alcohol consumption – II', *Addiction*, *88*, 791–804, 1993.

Skinner, H., 'The Drug Abuse Screening Test', *Addictive Behaviors*, *7*, 363–71, 1982.

Sobell, L. C. and Sobell, M. B., 'Timeline follow-back: A technique for assessing self-reported alcohol consumption', in Litten, R. and Allen, J., eds, *Measuring Alcohol Consumption: Psychosocial and Biochemical Methods*, pp. 41–72. Totoa, NJ: Humana Press, 1992.

Staley, D. and el-Guebaly, N., 'Psychometric properties of the Drug Abuse Screening Test in a psychiatric patient population', *Addictive Behaviors*, *15*, 257–64, 1990.

Velleman, R., *Counselling for Alcohol Problems*, 2nd ed. London: Sage, 2001.

WHO ASSIST Working Group, 'The Alcohol, Smoking and Substance Involvement Screening Test (ASSIST): Development, reliability and feasibility', *Addiction*, *97*, 1183–94, 2002.

Zanis, D., McLellan, A. and Corse, S., 'Is the Addiction Severity Index a reliable and valid assessment instrument among clients with severe and persistent mental illness and substance abuse disorders?' *Community Mental Health Journal*, *33*, 213–27, 1997.

Chapter 3

Motivational interviewing

David J. Kavanagh and Jennifer M. Connolly

KEY POINTS

1   Motivational interviewing (MI) is a client-centred, therapist-directed style of interviewing that seeks to accentuate client awareness of their ambivalence about current dysfunctional behaviour and to develop a functional resolution of this ambivalence.
2   MI is potentially brief, avoids risks of confrontation and is tailored to the needs and concerns of the individual.
3   MI has strong support as a method of engaging clients in behaviour change, both in the general population and in people with co-existing mental and substance use disorders, although it is not necessarily more effective than other active treatments.
4   Evidence supports the use of MI as a stand-alone intervention in substance misuse, in contrast to confrontation, which has negative net effects. In co-existing disorders, support for stand-alone MI is less strong than in the general community.
5   In people with severe mental disorders, greater emphasis is often needed on building rapport, adjusting for cognitive deficits, building self-efficacy and perceived control, addressing dysphoria and dealing with multiple concerns.

INTRODUCTION

In some past programs for co-existing mental and substance use disorders, a requirement for entry has sometimes been a demonstration of control over substance use and a stabilization of symptoms. Unless supported by other services, such programs abrogate responsibility for eliciting motivation and assisting the person in the earliest and often hardest stages of their attempt. This policy leads to some of those who most need the treatment being excluded. The focus of this chapter is on the generation of commitment to address jointly-occurring problems of substance misuse and mental disorder, and the development of a collaborative therapeutic relationship to achieve that end.

Within forensic settings and with some individuals who put themselves or others at unacceptably high and immediate risks of harm, change in substance use or management of their mental disorder may be mandated, and incentives or disincentives may be applied to obtain behaviour control. However, within this chapter we emphasize the clarification and fostering of the client's own goals for their lives and, within that context, their goals in relation to mental health, substance use and other physical health maintenance. There is no assumption by therapists that any substance use is necessarily dysfunctional, despite their knowledge that even low consumption levels tend to be problematic or unstable for many people with severe mental health problems, cognitive deficits or limited financial resources (Drake and Wallach 1993; Kavanagh *et al.* 1999). Individual variations in effects of given doses have been observed, even within the same diagnostic group. These considerations suggest that individual tailoring and a client-centred focus should form the framework in which engagement and motivation are developed.

As in substance misuse more generally, assessment feedback and directive advice to clients by a therapist are often effective in generating commitment to change (Miller and Rollnick 2002). This type of brief intervention relies on the person integrating the information into existing motivational structures. However, there is a risk that such an approach may become confrontational, increasing resistance to change or exacerbating symptoms in emotionally vulnerable individuals (Siegfried 1998). More consistent with the emphasis of this chapter is a motivational interviewing (MI) approach (Miller 1983).

Miller and Rollnick (2002) defined MI as 'a client centred, directive method for enhancing intrinsic motivation to change by exploring and resolving ambivalence' (Miller and Rollnick 2002: 25). The approach sees ambivalence as characteristic of the contemplation of change, and strives to increase the likelihood of change by communicating respect for the client's autonomy and a collaboration to help them resolve the ambivalence. Four general principles within MI are:

- the expression of empathy and acceptance;
- the development of discrepancy (eliciting cognitive dissonance between current behaviours and key values or goals);
- rolling with resistance (i.e. the therapist avoids arguing for change and uses resistance as a signal to emphasize autonomy); and
- supporting self-efficacy (e.g. by drawing attention to past achievements).

Clients explore their feelings about behavioural alternatives, and therapist summaries bring the bases of ambivalence into focus. While MI is particularly relevant to the 'contemplation' phase of the descriptive stages of change model of Prochaska and DiClemente (1982), MI can be applied to elicit or consolidate commitment at any stage.

Evidence of MI efficacy

There is now substantial evidence in favour of MI (or MI plus assessment feedback) as a way of eliciting commitment to further treatment, and as a stand-alone intervention for substance misuse (Burke *et al.* 2003; Dunn *et al.* 2001; Moyer *et al.* 2002). In the Miller and Wilbourne (2002) meta-analytic review of alcohol treatments, motivational interviewing had very strong evidentiary support, with 71 per cent of 17 available trials showing positive results. There were no studies supporting confrontational counselling, which had a negative average effect over control conditions. The strongest support for MI is in relation to no treatment or standard care. It is typically of about equal efficacy to other active treatments (Burke *et al.* 2003). In some cases these comparative treatments require substantially greater investment of time (Holder *et al.* 2000). In others, the interventions are similarly brief, and here the finding probably reflects the power of assessment feedback and authoritative advice to effect change in some individuals.

While most MI trials have been with adults with substance misuse (especially alcohol; Burke *et al.* 2003), there is evidence supporting the use of MI with substance-misusing adolescents (Tevyaw and Monti 2004). Current evidence does not support MI for smoking or HIV risk (Burke *et al.* 2003).

We now have several trials of MI to elicit motivation in people with coexisting substance misuse and mental disorder to attend subsequent therapy which show that even with psychiatric inpatients MI is more effective than standard care (Martino *et al.* 2000; Swanson *et al.* 1999), advice or psychoeducation (Baker *et al.* 2002a, 2002b; Steinberg *et al.* 2004). In one study, a motivational intervention promoted greater subsequent adherence than treatment as usual among inpatients with cocaine dependence and depression, and they spent fewer days in hospital over the next 12 months (Daley *et al.* 1998).

There is also evidence regarding MI variants as stand-alone interventions for substance misuse among psychiatric inpatients. Baker *et al.* (2002b) undertook a randomized controlled trial, comparing the impact of a single individual motivational interview of 30–45 minutes ($n = 79$) with the effects of a self-help booklet ($n = 81$) on hospitalized psychiatric inpatients with coexisting substance use disorder. There was a significantly greater effect from the interview on an aggregate measure of substance use, although the relative benefit dissipated over the follow-up period, and cannabis use was not substantially changed by either intervention. Hulse and Tait (2002) randomized psychiatric inpatients scoring problematic alcohol use at screening, but low levels of alcohol dependence, to MI plus feedback or an information pack. At six months, those receiving MI had lower alcohol use than those receiving education. At five years, there was no difference between the groups in terms of time spent hospitalized for any reason, but both groups fared better than matched controls (Hulse and Tait 2003). Significantly fewer drinking days and higher abstinence rates at six months were associated with MI than with educational treatment in Graeber *et al.*'s (2003) study of people with schizophrenia and alcohol use disorders. Brown *et al.* (2003) showed that two 45-minute sessions of MI were no more effective than 5–10 minutes of advice at addressing the smoking of hospitalized adolescents. However MI was more effective if the adolescents did not initially intend to address their smoking, while advice was more effective in those already committed to change.

A pilot study for young inpatients within three years of their first episode (Kavanagh *et al.* 2004) compared a variant of MI for substance misuse called 'Start Over and Survive' (SOS) with standard care, using a randomized design and intention-to-treat analyses. SOS had a maximum three hours of face-to-face contact, plus brief telephone follow-up. Four participants in SOS only received rapport-building sessions, which preceded MI and response planning. Eleven (85%) participants in SOS, and all eight who actually received MI, showed substantial improvement in their substance use at six months. This compared with seven (58 per cent) in the control condition. However, significantly more SOS patients were living with a family member, and this variable was associated with better outcomes. A second, as yet unpublished, trial with psychiatric inpatients by the same group compared SOS with an intervention of equal length that included only rapport-building. Preliminary analyses show that both approaches were equally successful. This may suggest that, in the context of an inpatient admission and ongoing assessment of substance use and psychotic symptoms, simple processes of empathy and reflection may be enough to trigger change in some people.

Overall, the current evidence provides strong support for the applicability of MI in promoting engagement in people with co-existing mental and substance use disorders. There is more modest and less consistent evidence for MI as a sole intervention, with greater relative effects often in the shorter term, and some alternatives (such as rapport building) sometimes showing comparable impact, at least in the context of repeated assessments.

CONTEXT OF THERAPY

Therapist variables

Surveys of mental health and alcohol and other drug services demonstrate that staff in each service perceive that they lack knowledge and skills in dealing with problems that are usually seen by the companion service (e.g. Kavanagh *et al.* 2000a), although they report a willingness to undergo training (Siegfried *et al.* 1999). Service structures and priorities inhibit collaboration and consultation in dealing with co-existing problems (Kavanagh *et al.* 2000b), while current evidence supports integration of treatment (Drake *et al.* 2004). MI is a procedure that in principle may be taught to and implemented by mental health staff who are not addiction specialists. (A dissemination trial by the authors to demonstrate this is in progress.)

Client variables

People with these co-existing disorders frequently have multiple socio-economic, social and emotional issues (Laudet *et al.* 2000). Many with severe disorders are unemployed and have few leisure activities or non-user friends (Hadzi-Pavlovic *et al.* 1992; Jackson and Edwards 1992; MacDonald *et al.* 2004), so they have little in their lives apart from substance use. Resolution of other issues often appears critical to the success of treatment for the focal disorders. Depression is endemic in this population. We know that dysphoria has a powerful effect on self-efficacy and achievements (Kavanagh 1992), particularly where persistence in the face of setbacks is required, as is often the case with multiple co-existing disorders. In addition, substantial cognitive deficits may be seen, although even in schizophrenia there is substantial variability in cognitive function (Heinrichs 2004). Application of MI to these populations needs to be tailored accordingly.

TREATMENT OF CO-EXISTING MENTAL HEALTH AND DRUG AND ALCOHOL PROBLEMS WITH MOTIVATIONAL INTERVIEWING

Detailed description of MI

MI is a style of interaction rather than a set of techniques. It requires that therapists suspend a convergent question-and-answer approach, so familiar in the context of rapid screening and assessment, and instead use open-ended questions and reflective listening to draw out the perspectives of clients (Miller and Rollnick 2002). Therapists should refrain from trying to influence clients directly, adopting instead a neutral stance. They may occasionally play 'devil's advocate', raising an alternative explanation for a negative effect of substance use, encouraging clients to argue for change and inoculating against later doubts. The topic of conversation, at least initially, is the issue that most concerns the client already.

Therapists avoid apportioning blame or guilt, since these issues provoke defensiveness and lead down unproductive reattributional paths. They refrain from negative judgments about behaviour, focusing responses on client perceptions of functionality in relation to their own goals. However, therapists do elicit clients' concerns about their current situation and the perceived importance of issues, since dissatisfaction (i.e. discrepancy from valued outcomes) is the primary catalyst of change.

Information is provided in answer to specific questions and to reinforce or correct the accuracy of factual statements. However, this is done sparingly, because information is not the key to change (think about how well-informed many substance users already are), and because an 'expert' role for therapists puts clients in a passive position.

One reason for the persistence of dysfunctional behaviours like substance use is the salience of proximal consequences (Bandura 1986). When decisions to use drugs are made, immediate positive expectations swamp the attentional field. So, one aspect of MI involves encouraging clients to consider things they like about substance use, and things that are not as appealing to them. Talking about the things they like is attractive even when clients are not contemplating change, and later discussion of the 'downside' is rendered more acceptable. Omitting detailed articulation of the advantages of substance use can render commitment to change unrealistic, in not taking account of the difficulties clients subsequently face.

Therapists encourage elaboration of concerns, and ascertain clients' own responses to them, especially when they suspect they are repeating the statements or concerns of others. For example, in response to, 'Well, I know that drinking this much is not good for my health,' therapists may say, 'Is there something *you* are worried will happen?' While therapists encourage consideration of delayed (and potentially extreme) risks or benefits, they also elicit proximal aspects relating to those issues. In the previous example, they may ask: 'Have you already had a health problem from drinking that you are concerned about?' or 'Has anything happened already that suggests you are at risk of that?' then 'Does that concern you?' Should a client say, 'If I fix my drinking, I may even be able to get married eventually,' the therapist may ask, 'Would it make any difference to the relationships you have now?' and then 'Is *that* something you would like to happen?'

Some issues can be omitted when people only think about their current situation. So, therapists also encourage clients to think about what they would miss if they did make a change, and what may be gained. 'I suppose I would miss seeing my drinking buddies as much. I hadn't thought of that before.'

Consideration of changes to current behaviour is within the context of the person's overall goals and values. So, in MI, clients are encouraged to articulate these values, and consider how they fit with their current substance use.

Summaries are important in MI, since they clarify complex issues, help to hold multiple issues in awareness and accentuate cognitive dissonance. They are used throughout the interview. Clients' reactions to summaries are sought. If clients say they do not want to change their behaviour, therapists do not press the issue ('rolling with resistance'), although they may ask what would need to happen before change was more attractive. If that situation occurred in the future, timing may then be better for MI than at present.

The primary barrier to change is sometimes perceived ability rather than desire. Throughout the process, therapists draw attention to early steps clients have taken (e.g. coming to this interview), reinforce statements of intention to change and express optimism about potential for future success. Since past performance is the most powerful information source for self-efficacy (Bandura 1986), successful aspects of relevant past attempts are emphasized. When clients are thinking about starting an attempt, therapists encourage them to break tasks into steps they are confident of achieving. If they become committed to changing their behaviour, a specific plan is developed and commitment to it is elicited.

Throughout MI, therapists maintain empathy for the difficulties clients have in resolving their ambivalence about behaviour change and in sustaining these changes in the face of obstacles and setbacks. They remind themselves that successful behaviour change often requires multiple attempts (Marlatt *et al.* 1990), and that they themselves have found significant behaviour change difficult to contemplate and attempt.

Application to co-existing psychosis and substance misuse

In order to provide a concrete description of MI for co-existing problems, the approach described here (SOS) adapts MI to the context of inpatients under-going an acute episode of psychosis who also have a substance use disorder. Applications of MI to less severe contexts may be closer to MI as described by Miller and Rollnick (2002).

SOS was designed to be consistent with a busy standard psychiatric ward, so we limited maximum contact to three hours, plus a family session (aimed at promoting empathy and maintaining client support). We also gave fortnightly five-minute telephone calls to the experimental and control groups in our controlled trial. For the experimental group this included reviewing material from the intervention and providing encouragement to continue or renew their attempt. Controls received continued rapport only. The calls ensured a minimum of support even in the absence of case manager involvement. These aspects of SOS are not prototypical of MI.

Modifications for psychosis

When MI is applied within an acute psychotic episode, some modifications to the procedure are needed (see also Chapter 13 of this volume; Martino *et al.* 2002).

Consider inclusion of rapport building

Often, therapists on an inpatient ward have no prior relationship with the person and were not involved in assessments at admission. Clients are often distressed, preoccupied with other issues and suspicious. Under these circumstances, we precede MI with frequent, brief contacts (once or twice a day, for one to five minutes), which aim to build rapport, trust and engagement (cf. the treatment stage of 'engagement in a working alliance'; Osher and Kofoed 1989). We talk about their interests (e.g. football, music, what they want to do when they leave hospital). These discussions also identify values and goals that may enter MI. When trust has been generated, other urgent issues have been addressed and they are able to maintain attention on a topic for 5–10 minutes with prompting (usually two to three days after admission), we ask whether we can talk about substance use.

Adjust for cognitive deficits

Since attention is often compromised in acute episodes, therapists minimize potential distractions, simplify question constructions (avoiding multiple clauses, multiple questions or alternatives) and, if necessary, remind the person about the topic and task. If other concerns are raised, therapists negotiate which issue should be delayed until a later time. When 'good' and 'not so good' aspects are elicited, information is written down, using the client's words. The most highly valued aspects are starred, and those of little concern or uncertain status are placed in brackets. Clients keep a copy of lists and information handouts to review. Sessions are usually short with in-patients, typically 10–20 minutes, and often MI is carried out over several brief sessions. Summaries and reviews are used extensively.

When the person has limited reading or writing skills, recorded items comprise simple drawings plus one or two words. Relative lengths of lists and number of starred items provide a visual aid for summaries when clients are unable to hold multiple items in working memory. Assessment feedback and information from the rapport phase are integrated into MI, reinforcing the issues clients raise, or introducing ideas after they have exhausted their own: for example, 'You said the other day that sometimes there are arguments when you have a drink, should that be on the list? . . . Is that something that you are concerned about?' Relationships between substance use and psychiatric symptoms are routinely explored (in terms of both relief and exacerbation). When poverty of speech or content is inhibiting the generation of ideas, therapists may ask whether the client shares a particular common experience of substance use (see Figure 3.1 for a form with some prompts). However, prompts are used sparingly, to avoid the session becoming a series of questions and answers rather than a personal exploration by the client.

Misinterpretation of therapist statements or intent sometimes occurs.

There are many reasons why people use ...., and many reasons why people cut down their use of ....
One reason why people keep using drugs a lot is that they have never really thought about what drugs are doing for them.
What have been the good things, and less good things about using ....?

Good things	Less good things
'It helps me relax'	'I have put on weight'
'I enjoy the taste'	'I have lost weight'
'It helps me fit in with other people'	'I tend to get into arguments and fights'
'It helps me celebrate'	'I make a fool of myself'
'It helps me work/study'	'It is damaging my health'
'It makes me feel good'	'I have more symptoms when using drugs'
'It helps me forget'	'I have had problems with relationships due
'I feel less anxious when with other people'	to using drugs'
'It helps with boredom'	'I have been in trouble with the police'
Other:	'It costs a lot of money'
	Other:

Figure 3.1 Form to assist motivational interviewing for clients with psychosis.

Therapists check client understanding of their statements more frequently than in standard MI, and examine the cognitions underlying mood changes during the session, encouraging clients to test the accuracy of their beliefs.

Take account of setting

Given that an inpatient admission is an extremely disempowering experience, personal choice is emphasized, including wishes to terminate sessions or not to disclose. Typically, clients find even the most caring and positive inpatient environments very unpleasant and at least some of their symptoms are very distressing. Key objectives are usually to secure release and recovery and to avoid re-admission. An advantage for MI is that this is a crisis that cannot be denied, and to the extent that clients relate substance misuse to their admission, there are substantial incentives to address it. However, compliance during

MI may be seen as accelerating discharge, and stated intentions to change sometimes reflect a desire to please rather than true commitment. Furthermore, the person is away from their usual environment, and both the advantages of substance use and their difficulties with control may seem less keen to them. Although SOS attempts to minimize these influences, it is often necessary to review MI and confirm commitment after discharge contingencies are removed.

Given the challenges of adapting MI to inpatients and the average brevity of admissions, we conduct inpatient MI on an individual basis. In outpatient or extended admissions settings, MI is sometimes adapted to a group format (Mueser *et al.* 1998; Chapter 6 of this volume). This allows modelling of disclosure and of positive changes, and can help in generation of ideas. However, clients with social anxiety, poverty of speech or attentional problems can find group sessions difficult or distressing and group MI may need to be adjusted accordingly.

People with psychosis often have difficulty meeting outpatient appointments. This does not necessarily imply lack of interest or active avoidance: more often it reflects pervasive difficulties with planning and initiating activities. Assertive follow-up, often with home visits, may be necessary. Provided that clients can decline to participate in MI, therapist-initiated contact is not inconsistent with its principles.

Address dysphoria

Given that anxiety or depression are typically present, attention to positive contributions and past achievements becomes more important than usual. Cognitive techniques (Beck *et al.* 1979) are applied to negative cognitions about potential for success. This may include suggestions of behavioural experiments.

Take account of limited alternatives and complexity of problems

Many people with severe co-existing disorders have a narrow repertoire of leisure activities, are unemployed and have few or no friends apart from other substance users. They often have few financial resources, families are often critical of them or out of contact, and many have difficulty maintaining stable accommodation. Attractive alternative activities or new opportunities are often critical to successful control of symptoms and substance use, and belief that these are possible can be critical to MI.

Commitment, planning and preparation within SOS

Consistent with MI, if and only if the person expresses a commitment to address substance misuse, discussion proceeds to defining behavioural goals and detailing how and when the attempt will start. The person is given a written summary of their plan, and encouraged to sign it (as an agreement with themselves). They discuss likely challenges during the first week of their attempt and apply problem-solving to those issues. Within SOS, they receive personalized handouts reflecting these issues, recording their plans. If indicated, we undertake brief role-played practice of substance refusal, or discuss short-term strategies for control of symptoms without using drugs. A personalized handout with an emergency plan to engage if they do have a lapse is also given to the client.

CASE STUDY

Some potentially identifying features in the case below have been changed to protect confidentiality. F was identified as a candidate for SOS on first admission to hospital at the age of 48. He presented with persecutory delusions and occasional visual hallucinations, which he reported experiencing for 18 months. He was diagnosed with late-onset paranoid schizophrenia and medicated with 2 mg of risperidone twice daily.

F reported a long history of polysubstance misuse, having commenced drinking alcohol at age 17 and smoking cannabis at 19. At the time of assessment, F reported having up to eight drinks, four times per week. He scored 27 on the AUDIT (Saunders *et al.* 1993), indicating probable alcohol dependence. A diagnosis of DSM-IV alcohol dependence was confirmed by standardized interview (World Health Organization 1997). F reported a substantial functional impact from alcohol use in the three months preceding admission, resulting in a score of 22 out of a possible maximum of 26 on the DrugCheck Problem List (Kavanagh *et al.* 1999). F reported smoking three or four 'cones' of cannabis three times per week and had used amphetamines once in the preceding three months.

After some rapport building, the therapist was able to proceed directly to MI. F reported that alcohol gave him confidence, relaxed him and helped him to talk to people. He stated that it took away his inhibitions, which was good for meeting people. F reported a troubled childhood and a lifetime of hardship, and said that alcohol helped him to escape from those memories and from family disharmony. Under 'not so good things' about alcohol, F reported concern about not remembering what had happened the night before and disturbances to his family, including swearing and violence resulting in domestic violence orders and assault charges. He said his drinking led to risky behaviours including driving while intoxicated, which had resulted in disqualifications from driving. He felt that drinking excessively gave him a bad reputation and had resulted in loss of friendships. The effects on his family seemed particularly important to F. The discrepancy between these concerns and his continued drinking was highlighted by more detailed exploration of the meaning and importance of family and his hopes and aspirations for family relationships in the future.

Throughout the session, F experienced difficulties focusing on the topic and would often introduce tangential ideas. This was overcome by summarizing points as they were made, reminding him about the task, and summarizing each segment before moving onto the next.

F was then asked to list the good things about reducing alcohol use. He said he would gain respect from other people if he were a non-drinker. He also said that he would be able to do things with his family and hold down a job, and that people (and his family in particular) would be proud of him, that he would feel proud being able to say that he is a non-drinker, that he would be invited to social events again and would be able to get his licence back and drive once more. F was assisted in developing this list by referring back to his list of 'not so good' things and asking if they would be different if he reduced his alcohol consumption. After summarizing the good things about changing his use, F was asked to list the less good things about changing. These included concern that becoming a non-drinker would seem judgmental to his friends who drank a lot, and having to change his lifestyle. The therapist acknowledged these concerns and the difficulty they would create.

After summarizing these points, the therapist summarized the whole session and asked F what he thought about the lists. He said he wanted to stop drinking, and eagerly completed a contract for abstinence, saying that he did not want to die an alcoholic and that he wanted to quit for his family. He elected to begin immediately and scheduled another session to discuss it further.

In this case, MI was conducted in a single 45-minute session. In other cases, MI may extend over four to six sessions totalling 90 minutes or more, and it may not of course result in such clear behaviour change immediately. Further negative experiences or a greater awareness of negative impact may be needed before the balance of perceived incentives is tipped towards change.

After MI, F developed plans for reducing his alcohol intake over an additional five sessions totalling two hours and 40 minutes. His expectations surrounding alcohol use were explored, with F acknowledging that outcomes of consumption were often more negative than anticipated. F and the therapist listed potentially difficult or risky situations and developed strategies for responding to these situations without having a drink. For example, F identified being with other drinkers as a risky situation. Problem-solving and role-played practice in how to refuse alcohol in these situations were conducted. Additional problem-solving for coping with symptoms without alcohol, and strategies to identify and prevent relapse, were also explored.

Throughout post-MI sessions, F was reminded of his reasons for change and encouraged to review them between sessions to maintain motivation. F was discharged from the inpatient unit after a 14-day admission, two days after completing the intervention. F's progress with his substance use was monitored by the therapist for 12 months, with fortnightly five-minute supportive telephone contacts and more lengthy assessments at one, three, six, nine and 12 months. At each contact, the therapist assessed F's progress and provided support when needed, by reviewing the content of the initial sessions.

One month after discharge, F reported that his weekly alcohol consumption was 12 per cent of baseline. He identified boredom as an ongoing risk, and problem-solving to address this issue was conducted. At three months, F reported a relapse comprising a 16.7 per cent increase in alcohol intake over baseline levels, but at six months his reported intake had dropped to five per cent of baseline. He had a further relapse after nine months that was triggered by several stressful events, but by the 12-month assessment he had ceased drinking altogether. He also reported that his cannabis intake had decreased by 95 per cent over the 12 months, and that he had not used any amphetamines at all after the initial MI.

We have found that this type of pattern, with some setbacks but an overall positive trajectory, is a common one. While F had some way to go before achieving stable alcohol abstinence, the impact of a relatively short initial intervention plus brief, regular contacts in the context of the more detailed quarterly assessments appeared substantial.

CONCLUSION

MI is applicable and effective, even in people with substance use disorders who also have severe mental disorders. Some modifications to MI are needed to take account of their emotional and cognitive state and to provide integrated treatment. There is evidence that some people with severe mental disorders may benefit from motivational treatment that is applied as a stand-alone, brief intervention. This suggests that, in common with the general population, many already have the skills that are needed to address their substance-related problems successfully. However, for others, MI is merely the first stage in a more extended and wide-ranging treatment.

KEY RESOURCES

Baker, A., Bucci, S. and Kay-Lambkin, F., *Intervention for Alcohol, Cannabis and Amphetamine Use among People with a Psychotic Illness* (NDARC Technical Report No. 193). Sydney: National Drug and Alcohol Research Centre, 2004. Available at http://www.med.unsw.edu.au/ndarc (accessed 16 September 2005).

Kavanagh, D. J., White, A., Young, R. M., Saunders, J. B., Wallis, G., Shockley, N. and Clair, A., *Start Over and Survive (SOS) Treatment Manual Mark II: A Brief Manualized Intervention for Substance Use in Psychosis.* Brisbane: University of Queensland, 2000.

Miller, W. R. and Rollnick, S., eds, *Motivational Interviewing: Preparing People for Change*, 2nd ed. New York: Guilford Press, 2002.

Miller, W. R., Zweben, A., DiClemente, C. C. and Rychtarik, R. G., *Motivational Enhancement Therapy Manual: A Clinical Research Guide for Therapists Treating Individuals with Alcohol Abuse and Dependence* (NIAAA Project MATCH Monograph Vol. 2, DHHS Publication No. ADM 92–1894). Washington: Government Printing Office, 1992.

Wagner, C., Conners, W., Miller, W. R. and Rollnick, S., *Motivational Interviewing (Resources for Clinicians, Researchers, and Trainers)*. Mid-Atlantic Addiction Technology Transfer Center, 2005. Available at http://motivationalinterview.org (accessed 1 June 2005).

REFERENCES

Baker, A., Lewin, T., Reichler, H., Clancy, R., Carr, V., Garrett, R. *et al.*, 'Motivational interviewing among psychiatric in-patients with substance use disorders', *Acta Psychiatrica Scandinavica*, *106*, 233–40, 2002a.

Baker, A., Lewin, T., Reichler, H., Clancy, R., Carr, V., Garrett, R. *et al.*, 'Evaluation of a motivational interview for substance use within psychiatric inpatient services', *Addiction*, *97*, 1329–37, 2002b.

Bandura, A., *Social Foundations of Thought and Action: A Social Cognitive Theory.* Englewood Cliffs: Prentice-Hall, 1986.

Beck, A., Rush, A., Shaw, B. and Emery, G., *Cognitive Therapy of Depression.* New York: Guilford Press, 1979.

Brown, R., Ramsey, S., Strong, D., Myers, M., Kahler, C., Lejuez, C. *et al.*, 'Effects of motivational interviewing on smoking cessation in adolescents with psychiatric disorders', *Tobacco Control*, *12* suppl. 4, 3–10, 2003.

Burke, B., Arkowitz, H. and Menchola, M., 'The efficacy of motivational interviewing: A meta-analysis of controlled clinical trials', *Journal of Consulting and Clinical Psychology*, *72*, 843–61, 2003.

Daley, D., Salloum, I., Zuckoff, A., Kirisci, L. and Thase, M., 'Increasing treatment adherence among outpatients with depression and cocaine dependence: Results of a pilot study', *American Journal of Psychiatry*, *155*, 1611–3, 1998.

Drake, R., Mueser, K., Brunette, M. and McHugo, G., 'A review of treatments for people with severe mental illnesses and co-occurring substance use disorders', *Psychiatric Rehabilitation Journal*, *27*, 360–74, 2004.

Drake, R. and Wallach, M., 'Moderate drinking among people with severe mental illness', *Hospital and Community Psychiatry*, *44*, 780–2, 1993.

Dunn, C., Deroo, L. and Rivara, F., 'The use of brief interventions adapted from motivational interviewing across behavioural domains: A systematic review', *Addiction*, *96*, 1725–42, 2001.

Graeber, D., Moyers, T., Griffith, G., Guajardo, E. and Tonigan, S., 'A pilot study comparing motivational interviewing and an educational intervention in patients with schizophrenia and alcohol use disorders', *Community Mental Health Journal, 39*, 189–202, 2003.

Hadzi-Pavlovic, D., Rosen, A. and Parker, G., 'The relevance and use of life skills assessments', in Kavanagh, D.J., ed., *Schizophrenia: An Overview and Practical Handbook*, pp. 206–20. London: Chapman & Hall, 1992.

Heinrichs, R. W., 'Meta-analysis, and the science of schizophrenia: Variant evidence or evidence of variants?' *Neuroscience and Biobehavioural Reviews, 28*, 379–94, 2004.

Holder, H., Cisler, R., Longabaugh, R., Stout, R., Treno, A. and Zweben, A., 'Alcoholism treatment and medical care costs from Project Match', *Addiction, 95*, 999–1013, 2000.

Hulse, G. K. and Tait, R. J., 'Six-month outcome associated with a brief alcohol intervention for adult in-patients with psychiatric disorders'. *Drug and Alcohol Review, 21*, 105–12, 2002.

Hulse, G. K. and Tait, R. J., 'Five-year outcomes of a brief alcohol intervention for adult in-patients with psychiatric disorders', *Addiction, 98*, 1061–8, 2003.

Jackson, H. J. and Edwards, J., 'Social networks and social support in schizophrenia: Correlates and assessment', In Kavanagh, D., ed., *Schizophrenia: An Overview and Practical Handbook*, pp. 275–92. London: Chapman & Hall, 1992.

Kavanagh, D., 'Self-efficacy and depression', in Schwartzer, R., ed., *Self-efficacy: Thought Control of Action*, pp. 177–93. New York: Hemisphere, 1992.

Kavanagh, D., Greenway, L., Jenner, L., Saunders, J., White, A., Sorban, J., Hamilton, G. and members of the Dual Diagnosis Consortium, 'Contrasting views and experiences of health professionals on the management of co-morbid substance abuse and mental disorders', *Australian and New Zealand Journal of Psychiatry, 34*, 279–89, 2000a.

Kavanagh, D., Saunders, J., Young, R., White, A., Wallis, G., Jenner, L. and Clair, A., *Evaluation of Screening and Brief Intervention for Substance Abuse in Early Psychosis*. Adelaide: Auseinet, 1999.

Kavanagh, D., White, A., Young, R., Saunders, J., Wallis, G., Shockley, N. and Clair, A., *Start Over and Survive (SOS) Treatment Manual Mark II: A Brief Manualized Intervention for Substance Use in Psychosis*. Brisbane: University of Queensland, 2000b.

Kavanagh, D., Young, R., White, A., Saunders, J., Wallis, G., Shockley, N. *et al.*, 'A brief intervention for substance abuse in early psychosis', *Drug and Alcohol Review, 23*, 151–5, 2004.

Laudet, A., Magura, S., Vogel, H. and Knight, E. L., 'Recovery challenges among dually diagnosed individuals', *Journal of Substance Abuse Treatment, 18*, 321–9, 2000.

MacDonald, E., Luxmoore, M., Pica, S., Tanti, C., Blackman, J., Catford, N. and Stockton, P., 'Social networks of people with dual diagnosis: The quantity and quality of relationships at different stages of substance use treatment', *Community Mental Health Journal, 40*, 451–64, 2004.

Marlatt, G., Curry, S. and Gordon, J., 'A longitudinal analysis of unaided smoking cessation', *Journal of Consulting and Clinical Psychology, 58*, 310–26, 1990.

Martino, S., Carroll, J., O'Malley, S. and Rounsaville, B., 'Motivational interviewing with psychiatrically ill substance abusing patients', *American Journal on the Addictions*, *9*, 88–91, 2000.

Martino, S., Carroll, K., Kostas, D., Perkins, J. and Rounsaville, B., 'Dual diagnosis motivational interviewing: A modification of motivational interviewing for substance-abusing patients with psychotic disorders', *Journal of Substance Abuse Treatment*, *23*, 297–308, 2002.

Miller, W., 'Motivational interviewing with problem drinkers', *Behavioural Psychotherapy*, *11*, 147–72, 1983.

Miller, W. and Rollnick, S., *Motivational Interviewing: Preparing People for Change*, 2nd ed. New York: Guilford Press, 2002.

Miller, W. and Wilbourne, P., 'Mesa Grande: A methodological analysis of clinical trials of treatments for alcohol use disorders', *Addiction*, *97*, 265–77, 2002.

Moyer, A., Finney, J., Swearingen, C. and Vergun, P., 'Brief interventions for alcohol problems: A meta-analytic review of controlled investigations in treatment-seeking and non-treatment-seeking populations', *Addiction*, *97*, 279–92, 2002.

Mueser, K., Drake, R. and Noordsy, D., 'Integrated mental health and substance abuse treatment for severe mental disorders', *Journal of Practical Psychiatry and Behavioral Health*, *4*, 129–39, 1998.

Osher, F. and Kofoed, L., 'Treatment of patients with psychiatric and psychoactive substance use disorders', *Hospital and Community Psychiatry*, *40*, 1025–30, 1989.

Prochaska, J. and DiClemente, C., 'Trans-theoretical therapy: Toward a more integrative model of change', *Psychotherapy: Theory and Research*, *19*, 276–88, 1982.

Saunders, J., Aasland, O., Babor, T., de la Fuente, J. and Grant, M., 'Development of the Alcohol Use Disorder Identification Test (AUDIT): WHO collaborative project on early detection of persons with harmful alcohol consumption – II', *Addiction*, *88*, 791–804, 1993.

Siegfried, N., 'A review of comorbidity: Major mental illness and problematic substance use', *Australian and New Zealand Journal of Psychiatry*, *32*, 707–17, 1998.

Siegfried, N., Ferguson, J., Cleary, M., Walter, G. and Rey, J. M., 'Experience, knowledge and attitudes of mental health staff regarding patients' problematic drug and alcohol use', *Australian and New Zealand Journal of Psychiatry*, *33*, 267–73, 1999.

Steinberg, M., Ziedonis, D., Krejci, J. and Brandon, T., 'Motivational interviewing with personalised feedback: A brief intervention for motivating smokers with schizophrenia to seek treatment for tobacco dependence', *Journal of Consulting and Clinical Psychology*, *72*, 723–8, 2004.

Swanson, A., Pantalon, M. and Cohen, K., 'Motivational interviewing and treatment adherence among psychiatric and dually diagnosed patients', *Journal of Nervous and Mental Disease*, *187*, 630–5, 1999.

Tevyaw, T. and Monti, P., 'Motivation enhancement and other brief interventions for adolescent substance abuse: Foundations, applications and evaluations', *Addiction*, *99* suppl. 2, 63–75, 2004.

World Health Organization, *Composite International Diagnostic Interview, CIDI-Auto Version 2.1*. Sydney: WHO, 1997.

Chapter 4

Cognitive behaviour therapy for people with co-existing mental health and drug and alcohol problems

Amanda Baker, Sandra Bucci, Frances J. Kay-Lambkin and Leanne Hides

KEY POINTS

1   CBT has documented efficacy in the treatment of a variety of single disorders in mental health and drug and alcohol domains.
2   The general principles of CBT are applicable to the treatment of people with co-existing mental health and drug and alcohol problems.
3   Integrated CBT approaches are recommended.
4   Integrated CBT is formulation driven. It emphasizes links between cognitions about mental health problems and drug and alcohol problems.

INTRODUCTION

In Chapter 1 of this book it was noted that cognitive behaviour therapy (CBT) has documented efficacy in the treatment of a variety of single disorders, including depression (APA 2000), psychosis (Kopeloxicz and Liberman 1998), anxiety (Andrews *et al.* 2003), problem drinking (Shand *et al.* 2003), cannabis misuse/dependence (Copeland *et al.* 2001) and amphetamine use (Baker and Dawe 2005). Indeed, CBT performs as well as many pharma-cotherapies, and is often preferred by clients (Baker and Wilson 1985). Numerous texts describe the general principles of CBT (e.g. Beck *et al.* 1979), its application to mental health problems (e.g. Hawton *et al.* 1989) and its use among people with drug and alcohol problems (e.g. Jarvis *et al.* 1995; Monti *et al.* 1989). Several treatment manuals have recently been published describing the process of CBT among people with severe mental disorders and co-existing drug and alcohol problems (Baker and Dawe 2005; Baker *et al.* 2005; Graham *et al.* 2004; Mueser *et al.* 2003), reflecting the current emphasis on psychosis as it co-exists with other disorders. The purpose of this chapter is to provide an overview of the processes commonly involved in the application of CBT to a variety of co-existing mental health and drug and alcohol problems. This will serve as a basis for the more specific descriptions of CBT, as applied to particular combinations of co-existing disorders, in many of the chapters in Section 3 of this book.

The general principles of CBT apply in the treatment of people with co-existing mental health and substance use problems. Treatment is based on the here and now, and specified in operational terms; evaluation using a variety of valid and reliable measurements is emphasized; and the main goal of therapy is to help the client achieve desired changes in their lives (Hawton *et al.* 1989). Therapy is time-limited, and focuses on client acquisition of new skills and producing changes in the real world outside the therapy setting (Hawton *et al.* 1989).

Kavanagh *et al.* (2003) reviewed the evolving evidence for the efficacy of CBT among people with co-existing mental health and drug and alcohol problems. They concluded that interventions for non-psychotic problems, delivered by different clinicians, either sequentially or in parallel, may be feasible, but:

1   Integrated treatment for depression and co-existing drug and alcohol problems is often indicated due to features shared by both disorders such as low self-efficacy, pessimism, substance use to enhance mood, etc.
2   In the case of co-existing anxiety and substance use disorders, it is unclear whether integrated treatment is more effective than parallel or sequential approaches, but integrated treatment may result in more substantial treatment effects.

In addition, integrated treatments produce better outcomes than parallel or sequential approaches to severe mental disorders (such as psychosis) and co-existing drug and alcohol problems (Kavanagh *et al.* 2003).

Integrated CBT emphasizes the links between cognitions about mental health problems and substance use problems (Beck *et al.* 1993; Graham *et al.* 2004). Consideration is given to how such beliefs combine with the individual's positive expectations of drug and alcohol use, interact with underlying core beliefs about themselves, others and the future, and relate to specific affective and behavioural outcomes.

CONTEXT OF INTEGRATED CBT FOR CO-EXISTING MENTAL HEALTH AND DRUG AND ALCOHOL PROBLEMS

Therapist variables

Engagement in therapy is a prerequisite for effective CBT. Motivational interviewing (MI; see Chapter 3) is often an essential precursor to treatment with this population, given that many people present at the pre-contemplation and early contemplation stages of change (Prochaska and DiClemente 1982) for mental health and/or drug and alcohol problems. Training and supervised clinical experience in CBT with either mental health or drug and alcohol problems, and some experience in both areas, is beneficial before commencing an integrated approach to CBT for co-existing problems. Professional development will help build confidence and improve knowledge, particularly when it involves exposure to advances in the treatment of co-existing problems. As a key aim of CBT is to help the client achieve their chosen goals for change, a harm reduction perspective is important. In addition, as mental health and drug and alcohol problems can sometimes severely compromise functioning, the therapist should be familiar with reporting procedures if the client is at risk of harming themselves or others, including their children. Therapists should hold a good basic knowledge of the biomedical and pharmacological aspects of different substances and routes of administration.

Client variables

Issues of motivation and stigma, compounded by the combination of disorders, may impact on the client's ability to follow through with a treatment plan, necessitating assertive homework checks and follow-up procedures. Therapists may need to establish rules such as postponing sessions if the client attends while intoxicated or is using substances with other clients, and will also need to establish a safety protocol for clinic- and home-based sessions.

Therapists will need to consider the type and severity of mental health and drug and alcohol problems and possible effects on cognitive functioning. Among clients with more severe problems, an initial focus on behavioural elements of therapy, simplifying therapeutic material and writing down key points and homework, is often helpful, with cognitive therapy elements introduced slowly.

TREATMENT OF CO-EXISTING MENTAL HEALTH AND DRUG AND ALCOHOL PROBLEMS WITH INTEGRATED CBT

An integrated approach to treatment is recommended, where treatment strategies addressing mental health and drug and alcohol problems are introduced to the client simultaneously, allowing him/her scope to explore the relationship between the co-existing conditions. Ideally, integration occurs from the outset with assessment, and continues through the phases of treatment, which is preferably conducted by the one therapist. CBT can be complemented by pharmacological and other non-pharmacological treatment approaches. The therapist's aim is to tailor an individual treatment plan for the client based on a detailed case formulation of the co-existing problems.

Case formulation specific to co-existing mental health and drug and alcohol problems

Following assessment, the therapist and client should work together to develop a shared understanding of the client's co-existing mental health, drug and alcohol and other problems and to formulate hypotheses about their development, maintenance and inter-relationships (Persons *et al.* 2001). This case formulation has several key parts.

Step 1: List of co-existing problems

A comprehensive problem list is generated, which includes psychological, interpersonal, occupational, medical, legal, financial and social problems (Persons *et al.* 2001). Psychological problems should be described in terms of their mood, behavioural and cognitive components, as doing so fits well with a CBT rationale for treatment.

Step 2: Diagnosis specific to co-existing mental health and drug and alcohol problems

The client is provided with feedback about any diagnostic assessment that has been completed in both domains, including the sequelae of their mental health and alcohol/other drug problems (i.e. primary versus secondary diagnoses, if known, and implications for treatment). However, treatment can proceed without a formal primary diagnosis being confirmed (Schuckit *et al.* 1997). From a public health perspective, it is also important that the therapist provide brief advice about health authority recommendations regarding consumption of alcohol, tobacco and other drugs.

Step 3: Working hypothesis for co-existing mental health and substance use problems

This step has several components. The therapist summarizes ideas about the client's current life situation, including the factors that have contributed to their current state.

Beliefs

First, the therapist describes for the client what he/she understands about the role of substance misuse and mental health problem(s) in the client's life. This information can be taken from questionnaires completed during the assessment, and/or from discussions with the client. The client's answers will provide valuable triggers for MI.

High-risk situations

External events can activate problematic thoughts and feelings that then give rise to mental health problems (e.g. psychosis, depression, anxiety) and substance misuse. These events can be large-scale precipitants to an acute episode and/or problematic substance use (e.g. events that have caused the client to seek treatment), or small-scale situations such as negative thoughts (Persons *et al.* 2001). These high-risk situations will serve as important foci for treatment, and will often be the targets of both behavioural and cognitive activities taught to the client.

Origins

Information about how the client has developed or learned their problematic beliefs is useful in forming hypotheses about their current situation. As such, a discussion about the origins of the client's substance use and mental health problems is valuable. Although information about origins may already be evident from the assessment phase, extra discussion might be necessary. Therapists should also discuss early learning experiences that may have contributed not only to the formation of beliefs, but also to the use of maladaptive behaviours (e.g. drug and alcohol use, negative styles of thinking; Persons *et al.* 2001).

Working hypothesis

Here the therapist 'tells the story' that summarizes how the person came to be in their current state of distress. Key issues to guide the discussion will include the relationship between substance use and mental health problems (such as links between the client's beliefs about both issues) and how the client explains current difficulties (e.g. work, relationships, legal etc; Graham *et al.* 2004). The idea is to create a 'chain' of events and experiences that have contributed to the client's current situation. Generally, this 'working hypothesis' takes the following format (Beck *et al.* 1979; Persons *et al.* 2001):

> Your childhood experiences (origins) led to the formation of certain beliefs you hold about yourself (list beliefs). These beliefs have given rise to other problems in later life (e.g. relationship difficulties, social awkwardness, inadequacy at work etc. – see problem list) which reinforce these beliefs. You then turned to (alcohol, other drugs) in the belief that it would (reasons for substance use), however this has been associated with further problems (as per the problem list). These additional problems feed back into the problematic cycle of beliefs (e.g. depression, low self-worth), which has led you to believe more strongly that you need (alcohol/other drugs) to help cope with this situation. In addition, your

friends believe that . . . which (either reinforces the use of drug/alcohol or isolates the client further). As a result, your problems have continued to worsen.

The above summary will be the basis on which the treatment plan is created, and will help guide the therapist's choice of treatment strategies in subsequent sessions.

Step 4: Treatment plan

Research suggests that a person's perception of the effectiveness and usefulness of treatment strongly predicts their response (Agnew-Davies *et al.* 1998). As such, clients should be allowed to voice their prior experiences with therapy and clarify their expectations and concerns. This is particularly pertinent given the difficulties people with co-existing problems often face in accessing treatment, partly due to the separation of mental health and drug and alcohol services.

At this stage it may be premature to ask the person to set goals for therapy, particularly in terms of reducing substance use. However, they may have ideas about how they want to change their current state (e.g. reduce depressive symptoms, have fewer arguments with family etc.). These goals serve as potential areas for identifying discrepancy later on in therapy, between the person's current behaviour (e.g. substance use) and their plans/goals (e.g. reducing depression, fewer arguments). Together, therapist and client can develop a treatment plan that focuses on particular issues within the CBT program. Following this, a brief explanation of the premises of CBT for co-existing problems is useful, and should include a focus on thoughts, the importance of homework activities and the integration of strategies for mental health and drug and alcohol problems.

Integrated behavioural strategies

As in CBT for single disorders, the early focus of integrated CBT for co-existing problems is usually on behavioural activities and restoring client functioning to appropriate levels (Beck *et al.* 1979) in both mental health and substance use domains. This is enhanced using the following techniques.

Increasing activity levels (behavioural activation) and avoiding high-risk situations

When taking an integrated approach, the steps of diary-keeping, identifying enjoyment and achievement tasks, and planning an activity schedule are undertaken with a focus on situations with a high risk for experiencing mental health symptoms and experiencing cravings/using substances (Westermeyer

2003). When planning activities, the client needs to consider possible consequences for both mental health and drug and alcohol use. For example, while visiting a friend's place may elevate depressed mood, if the friend uses drugs the visit may result in drug use. At this stage of treatment, the client could be encouraged to avoid or reduce exposure to high-risk situations for substance misuse/mental health symptoms until there are some strategies in place for coping with them (Graham *et al.* 2004; Monti *et al.* 1989).

Self-monitoring

Monitoring fluctuations in mental health symptoms and drug and alcohol cravings/use on a daily basis is an important first step in addressing problematic thoughts and behaviours. For many clients, the mere act of monitoring these patterns will result in some improvement in both of these domains, and will permit better understanding of the more cognitively-based strategies introduced in later sessions. Clients should monitor examples of triggers and thoughts associated with mental health symptoms and substance use/cravings that are independent of one another (e.g. low mood associated with a cancelled outing, craving for a drink when walking past the pub) and that are linked (e.g. drinking in response to low mood) (Myrick and Brady 2001; Westermeyer 2003). This will demonstrate the need to address both problems separately and together, enhancing the client's ability to avoid relapse to either or both in future.

Setting goals

Once it is apparent that the client is prepared to take some action towards changing, clear goals for this change should be set. Ideally, the client will see that their mental health and drug and alcohol problems can be worked on simultaneously, with goals established for each.

Integrated cognitive therapy

Introduction to the integrated ABC model

A clear rationale for integrated cognitive treatment should be provided, addressing antecedents, beliefs and consequences (ABC model; Beck *et al.* 1979) associated with examples of the client's mental health and drug and alcohol problems, separately and linked.

Identifying negative or distressing thoughts and positive expectations regarding drug and alcohol use

The person is taught how to identify and monitor negative or distressing thought patterns and positive expectations regarding drug and alcohol use (Beck *et al.* 1979; Myrick and Brady 2001; Westermeyer 2003), based on the ABC model. This involves noting the activating events, beliefs and emotional/ behavioural consequences associated with symptoms such as voices, negative mood states and/or cravings/use of substances (see the monitoring form in Figure 4.1, columns 1–4). The client is asked to observe the times of day when they experience cravings for alcohol/other drugs, are feeling at their most negative and positive, or experience the most distressing or frequent symptoms such as voices. It may also be useful to request that the person notes the quantity and frequency of their substance use on the monitoring form, as this has been found to be effective in reducing drug and alcohol use. It is helpful to note when negative moods or symptoms have led to substance use and vice versa.

Challenging negative or distressing thoughts and positive expectations regarding drug and alcohol use

The next step is for the client to learn how to modify and challenge negative or distressing beliefs, so that they can develop more helpful ways of thinking (Beck *et al.* 1979; Persons *et al.* 2001; Segal *et al.* 2002). The procedure is the same as in single-disorder cognitive therapy: define the problem in specific terms; use mindfulness or other skills to distance one self from the thoughts (e.g. thoughts are not facts, not to be evaluated or given control) (Segal *et al.* 2002); challenge the thoughts (see Figure 4.1, columns 5–9) (Beck *et al.* 1979; Free 1999; Persons *et al.* 2001); and generate more helpful beliefs and alternative emotional/behavioural consequences (Beck *et al.* 1979; Free 1999; Persons *et al.* 2001).

Schema modification across multiple domains, including negative mood and substance misuse

According to the cognitive model, client problems will occur on two levels (overt, surface-level symptoms and underlying schema; Persons *et al.* 2001). The treatment strategies described above assist the client at the overt symptom level. The downward/vertical arrow technique is useful in identifying the schema/core beliefs that underlie mental health and substance use problems. The therapist asks a series of questions about commonly occurring negative or distressing automatic thoughts (e.g. 'If that thought was true, what would it mean about you?'). This process continues until the client reaches their core belief, usually indicated by high levels of affective arousal (Free 1999). Then,

A Situation/Trigger	B Beliefs/Thoughts	C Feelings/Emotions	C Behaviours		What exactly do you mean? Do I hold the same rule for other people?	Does it fit the facts? What is the evidence for and against this belief? For	Against	Is there another way of looking at it?	Feelings now
Watching TV, bored.	Life sucks. Nothing ever changes.	Sad.	Drank a bottle of wine.	This is just a thought Thoughts are not facts	I'm stuck in a rut and can't escape, nothing will ever change. No, I wouldn't hold the same rule for others.	Unemployed. No hobbies.	I did OK at school. I've got some good friends and used to have hobbies.	Just because I'm bored doesn't mean I'm completely stuck in a rut. I can change something small, like going for a walk, and slowly build up my activities.	OK
Feeling down, with a hangover when I woke up.	I need a smoke (cannabis) to get going.	Down.	Smoked a joint.	I am not my thoughts	I have to get stoned to feel better.	I sometimes feel better when I have a smoke.	Usually I just end up feeling paranoid.	I can deal with a hangover without having a smoke. I'll see how I feel after having something to eat.	OK

Figure 4.1 Thought monitoring and challenging form.

the client tests the validity of their core belief across different domains (e.g. work, social, family, mood, substance use) by rating themselves on these characteristics as well as on their overall schema (see Figure 4.2; Persons *et al.* 2001). Usually, clients will be more objective about their ratings on specific domains than on their more general schema. The overall objective of this exercise is to identify these discrepancies and develop a more balanced, rational belief.

My core belief is: (put core belief here, e.g. *I'm hopeless and useless***)**

Where do I fit along the scale from 0 to 100 of this core belief?

X

0%	100%
Totally hopeless	Hopeful in every way
No good at all	Useful in every way

How would I describe _____ **(put core belief here, e.g.** *hopelessness***) at:**

WORK   X

0%	100%
No job	*The perfect job*
If job, always in trouble with boss	*Always praised for good work*

SOCIAL OCCASIONS   X

0%	100%
No friends at all	*Loads of friends*
Never invited anywhere	*Always invited everywhere*
Not liked at all by anyone	*Liked by everyone*
Always alone	*Never alone*

HOBBIES   X

0%	100%
No interests at all	*Loads of interests*
No hobbies at all	*Loads of hobbies*
Never anything to do	*Always busy with something*

FAMILY FUNCTIONS   X

0%	100%
Totally hated by all family members	*Loved by every family member*
Never included in any family events	*Always attends every family event*
Excluded all the time by all family	*Always included in every family event*
Never contributes anything to family	*Always contributes in every way to family*

Now, where do you put yourself on these domains of work, social occasions, interests/hobbies and family functions?

Alternative core belief: *I'm not really hopeless or useless as I have some friends to socialize with and who include me in their plans, I have several interests/hobbies that I could do more of, I have a job and, although I don't like it much, I'm able to do most of what is asked of me. Also, my family love me and include me in all their activities.*

Figure 4.2 Schema challenge.

Once the client has identified an alternative, balanced belief they need to develop evidence for its accuracy and validity by learning to pay attention to information that confirms this new, more balanced view. However, the long-term nature of schema change should be emphasized, as well as the need to challenge each core belief associated with their mental health problem and substance misuse.

Integrated relapse prevention

Throughout treatment, the client is encouraged to avoid or reduce exposure to high-risk situations for substance misuse and mental health symptoms (Graham *et al.* 2004; Marlatt and Gordon 1985; Monti *et al.* 1989), which can be identified during activity scheduling exercises. However, as some high-risk situations are unavoidable, it is useful to identify and practice appropriate skills for managing these situations, thoughts and feelings in order to enhance self-efficacy. Clients may also benefit from cue exposure techniques, in which a graded hierarchy of high-risk situations and associated cues is developed, with subsequent progressive exposure to these situations while using appropriate coping strategies (Rohsenow *et al.* 2001).

Coping skills

Often clients have been managing their symptoms for a while before they present for treatment. It is useful to identify the client's pre-existing coping strategies and build on these. For example, drug and alcohol use may improve with specific sessions on coping with cravings and/or communication skills (assertiveness, drink/drug refusal; Monti *et al.* 1989; Myrick and Brady 2001). Specific strategies to deal with aspects of co-existing mental health problems (e.g. coping strategy enhancement in the case of psychotic symptoms; Tarrier and Haddock 2002) may also be part of treatment.

CASE STUDY

Jamie is an 18-year-old male high school student, about to sit his end of school exams. He sought treatment after experiencing perceptual disturbances (e.g. hearing voices), sleep difficulties, changes in mood and ideas of reference (e.g. being kept under electronic surveillance). He believed that love songs on the radio were sending him special messages and was convinced that his teacher could read his mind. Jamie also reported regular amphetamine use, injecting at least four times a week. He said this got him 'through the day'. Jamie's condition escalated when he was waiting to catch the train to school and he verbally abused by-standers for staring at him. Rail security called the police, who took him to the nearby psychiatric hospital for assessment. Jamie was admitted to an inpatient unit at the local psychiatric hospital with an acute psychotic episode and amphetamine dependence.

The above information was gathered by a psychologist in the initial interview, which lasted around one hour. The therapist decided that, at the time of initial presentation, Jamie was in the contemplation stage of change for his substance use, and he was informed he was experiencing a drug-induced psychosis. While angry about the diagnosis and the need for hospitalization, he was willing to entertain the idea that his beliefs were possibly a function of his imagination rather than 'real' events.

Rationale for integrated CBT

The therapist initially sought information from Jamie about his symptoms, including the voices, sleep patterns, performance at school, social relations and ideas of reference. Jamie did not make eye contact with the therapist during the interview. Given that he was distressed about his diagnosis, the therapist concentrated on building rapport and engaging Jamie into treatment. When the therapist had validated and explored Jamie's concerns, the subject of substance use was gently raised and discussion ensued. Following a case formulation session, Jamie was able to reflect on his thoughts and past behaviours and was seen for a further 10 weekly sessions. CBT commenced with an explanation of psychosis and the possible effects that substances can have on mental health symptoms:

Therapist: I think it's important that we talk about the treatment model we are going to be working with. The treatment is called cognitive behavioural therapy, or CBT, and it can help people who might want to stop using substances who also have some distressing thoughts. Is it OK if I talk about CBT with you?

Jamie: Yeah, whatever.

Therapist: OK. Once people start using a lot of speed they sometimes learn that it changes the way they feel. For example, you mentioned earlier that using speed helps you get through the day. Other people think it will make them more confident or it will keep them from thinking about their worries.

Jamie: Yeah, that's one of the good things about it for me. I totally zone out and just party. I don't give a stuff about anything else.

Therapist: Right. And after a while, things in the environment, sometimes without you realizing it, can trigger using. Triggers include things like seeing other people use or being in stressful situations, like exams. You may have found that you've developed your own views about using, for example, 'Life is boring without speed'.

Jamie: Well, giving up isn't as easy as I thought it would be. After our last appointment, I tried to not have any on the weekend but I couldn't help it. The party was rocking and I couldn't keep up without it.

Therapist: So you tried not to have any speed on the weekend, that's great. That's a pretty big thing you did, and a decision you made on your own. Giving up something that is a regular part of your life is going to be tough for a little while, but eventually you'll get used to the feeling of not needing speed and be able to enjoy life without it.

Jamie: I hope so.

Therapist: Using speed can really change the way a person thinks, feels and acts. This can make using very easy to start and very hard to stop. I'd like you to think about what you want from our sessions together.

Jamie: I don't know what else to do but use. It's a habit.

Therapist: Well, maybe one of our goals could be looking at ways to help you cope better with situations in which you tend to use. This treatment will also help you manage the distressing thoughts you have such as thinking people are following you. What do you think so far about what I've said?

Jamie: It makes sense. Maybe those things are in my head, the doctors said they were, but they seem so real. I didn't realize speed could do that to you.

Therapist: What happens with psychosis is that people have trouble knowing what's real and what isn't. What CBT says is that by changing the way we think about things, we can change how we feel and behave. We don't worry quite as much.

Jamie: So if I think differently, I'll feel differently.

Therapist: It probably sounds easier than it really is. It takes time and practice to challenge the way you think, much like learning a new sport takes practice. Everyone who is trying to use less, for example, will have urges to use. Also, people trying to manage their worries may have automatically learned to think and respond to situations in a particular way. It's not really the situations that are the problem, rather it's the way you respond to the situation that will affect how you feel. It sounds like the way you respond to seeing a person in the street, for example, is, 'They're out to get me.' Is that fair to say?

Jamie: Yeah. I think everyone's out to get me.

Therapist: So for you, the world is a dangerous place. And thinking this way makes you feel paranoid and afraid to the extent that you don't want to leave the house.

Jamie: That's right.

Therapist: Often these negative or paranoid thoughts happen so quickly that you're not even aware of it. You believe it to be true without really questioning the thought. That's why we call these thoughts automatic. . . . It's as though suddenly you realize that you're feeling bad, or you're having the urge to use speed.

Self-monitoring speed use and distressing thoughts

The therapist then asked Jamie to identify a period during the week when he had had an urge to use speed and when he thought he was being followed. The therapist helped him identify the thoughts, feelings and behaviours in those situations. Jamie's homework following this session was to monitor his thoughts to help identify triggers to use or to feel paranoid.

Assessing and avoiding high-risk situations for substance misuse and paranoid symptoms plus relapse prevention

An assessment of high-risk situations was conducted.

Therapist: In what kinds of situations do you use speed?
Jamie: Well, I use when I'm at parties.
Therapist: Can you remember what kinds of thoughts you have when you are at parties?
Jamie: I know if I don't use I feel left out. Everyone looks like they're having such a good time and I don't like to miss out.
Therapist: If you don't use at parties you feel pretty isolated. You also don't feel like you can join in and have a good time without using speed. Is that right?
Jamie: Yeah, it's just not the same.
Therapist: So going to parties is what we call a high-risk situation for you. Being at parties is when you are likely to have the urge to use speed. What about feeling paranoid? In what kinds of situations do you feel paranoid?
Jamie: When I'm around others, like at the shops or at school. I think people are talking about me. And the radio, that's a big one. I always think that those stupid love songs are about me, it's like they're making fun of me because I've never had a girlfriend.
Therapist: So being around others and listening to the radio are also examples of high-risk situations that lead you to feeling paranoid.
Jamie: But I've already stuffed it. This week I tried not to use and I did. It's no use. I may as well stop trying.
Therapist: Jamie, it's hard to stay motivated when you're not getting the rewards of not using yet. The benefits of not using are definitely not immediate. You have to trust that it will come.
Jamie: Well, I've blown it haven't I? I knew I wouldn't be able to stop!

Therapist: I think you've touched on a very interesting point Jamie. Often people tell me they feel bad about themselves if they've had a lapse, and they see it as the end of the world and of further attempts at cutting down or quitting. I wonder if you could think about this slip-up as just that – a slip-up. Changing your behaviour is going to take a lot of practice, and you may slip up now and then, but that doesn't mean it's all over for you. I tend to see it as something you can learn from. It's an opportunity for us to talk about what you were struggling with and see if we can strengthen some of the strategies we've talked about so far so that they make sense for you.

Jamie: I just felt so bad at having used again.

Therapist: I take that as meaning you're committed to this. If you weren't committed to changing or didn't really care then you wouldn't be so disappointed in yourself. That's really positive to see.

Jamie: Thanks. I never thought of it like that.

Therapist: What kinds of things do you think you can say to yourself then if you have another slip-up? Rather than, 'That's it. I've blown it,' what else do you think you could say to yourself?

Jamie: Maybe I could say I've just had a slip-up and I can get back on track.

Therapist: Sounds good. Do you have any other thoughts?

Jamie: I've just slipped up and I can learn from it and keep going.

The therapist continues to encourage Jamie to reframe a lapse and writes down these positive statements for Jamie to refer to in the future.

Coping strategy enhancement

Jamie discussed new ways of coping with the feeling of being followed with the therapist, who set him a homework task around this.

Therapist: So, you had a task to do during the week. You were going to try to do some schoolwork in the study with your Walkman on. How did that go?

Jamie: Well, I gave it a go and it went OK. I lasted half an hour until I started to wonder if they would know what I was up to because I wasn't in my room.

Therapist: So you were able to go to the study for half an hour and concentrate on some schoolwork. That's great. Can you imagine having done that a few weeks ago?

Jamie: No way.

Therapist: It strikes me that when you put your mind to something you really pull through.

Jamie: Actually, Mum's always said that to me. If I put my mind to something then I can do it.

Over time, Jamie was able to understand the interaction between thinking patterns, symptoms and drug use. By reframing his thinking patterns and behaviours, the therapist was able to help Jamie identify and challenge his thoughts and develop more productive strategies to manage stress. Jamie was followed up regularly at increasingly less frequent intervals. He continued to challenge his beliefs and use the coping strategies discussed in therapy. This, along with support from his family, helped him remain abstinent from speed and recover from his psychotic episode.

CONCLUSION

Integrated CBT for co-existing mental health and drug and alcohol problems is based on a comprehensive assessment and a case formulation that considers each issue. Therapists can then adapt behavioural and cognitive strategies for the co-existing disorders in flexible ways, tailoring interventions to the individual's presentation. Further evidence regarding the efficacy and effectiveness of CBT for people with co-existing problems is required. Trials of CBT in laboratories and mental health and drug and alcohol settings should include people with co-existing problems, and report on their characteristics and treatment outcomes across these domains. Many of the chapters in Section 3 describe the application of integrated CBT approaches to specific groups with co-existing mental health and alcohol/other drug use problems.

KEY RESOURCES

Ten-session CBT manual for alcohol/other drug use problems and psychotic illnesses

Baker, A., Bucci, S. R. and Kay-Lambkin, F. J., *Intervention for Alcohol, Cannabis and Amphetamine Use among People with a Psychotic Illness* (NDARC Technical Report No. 193). Sydney: University of New South Wales, 2004. Available at www.med.unsw.edu.au/NDARCWeb.nsf/page/Publications (accessed 16 October 2006).

Eight-session CBT manual for tobacco reduction among people with psychotic illnesses

Baker, A., Kay-Lambkin, F. J., Bucci, S. R., Haile, M., Richmond, R. and Carr, V. J., *Intervention for Tobacco Dependence among People with a Mental Illness* (NDARC Technical Report No. 192). Sydney: University of New South Wales,

2004. Available at www.med.unsw.edu.au/NDARCWeb.nsf/page/Publications (accessed 16 October 2006).

Four-session CBT manual for regular users of amphetamines

Baker, A., Kay-Lambkin, F. J., Lee, N. K., Claire, M. and Jenner, L., *A Brief Cognitive Behavioural Intervention for Regular Amphetamine Users*. Canberra: Australian Government Department of Health and Ageing, 2003. Available at www.nationaldrugstrategy.gov.au/publications/illicit.htm (accessed 8 August 2005).

CBT guide for alcohol dependence

Monti, P. M., Abram, D. B., Kadden, R. M. and Cooney, N. L., *Treating Alcohol Dependence: An Introductory Guide*. New York: Guilford Press, 1989.

CBT guide for alcohol/other drug use

Jarvis, T. J., Tebbutt, J. T. and Mattick, R. P., *Treatment Approaches for Alcohol and Drug Dependence: An Introductory Guide*. Chichester: John Wiley, 1995.

CBT guide for co-occurring substance use problems and psychosis

Graham, H. L., Copello, A., Birchwood, M. J., Mueser, K. T., Orford, J., McGovern, D. *et al.*, *Cognitive-Behavioural Integrated Treatment (C-BIT): A Treatment Manual for Substance Misuse in People with Severe Mental Health Problems*. Chichester: John Wiley, 2004.

Guide for integrated treatment of co-occurring substance use problems and serious mental illnesses

Mueser, K. T., Noordsy, D. L., Drake, R. E. and Fox, L., *Integrated Treatments for Dual Disorders: A Guide to Effective Practice*. New York: Guilford Press, 2003.

Guide for integrated treatment of co-occurring mood and substance use problems

Westermeyer, J. J., *Addressing Co-occurring Mood and Substance Use Disorders*. London: Johns Hopkins University Press, 2003.

REFERENCES

Agnew-Davies, R., Stiles, W. B., Hardy, G. E., Barkham, M. and Shapiro, D. A., 'Alliance structure assessed by the Agnew Relationship Measure', *British Journal of Clinical Psychiatry*, *37*, 155–72, 1998.

American Psychiatric Association (APA), 'Practice guideline for the treatment of patients with major depressive disorder (revision)', *American Journal of Psychiatry*, *157*, 1–45, 2000.

Andrews, G., Creamer, M., Crino, R., Hunt, C., Lampe, L. and Page, A., *The Treatment of Anxiety Disorders, Second Edition. Clinician Guides and Patient Manuals*. Port Melbourne: Cambridge University Press, 2003.

Baker, A. and Dawe, S., 'Amphetamine use and co-occurring psychological disorders: A review of the literature and implications for treatment', *Australian Psychologist*, *40*, 87–94, 2005.

Baker, A., Lee, N. K., Claire, M., Lewin, T. J., Grant, T., Pohlman, S. *et al.*, 'Brief cognitive behavioural interventions for regular amphetamine users: A step in the right direction', *Addiction*, *100*, 367–78, 2005.

Baker, A. and Wilson, P. H., 'Cognitive therapy for depression: The effect of booster sessions on relapse', *Behaviour Therapy*, *6*, 335–44, 1985.

Beck, A. T., Rush, A. J., Shaw, B. F. and Emery, G., *Cognitive Therapy of Depression*. New York: Guilford Press, 1979.

Beck, A. T., Wright, F. D., Newman, C. F. and Liese, B. S., *Cognitive Therapy of Substance Abuse*. New York: Guilford Press, 1993.

Copeland, J., Swift, W. and Rees, V., 'Clinical profile of participants in a brief intervention program for cannabis use disorder', *Journal of Substance Abuse Treatment*, *20*, 45–52, 2001.

Free, M. L., *Cognitive Therapy in Groups: Guidelines and Resources for Practice*. New York: John Wiley, 1999.

Graham, H. L., Copello, A., Birchwood, M. J., Mueser, K. T., Orford, J., McGovern, D. *et al.*, *Cognitive-Behavioural Integrated Treatment (C-BIT): A Treatment Manual for Substance Misuse in People with Severe Mental Health Problems*. Chichester: John Wiley, 2004.

Hawton, K., Salkovskis, P. M., Kirk, J. and Clark, D. M., *Cognitive Behaviour Therapy for Psychiatric Problems: A Practical Guide*. London: Oxford University Press, 1989.

Jarvis, T. J., Tebbutt, J. T. and Mattick, R. P., *Treatment Approaches for Alcohol and Drug Dependence: An Introductory Guide*. Chichester: John Wiley, 1995.

Kavanagh, D., Mueser, K. and Baker, A., 'Management of co-morbidity', in Teesson, M., ed., *Co-morbid Mental Disorders and Substance Use Disorders: Epidemiology, Prevention and Treatment*, pp. 78–107. Canberra: Commonwealth of Australia, 2003.

Kopeloxicz, A. and Liberman, R. P., 'Psychosocial treatments for schizophrenia', in Nathan, P. E. and Gorman, J. M., eds, *A Guide to Treatments that Work*. New York: Oxford University Press, 1998.

Marlatt, G. and Gordon, J. R., *Relapse Prevention*. New York: Guilford Press, 1985.

Monti, P. M., Abram, D. B., Kadden, R. M. and Cooney, N. L., *Treating Alcohol Dependence: An Introductory Guide*. New York: Guilford Press, 1989.

Mueser, K. T., Noordsy, D. L., Drake, R. E. and Fox, L., *Integrated Treatments for Dual Disorders: A Guide to Effective Practice*. New York: Guilford Press, 2003.

Myrick, H. and Brady, K. T., 'Management of comorbid anxiety and substance use disorders', *Psychiatric Annals, 31*, 265–71, 2001.

Persons, J. B., Davidson, J. and Tompkins, M. A., *Essential Components of Cognitive-Behaviour Therapy for Depression*. Washington: American Psychological Association, 2001.

Prochaska, J. O. and DiClemente, C. C., 'Transtheoretical therapy: Toward a more integrative model of change', *Psychotherapy: Theory, Research and Practice, 19*, 276–88, 1982.

Rohsenow, D. J., Monti, P. M., Rubonis, A. V., Gulliver, S. B., Colby, S. M., Binkoff, J. A. and Abrams, D. B., 'Cue exposure with coping skills training and communication skills training for alcohol dependence: 6- and 12-month outcomes', *Addiction, 96*, 1161–74, 2001.

Schuckit, M. A., Tipp, J. E., Bergman, M., Reich, W., Hesselbrock, V. M. and Smith, T. L., 'Comparison of induced and independent major depressive disorders in 2,945 alcoholics', *American Journal of Psychiatry, 154*, 948–57, 1997.

Segal, Z. V., Williams, J. M. G. and Teasdale, J. D., *Mindfulness-based Cognitive Therapy for Depression: A New Approach to Preventing Relapse*. New York: Guilford Press, 2002.

Shand, F., Gates, J., Fawcett, J. and Mattick, R., *The Treatment of Alcohol Problems: A Review of the Evidence*. Canberra: Australian Commonwealth Department of Health and Ageing, 2003.

Tarrier, N. and Haddock, G., 'Cognitive-behavioral therapy for schizophrenia: A case formulation approach', in Hofmann, S. G. and Tompson, M. C., eds, *Treating Chronic and Severe Mental Disorders: A Handbook of Empirically Supported Interventions*, pp. 69–95. New York: Guilford Press, 2002.

Westermeyer, J. J., *Addressing Co-occurring Mood and Substance Use Disorders*. London: Johns Hopkins University Press, 2003.

Chapter 5

Family intervention for co-existing mental health and drug and alcohol problems

Gina Smith and Richard Velleman

KEY POINTS

1   Research shows that family work is important in families either where someone has severe mental health problems or where there are alcohol or drug problems. This chapter shows its importance when there are co-existing problems: family approaches can be just as effective when applied to cases where co-existing problems arise as they are when either problem presents on its own.

2   Many of the ideas and skills utilized in mental health-related approaches are the same as those utilized in alcohol- or drug-related approaches. Where there are differences, each set of approaches can be developed as we learn from these differences, and hence produce a family intervention which draws on the best ideas of both traditions.

3   Family work with co-existing problems focuses on the process of change, attributions, motivation and coping.

4   Family workers aim to create an atmosphere that is conducive to change by being respectful, supportive and persuasive, not coercive or argumentative, with the assumption being that the family members are the 'experts', not the professionals.

5   The process of family intervention tends to go through a number of phases: promoting awareness of family interventions, referral, initial meeting, assessments, education, problem-solving/goal-setting, evaluation and booster sessions.

INTRODUCTION

'Family work' has been shown to be important in engaging and intervening among people with psychosis (Pharoah *et al.* 2003; Pitschel-Walz *et al.* 2001), depression and anxiety (Asen 2002) and alcohol and drug problems (Copello *et al.* 2005). This chapter will demonstrate that such work is also vital when working with people who have both mental health and drug and alcohol problems at the same time.

There is a long history of working with the families of people with severe mental disorders. Brown and Rutter (1966) introduced the term 'high expressed emotion' to describe the emotionally charged environments, characterized by high levels of criticism and hostility or over-involvement, which were associated with an increased risk of relapse for a person suffering from schizophrenia (Brown *et al.* 1962). This led to the development of a number of intervention models based on the hypothesis that the course of schizophrenia could be improved by reducing expressed emotion (EE). Many systematic reviews of subsequent family intervention studies (e.g. Pitschel-Walz *et al.* 2001) have shown this to be true. These psycho-educational approaches, known as 'family work' (Gamble and Midence 1994), aim to help the family to understand the disorder, and attribute the symptoms to the disorder rather than seeing them as awkwardness or behaviours that the client can easily control (Kuipers *et al.* 2002). The impact of high EE on many chronic conditions (both physical and psychiatric) has been recognized (Leff 1998). Although it is likely that family work for these would mirror the effectiveness shown in reducing relapse in schizophrenia, as yet there is no body of research to guide practice.

There has been a similarly long history within the alcohol and drug area of approaches which focus on the influence of the family. It has been known for some time that the quality of family relationships impacts on alcohol or drug use, and that positive marital and family adjustment is related to positive treatment outcomes (Moos and Moos 1984; Orford and Edwards 1977). There have been many examples (Copello *et al.* 2005) of studies showing that the involvement of family members can lead to improved engagement (e.g. Smith and Meyers 2004) and outcomes, in both alcohol treatment (e.g. O'Farrell *et al.* 1998) and drug treatment (e.g. Higgins and Budney 1994). It is also known that if interventions are offered to family members in their own right (e.g. to help them cope better, or help them develop improved social networks), there are significant benefits in terms of reduced levels of psychological and physical symptoms and altered coping mechanisms in these family members (Copello *et al.* 2000a, 2000b; Velleman and Templeton 2003), which in turn impact on the drinker's or drug user's behaviour.

Family environments which are tolerant influence motivation. Brown and colleagues (1972) found that families who were more tolerant of deviant behaviour in their relative suffering from schizophrenia created an atmosphere that helped maintain the relative's wellbeing. Tolerance is thought to be informed by attributions which relatives make about deviance. External attributions (believing that the client cannot control their behaviour) relate to more relaxed attitudes (Barrowclough *et al.* 1996), as long as such attributions do not extend to seeing the client as very fragile, which can lead to emotional over-involvement. Internal attributions (whereby the client is perceived as being able to control mental health or substance use) can induce critical comments as the relative attempts to prompt recovery.

Where there are co-existing mental health and drug and/or alcohol problems, family intervention differs from the first-generation family intervention models (Lam 1991) by incorporating into the education process the model of change developed by Prochaska and DiClemente (1986), and the ideas of motivational interviewing developed by Miller and Rollnick (1991, 2002). An attempt is made to help the family move away from blaming substance misusers for their behaviour (Turner 1998). A model of family intervention for substance misuse and psychosis has since been shown to be effective through a small scale randomized controlled trial, based on the assumption that 'patients' motivational state as regards changing their substance use could be influenced by the family environment' (Barrowclough 2003: 232).

Through family work meetings, people are encouraged to share their experiences and discuss their attributions. Everyone's coping responses and strategies (including substance misuse) are recognized, with coaching given (if necessary) to improve the family's ability to solve problems and deal with stress by encouraging clear communication. As understanding increases, tension and stress throughout the family decrease, improving the quality of life for all concerned (Barrowclough and Tarrier 1997). Altered attributions (Brewin 1994), reduced EE and reduced ambient stress level in the family enable the client to cope better with unavoidable life stresses. This lessens the risk of relapse of their disorder (Falloon *et al.* 1984) and reduces the client's need to misuse drugs or alcohol (Macdonald *et al.* 2002; Meyers and Miller 2001).

CONTEXT OF THERAPY

Therapist variables

Promoting awareness of family intervention

Three levels of clinician competence are needed within the workforce in order to provide family interventions within routine clinical practice (Smith and Velleman 2002). The first of these is an awareness of family work, needed by all staff in contact with families who have to cope with psychosis or with co-existing problems. Without such awareness of family work on the part of staff there will be few or inappropriate referrals. Appropriate referrals are more likely to lead to high levels of engagement.

Staff need (i) sufficient knowledge of family interventions to see when a family may benefit from this type of help; (ii) the skill to introduce the idea to families; and (iii) knowledge of how to refer to those who will provide the intervention. This level of competence can be achieved by attending a relevant presentation, discussion with trained family workers or careful reading of the available practical guides (e.g. Kuipers *et al.* 2002). A short summary of the intervention (based on the steps on the flowchart in Figure 5.1) can also be useful to give to new staff and family members to promote a clear understanding (see Figure 5.2).

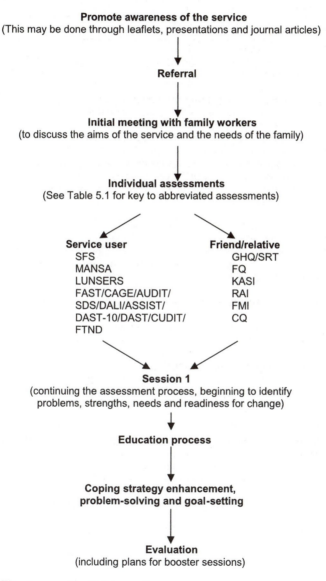

Figure 5.1 The process of family intervention.

FAMILY WORK FOR PSYCHOSIS

We know that families can do a great deal to help their relative recover from a psychotic episode. This service aims to support families in this process by sharing information and ways of working, to help you to improve the things you can, and accept things you cannot change.

HOW THE SERVICE WORKS

How do you find out about the service?
This may be from your GP or care coordinator, or through a leaflet, a friend, a voluntary agency or some other source.

⇓

How do you and your family get referred for family work?
This could be by your care coordinator or another family member.

⇓

What happens at the initial first meeting for you and your family with the family workers?
This provides an opportunity to discuss the needs of the family and how this service could help. You will also get a copy of the *Commitment to Carers* booklet. This initial meeting may be with the whole family, or with some of it, or as an individual meeting, depending on what seems best to you.

⇓

Do you all get a chance to put your views across?
Each member of the family is offered a private meeting to discuss how psychosis affects their life. Workers will help you look at how you cope day to day, and the resources you have, including your knowledge about the illness, medication and other possible treatments such as cognitive behaviour therapy.

⇓

What happens in the first family work session? (ie the one after the initial meeting)
This carries on from your initial meeting, and continues to assess the situation and identify problems, what you do that works and where you need help.

⇓

What happens in the following sessions?
The work continues, building on the family's skills and knowledge, helping you to feel more able to cope and manage problems. To start with, sessions for all family members to attend will usually take place fortnightly, tailing off gradually in step with the family's confidence.

⇓

Do you all get to comment on the sessions and if the service was helpful?
The service is always keen to receive any comments, good or bad, to ensure that it develops and evolves to continue to meet the needs of families.

For further information please contact :
Gina Smith, Consultant Nurse for Family Interventions

Figure 5.2 Leaflet given to new staff and family members: *A Short Summary of the Family Work Intervention.*

Undertaking family intervention

Our integrated family work model (Smith *et al.* 2007) is based upon a respectful stance towards family members. Miller (1983) found that an accepting attitude built a therapeutic alliance that supported clients' self-esteem, a prerequisite for change. Engagement is achieved through empathic warmth and reflective listening (or accurate empathy; Rogers 1959), underpinned by an attitude of acceptance, as family workers try to understand, without judging, the individual's feelings and perspectives. In family work, as in motivational interviewing, workers aim to create an atmosphere that is conducive to change by being supportive and persuasive, rather than coercive or argumentative (Miller and Rollnick 1991, 2002).

Early sessions within our model explore the reasons for change and make it explicit that change is possible, rather than teaching the skills to bring about change. An early focus on skills before a readiness for change has been established can be problematic. Through support and persuasion the client is encouraged to present their own reasons for change: individuals are usually more convinced by their own words than what others tell them.

Therapists providing family interventions should work in pairs, allowing them to model clear communication skills through discussions between themselves during sessions, and showing that it is possible to resolve a difference of opinion without conflict. It may sometimes be useful for one worker to ally with one family member, while the other worker supports another individual or several relatives in order to bolster new coping strategies. It is important that these alliances do not become fixed as this can lead to individuals imagining that only one worker understands them (Kuipers *et al.* 2002).

Between them, the workers need to have a sound working knowledge of mental health and substance misuse, as well as a willingness to learn from the family's experience. The workers' gender does not appear to impact on the effectiveness of the intervention (Gamble 2000).

Client variables

Family members often seek help before the client recognizes a problem, but effective family intervention necessitates that the client is present for at least some sessions (Fadden 1998).

We have not found it possible to offer family work for co-existing problems in a group setting.

Rather than aiming to assess 'suitable' families, it is more useful in practice to ensure that intervention is offered in a timely way (Smith and Velleman 2002). Nonetheless, establishing ground rules will maximize the usefulness of family meetings. These are likely to include not attending a meeting under the influence of drugs or alcohol, and listening to everybody's point of view.

Substance use problems often re-occur across generations. Hence it is possible that one or both parents of someone with co-existing substance and mental health problems will also be drinking alcohol problematically. The same techniques of feedback, motivational interviewing, reframing, problem-solving etc. – utilizing the same accepting and respectful stance – can also be used in such cases, enabling the workers to address both generations of substance misuse.

TREATMENT OF CO-EXISTING MENTAL HEALTH AND DRUG AND ALCOHOL PROBLEMS WITH FAMILY INTERVENTION

The process of family intervention

Family work takes place in addition to routine care within the context of case management. One of the family workers may be the case manager; if not, clear communication between family workers and the case manager is vital (Smith and Velleman 2002). The flowchart in Figure 5.1 represents the simplest process of family intervention. There are occasions when it may be necessary due to an actual or impending crisis to begin with some problem-solving. Nevertheless, it is important to conduct the assessments at the earliest opportunity to ensure that workers gain a picture of everyone's strengths and resilience as well as their problems and needs. Without the information gathered through a thorough assessment it is impossible to create the collaboration upon which effective family intervention is based.

Referral

Having discussed with clients and family members the potential benefits of family intervention, and agreed it may be useful, a formal referral is made. A simple referral form is best, sent to whoever allocates the work to clinicians (e.g. team leader or service coordinator) and knows who is in a position to provide a prompt response. In most cases, leaving a family without family intervention for more than two or three weeks once the need has been identified is strongly correlated with a refusal to engage in family work.

Following allocation, one of the workers should make contact with the client, to ensure they have a clear idea of what is on offer. Any ambivalence about sharing personal information and accepting help must be explored with the individual before the family meeting. Failure to do so can cause the client to feel overwhelmed and liable to refuse to engage in family intervention. Non-engagement is particularly likely if a client who is misusing drugs or alcohol sees the intervention as a means of the workers allying with and helping the family to persuade him or her change this behaviour (Miller and

Rollnick 2002). Family intervention is unlikely to be successful if the client does not feel safe. Building a therapeutic alliance is vital (Vaccaro and Roberts 1992).

Initial meeting

This occurs before the individual assessments (see Figure 5.1), and is an opportunity for the family's main needs to be expressed, and for the therapists to convey optimism and hope, start to deal with ambivalence and present themselves to the family as a resource to assist the family in moving on. An important component of successful family intervention is the hope it brings that things can improve (Drage et al. 2005). Family workers can convey optimism from their experience of work with other families and through stating their belief in the client's self-efficacy (Bandura 1977), which is also influenced by the therapists' expectations of the client's recovery (Miller 1983).

Families, and especially the client, will often be ambivalent about engaging in family intervention. It is important to make explicit that ambivalence is normal (Miller and Rollnick 2002), particularly in situations when investing in change presents some risks. These include the risk to the client of exacerbating psychotic symptoms or behaviour by engaging in new strategies or relationships, and the risk of disappointment for all concerned if a hoped-for change does not occur.

Assessments

The family's needs are assessed generally in the initial meeting, and then more precisely via each individual being formally assessed (see below). It is recommended that each family member, including the client, has at least one individual interview to express their concerns in private. How much of this information is then shared with other family members is a matter for negotiation, with the power of veto ultimately remaining with whoever provided the material. Workers strongly encourage the sharing of information, as 'secrets' appear to cause a feeling of tension – but unless there is a risk of ongoing abuse (about which people are warned), workers will not override an individual's wish for privacy.

There are several specific assessment tools designed to elicit the background information required in most cases of family intervention with co-existing problems. Some are validated for use with carers, others for clients (see the flowchart in Figure 5.1). These assessment scales are listed in Table 5.1. The overall purpose of the assessment process is to develop further a therapeutic alliance with each family member, while gathering details of their particular strengths and needs, and areas where they would like help.

Table 5.1 Assessments

Family assessments
General Health Questionnaire (GHQ; Goldberg 1972)
Symptom Rating Test (SRT; Kellner and Sheffield 1973)
(both of the above measure the general health of the family member)
Family Questionnaire (FQ; Barrowclough and Tarrier 1997)
Knowledge About Schizophrenia Interview (KASI; adapted by Barrowclough 2003 from Barrowclough *et al.* 1987; including Section 7 which relates to substance misuse)
Relative's Assessment Interview (RAI; Barrowclough and Tarrier 1997)
Family Member Impact scale (FMI; Orford *et al.* 2005; which examines the impact that a relative's alcohol or drug misuse has had on other family members)
Coping Questionnaire (CQ; Orford *et al.* 1975, 1976, 2005; which examines how other family members cope with their relative's alcohol or drug misuse)

User assessments
Re psychosis: see Chapter 2 for screening instruments, including:

Social Functioning Scale (SFS; Birchwood *et al.* 1990)
Manchester Short Assessment of Quality of Life (MANSA; Priebe *et al.* 1999)
and also the Liverpool University Neuroleptic Side Effects Rating Scale (LUNSERS; Day *et al.* 1995)
Re substance misuse: see Chapter 2 for screening instruments, including:

for alcohol:
Fast Alcohol Screening Test (FAST; Hodgson *et al.* 2002)
Cut down, Annoyed, Guilty, Eye-opener questionnaire (CAGE; Rydon *et al.* 1992)
Alcohol Use Disorders Identification Test (AUDIT; Saunders *et al.* 1993)

for either drug or alcohol problems:
Severity of Dependence Scale (SDS; Gossop *et al.* 1995, 1997)
Dartmouth Assessment of Life Instrument (DALI; Rosenberg *et al.* 1998)
Alcohol, Smoking and Substance Involvement Screening Test (ASSIST; WHO ASSIST Working Group 2002)
10-item Drug Abuse Screening Test (DAST-10; Skinner 1982)
28-item Drug Abuse Screening Test (Staley and el-Guebaly 1990)
Cannabis Use Disorders Identification Test (CUDIT; Adamson *et al.* 2003)
Fagerstrom Test for Nicotine Dependence (FTND; Heatherton *et al.* 1991)

Screening tools are useful, but further questionnaires may be needed to determine problem severity: more comprehensive assessment instruments are discussed in Chapter 2, and include:

Clinicians' Rating Scale for Alcohol Use (CAUS) and Drug Use (CDUS; Drake *et al.* 1996)
Substance Abuse Treatment Scale (SATS; Drake *et al.* 1996)
Readiness to Change Questionnaire – Treatment Version (RCQ; Heather *et al.* 1999)
Chemical Use, Abuse and Dependence Scale (CUAD; Appleby *et al.* 1996)

Education where there are co-existing psychosis and drug and alcohol problems

In families where there are co-existing psychosis and drug and alcohol problems, there is frequently a lack of knowledge around ambivalence and readiness for change. The Prochaska and DiClemente (1986) model of change can provide a useful framework for everyone to understand their role within problem-solving and goal-setting. All family members are taught about the stages of change (which range from pre-contemplation, where there is no acceptance of a problem, through contemplation when it becomes possible to consider the pros and cons of changing, to action and finally maintenance of the desired change). We explain why one should avoid trying to be persuasive or helpful before someone is ready to accept help, as this is almost always counter-productive. This way of thinking about changing behaviour can as usefully be applied to a relative's emotional over-involvement, for example, as to the client's substance misuse, which neatly demonstrates the family worker's interest in the whole family's wellbeing.

Lack of knowledge about drugs, psychosis, the effects of these and possible interactions with the client's personality are also common. Here there is often a need to provide basic information about drugs and alcohol and their effects, and about psychosis.

Throughout the family intervention process family workers employ reframing techniques, and it is useful to make this explicit during the education stage. Workers initially seek to provide an alternative explanation for EE, such as care or concern, which in itself reduces levels of ambient stress. Family members are encouraged to adopt this strategy themselves, and look for the positive motivation that underlies their criticism or intrusiveness. In time they will become skilful enough to be able to spontaneously articulate just the positive reframe. Miller and Rollnick (2002) suggest that reframing can also be a useful way to deal with the resistance of someone who is providing reasons to support their assertion that they do not have a problem with their substance use. The approach validates the client's observations while offering an alternative explanation, which may support their motivation to change.

Problem-solving/goal-setting

It is vital for family workers to leave the responsibility for change with the client and their family, while offering themselves as a resource for the family as required. We must work with the family to help them learn to help themselves, not try to solve their problems ourselves. It is possible that others in mainstream services will adopt a different approach. In order to ensure that those who use services do not experience a conflict, family workers may need to work with their colleagues to promote an overall approach to mental health practice that sees clients, and not professionals, as the experts (Repper and Perkins 2003).

The aim of problem-solving is to develop creative solutions that avoid confrontation or unspoken conflicts and therefore reduce tension in the environment. Individual family members' approaches to dealing with difficulties will have been explored during the assessment process, so family workers should have an idea of each person's strengths. It is important that these are acknowledged before the workers attempt to teach any new skills. It is also useful to note that even those who are adept at solving problems and achieving goals within their professional life are usually less skilled at home when faced with an emotional situation. Normalizing this position can pave the way to introducing the structured problem-solving approach (Falloon *et al.* 1984) we advocate, where a repeated cycle of goal-setting and experimentation is undergone until the process is incorporated within the family's usual way of working.

The first stage of this process is to ask the family to define a problem that they wish to work on together. It is inadvisable to start with a difficult or entrenched problem, but rather to gain familiarity with a relatively trivial example. Unless specifically requested by the client, anything related to drug or alcohol misuse should be avoided. Encouragement is then given by the workers to reframe the problem as a goal, with a positive outcome. Often, gaining agreement on exactly how the problem or goal is defined will take much discussion and negotiation. The workers should support this interaction, but must resist any temptation to take over, as this would provide evidence that they are, after all, the experts. At this and every other stage of the process, everyone's opinion is sought. It is also useful to nominate a chairperson to manage the process and take notes. This may be one of the workers in the first instance but they should not maintain the role, as this would leave the family less likely to adopt the process when the workers leave.

Having established the goal that they are working towards, the family is encouraged to make a list of possible solutions, avoiding any discussion about their feasibility or utility; only when the list is complete is there a conversation about the advantages and disadvantages of each one. When the pros and cons have been considered the family chooses one option or a combination of several. Although it is unlikely to be apparent in the early stages, this specificity is very valuable when the client wants help to change addictive behaviour. Miller and Rollnick (1991: 20) describe 'active helping' – a component of effective motivational approaches. Being clear about exactly what is wanted allows family members to take on this role.

The final stages involve deciding how the solution (which should be measurable and take into account what resources are available) will be carried out and how it will be reviewed. Calling this plan 'an experiment' promotes the suggestion that any result is interesting, and removes the idea of success or failure. Careful attention should be paid to the review so that lessor can be incorporated into future plans. The cycle is then repeate different problem/goal.

Evaluation, endings and booster sessions

Within family intervention the concepts of evaluation and endings are not left to the final sessions, but are embraced from the beginning. At the first meeting it is likely that workers will be introducing the notion that, while this is not necessarily a brief intervention, it is time limited. The average length of intervention is between nine months and three years (Kuipers *et al.* 2002), with the interval between meetings increasing over time and an agreement between the family and the workers when the work is complete. However, it is emerging (Drage *et al.* 2005) that families would appreciate the opportunity for further 'booster sessions' to help them revitalize their skills when they find themselves confronted by new challenges.

CASE STUDY

Simon T has a long and troublesome history of substance misuse, as well as a diagnosis of paranoid schizophrenia. The first author of this chapter (GS) was one of the family workers.

Case history

Simon is 22 years old and has a brother aged 25. There is no known history of severe mental disorder in the family. In order to focus on the family intervention here, only a brief summary of his history is provided. Briefly, Simon was described as a clingy infant, had received diagnoses of learning disability and dyslexia at primary school, and had excelled at sports at secondary school. At age 14, without apparent reason, Simon's behaviour changed. He quit sporting activities and became generally destructive. Difficulties escalated, with problems maintaining employment, involvement with petty criminals and stealing from friends and family. His parents continued to offer assistance, providing money, helping with rent and buying him food. His mother now admits she was very frightened of him but could not obtain help from any agency despite many requests and assessments.

At the age of 19, Simon was diagnosed with schizophrenia and, following his continued refusal of treatment, he was admitted involuntarily to hospital. Three years later he remained an inpatient, having progressed from an acute ward to living almost independently within the hospital rehabilitation unit. He remained paranoid and was unwilling to accept any suggestion that he could cope outside the haven that hospital had become. Medication had been helpful to Simon, but his unwillingness to move on caused the staff great frustration. Once, with the family's agreement, he was pushed towards discharge and a flat was found. However, he became acutely psychotic again before the move took place and he was assured this would not happen again in the future.

Referral

Although Simon had been in hospital for three years, he had not responded to treatment to the extent that he could leave, possibly due to continuing use of cannabis and amphetamines. No formal help had been available to families during this time.

In 1998, GS was employed to devise and implement a local strategy to apply family interventions (Mari and Streiner 1996) in routine practice. Having attended a presentation by GS on the new strategy, staff caring for Simon quickly recognized the family's need and a formal referral for family work was made.

Initial meeting

GS visited the rehabilitation unit and discussed with Simon what family work could offer and whether or not he wished to engage. Simon said he had been diagnosed with schizophrenia although he was not sure what this meant. GS explained how family work could help him to understand more – both about how it was affecting him personally and about how to negotiate how his family could best support him. She was careful to avoid giving any impression that he was obliged to accept this intervention and made it explicit that ambivalence was normal. He was quite non-committal, but recognized that it could be useful to have help to improve his parents' understanding, especially as he did not always find their advice useful. At this stage there was no mention of drug or alcohol misuse.

With Simon's permission GS then contacted his parents to offer family work. This was instantly accepted and appointments were made with each of them to conduct the Relative's Assessment Interview (RAI), the Knowledge about Schizophrenia Interview (KASI) and the General Health Questionnaire (GHQ) (see Table 5.1). A nurse from the hospital rehabilitation unit agreed to co-work and carried out the assessment with Simon while GS assessed his parents.

Assessments

Simon

Simon accepted his diagnosis of schizophrenia and was willing to take medication (Olanzapine), which he found partially helpful. His psychiatrist had recommended Clozapine, which Simon was unwilling to take because people he knew who took it complained of nausea. He felt criticized for his decision, but at this stage had no idea that any other treatments were available. He clearly stated that he wanted to increase his parents' knowledge of his experiences and coping strategies, so that they could stop worrying about him. He was ambivalent about leaving hospital 'because it's too dangerous out there', but would not elaborate as this would 'increase the risk'.

Simon was quite reluctant to discuss 'street drugs' and alcohol use, as he knew their use was not permitted by the hospital. He did say however that he had 'found a number of substances helped [him] to chill out in the past'; he did not recognize that his use was connected in any way with his current mental health problems.

Mr T

Mr T worked as a personnel manager for a local furniture manufacturer. He described the traumas experienced by the family before Simon's disorder was recognized, and how Simon was later involuntarily admitted to hospital, where his paranoia developed to include fears about family members conspiring against him. A diagnosis of schizophrenia had been made, which they found helpful, but Simon was not responding to treatment, possibly due to continuing use of cannabis and amphetamines, and was still an inpatient on the rehabilitation unit. No help had been offered to the family. With his wife, he had spent many hours prior to the hospital admission seeking information to explain Simon's behaviour; he scored very highly on the KASI. He agreed with the medical diagnosis and was disappointed that the medication had not been more effective. He thought that Simon should be made to take part in a structured programme of activities and was angry that nursing staff could not enforce this.

He was also angry that Simon was apparently still misusing 'street drugs' while in hospital, as he expected the charge nurse to ensure prohibition. He recognized when Simon used amphetamines because he became over-active and aggressive; cannabis, he said, caused Simon to become disorganized and unmotivated for days. Both seemed to increase his paranoia. Alcohol also seemed to lead to increased disorganization. He had tried, unsuccessfully, to point out his observations and concerns to Simon, who just accused his father of always being critical and not understanding. Communication between them was almost non-existent, which Mr T found quite upsetting.

The GHQ showed that coping with Simon's condition was impacting on Mr T's health. He recognized this, but was adamant that he must 'do anything' that would help Simon and would not consider GS's suggestion that he may need to consider his own needs too.

Mrs T

Mrs T worked as a health visitor, so had some understanding of schizophrenia before Simon's diagnosis. She too scored highly on the KASI and held similar views to her husband about the need for structured activity. She was not as specific as her husband about their impact, but she also wanted Simon to be forced to discontinue his use of 'street drugs', seeing no hope of recovery if this was not achieved. She did not see Simon as being able to look after himself. Her score on the GHQ suggested she was herself unwell and she agreed to see her general practitioner.

Education

Having established their willingness to work together, the initial family work sessions were generally focused on education. Simon was able to use sessions to explain something of his experience of schizophrenia, and his parents learned to be facilitative rather than challenging as they recognized his attempts to cope. This demonstrates how quickly attributions can change within the context of family intervention. Providing information about Prochaska and DiClemente's (1986) model of change gave Mr and Mrs T the framework they needed to demonstrate their care and concern without giving advice. Simon openly acknowledged that he appreciated the change in their behaviour and said that hearing their fears about his safety helped him to consider how he might become more responsible and indulge less frequently in risky behaviours such as misusing drugs and getting drunk.

However, the workers were aware of how little detail Simon was willing to disclose. For example, he was able to say that he heard voices that upset him, but would not discuss the content of what they said, leaving his parents frustrated at being denied the information that could help them really understand the barriers to Simon's recovery. The workers regularly described and modelled the skills of motivational interviewing during these early sessions to help Mr and Mrs T to avoid exerting pressure to change upon him. When praise was given by his parents Simon obviously appreciated their approval; the workers tried to ensure this did not go unnoticed.

In order for the family work to progress, the workers felt that Simon needed to extend on a one-to-one basis his understanding of his symptoms and coping strategies, and gather further ideas of what could help, before trying to share his insights with his parents. It was agreed that cognitive behaviour therapy (CBT) would be the most appropriate means to help him achieve this due to its structured approach (Kinderman and Cooke 2000). Simon understood this and agreed to accept the therapy, which was provided by GS.

Individual CBT

CBT approaches to co-existing problems are described in Chapter 4. The details of Simon's individual CBT are beyond the scope of this chapter. Instead, a summary of his learning is provided:

- recognition of his jumping to conclusions and 'absolutist' thinking, leading to a willingness to accept alternative possibilities rather than a single position;
- understanding of how his paranoia developed;
- understanding that his substance misuse was linked to his anxieties, and that both were linked to feeling out of control;
- understanding that anxiety and low self-esteem increases paranoia; and
- acceptance that alcohol, cannabis and amphetamines all have a negative impact on his mental health.

Simon summed up the therapy as helping him to 'see the bigger picture'.

Family problem-solving/goal-setting

Most problem-solving sessions were focused on helping Simon to manage his anxieties, within the context of the stress-vulnerability model (Zubin and Spring 1977). Without feeling obliged to disclose any detail, Simon was able to share with his parents much of what he had learned through individual therapy. He explained his tendency to jump to conclusions and asked that, if they noticed him doing this, rather than telling him he was wrong they should encourage him to gather further evidence to back up his reasoning. They reported that it was 'good to know how to help'. He also explained how he felt anxious when leaving the hospital in case he was burgled. Using the structured problem-solving approach, this led to conversations about how one protects one's possessions; the previous pattern had been simply to pressurize him to go out more. Mr and Mrs T were also able to let Simon know how delighted they were that he had possessions he cared about.

Without much overt discussion about his drug and alcohol misuse Simon and his parents were able to consider the benefits of his increasing abstinence. A link was made between Simon's ability to think logically and the effectiveness of family meetings, so if he came to a meeting and was obviously muddled the meeting was adjourned to another time. In fact this happened on fewer and fewer occasions as Simon took charge of organizing the agendas for the meetings himself, providing further confirmation for him that his anxieties (and substance misuse) were linked to his feeling out of control.

Evaluation and booster sessions

Gradually Simon began to realize that those who he found most helpful were people he had confided in. He acknowledged that being clear about what he found helpful enabled his parents to adopt an 'active helping' position which they all enjoyed.

Simon now recognizes why he used drugs and alcohol and is pleased to have developed alternative coping strategies to manage his anxiety. He has used family work sessions to learn to check his perceptions against those of people that he trusts, and through this he has gained the confidence to make new friends to widen his support network.

After about 15 sessions – about half of which took place every fortnight, while the rest had a six-week gap between – the regular meetings ceased. Now if Simon feels his paranoia returning he convenes a family meeting to provide an opportunity for 'a reality check'. These booster sessions occur approximately twice per year and appear to be a very positive means to provide on-going family support without creating a sense of dependence or failure.

CONCLUSION

Although family approaches have been shown to be effective both with families where there are severe mental health problems and with families where there are severe alcohol or drug problems, many workers shy away from using these approaches when there are co-existing problems. This may be due to each set of workers feeling unskilled in the other area (substance misuse work or work with serious mental health problems). This chapter has demonstrated three things:

1   Family approaches can be just as effective when applied in cases where co-existing problems arise.
2   Many of the ideas and skills utilized in mental health-related approaches are the same as those utilized in alcohol- or drug-related approaches.
3   There *are* some differences, and we can learn from these differences and hence produce a family intervention which draws on the best ideas of both traditions.

KEY RESOURCES

Integrated family work model

Barrowclough, C., 'Family intervention for substance misuse in psychosis', in Graham H., Copello, A., Birchwood, M. and Mueser, K., eds, *Substance Misuse in Psychosis*, pp. 227–43. Chichester: Wiley, 2003.

Smith, G., Gregory, K. and Higgs, A., *Integrated Approaches to Family Intervention: A Manual for Practice*. London: Jessica Kingsley Publishers, 2007.

Motivational interviewing

Miller, W. and Rollnick, S., *Motivational Interviewing, Preparing People for Change*, 2nd ed. New York: Guilford Press, 2002. Available at http://www.motivational interview.org/ (accessed 26 August 2005).

Family work with psychosis

Barrowclough, C. and Tarrier, N., *Families of Schizophrenic Patients*, 2nd ed, Cheltenham: Stanley Thornes, 1997.

The Early Psychosis Prevention and Intervention Centre, *Family Work*. Melbourne: EPPIC, 2004. Available at http://www.eppic.org.au/mhp/eppic/family_work.htm (accessed 26 August 2005).

Kuipers, E., Leff, J. and Lam, D., *Family Work for Schizophrenia*, 2nd ed. London: Gaskell, 2002.

REFERENCES

Adamson, S. and Sellman, J., 'A prototype screening instrument for cannabis use disorder: The Cannabis Use Disorders Identification Test (CUDIT) in an alcohol dependent clinical sample', *Drug and Alcohol Review*, *22*, 309–15, 2003.

Appleby, K., Dyson, V., Altman, E., McGovern, M. and Luchins, D., 'Utility of the Chemical Use, Abuse and Dependence Scale in screening patients with severe mental illness', *Psychiatric Services*, *47*, 647–9, 1996.

Asen, E., 'Outcome research in family therapy', *Advances in Psychiatric Treatment*, *8*, 230–8, 2002.

Bandura, A., 'Self-efficacy', *Psychological Review*, *84*, 191–215, 1977.

Barrowclough, C., 'Family intervention for substance misuse in psychosis', in Graham, H. L., Copello, A., Birchwood, M. J. and Mueser, K. T., eds, *Substance Misuse in Psychosis*, pp. 227–43. Chichester: Wiley, 2003.

Barrowclough, C. and Tarrier, N., *Families of Schizophrenic Patients*, 2nd ed. Cheltenham: Stanley Thornes, 1997.

Barrowclough, C., Tarrier, N. and Johnson, M., 'Distress, expressed emotion and attributions in relatives of schizophrenia patients', *Schizophrenia Bulletin*, *22*, 691–702, 1996.

Barrowclough, C., Tarrier, N., Watts, S., Vaughn, C., Bamrah, J. and Freeman, H., 'Assessing the functional value of relatives' knowledge about schizophrenia: A preliminary report', *British Journal of Psychiatry*, *151*, 1–8, 1987.

Birchwood, M., Smith, J., Cochrane, R., Wetton, S. and Copestake, S., 'The Social Functioning Scale. The development and validation of a new scale of social adjustment for use in family intervention programmes with schizophrenic patients', *British Journal of Psychiatry*, *157*, 853–9, 1990.

Brewin, C., 'Changes in attribution and expressed emotion in relatives of patients with schizophrenia', *Psychological Medicine, 24*, 905–11, 1994.

Brown, G., Birley, J. and Wing, J., 'Influence of family life on the course of schizophrenia disorders: A replication', *British Journal of Psychiatry, 121*, 241–58, 1972.

Brown, G., Monck, E. and Carstairs, G., 'Influence of family life on the course of schizophrenic illness', *British Journal of Preventive and Social Medicine, 16*, 55–68, 1962.

Brown, G. and Rutter, M., 'The measurement of activities and relationships: A methodological study', *Human Relations, 19*, 241–63, 1966.

Copello, A., Orford, J., Velleman, R., Templeton, L. and Krishnan, M., 'Methods for reducing alcohol and drug related family harm in non-specialist settings', *Journal of Mental Health, 9*, 329–43, 2000a.

Copello, A., Templeton, L., Krishnan, M., Orford, J. and Velleman, R., 'A treatment package to improve primary care services for the relatives of people with alcohol and drug problems: Feasibility and preliminary evaluation', *Addiction Research, 8*, 471–84, 2000b.

Copello, A., Velleman, R. and Templeton, L., 'Family interventions in the treatment of alcohol and drug problems', *Drug and Alcohol Review, 24*, 369–85, 2005.

Day, J., Wood, G., Dewey, M. and Bentall, R., 'A self-rating scale for measuring neuroleptic side-effects: Validation in a group of schizophrenic patients', *British Journal of Psychiatry, 166*, 650–3, 1995.

Drage, M., Floyd, S., Smith, G. and Cocks, N., *Evaluating Family Interventions: A Qualitative Investigation.* Bath: University of Bath (Mental Health R&D Unit), 2005.

Drake, R., Mueser, K. T. and McHugo, G. J., 'Clinician rating scales: Alcohol Use Scale (AUS), Drug Use Scale (DUS) and Substance Abuse Treatment Scale (SATS)', in Sederer, L. and Dickey, B., eds, *Outcomes Assessment in Clinical Practice*, pp. 113–16. Baltimore: Williams and Wilkins, 1996.

Fadden, G., 'Family intervention', in Brooker, C. and Repper, J., eds, *Serious Mental Health Problems in the Community: Policy, Practice and Research*, pp. 159–83. London: Ballière–Tindall, 1998.

Falloon, I., Boyd, J. and McGill, C., *Family Care of Schizophrenia.* New York: Guilford Press, 1984.

Gamble, C., 'Using a low expressed emotion approach to develop positive therapeutic alliances', in Gamble, C. and Brennan, G., eds, *Working with Serious Mental Illness: A Manual for Practice.* Edinburgh: Ballière–Tindall, 2000.

Gamble, C. and Midence, K., 'Schizophrenia family work: Mental health nurses delivering an innovative service', *Journal of Psychosocial Nursing, 32*, 13–16, 1994.

Goldberg, D., *The Detection of Psychiatric Illness by Questionnaire.* London: Oxford University Press (Maudsley Monograph Series), 1972.

Gossop, M., Best, D., Marsden, J. and Strang, J., 'Test–retest reliability of the Severity of Dependence Scale', *Addiction, 92*, 353, 1997.

Gossop, M., Darke, S., Griffiths, P., Hando, J., Powis, B., Hall, W. and Strang, J., 'The Severity of Dependence Scale (SDS): Psychometric properties of the SDS in English and Australian samples of heroin, cocaine and amphetamine users', *Addiction, 90*, 607–14, 1995.

Heather, N., Luce, A., Peck, D., Dumbar, B. and James, I., 'Development of a treatment version of the Readiness to Change Questionnaire', *Addiction Research and Theory, 7*, 63–83, 1999.

Heatherton, T. F., Kozlowski, L. T., Frecker, R. C. and Fagerstrom, K. O., 'The Fagerstrom test for nicotine dependence: A revision of the Fagerstrom Tolerance Questionnaire', *British Journal of Addiction, 86*, 1119–27, 1991.

Higgins, S. T. and Budney, A. J., 'Participation of significant others in out-patient behavioural treatment predicts greater cocaine abstinence', *American Journal of Drug and Alcohol Abuse, 201*, 47–56, 1994.

Hodgson, R., Alwyn, T., John, B., Thom, E. and Smith, A., 'The FAST (Fast Alcohol Screening Test)', *Alcohol and Alcoholism, 37*, 61–6, 2002.

Kellner, R. and Sheffield, B., 'A self-rating scale of distress', *Psychological Medicine, 3*, 88–100, 1973.

Kinderman, P. and Cooke, A., *Recent Advances in Understanding Mental Illness and Psychotic Experiences*. Leicester: The British Psychological Society, 2000.

Kuipers, E., Leff, J. and Lam, D., *Family Work for Schizophrenia*, 2nd ed. London: Gaskell, 2002.

Lam, D., 'Psychosocial family interventions in schizophrenia: A review of empirical studies', *Psychological Medicine, 21*, 423–41, 1991.

Leff, J., 'Needs of the families of people with schizophrenia', *Advances in Psychiatric Treatment, 4*, 277–84, 1998.

Macdonald, D., Russell, P., Bland, N., Morrison, A. and De la Cruz, C., *Supporting Families and Carers of Drug Users: A Review*. Edinburgh: Scottish Executive – Effective Interventions Unit, 2002.

Mari, J. and Streiner, D. L., *The Effects of Family Intervention for those with Schizophrenia (Cochrane Review)*. The Cochrane Library, Oxford: Update Software, 1996.

Meyers, R. and Miller, W., *A Community Reinforcement Approach to the Treatment of Addiction*. Cambridge: Cambridge University Press, 2001.

Miller, W., 'Motivational interviewing with problem drinkers', *Behavioural Psychotherapy, 11*, 147–72, 1983.

Miller, W. and Rollnick, S., *Motivational Interviewing: Preparing People for Change*. New York: Guilford Press, 1991.

Miller, W. and Rollnick, S., *Motivational Interviewing: Preparing People for Change*, 2nd ed. New York: Guilford Press, 2002.

Moos, R. H. and Moos, B. S., 'The process of recovery from alcoholism. III. Comparing functioning in families of alcoholics and matched control families', *Journal of Studies on Alcohol, 45*, 111–8, 1984.

O'Farrell, T. J., Choquette, K. A. and Cutter, H. S., 'Couples relapse prevention sessions after behavioral marital therapy for male alcoholics: Outcomes during the three years after starting treatment', *Journal of Studies on Alcohol, 59*, 357–70, 1998.

Orford, J. and Edwards, G., *Alcoholism: A Comparison of Treatment and Advice, with a Study of the Influence of Marriage*. Oxford: Oxford University Press (Maudsley Monograph 26), 1977.

Orford, J., Guthrie, S., Nicholls, P., Oppenheimer, E., Egert, S. and Hensman, C., 'Self-reported coping behaviour of wives of alcoholics and its association with drinking outcome', *Journal of Studies on Alcohol, 36*, 1254–67, 1975.

Orford, J., Oppenheimer, E., Egert, S., Hensman, C. and Guthrie, S., 'The cohesiveness of alcoholism-complicated marriages and its influence on treatment outcome', *British Journal of Psychiatry*, *128*, 318–39, 1976.

Orford, J., Templeton, L., Velleman, R. and Copello, A., 'Family members of relatives with alcohol and drug problems: A set of standardised questionnaires for assessing stress, coping and strain', *Addiction*, *100*, 1611–24, 2005.

Pharoah, F. M., Rathbone, J., Mari, J. and Streiner, D., *Family Intervention for Schizophrenia (Cochrane Review)*. The Cochrane Library. Oxford: Update Software, 2003.

Pitschel-Walz, G., Leucht, S., Bauml, J., Kissling, W. and Engel, R., 'The effect of family intervention on relapse and rehospitalisation in schizophrenia: A meta-analysis', *Schizophrenia Bulletin*, *27*, 73–92, 2001.

Priebe, S., Huxley, P., Knight, S. and Evans, S., 'Application and results of the Manchester Short Assessment of quality of life (MANSA)', *International Journal of Social Psychiatry*, *45*, 7–12, 1999.

Prochaska, J. O. and DiClemente, C. C., 'Toward a comprehensive model of change', in Miller, W. R. and Heather, N., eds, *Treating Addictive Behaviors: Processes of Change*, pp. 3–27. New York: Plenum Press, 1986.

Repper, J. and Perkins, R., *Social Inclusion and Recovery*. Edinburgh: Ballière–Tindall, 2003.

Rogers, C., 'A theory of therapy, personality and interpersonal relationships, as developed in the client-centered framework', in Koch, S., ed., *Psychology: A Study of a Science, Volume 3*, pp. 186–256. New York: McGraw-Hill, 1959.

Rosenberg, S. D., Drake, R., Wolford, G. L., Mueser, K. T., Oxman, T. E., Vidaver, R. M. *et al.*, 'Dartmouth Assessment of Lifestyle Instrument (DALI): A substance use disorder screen for people with severe mental illness', *American Journal of Psychiatry*, *155*, 232–8, 1998.

Rydon, P., Redman, S., Sanon-Fisher, R. W. and Reid, A. L., 'Detection of alcohol related problems in general practice', *Journal of Studies in Alcohol*, *50*, 197–202, 1992.

Saunders, J., Aasland, O. G., Babor, T. F., de la Fuente, J. R. and Grant, M., 'Development of the Alcohol Use Disorder Identification Test (AUDIT): WHO collaborative project on early detection of persons with harmful alcohol consumption – II', *Addiction*, *88*, 791–804, 1993.

Skinner, H., 'The Drug Abuse Screening Test', *Addictive Behaviors*, *7*, 363–71, 1982.

Smith, G., Gregory, K. and Higgs, A., *Integrated Approaches to Family Intervention: A Manual for Practice*. London: Jessica Kingsley Publishers, 2007.

Smith, G. and Velleman, R., 'Maintaining a family work for psychosis service by recognising and addressing the barriers to implementation', *Journal of Mental Health*, *11*, 471–9, 2002.

Smith, J. and Meyers, R., *Motivating Substance Abusers to Enter Treatment: Working with Family Members*. New York: Guilford Press, 2004.

Staley, D. and el-Guebaly, N., 'Psychometric properties of the Drug Abuse Screening Test in a psychiatric patient population', *Addictive Behaviors*, *15*, 257–64, 1990.

Turner, S., 'Comments on expressed emotion and the development of new treatments for substance abuse', *Behaviour Therapy*, *29*, 647–54, 1998.

Vaccaro, J. V. and Roberts, L., 'Teaching social and coping skills', in Birchwood, M. J. and Tarrier, N., eds, *Innovations in the Psychological Management of Schizophrenia*. Chichester: Wiley, 1992.

Velleman, R. and Templeton, L., 'Alcohol, drugs and the family: Results from a long running research programme within the UK,' *European Addiction Research*, *9*, 103–12, 2003.

WHO ASSIST Working Group, 'The Alcohol, Smoking and Substance Involvement Screening Test (ASSIST): Development, reliability and feasibility', *Addiction*, *97*, 1183–94, 2002.

Zubin, J. and Spring, B., 'Vulnerability: A new view of schizophrenia', *Journal of Abnormal Psychology*, *86*, 260–6, 1977.

Chapter 6

Group interventions for co-existing mental health and drug and alcohol problems

Kim T. Mueser and Steven C. Pierce

KEY POINTS

1 The rationale for using group interventions lies in the social context of this treatment modality. Since drug and alcohol use is fundamentally a social behaviour, the social format of group interventions promotes exploration of the social (and other) benefits and negative impacts of substance use. Group settings also provide opportunities for the influence of role modelling, as well as increasing connections with friends who do not use drugs and alcohol problematically, replacing the substance-using social network.

2 Self-help groups are widely used by people recovering from addiction. They are frequently recommended by professionals, and there is research suggesting they are beneficial. However, individuals with severe mental disorders often have social anxiety and impairments in social judgment and social skills, which may make them appear and feel awkward in the self-help group setting. Self-help groups should be presented to people with co-existing disorders at a point in their recovery when they have sufficient motivation to pursue them, with special consideration given to groups designed for persons with both disorders.

3 Stage-wise treatment groups are professionally facilitated groups based on the concept of the *stages of change* or the *stages of treatment* of co-existing disorders. Most stage-wise groups focus on the persuasion stage (developing motivation to work on substance misuse), the active treatment stage (reducing substance use), or the relapse prevention stage of treatment (preventing substance misuse relapses). Within each of these stage-wise groups, the leader depends primarily on group process to foster change, but also integrates education and skills development into the group structure.

4 Social skills training can either be incorporated into stage-wise treatment groups, or run as separate groups. Skills training groups focus on developing a healthier lifestyle through learning new and more effective social skills for connecting with people and dealing with overtures from others

to use substances. Skills are taught through a combination of social modelling, behavioural rehearsal and feedback, and practice in real-world situations.

5   Research shows benefits from participating in group intervention for those with co-existing disorders. Across different studies, there is evidence that clients who attend groups consistently (e.g. for a year or more) have better outcomes. Even participating in shorter-term groups focused on motivational enhancement has been found to have positive outcomes.

INTRODUCTION

Group interventions are among the most common types of psychotherapy provided to individuals with substance use and mental disorders (co-existing disorders). Furthermore, group interventions for co-existing disorders have been more extensively studied than any other treatment modality (e.g. individual, family), with findings indicating that a variety of different group treatment approaches (e.g. motivational enhancement, cognitive-behavioural counselling) are more effective at improving substance misuse outcomes than no group treatment or standard 12-step approaches (Mueser *et al.* 2005). Therefore, provision of group treatment is both an efficacious and cost-effective approach to clients with severe mental disorder and substance misuse.

This chapter describes different approaches to group work for persons with co-existing disorders. We begin with a discussion of the rationale for group intervention for co-existing disorders, and consider some of the advantages of this approach over other modalities. Next, we describe different models of group intervention for co-existing disorders, including self-help groups, stage-wise (motivation-based) treatment groups, and social skills training groups. We conclude with a summary of research into the effectiveness of group intervention for persons with co-existing disorders.

Rationale for group intervention

There are a number of reasons for considering group interventions for co-existing disorders as a primary treatment option in this population.

First, both alcohol and drug use are fundamentally social behaviours that develop and are often maintained in a social context. People are usually introduced to alcohol and drugs by other individuals, and their use often serves celebratory and social purposes, especially before such use becomes problematic. In addition, some individuals with severe mental health problems specifically use substances to facilitate social contacts and overcome the social stigma associated with mental disorder (Carey and Carey 1995; Test *et al.* 1989). Considering the social nature of substance use, group interventions have the natural advantage of capitalizing on this social function while using this format to explore and challenge beliefs regarding the social (and other) benefits of using substances.

Second, addressing substance misuse in groups can provide people who are early in the process of coming to grips with their substance use problems with exposure to others who have made more progress in overcoming their problems, and have begun to turn their lives around by endorsing abstinence or non-problematic use. These individuals can serve as role models to others who are still in the throes of problematic use, motivating them and providing them with hope that they too can pull their lives together.

Third, a group intervention for co-existing disorders can provide participants with connections to other people who are not misusing substances, thereby replacing people with substance use problems in those individuals' social networks. Research shows that a large number of substance misusers in the social network of a person with co-existing disorders predicts a worse outcome over the course of integrated treatment (Trumbetta *et al.* 1999). Friends who do not use substances problematically can replace substance-misusing friends in an individual's social network, and then support that person's reduced use or abstinence and efforts to develop a new life.

Fourth, group work offers the advantage of preparing some clients for self-help groups and connecting them with those groups. Self-help groups such as Alcoholics or Narcotics Anonymous play an important role in recovery from addiction for many individuals, including those with co-existing disorders (Humphreys *et al.* 2004). However, severe mental disorders often interfere with the participation of clients with co-existing disorders in self-help groups (Noordsy *et al.* 1996). Group intervention can help prepare these clients to participate in self-help groups, and can connect them with groups in their community that meet their personal needs. Facilitating involvement in self-help groups for persons with co-existing disorders can enable them to take advantage of these resources, which are available in most communities.

Finally, compared to individual and family modalities, group-based intervention may be more cost-effective for those who choose to participate. Providing treatment in a group format allows one or two clinicians to work simultaneously with four to eight clients, decreasing the intensity of services provided while simultaneously capitalizing on the aforementioned advantages of group intervention. It should be noted that while cost-effectiveness is a presumed advantage of group intervention, clients participating in such groups nevertheless need individual work to engage them, and many require ongoing individual work to address their personal treatment needs.

CONTEXT OF INTERVENTION

Therapist variables

It is easier, but not essential, to conduct groups with two co-leaders. One can focus on presenting material and facilitating interactions among group members, while the other can attend to group process. Leaders should strive to acknowledge, involve, and validate all group participants, while also structuring the group in order to accomplish the planned teaching. Refreshments are a helpful way of rewarding attendance at groups and making clients feel comfortable in the group setting.

Client variables

It is feasible to conduct groups with a diagnostically heterogeneous mix of clients (e.g. schizophrenia, bipolar disorder, major depression). However, it is best if groups of clients are similar in their level of functioning, as evidenced by capacity for independent living, cognitive functioning, and social skill. Some variability in functional level of clients is inevitable, and this is not problematic. In fact, clients who function at a higher level can serve as role models for other clients with more impaired functioning. Relative similarity in functioning enables group leaders to pace the group in a way that avoids going too fast or too slow for some participants.

The decision about whether to include clients with different motivations to stop using substances in the group depends on the nature of the group. As described later in this chapter, groups that focus on a particular stage of substance misuse treatment require a selection of clients at the corresponding or later stages of treatment, but not clients at the earlier stages of treatment (e.g. avoid engaging clients who are not motivated to stop using substances in groups focused on substance use reduction or relapse prevention).

GROUP INTERVENTIONS FOR CO-EXISTING MENTAL HEALTH AND DRUG AND ALCOHOL PROBLEMS

Self-help groups

Group-based self-help approaches such as Alcoholics Anonymous (AA) are among the most commonly utilized treatment modalities for addiction throughout the world (Emrick et al. 1993). Self-help groups have several distinct advantages for people with co-existing disorders, including their widespread availability, predictable structure, and potential for helping individuals with co-existing disorders replace substance-abusing peers with social supports who endorse sobriety. However, there are also some disadvantages to self-help groups for individuals with co-existing disorders (Noordsy et al.

1996). Prominent impairments in social judgment and social skill in clients with disorders such as schizophrenia may make them appear awkward in self-help group meetings, and interfere with establishing supportive relationships with others.

Some individuals with co-existing disorders may not relate to the losses described by other participants in self-help groups. People with severe mental disorders have often suffered severe impoverishment throughout their lives, in contrast to some self-help participants who may have functioned better in their lives, but due to their addiction have lost well-paid jobs, close family relationships, and material possessions such as houses and cars. Finally, some people with co-existing disorders have difficulty with the strong spiritual focus of many self-help groups and such a focus may be especially problematic for individuals who have religious delusions. On the other hand, many individuals with severe mental disorders report having significant spiritual needs (Corrigan *et al.* 2003), and self-help groups can be consonant with their beliefs and needs (McDowell *et al.* 1996).

Self-help groups are an important option for clients with co-existing disorders, but they should not be forced on reluctant participants. Several strategies may be useful in helping people explore whether participation in self-help groups might be useful (Mueser *et al.* 2003). First, the availability of self-help groups specifically tailored for individuals with co-existing disorders should be explored, such as Dual Recovery Anonymous. Second, it can be helpful to prepare an individual who is interested in participating in a self-help group by describing how these groups run, and participating in a simulated self-help group meeting. Third, because multiple self-help groups may be available and each group differs in terms of individual culture and participants, attending different self-help groups with a client ('meeting shopping') can help that person decide whether one group appears likely to meet their needs. Finally, self-help groups need to be presented to people with co-existing disorders at a point in their recovery when they have sufficient motivation to pursue them, for example when individuals are actively contemplating cutting down or stopping, or have made progress towards sobriety.

Stage-wise treatment groups

Stage-wise treatment groups are professionally facilitated groups based on the concept of the *stages of change* (Prochaska 1984; Prochaska and DiClemente 1984) or the *stages of treatment* (Mueser *et al.* 2003; Osher and Kofoed 1989) of co-existing disorders. The stages of change theory was developed from the observation that individuals with addictive and other harmful behaviours often go through a sequence of discrete changes as they develop an awareness of their substance use problems and proceed to change their harmful lifestyles. The stages of change include: precontemplation (the individual is not thinking about changing his/her substance use habits), contemplation (the individual is thinking about changing), preparation (the person is planning on making specific changes), action (the individual is changing his or her behaviour), and maintenance (the individual is maintaining his or her behaviour change).

The stages of change have been adapted to describe the stages of treatment that individuals with co-existing disorders go through when they change their behaviour with professional help. The following stages of treatment have been identified: engagement (the clinician does not have a therapeutic relationship with the client, and the goal is to establish an alliance), persuasion (the client has a relationship with the clinician, but is not motivated to work on substance misuse, and the goal is to instil such motivation), active treatment (the client is motivated to reduce their substance misuse, and the goal is to facilitate such reduction and attainment of stable change), and relapse prevention (the person no longer misuses substances and the goal is to prevent relapses and to expand recovery to other areas of functioning). Stage-wise treatment groups specifically focus on helping clients achieve the goal of a specific stage of treatment.

In practice, most stage-wise treatment groups focus on achieving the goals of the persuasion stage, active treatment stage, or relapse prevention stage of treatment. The distinction between the persuasion stage and the later stages of treatment is especially critical because, by definition, clients in the persuasion stage lack the motivation to change their substance use or lifestyle, and therefore tend to have relatively little tolerance for interventions aimed at reducing substance use and achieving a sober lifestyle. In contrast, individuals in the active treatment or relapse prevention stages are motivated to reduce substance use or to maintain abstinence, and therefore have a strong motivation to learn how better to resist the temptations of substance misuse. Because the goals of the persuasion stage and the latter stages of treatment differ so greatly, having separate groups that address these goals is a convenient way of using groups to help people make progress in the stages of their co-existing disorder treatment.

Persuasion groups

Persuasion groups are designed to help members move into and through the contemplation stage and finally into the preparation stage of change. As individuals move from the engagement to the persuasion stage of treatment, they begin to talk openly about their substance use, though they often express little or no desire to reduce or stop their use. In order to enhance motivation towards change, group leaders create an atmosphere within the group that promotes self-exploration regarding the function and impact of substances within each member's life.

The group leader depends primarily on group process to foster change, but education and skills development are also important interventions, which are thoughtfully integrated into the group process. These processes and techniques are not only utilized within the persuasion group, but also within the active treatment and relapse prevention groups. Within each of these stage-wise groups, group process is based upon the principle that peer interactions lead to insights and motivation to address substance misuse problems. It is typical for group members to view each other's comments and feedback as more valuable than the leader's. Therefore, in order to promote group process, leaders limit their involvement and promote peer interaction. They also keep the group on topic and promote personal exploration among members. Education and skills development are judiciously interspersed into the group process.

Psycho-education plays an integral role within all the stage-wise groups. Leaders are constantly searching for opportunities to provide psycho-education in areas of addiction, mental disorder, and especially the interactions between them. In providing education, the leader is careful not to present information in a purely didactic manner. Instead, the leader fosters member interaction around educational topics and elicits their experiences whenever possible. This becomes essential within the persuasion group as members with active addictions are often more symptomatic and have difficulty attending to didactic presentations.

Leaders should be prepared with discussion topics or exercises to facilitate group discussions and address psycho-educational needs. These may include social skills training, guest speakers, education (with interactive exchange), art projects, and motivational enhancement exercises (Mueser *et al.* 2003). Leaders often utilize these during the initial development of a persuasion group, when the group has not yet established the norms that foster group process.

As the group matures and establishes norms for group process, the need for leaders to intervene with an exercise greatly decreases. In the mature persuasion group, the discussion topics are often found within the 'check-in' phase of the group. During this phase, each member discusses their substance use and other significant events within the past week and leaders often find related issues between two or more members. One or two of these issues then can be brought into the 'discussion topic' phase of the group. At the end of the group, the leader makes closing remarks, commenting on the group's processing of the discussion topic, and also giving members a chance to make their last comments on that session's topic.

Unlike some of the more traditional treatment models for addictions, a non-confrontational atmosphere is essential within persuasion groups. The leader does not confront members on issues that would typically be confronted in other stage-wise groups. For example, when members enter a group intoxicated, they are allowed to remain and participate as long as they are not disruptive to the group process. Instead of confronting their intoxication, the leader may offer support and encouragement for attending that group session. The leader's role also includes the modulating of confrontation by other members. For example, if other members confront an intoxicated member in an emotionally charged manner, the leader intervenes, promoting a sense of tolerance between members and a recognition that different members may be at different points regarding their substance misuse. The leader creates a group norm of non-confrontation and acceptance.

Leaders utilize this accepting, non-confrontational approach when addressing attendance issues. In the early persuasion stage, many individuals are still developing their commitment to treatment and consistent attendance. When members are absent from the group, they are not confronted. Instead, they are encouraged to attend and are positively reinforced when they come to the next group. With this low level of expectation, but strong support for attendance, some of these groups take on a 'drop-in' quality.

This accepting, non-confrontational atmosphere within the persuasion group sets the groundwork for motivational approaches. A natural barrier to utilizing groups for the reduction of substance use is the social-psychological phenomenon of reactance. As defined by Brehm (1976: 15), reactance is 'an individual's concern with his freedom to behave as he wishes and his desire to avoid being subject to another person's directives'. Often persuasion group members have had experiences in which treatment providers, family members, or others have told them to stop their substance use and change their lives. This external pressure has often been presented with a focus on the negative impact of substance use, never acknowledging reasons or benefits of use. These experiences have often left people feeling defensive and invalidated, fostering continued use. Leaders can reduce reactance through strongly validating the benefits of substance use as expressed by the group members and avoiding pressure towards abstinence. Through this, the leader creates a non-judgmental atmosphere, allowing members to process all aspects of their substance use. The following dialogue is an example of how group leaders validate a member's positive experiences associated with substance misuse. Leading up to this dialogue, the group members had been discussing reasons for their misuse:

Gerald: I sit around all day doing nothing, watching TV. . . . So I go have a beer over my friend's.
Leader: Paula, what do you imagine Gerald goes through in his apartment, doing nothing?
Paula: I think he's probably bored and lonely. When I feel like that, sometimes I feel I can't get out of my chair, like I'm not even alive.
Gerald: Yeah, I'm bored, there's no one else there. . . . So I go to my friend's.
Leader: What happens then?
Gerald: I either bring beer or he has some. [Gerald and a few other

members begin smiling.] Yeah, and we sit around . . . have fun. [Other members are laughing with Gerald.]

Leader: It sounds like you have fun, what do you do together?

Gerald: [Still smiling] Nothing, we just joke around and have beers. We've been friends for years. We have a good time.

Leader: Have you ever gone over to your friend's without drinking?

Gerald: No, he drinks all the time, I'd feel weird going there and not drinking.

Leader: We all have a need to be connected with others; boredom and loneliness can be quite painful experiences. It's important to get some relief from them, and drinking is an effective way you deal with boredom and spend time with friends. . . . Have any of the rest of you found it easy to connect with others while using drugs or alcohol?

[After the group members have processed their own positive experiences of substance use with non-judgmental validation from the leader, they become more open in their discussion of negative aspects of use. The leader then asked a provocative question.]

Leader: With drugs and alcohol meeting such important needs, why would anyone consider not using?

Gerald: [After a pause] Sometimes I run out of money. . . . Beer can be expensive. . . . [Other members support this and join in, leading to an open discussion of the negative consequences of use.]

In this example, the leader strongly validated Gerald's experience, stimulating others to talk openly about the benefits of use. Once members experience the leader as validating their reasons for misusing substances, their reactance is reduced. They feel understood and no longer fear that the leader will use their statements to pressure them towards change. The members then feel freer to express the negative consequences of their misuse.

As persuasion group members begin to discuss openly the negative consequences of substance misuse, leaders can assist them in their exploration. To avoid stimulating reactance, leaders must be careful not to over-emphasize the negative side of substance misuse beyond how the members experience it. Instead, leaders should validate the negative experiences and make inquiries that promote self-exploration. As members increase their focus on and awareness of the negative consequences, they tend to move towards the preparation stage of change.

Another way in which leaders develop motivation towards stopping misuse entails cognitive dissonance (Miller and Rollnick 2002). The leader creates cognitive dissonance through assisting members in exploring and defining their goals, both short-term and long-term. It is critical that the therapist does not push his/her own sense of 'healthy' goals, but instead supports members in identifying their own goals. This allows them to take full ownership of their goals, making them more difficult to put aside. As members focus upon their goals and the steps towards those goals, leaders help them identify barriers, which often include their substance use. Cognitive dissonance is created as they experience their behaviours (i.e. substance use) as interfering with their goals. The group is now in a position to problem-solve actively on how to minimize or remove the barriers associated with substance misuse. Although abstinence may be one of the potential solutions, leaders should refrain from pushing this as the only viable option. Instead, they should support the plan to stop misuse that members adopt. They may adopt any number of plans, including reduction of use, switching the time of use, changing the substance of use, etc. Any success towards modified use should be reinforced. After implementing their modifications, members often find that their substance use continues to impede attainment of their goals. At this point, the group can assist the members in re-examining their plans and making the changes necessary to reduce the impact of substance misuse on goal attainment.

As group members identify abstinence or reduced use as a goal, they move into the preparation stage of change. At this stage, leaders should be sensitive to the members' fears associated with a changed lifestyle. Often these fears include the anticipation of: rejection by substance-using friends; inability to make substance-free friends; difficulty dealing with emotions that have been managed through substance misuse, such as anxiety, anger, boredom, loneliness, etc.; inability to have fun; expectations of increased responsibility from others; expectation of failure by others; and fear of withdrawal. The group leader looks for opportunities in the group to plan for and address these fears. Often the members' successful transition from contemplation to the preparation and action stages of change depends on the successful management of these concerns.

Active treatment groups

Active treatment groups share some general therapeutic principles with persuasion groups (e.g. group process, psycho-education, and skills development), but they differ in critical ways. Active treatment groups are for individuals who are in the process of significantly reducing or stopping their substance misuse, or have already significantly reduced or stopped. These individuals are moving through the preparation stage of change or have entered the action stage. Their motivation to stop misuse of substances has solidified. It is expected that members who have recently stopped or reduced substance use may experience a relapse to previous levels of use. If relapses are brief and followed by re-established abstinence or reduced use, it is likely that those members will benefit from remaining in the group. When members experience a sustained relapse, it is likely that they will not benefit from remaining in the group, and they may be harmful to the group's integrity. In these situations, it is often beneficial to recommend a temporary move to a persuasion group until they re-establish reduced use or abstinence.

Active treatment groups focus upon the development of strategies, skills, and a lifestyle that will support efforts towards reducing use or maintaining abstinence. At this stage of treatment, many of the skills and strategies presented are taken from the addictions treatment field and adapted. They include such things as de-activation of cravings, preparation for stressful situations, saying 'no' to common drug offers, and developing a plan to interrupt and manage a relapse. Other topics for education and self-exploration include identifying and understanding triggers and dangerous situations, the problems of secondary substance use (i.e. substances members have not yet identified as problematic), and issues of the recovering family. Although members at this stage often tolerate didactic presentations better than members in the persuasion stage, the leader still emphasizes the active involvement of the members and their expression of personal experiences.

Although psycho-education and group exercises are integral within this group, the leader focuses upon the development of group process. Members within the active treatment stage are less vulnerable or fragile, and therefore they can manage a greater degree of confrontation. This allows for a more direct focus on the issues of substance misuse. As group members may struggle with denial and pre-relapse behaviour, these issues often become the focus of confrontation between members. Although moderate confrontation is often beneficial, the leader is careful to intervene if the emotional intensity causes excessive stress. Some members of the group who are abstinent may tend to push the message of recovery aggressively. Excessive stress levels tend to shut down the group process, leaving the more vulnerable members feeling unsafe and unwilling openly to discuss relapse or pre-relapse issues. There are various ways in which a leader can intervene to manage excessive confrontation. The following example demonstrates how a group leader helped a member, Bill, communicate his concerns for another member without excessive confrontation and stress:

George: [After being confronted on his reluctance to attend Narcotics Anonymous (NA) meetings] I don't want to hear other people's problems. It makes me want to use.

Bill: [With raised voice and frustration] That's crap! You've never gone to a meeting. You're going to use. That leads to jails, institutions, and death. You're going to end up dead! [George appears distressed]

Leader: [Interrupts] Bill, you seem angry.

Bill: He needs to go to meetings or he'll relapse.

Leader: It sounds like you care what happens to George, that you're concerned.

Bill: I am.

Leader: I think it would be important for George to hear that you're concerned and care about him. Can you tell George what you wish for him?

Bill: [In a more modulated, caring voice] Yeah . . . I wish that you would attend meetings so you can stay clean.

Following this verbal exchange, a leader could guide the group in a few useful directions. The leader could have focused on the topic of how to communicate one's concerns effectively. The focus could also have been on the need to tolerate individual differences among members. The important outcome in this dialogue was the reduction of excessive stress associated with the confrontation as well as the introduction of a more sensitive manner of communicating one's concerns.

The boundaries of active treatment groups are somewhat firmer and expectations somewhat higher than in persuasion groups. Within these groups, there is a more formal expectation regarding attendance. Whereas the persuasion group may take on a 'drop-in' quality, members of active treatment groups often have clear group norms regarding consistent attendance. When members have been absent, confrontation can be used to motivate attendance. Also, active treatment groups have a clear focus on reducing or stopping substance misuse, and therefore intoxication within group is not tolerated. If a member is obviously inebriated within group, that member should be escorted out by a leader. The leader should have a brief discussion with that member regarding the impact his/her intoxication may have on the rest of the group. The member then should be strongly encouraged to return to the next group meeting, without using substances prior to the meeting. These situations lend support to the argument that stage-wise groups should be run by two leaders.

As this group focuses on developing a lifestyle that promotes abstinence, self-help groups such as AA or NA are encouraged. It is recognized that for individuals with co-existing disorders who can participate within the 12-step model, it can provide a significant support for abstinence within the community. But it is also recognized that many individuals with co-existing disorders have not developed all the necessary skills needed to manage those social settings successfully. The active treatment group works to develop those skills and attempts to familiarize group members with the structure, expectations, and philosophy associated with those meetings. This can be done through social skills training, didactic education, conducting a session in an AA/NA meeting format, or having a speaker from those meetings speak to the group.

Relapse prevention groups

Relapse prevention groups, like active treatment groups, share some general therapeutic principles with persuasion groups (i.e. group process, psycho-education, and skills development). Although these groups are similar to active treatment groups and at times may take on a similar appearance, there is a difference in the direction and focus. Relapse prevention groups are for individuals who have stopped misuse of substances for more than six months. These individuals are moving through the action stage of change or have entered the maintenance stage. They have developed the necessary skills to prevent relapse, and they have made alterations in their lifestyle to support their change goal. As in the active treatment groups, when a member experiences a brief relapse followed by a solidified abstinence or reduction, that member will probably benefit from remaining in the group. When a member experiences a sustained relapse, that member will benefit from a move to a persuasion group.

Beyond maintaining and enhancing the relapse prevention skills and social supports developed within the active treatment group, the relapse prevention group focuses upon life fulfillment and integration into the community without active addiction. It is not uncommon for individuals with co-existing disorders to struggle for and achieve abstinence, only to be left with a sense of increased loneliness and general dissatisfaction with their lives. This is addressed through a focus on developing substance-free leisure time activities, assessing one's social life, developing new friendships and intimate relations, and developing a more open recovery. Within this group, members focus on their dreams and goals, and begin taking the steps to achieve them. The development of a productive, socially rewarding lifestyle becomes an essential part of sustaining and enhancing recovery.

Social skills training groups

As previously described, many individuals with co-existing disorders use substances partly to facilitate social contact (Salyers and Mueser 2001). While substance use can facilitate social connections and interactions with others, it is often at a high cost, and when substance misuse is extreme, the addiction can paradoxically lead to social exclusion (Alverson *et al.* 2001; Drake *et al.* 2002). For many people with co-existing disorders, developing a changed lifestyle involves learning new and more effective ways of connecting with people, and skills for dealing with overtures to use substances from friends and acquaintances.

Social skills training is a rehabilitation strategy for dealing with a wide range of interpersonal problems across a spectrum of different disorders, including addiction, schizophrenia, mood disorders, and anxiety disorders (Mueser 1998). Social skills training procedures are based on social learning theory (Bandura 1969), and posit that new and more effective social behaviours are most effectively taught through a combination of social modelling, behavioural rehearsal and feedback, and practice in real-world situations. The steps of social skills training are summarized in Table 6.1.

Table 6.1 The steps of social skills training

1	Establish a rationale for learning the skill
2	Discuss the component steps of the skill
3	Model (demonstrate) the skill in a role play
4	Engage client in a role play
5	Provide positive feedback
6	Provide corrective feedback
7	Engage the client in another role play of the same situation
8	Provide more positive and corrective feedback
9	Engage other clients in role plays, positive feedback, and corrective feedback
10	Assign homework to practise the skill

A variety of social skills training manuals are available for people with co-existing disorders (Bellack *et al.* 2004; Mueser *et al.* 2003; Roberts *et al.* 1999). Skills training groups typically involve between four and eight individuals, with sessions lasting approximately an hour conducted more than once per week. Skills training is highly structured in approach, with sessions focused on teaching specific skills based on a pre-determined curriculum, and an emphasis on helping clients adapt and apply these skills to their personal situations.

Two types of interpersonal skills are taught: establishing and deepening interpersonal connections with others; and dealing with social situations involving offers or pressure to use substances. As previously discussed, people with an addiction often use substances in order to establish social connections with others, and to experience closeness and intimacy. If the clients are to be successful in developing sober and rewarding lives, they will need new and more effective interpersonal skills for getting their affiliative needs met. Examples of skills for connecting and getting closer to people taught in social skills training groups for clients with co-existing disorders are provided in Table 6.2.

In addition, people with co-existing disorders also need to know how to manage common social situations involving substance use. Almost no person with an addiction can successfully avoid all social situations involving substance use. Therefore, teaching assertiveness skills for dealing with substance use situations is of critical importance in skills training groups for co-existing disorders. Examples of social skills for dealing with substance use situations are also provided in Table 6.2.

Table 6.2 Examples of social skills taught in groups for co-existing disorders

Skills for establishing relationships and getting closer to people:
Initiating, maintaining, and ending conversations
Listening skills
Expressing positive feelings
Making a request
Monitoring disclosure
Giving and receiving compliments
Expressing affection
Finding common interests
Expressing unpleasant feelings
Compromise and negotiation
Asking someone to do something with you

Skills for dealing with substance misuse situations
Refusing offers to drink or use drugs
Levelling with the person about your change goals
Suggesting an alternative activity
Resisting offers/pressure to use from a former drug connection

CONCLUSION

In conclusion, group treatment can be very effective for persons with co-existing disorders. Across different studies, there is some evidence that clients who attended groups consistently (e.g. for a year or more) had better outcomes, although even some shorter-term groups had positive outcomes (James *et al.* 2004). The better outcomes associated with longer-term participation in group intervention could reflect the impact of group work on outcomes, or the fact that clients who achieve and maintain change goals are more likely to stay in substance misuse treatment of any kind, a finding widely reported in the substance misuse treatment field (Moos *et al.* 2001; Simpson *et al.* 1986, 1996). It is noteworthy that despite the relatively large number of studies in this area, no replication studies of group interventions have been reported. Considering that the replication of research findings is at the very heart of science, replication of treatment effects is an important priority for future research in this area.

KEY RESOURCES

Bellack, A. S., Mueser, K. T., Gingerich, S. and Agresta, J., *Social Skills Training for Schizophrenia: A Step-by-Step Guide*. New York: Guilford Press, 2004.

Graham, H., Copello, A., Birchwood, M., Orford, J., McGovern, D., Maslin, J. and Georgiou, G., 'Cognitive-behavioural integrated approach for psychosis and problem substance use', in Graham, H.L., Copello, A., Birchwood, M.J. and Mueser, K.T., eds, *Substance Misuse in Psychosis: Approaches to Treatment and Service Delivery*, pp. 181–206. Chichester: John Wiley, 2002.

Graham, H. L., Copello, A., Birchwood, M. and Mueser, K. T., eds, *Substance Misuse in Psychosis: Approaches to Treatment and Service Delivery*. Chichester: John Wiley, 2002.

Mueser, K. T., Noordsy, D. L., Drake, R. E. and Fox, L., *Integrated Treatment for Dual Disorders: A Guide to Effective Practice*. New York: Guilford Press, 2003.

Roberts, L. J., Shaner, A. and Eckman, T. A., *Overcoming Addictions: Skills Training for People with Schizophrenia*. New York: W. W. Norton, 1999.

Websites

Centre for Mental Health Services, *Integrated Dual Disorder Treatment Implementation Resource Kit*. United States Department of Health and Human Services, 2005. Available at http://www.mentalhealth.samhsa.gov

DRA World Service Central Office, *Dual Recovery Anonymous Online Resource Center*. Kansas: Dual Recovery Anonymous World Services Inc., 2004. Available at http://www.draonline.org/

Psychiatric Rehabilitation Consultants, *Psychiatric Rehabilitation Consultants – Products and Services for Biobehavioral Rehabilitation*. California, 2000. Available at http://www.psychrehab.com

REFERENCES

Alverson, H., Alverson, M. and Drake, R. E., 'Social patterns of substance use among people with dual diagnoses', *Mental Health Services Research, 3*, 3–14, 2001.

Bandura, A., *Principles of Behavior Modification*. New York: Holt, Rinehart and Winston, 1969.

Bellack, A., Mueser, K., Gingerich, S. and Agresta, J., *Social Skills Training for Schizophrenia: A Step-By-Step Guide*, 2nd ed. New York: Guilford Press, 2004.

Brehm, S. S., *The Application of Social Psychology to Clinical Practice*. Washington: Hemisphere, 1976.

Carey, K. B. and Carey, M. P., 'Reasons for drinking among psychiatric outpatients: Relationship to drinking patterns'. *Psychology of Addictive Behaviors, 9*, 251–7, 1995.

Corrigan, P., McCorkle, B., Schell, B. and Kidder, K., 'Religion and spirituality in the lives of people with serious mental illness', *Community Mental Health Journal, 39*, 487–99, 2003.

Drake, R., Wallach, W., Alverson, H. and Mueser, K., 'Psychosocial aspects of substance abuse by clients with severe mental illness', *Journal of Nervous and Mental Disease*, *190*, 100–6, 2002.

Emrick, C. D., Tonigan, J. S., Montgomery, H. and Little, L., 'Alcoholics Anonymous: What is currently known', in McCrady B. S., and Miller, W. R., eds, *Research on Alcoholics Anonymous*, pp. 41–76. New Brunswick: Rutgers Centre of Alcohol Studies, 1993.

Humphreys, K., Wing, S., McCarty, D., Chappel, J., Gallant, L., Haberle, B. *et al.*, 'Self-help organizations for alcohol and drug problems: Toward evidence-based practice and policy', *Journal of Substance Abuse Treatment*, *26*, 151–8, 2004.

James, W., Preston, N. J., Koh, G., Spencer, C., Kisely, S. R. and Castle, D. J., 'A group intervention which assists patients with dual diagnosis reduce their drug use: A randomised controlled trial', *Psychological Medicine*, *34*, 983–90, 2004.

McDowell, D., Galanter, M., Goldfarb, L. and Lifshutz, H., 'Spirituality and the treatment of the dually-diagnosed: An investigation of patient and staff attitudes', *Journal of Addictive Diseases*, *15*, 55–68, 1996.

Miller, W. and Rollnick, S., *Motivational Interviewing: Preparing People for Change*. New York: Guilford Press, 2002.

Moos, R., Schaefer, J., Andassy, J. and Moos, B., 'Outpatient mental health care, self-help groups, and patients' one-year outcomes', *Journal of Clinical Psychology*, *57*, 273–87, 2001.

Mueser, K. T., 'Social skill and problem solving', in Bellack, A. S. and Hersen, M., eds, *Comprehensive Clinical Psychology*, pp. 183–201. New York: Pergamon, 1998.

Mueser, K. T., Drake, R. E., Sigmon, S. C. and Brunette, M. F., 'Psychosocial interventions for adults with severe mental illnesses and co-occurring substance use disorders: A review of specific interventions', *Journal of Dual Diagnosis*, *1*, 57–82, 2005.

Mueser, K. T., Noordsy, D. L., Drake, R. E. and Fox, L., *Integrated Treatment for Dual Disorders: A Guide to Effective Practice*. New York: Guilford Press, 2003.

Noordsy, D. L., Schwab, B., Fox, L. and Drake, R. E., 'The role of self-help programs in the rehabilitation of persons with severe mental illness and substance use disorders', *Community Mental Health Journal*, *32*, 71–81, 1996.

Osher, F. C. and Kofoed, L. L., 'Treatment of patients with psychiatric and psychoactive substance use disorders', *Hospital and Community Psychiatry*, *40*, 1025–30, 1989.

Prochaska, J. O., *Systems of Psychotherapy: A Transtheoretical Analysis*. Homewood: Dorsey, 1984.

Prochaska, J. O. and DiClemente, C. C., *The Transtheoretical Approach: Crossing the Traditional Boundaries of Therapy*. Homewood: Dow-Jones/Irwin, 1984.

Roberts, L. J., Shaner, A. and Eckman, T. A., *Overcoming Addictions: Skills Training for People with Schizophrenia*. New York: W. W. Norton, 1999.

Salyers, M. P. and Mueser, K. T., 'Social functioning, psychopathology, and medication side effects in relation to substance use and abuse in schizophrenia', *Schizophrenia Research*, *48*, 109–23, 2001.

Simpson, D. D., Joe, G. W. and Brown, B. S., 'Treatment retention and follow-up outcomes in the Drug Abuse Treatment Outcome Study (DATOS)'. *Psychology of Addictive Behaviors*, *11*, 294–307, 1996.

Simpson, D. D., Joe, G. W., Lehman, W. E. K. and Sells, S. B., 'Addiction careers: Etiology, treatment, and 12 year follow-up procedures', *Journal of Drug Issues*, *16*, 107–21, 1986.

Test, M. A., Wallish, L. S., Allness, D. G. and Ripp, K., 'Substance use in young adults with schizophrenic disorders', *Schizophrenia Bulletin*, *15*, 465–76, 1989.

Trumbetta, S. L., Mueser, K. T., Quimby, E., Bebout, R. and Teague, G. B., 'Social networks and clinical outcomes of dually diagnosed homeless persons', *Behavior Therapy*, *30*, 407–30, 1999.

Chapter 7

A consultation-liaison service model offering a brief integrated motivational enhancement intervention

Hermine L. Graham, Derek Tobin and Emma Godfrey

KEY POINTS

1   A consultation-liaison service model that offers a brief integrated motivational enhancement intervention for those with severe mental health
problems and co-existing drug and alcohol problems is described. This
service is provided as part of a structured response to this client group
within an inner city area of the UK to improve engagement, motivation
and treatment outcome.

2   This chapter illustrates the uptake of this service and the characteristics
of the teams and service users who benefit from such an approach. A
range of teams utilised this service, typically primary care liaison,
rehabilitation and recovery community mental health teams, mental
health inpatient units and community drug teams.

3   The clients were mainly male with a mean age of 37 years and a schizophrenia spectrum disorder; the main substances used problematically
were cannabis, alcohol, opiates and crack-cocaine. Some case examples
are included to illustrate those using the service.

4   Following the intervention, clinician ratings indicated that clients were
more engaged in the treatment process of addressing their problematic
substance use.

INTRODUCTION

There is growing consensus of opinion in the treatment literature about the
key ingredients necessary for the engagement and treatment of people with
severe mental health and co-existing drug and alcohol problems (e.g.
Department of Health 2002; Drake *et al.* 2001; Mueser *et al.* 2003). However,
although there has been some agreement about the key ingredients, there has
been considerable debate about what model of service delivery should be
adopted. Some have argued for specialist 'dual diagnosis teams' or workers,
while others have highlighted the need for the treatment of substance use to

be integrated into mainstream mental health services (e.g. Department of Health 2002). In the United Kingdom the clear message from the Department of Health's *Mental Health Policy Implementation Guide: Dual Diagnosis Good Practice Guide* (Department of Health 2002) is that the treatment of people with severe mental health and co-existing drug and alcohol problems is the responsibility of mainstream mental health services. It also emphasises that the treatment of substance use should be integrated within the mental health co-ordinated care package. However, it also suggests that the service approach adopted should be tailored to local needs.

The aim of this chapter is to describe a consultation-liaison service model which was one part of a structured response to the treatment of those with combined psychosis and substance use problems in Birmingham, in the UK. Two illustrative case examples are included to bring to life the way in which the consultation-liaison service is utilised.

THE SERVICE CONTEXT

Since 1997, the model of service delivery developed within the Northern Birmingham Mental Health Trust (NBMHT) has been tailored to fit with local needs and the community-based mental health service model already in place (Graham *et al.* 2003a, 2003b). NBMHT is a statutory provider of mental health and substance misuse treatment services to a catchment population of approximately 570,000 in an urban, multi-cultural area of the UK. The catchment includes a large (309,000) inner city population with high levels of social deprivation. The Trust has evolved into the provider of a spectrum of community-based mental health services tailored to the range of service user needs. The area is divided into geographical localities, each of which has the range of functional community mental health teams (Department of Health 2000) and inpatient units. These teams include assertive outreach teams, which are based on the Programme in Assertive Community Treatment (PACT) model (Stein and Santos 1998; Stein and Test 1980), home treatment teams (Dean and Gadd 1990), rehabilitation and recovery teams and primary care liaison teams. Some specialist services cover all localities and these include early intervention services. Specialist substance misuse services provided by the Trust are primarily based on harm-reduction principles (e.g. Heather *et al.* 1993; Marlatt 1998) and community-based. They comprise locality-based community drug teams, a small number of more specialist services and an inpatient unit.

It became increasingly apparent that the needs of those with severe mental health and co-existing drug and alcohol problems were not being met by existing service provision. This significant unmet need for integrated substance misuse treatment for people with severe mental health problems was the backdrop for a fundamental shift in service provision. The response by the Trust was to develop a new initiative, spearheaded by the Combined Psychosis and Substance Use (COMPASS) Programme, which complemented existing service provision.

THE COMPASS PROGRAMME

Our position has been that the treatment of those with severe mental health and co-existing drug and alcohol problems should be fully integrated within mainstream mental health services. The philosophy of the COMPASS Programme is that integration of treatment is achieved by training staff within mental health settings to deliver treatment for substance misuse as an integral part of the treatment delivered for the mental health difficulties. Additional specialist supervision, consultation and co-working are provided by the COMPASS Programme team (Graham et al. 2003a, 2003b). Specialist substance misuse services are then accessed when clients are more motivated and engaged, where appropriate.

Hence, the COMPASS Programme is a specialist multidisciplinary team that trains and works alongside existing mental health and substance misuse services to facilitate the provision of integrated treatment. It does not, however, seek to function as an additional 'third' service that takes on a separate caseload.

We reviewed the situation across NBMHT and found differences between various services and teams – both in terms of the proportion of clients with co-existing mental health and drug and alcohol problems, and in terms of the training needed to deliver integrated treatment. As a result, the service model that emerged comprised two main arms: intensive input into the assertive outreach teams (Graham 2004; Graham et al. 2003b, 2004) and the development of a consultation-liaison service.

Therefore, each assertive outreach team was trained intensively, over six half days, to deliver a manualised cognitive-behavioural integrated treatment (C-BIT) for problematic substance use among those with psychosis (Graham 2004; Graham et al. 2004). In addition, members of the COMPASS Programme team worked alongside members of the assertive outreach teams on a weekly basis.

At the other end of the spectrum, we identified that although the assertive outreach teams did have the highest proportion of those with severe mental health and co-existing drug and alcohol problems, a number of clients with such combined problems were also present in the other mental health teams and substance misuse services (Graham et al. 2001). It was clear from consultation with these services that staff there did not require the intensive input given to assertive outreach teams. However, staff often experienced difficulties in accessing services. In addition, they felt they lacked the particular skills and knowledge to assess, engage and build motivation to change with their clients. As a result, they desired specialist support (Maslin *et al.* 2001). As a result, the approach developed for these services was a consultation-liaison service model, which offered training, an integrated brief motivational enhancement intervention in the community and a brief motivational group programme on inpatient units.

CONSULTATION-LIAISON SERVICE MODEL

The consultation-liaison service offered by the COMPASS Programme is based on an adaptation of a substance abuse consultation-liaison service model developed by Greenfield *et al.* (1995) in the United States. In that service, substance misuse staff offered consultation and liaison to all psychiatric inpatient units. Consultation-liaison staff (i.e. psychiatrists, social workers and psychologists) were experienced in both mental health and substance misuse services. They provided assessments and consultancy regarding the best treatment approach for clients with substance misuse issues who were admitted due to mental health problems.

The COMPASS Programme's consultation-liaison service model was developed to be accessible to both mental health (i.e. primary care liaison, home treatment and rehabilitation and recovery community mental health teams) and substance misuse services (i.e. community drug teams) in the community and on inpatient units. The two main interventions offered as part of the COMPASS Programme's consultation-liaison service in the community will be described in this chapter: (i) training in delivering the brief integrated intervention; and (ii) a service whereby requests can be made to the COMPASS Programme team for a brief intervention.

Training

Clinicians within the teams were provided with a two-stage training package (see Table 7.1). The first stage of training involved one session with whole teams. The focus of this training was psycho-educational, with awareness-raising of the reasons for substance use among those with severe mental health problems and its impact on mental health/functioning. The second stage of training involved a smaller number of clinicians from each team. These individuals had been identified by their managers as those to take a specialist lead and interest in this area and serve as the designated liaison person. This training was skills-based: clinicians were trained to deliver the integrated brief motivational enhancement intervention. The aim was for these clinicians to act as a point of contact for other services in an attempt to ease movement between mental health and substance misuse services, to offer the brief intervention to clients within their team and to support other clinicians within their team in working with this client group.

Table 7.1 Staff who received training

Team type	Type of training	No. of attendants
Primary care liaison		
Full team	Awareness raising	57
Identified staff	Brief intervention	15
Inpatient units		
Full team	Awareness raising	71
Identified staff	Brief intervention	22
Rehabilitation and recovery		
Full team	Awareness raising	17
Substance misuse		
Full team	Awareness raising	40
Total trained		222

Brief integrated intervention

In addition to training staff to deliver the intervention themselves, COM-PASS Programme team members also actually deliver the brief intervention alongside keyworkers to clients. Teams that have received the training can make specific requests to the COMPASS Programme for a specialist assessment and the brief intervention. This service is typically for those keyworkers who want support/supervision in delivering the intervention to clients when they have particular concern about the negative impact of drug and/or alcohol use on mental health, and for cases where there are problems accessing appropriate services. The brief integrated intervention offered has developed into a time-limited, structured and focused intervention. In line with developments in the area of brief interventions for substance use treatment (e.g. Franey and Thom 1995; Miller *et al.* 1995; Richmond *et al.* 1995) and the treatment of substance use in psychosis (e.g. Baker *et al.* 2002; Kavanagh *et al.* 1998, 2003), a number of principles were incorporated into this service.

Aims

The aim of the brief intervention is to engage clients in discussing their drug and/or alcohol use and its impact on mental health, and to mobilise motivation, so they are then able to make changes appropriate to their stage of change. The focus is on examining the reasons and beliefs that maintain problematic substance use and prevent change. The intervention seeks to increase awareness of both the 'positive' and adverse links between mental health and problematic drug/alcohol use. 'Significant others' – that is, families, carers or friends (if possible and appropriate) – and keyworkers are included in the process. Keyworkers are involved in the intervention from the outset to ensure that there is joint ownership and that they feel able to continue the work once the COMPASS Programme is no longer involved. The inclusion of significant others is to promote social support, through the client's social network, for change (e.g. Copello *et al.* 2002; Drake *et al.* 1993; Galanter 1993, 1999).

Structure

The brief intervention consists of six sessions carried out over a 12-week period, as seen in Table 7.2. It comprises two assessment sessions, two motivational enhancement intervention sessions and two follow-up sessions.

Content

Assessment

The treatment sessions are preceded by an in-depth assessment carried out over two sessions, which includes a semi-structured clinical assessment as outlined in Table 7.3 and a battery of assessment tools. During the assessment phase the staff member who made the request is asked to complete the Clinicians' Rating Scale for Alcohol Use (CAUS) and Drug Use (CDUS) (Drake *et al.* 1996). This scale is based on DSM-IV diagnostic criteria for substance-related disorders and has been reliably used to classify the severity of substance use in people with severe mental health problems. The staff member also completes the Substance Abuse Treatment Scale (SATS). This scale seeks to assess the extent to which clients are engaged in discussing their substance use or receiving substance abuse treatment (Drake *et al.* 1996). These measures are then repeated at the first and second follow-up sessions.

The client is also asked to complete a number of assessment tools during the assessment and follow-up sessions, where appropriate. These measures are repeated at the first and second follow-up sessions to monitor progress and to assess the client's motivation towards change in terms of their stage of change, drug/alcohol use, substance-related beliefs and confidence in making changes.

These include:

Table 7.2 Overview of sessions

Week	Session type
1 and 2	Assessment and formulation
3 and 4	Motivational enhancement
8	Follow-up 1
12	Follow-up 2

- The Readiness to Change Questionnaire – Treatment Version (Heather *et al.* 1999): a 15-item measure that seeks to assess motivational readiness to change alcohol use behaviour, is based on the stages of change model (Prochaska *et al.* 1992) and allocates drinkers to one of three stages: precontemplation, contemplation and action. For the purpose of another study, this questionnaire has been adapted for use with other drugs. However, the adapted version has not been subject to the same stringent reliability and validity tests as the original version.
- The Alcohol Use Disorders Identification Test (AUDIT; Babor *et al.* 1992; Saunders *et al.* 1993): a score of eight or more indicates a strong likelihood of hazardous/harmful alcohol consumption.
- The Severity of Dependence Scale (SDS; Gossop *et al.* 1995): a total score is calculated for all five questions in the scale, and a score of five or more is usually considered indicative of problem substance use.
- A substance-related beliefs questionnaire and a confidence and skills ruler (Graham *et al.* 2004).

Formulation and treatment planning

Based on the information gathered, a case formulation is developed. The aim of the case formulation is to generate hypotheses about how the client's problems developed and are maintained. It also examines the relationships between the various problems a client may have, particularly between drug/alcohol use and mental health problems (Beck *et al.* 1993; Graham *et al.* 2004). The formulation serves as a guide to treatment planning.

A number of key factors are taken into consideration when planning treatment and deciding on the most appropriate intervention. These include the case formulation, the stage of change that the client is in (Prochaska *et al.* 1992), their stage of engagement with treatment (Drake *et al.* 1996; Graham *et al.* 2004), their self-identified individualised goals and concerns, their short- and long-term treatment needs and their overall needs as recorded in their care plan.

The results of the assessment and a simplified version of the case formulation are fed back to the client. The aim of this is to discuss the formulation and negotiate the treatment plan with the client, to ensure that the client is in agreement with it, enhance motivation towards change and ensure that interventions included are appropriate to the client's stage of change.

Treatment sessions

The two motivational enhancement sessions include: identifying negative consequences associated with use; reviewing advantages and disadvantages of continued use; re-evaluation and modification of substance-related beliefs (Beck *et al.* 1993; Graham *et al.* 2004); and reviewing the pros and cons of

Table 7.3 Clinical assessment of drug/alcohol use and relationship with mental health

Current functioning
This includes an initial conversation with the client to enhance engagement. Information should be gathered about current mood, sleeping and eating patterns, concentration, general motivation and level of interest, daily activities/employment and the client's view of their current circumstances.

Current substance use
This includes current pattern of use (e.g. types of substances used, cost, quantity and frequency of use, route of use, triggers and moderating factors and social networks). Information is gathered regarding effects of use and problems related to use (e.g. withdrawal symptoms, impact on family and social networks, and problems with the following areas: mental health, financial/debts, social/relationships, physical/health, housing, legal/forensic, occupation and child care).

Reasons for using and beliefs about substance use
To help identify key beliefs/cognitions (e.g. pleasure, social/cultural or coping) about alcohol/drug use, questions such as 'What usually goes through your mind just before you use?' or 'What are the positive things about your use?' are asked.

Drug/alcohol use history
As well as a brief developmental and family history, information is gathered on age of first use of each substance and how this developed over time. Clients are guided through this process through discussing use at various ages or significant life events. Periods of abstinence and treatment are also discussed.

Relationship between substance use and mental health
The focus is on whether the mental health problems/symptoms exist in the absence or presence of substance use, and includes assessing whether the client's reasons for using substances are related to his/her mental health problems/symptoms or his/her experience of taking medication.

Motivation to change and goals
This includes assessment regarding whether the client perceives his/her use as problematic and regarding the client's motivational stage of change. Clients are encouraged to identify their own goals to enhance motivation towards change.

behaviour change and obstacles to behaviour change (Miller and Rollnick 1991). The aims of these motivational sessions are to get a decision for change, build commitment to change and increase awareness of the negative relationship between mental health and alcohol/drug use.

Follow-up sessions

During the two follow-up sessions, clients repeat the assessment tools completed during the assessment phase. Sessions focus on monitoring and encouraging progress, and evaluating behaviour change and changes in the client's substance-related beliefs. During these sessions the client's advantages/disadvantages of drug use and the pros and cons of change analysis are reviewed to highlight changes made and to help identify any difficulties clients may have experienced. Where difficulties have been experienced, clients are encouraged to complete a goal-setting and problem-solving exercise to build on motivation to change and implement a self-identified plan to achieve goals.

It is anticipated that the intervention will have enhanced the client's engagement with services that are appropriate to their needs. If appropriate, a referral may be made to specialist substance misuse or mental health services. The intervention aims to increase awareness so that clients can be linked into and engaged with appropriate services.

UPTAKE OF THE CONSULTATION-LIAISON SERVICE'S BRIEF INTERVENTION

Over approximately a 12-month period, a total of 122 requests were received by the COMPASS Programme to offer the brief integrated intervention alongside keyworkers.

Characteristics of the teams using the service

The main sources of referrals were primary care liaison community mental health teams, rehabilitation and recovery community mental health teams, mental health inpatient units and community drug teams (see Table 7.4).

Characteristics of service users

The demographic profiles of the 122 clients are illustrated in Table 7.5. At the referral stage the keyworker making the referral indicated the substances

Table 7.4 Source of referral

Team making referral	Number of clients	Percentage
Primary care liaison	38	31.1
Rehabilitation and recovery	23	18.9
Inpatient units	20	16.4
Community drug teams	16	13.1
Home treatment	11	9
Early intervention	7	5.7
Homeless team	3	2.5
Addictive behaviours centre	2	1.6
Afro-Caribbean service	1	.8
Manic depression service	1	.8
Total	122	100

Table 7.5 Clients' demographic profile

Demographic variables	Client characteristics (n = 122)
Mean age	37.25
Gender	
Male	99 (81%)
Female	23 (19%)
1991 racial cultural classifications	
White	71 (58%)
Indian, Pakistani and Bangladeshi	17 (14%)
Black	16 (13%)
Chinese and other Groups	5 (4%)
Missing data	13 (11%)
Mental health status (ICD-10 criteria)	
Schizophrenia, schizotypal and delusional disorders	90 (73.7%)
Major mood (affective) disorders	12 (10%)
Undiagnosed	20 (16.3%)

they perceived as being used in a problematic way by the client (see Table 7.6). The main substances used problematically were cannabis and alcohol.

Progression of clients through the brief integrated intervention

Of the initial 122 clients for whom keyworkers requested the brief integrated intervention, 24 completed the intervention. Figure 7.1 illustrates how clients progressed through this service.

Table 7.6 Substances used in a problematic pattern

Substance	Number of clients using problematically
Cannabis	54
Alcohol	53
Opiates	21
Crack	28
Amphetamines	6
Other drug	5
Solvents	5
Ecstacy	4
Benzodiazepines	3
Cocaine powder	2
Prescribed medication	1

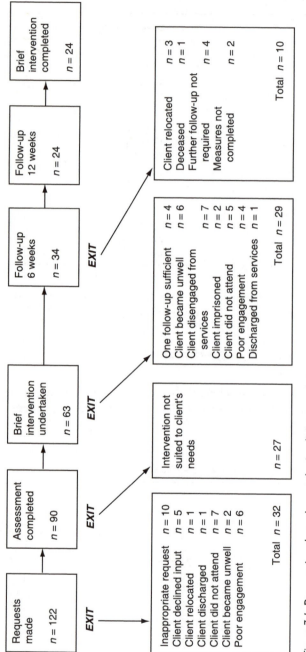

Figure 7.1 Progression through consultation-liaison service.

Table 7.7 Substances used problematically (*n* = 63)

Substance	Number of clients using problematically
Alcohol	22
Cannabis	21
Crack	15
Opiates	11
Ecstacy	5
Solvents	2
Amphetamines	2
Other drug	2
Prescribed medication	2
Benzodiazepines	1
Cocaine powder	1

The 27 individuals who exited the brief intervention between the assessment and intervention sessions were typically white males, aged between 25 and 29 years, with a diagnosis of schizophrenia and in contact with primary care teams. Following assessment, it was identified that the brief intervention was not suited to their needs. As Figure 7.1 indicates, of the 122 clients, 63 went on to be offered the brief intervention. The substances most commonly used in a problematic pattern (abuse or dependence) by these clients were cannabis and alcohol (see Table 7.7). Of these 63 individuals, 18 were polydrug users, using between two and four drugs.

The mean CAUS, CDUS and SATS scores, as rated by the clinicians, for the 24 clients who completed the intervention and follow-up sessions are reported in Table 7.8. No improvement was noted following the intervention or at follow-up in clinician ratings of clients' substance use problems. However, following the intervention, clinicians' SATS ratings indicated that clients were more engaged in the treatment process of addressing their problematic substance use (i.e. from 3 = 'early persuasion' to 4 = 'late persuasion'). This appears to persist at 12-week follow-up.

Table 7.8 Mean CAUS, CDUS and SATS scores of those who completed the full intervention (*n* = 24)

	Baseline	6 weeks	12 weeks
CAUS	2.27	1.95	1.73
CDUS	1.68	1.55	1.50
SATS	3.09	4.18	4.55

ILLUSTRATIVE CASE EXAMPLES

The following case examples illustrate how the consultation-liaison service has been used by substance misuse and mental health services. In the first case example, the consultation-liaison service served to improve assessment and access to appropriate mental health treatment for a client with mental health problems initially seen only within a community drug team setting. The second example illustrates the benefits of bringing substance misuse treatment into mental health treatment for someone with bipolar disorder who was ambivalent about changing his drug using behaviour.

Case example I

A request was made by one of the local community drug teams for the COMPASS Programme's consultation-liaison service for Marie, a 34-year-old woman with a history of heroin and crack-cocaine use. She had engaged well with the drug team and in the 12 months leading up to the request she had used crack on one occasion and heroin on three occasions. She was maintained on 40 mls of methadone daily. At this time Marie's mother was ill and Marie started to experience feelings of evil around her. She became suspicious of her partner and believed that he was going to harm her children. Following her mother's death there was deterioration in Marie's mental health and she became increasingly paranoid towards her partner and family. Her drug worker referred her to mental health services for assessment and treatment. However, following an initial assessment they felt that her behaviour was a result of her recent heroin use. A week later she was found trying to resuscitate her young daughter after trying to rid her of evil, leading to her daughter being injured and requiring hospital admission. As a consequence, her two children were taken into the care of social services and Marie was admitted to a psychiatric hospital. However, at that time it was still felt that her recent experiences were drug-related.

Following an assessment by the COMPASS Programme, carried out with Marie's drugs worker, information gathered from Marie and her family made it clear that she had been experiencing feelings of paranoia in the weeks leading up to her admission to a psychiatric inpatient unit. This period was eight weeks prior to her heroin use and was unlikely to be drug-induced. She said that she had recommenced her use of heroin in an attempt to 'calm down' and to 'cope with the symptoms' she was experiencing. The death of her mother had engendered strong feelings of loss; she felt that she had lost a major supportive person in her life and the life of her children.

Following this assessment, it was agreed that Marie would stay on the ward for a further period of psychiatric assessment and stabilisation. She was prescribed antipsychotic medication and a referral was made for follow-up by one of the community mental health teams. Care was co-ordinated by the mainstream mental health services (i.e. primary care community mental health team). A plan was put in place to meet with social services to ensure that Marie had access to her children, and to pursue occupational activities on discharge to promote recovery. Through this process Marie received appropriate access to mental health and substance misuse treatment services. As a result both services are working to an agreed co-ordinated care plan to support her recovery in both areas.

Case example 2

A referral was made to the consultation-liaison service from a primary care mental health team for Jack, a 32-year-old man with a history of bipolar disorder. There was concern that Jack's cannabis use was exacerbating his depressive symptoms. At the time of the request, Jack was low in mood. During the assessment, Jack reported using cannabis on a daily basis. He said that his reasons for using cannabis were a set of positive beliefs, such as: 'Cannabis helps me to feel better and more alert,' 'It gets me through the day,' and 'It helps me to relax.' However, his concerns about his cannabis use were: 'It makes me hide away from things from the past,' 'It's bad for my physical health,' and 'I'm spending too much money on cannabis.' He described triggers to his cannabis use as feeling low in mood and ruminating on events from the past. Another trigger was his social network. He said that he had cut himself off from friends who were not using and his current social network now consisted mainly of other cannabis users. At the time of the assessment, Jack believed that the advantages of his use outweighed the disadvantages. Therefore, his positive substance-related beliefs about cannabis left him vulnerable to maintaining a problematic cycle of cannabis use.

The treatment plan was to complete the brief integrated motivational enhancement intervention with Jack and, along with his keyworker, to build positive supportive networks and occupational activities, engage him in the specialist bipolar disorder services and encourage him in seeking psychological input regarding his early experiences and family life. Although Jack was still using cannabis on completion of the brief intervention, his use was dramatically reduced. There was also a shift in his cannabis-related beliefs: he no longer believed he needed cannabis to get through the day and found more enjoyment in voluntary work. He made attempts to re-engage with his non-cannabis-using social network with whom he had lost touch, and started to build a more supportive social network. His engagement with bipolar disorder services became more consistent.

The intervention facilitated Jack's ability to build on his motivation to change and served to enable him to make successful changes in relation to both his cannabis use and mental health. After re-evaluating his positive beliefs about cannabis, Jack was able to begin to manage his mood without believing that cannabis was the only thing that helped him. Making these changes enabled Jack to achieve additional goals to enhance the quality of his life.

CONCLUSIONS

The COMPASS Programme provides a consultation-liaison service which seeks to build on existing staff skills and expertise, and also delivers the brief integrated intervention itself alongside keyworkers. However, the ideal scenario is where teams are able to provide intervention themselves. Experience has demonstrated that teams tend to access the consultation-liaison service to access specialist help, broker services, access appropriate treatment services or where the issues appear more complex and/or the client is difficult to engage. The consultation-liaison service model described here has served to enhance a shared care approach between mental health and substance misuse services.

The uptake of the service highlights the need for a range of interventions to be developed for this client group to suit local needs, the specific needs of the teams and services, and the range of service users with severe mental health and co-existing drug and alcohol problems. Assessment of the progression of clients through this service indicates that the brief intervention was not always appropriate to the needs of all clients. However, the assessment sessions seemed to serve as a filter through which clients are able to move to more appropriate services, as in the case example of Marie. The intervention did not appear, from keyworker ratings, to make notable changes in substance use problems. However, the enhancement of engagement and motivation were the key targets of the brief integrated intervention. Hence, a positive outcome was that, following the intervention, clients were rated by clinicians as being on average, more engaged in the treatment process of addressing their problematic substance use and beginning to make changes in their substance use. This improvement in engagement appears to persist at 12-week follow-up.

KEY RESOURCES

Graham, H. L., Copello, A., Birchwood, M. J., Mueser, K., Orford, J., McGovern, D. et al., Cognitive-Behavioural Integrated Treatment (C-BIT): A Treatment Manual for Substance Misuse in People with Severe Mental Health Problems. Chichester: John Wiley, 2004.

Miller, W. R. and Rollnick, S., Motivational Interviewing: Preparing People to Change Addictive Behaviour. London: Guilford Press, 1991.

Miller, W. R., Zweben, A., DiClemente, C. C. & Rychtarik, R. G., Motivational Enhancement Therapy Manual: A Clinical Research Guide for Therapists Treating

Individuals with Alcohol Dependence. Rockville: NIAAA (Project Match Monograph Series 2), 1995.

REFERENCES

Babor, T. F., de la Fuente, J. R., Saunders, J. and Grant, M., *AUDIT. The Alcohol Use Disorders Identification Test. Guidelines for Use in Primary Health Care.* Geneva: World Health Organization, 1992.

Baker, A., Lewin, T., Reichler, H., Clancy, R., Carr, V., Garrett, R. *et al.*, 'Evaluation of a motivational interview for substance use within psychiatric in-patient services', *Addiction*, *97*, 1329–37, 2002.

Beck, A. T., Wright, F. D., Newman, C. F. and Liese, B. S., *Cognitive Therapy of Substance Abuse.* New York: Guilford Press, 1993.

Copello, A., Orford, J., Hodgson, R., Tober, G. and Barrett, C., 'Social behaviour and network therapy: Basic principles and early experiences', *Addictive Behaviors*, *27*, 345–66, 2002.

Dean, C. and Gadd, E. M., 'Home treatment for acute psychiatric illness', *British Medical Journal*, *301*, 1021–3, 1990.

Department of Health, *NHS Plan: A Plan for Investment, a Plan for Reform.* London: Department of Health, 2000.

Department of Health, *Mental Health Policy Implementation Guide: Dual Diagnosis Good Practice Guide.* London: Department of Health, 2002.

Drake, R., Bebout, R. R. and Roach, J. P., 'A research evaluation of social network case management for homeless persons with dual disorders', in Harris, M. and Bergman, H. C., eds., *Case Management for Mentally Ill Patients: Theory and Practice*, pp. 83–98. Pennsylvania: Harwood Academic Publishers, 1993.

Drake, R., Mueser, K. T. and McHugo, G. J., 'Clinician rating scales: Alcohol Use Scale (AUS), Drug Use Scale (DUS) and Substance Abuse Treatment Scale (SATS)', in Sederer, L. and Dickey, B., eds, *Outcomes Assessment in Clinical Practice*, pp. 113–16. Baltimore: Williams and Wilkins, 1996.

Drake, R. E., Essock, S. M., Shaner, A., Carey, K. B., Minkoff, K., Kola, L. *et al.*, 'Implementing dual diagnosis services for clients with severe mental illness', *Psychiatric Services*, *52*, 469–76, 2001.

Franey, C. and Thom, B., *The Effectiveness of Alcohol Interventions. Centre for Research on Drugs and Health Behaviour, Executive Summary 38.* London: Centre for Research on Drugs and Health Behaviour, 1995.

Galanter, M., 'Network therapy for substance abuse: A clinical trial', *Psychotherapy*, *30*, 251–8, 1993.

Galanter, M., *Network Therapy for Alcohol and Drug Abuse.* New York: Guilford Press, 1999.

Gossop, M., Darke, S., Griffiths, P., Hando, J., Powis, B., Hall, W. and Strang, J., 'The Severity of Dependence Scale (SDS): Psychometirc properties of the SDS in English and Australian samples of heroin, cocaine and amphetamine users', *Addiction*, *90*, 607–14, 1995.

Graham, H. L., 'Implementing integrated treatment for co-existing substance use and severe mental health problems in assertive outreach teams: Training issues', *Drug and Alcohol Review*, *23*, 463–70, 2004.

Graham, H. L., Copello, A., Birchwood, M. J., Mueser, K. T., Orford, J., McGovern, D. et al., *Cognitive-Behavioural Integrated Treatment (C-BIT): A Treatment Manual for Substance Misuse in People with Severe Mental Health Problems.* Chichester: John Wiley, 2004.

Graham, H. L., Copello, A., Birchwood, M. J., Orford, J., McGovern, D., Georgiou, G. and Godfrey, E., 'Co-existing severe mental health and substance use problems: Developing integrated services in the UK', *Psychiatric Bulletin, 27,* 183–6, 2003a.

Graham, H. L., Copello, A., Birchwood, M. J., Orford, J., McGovern, D., Maslin, J. and Georgiou, G., 'Cognitive-behavioural integrated approach for psychosis and problem substance use', in Graham, H. L., Copello, A., Birchwood, M. J. and Mueser, K. T., eds, *Substance Misuse in Psychosis: Approaches to Treatment and Service Delivery.* Chichester: John Wiley, 2003b.

Graham, H. L., Maslin, J., Copello, A., Birchwood, M. J., Mueser, K. T., McGovern, D. and Georgiou, G., 'Drug and alcohol problems amongst individuals with severe mental health problems in an inner city area of the UK'. *Journal of Social Psychiatry and Psychiatric Epidemiology, 36,* 448–55, 2001.

Greenfield, S. F., Weiss, R. D. and Tohen, M., 'Substance abuse and the chronically mentally ill: A description of dual diagnosis treatment services in a psychiatric hospital', *Community Mental Health Journal, 31,* 265–77, 1995.

Heather, N., Luce, A., Peck, D., Dumbar, B. and James, I., 'Development of a treatment version of the Readiness to Change Questionnaire', *Addiction Research, 7,* 63–83, 1999.

Heather, N., Wodak, A., Nadelman, E. and O'Hare, P., *Psychoactive Drugs and Harm Reduction: From Faith to Science.* London: Whurr, 1993.

Kavanagh, D. J., Young, R., Boyce, L., Clair, A., Siharthan, T., Clark, D. M. and Thompson, K., 'Substance treatment options in psychosis (STOP): A new intervention for dual diagnosis', *Journal of Mental Health, 7,* 135–43, 1998.

Kavanagh, D. J., Young, R., White, A., Saunders, J., Shockley, N., Wallis, J. and Clair, A., 'Start over and survive: A brief intervention for substance misuse in early psychosis', in Graham, H. L., Copello, A., Birchwood, M. J. and Mueser, K. T., eds, *Substance Misuse in Psychosis: Approaches to Treatment and Service Delivery,* pp. 244–58. Chichester: John Wiley, 2003.

Marlatt, G. A., *Harm Reduction: Pragmatic Strategies for Managing High-risk Behaviours.* New York: Guilford Press, 1998.

Maslin, J., Graham, H. L., Cawley, M., Copello, A., Birchwood, M. J., Georgiou, G. et al., 'Combined severe mental health and substance use problems: What are the training and support needs of a staff working with this client group?' *Journal of Mental Health, 19,* 131–40, 2001.

Miller, W. and Rollnick, S., *Motivational Interviewing: Preparing People for Change.* New York: Guilford Press, 1991.

Miller, W. R., Zweben, A., DiClemente, C. C. and Rychtarik, R. G., *Motivational Enhancement Therapy Manual: A Clinical Research Guide for Therapists Treating Individuals with Alcohol Dependence.* Rockville: NIAAA (Project Match Monograph Series 2), 1995.

Mueser, K. T., Noordsy, D. L., Drake, R. and Fox, L. W., *Integrated Treatment for Dual Disorders: A Guide to Effective Practice.* New York: Guilford Press, 2003.

Prochaska, J. O., DiClemente, C. C. and Norcross, J. C., 'In search of how people change: Applications to addictive behaviours', *American Psychologist*, *47*, 1102–14, 1992.

Richmond, R., Heather, N., Wodak, A., Kehoe, L. and Webster, I., 'Controlled evaluation of a general practice-based brief intervention for excessive drinking', *Addiction*, *90*, 119–32, 1995.

Saunders, J., Aasland, O. G., Babor, T. F., de la Fuente, J. R. and Grant, M., 'Development of the Alcohol Use Disorder Identification Test (AUDIT): WHO collaborative project on early detection of persons with harmful alcohol consumption – II', *Addiction*, *88*, 791–804, 1993.

Stein, L. and Santos, A., *Assertive Community Treatment of Persons with Severe Mental Illness*. New York: W. W. Norton, 1998.

Stein, L. and Test, M. A., 'Alternatives to mental hospital treatment: Conceptual model, treatment program and clinical evaluation', *Archives of General Psychiatry*, *37*, 392–7, 1980.

Chapter 8

Young people with co-existing mental health and drug and alcohol problems

Leanne Hides, Dan I. Lubman, Frances J. Kay-Lambkin and Amanda Baker

KEY POINTS

1   Adolescence and young adulthood are critical developmental periods that are associated with increased vulnerability to a range of mental health and substance use problems.
2   Current models of service delivery tend to focus on low prevalence disorders (such as psychosis) and often fail to address adequately the needs of young people with high prevalence co-existing conditions, such as substance misuse and depression.
3   Despite high rates of co-existing mental health disorders among young people with drug and alcohol problems, little evidence exists to suggest which treatments are most effective for this population. This is especially true for the highly prevalent co-existing conditions of depression and problematic substance use.
4   Cognitive behaviour therapy has the potential to benefit youth with co-existing depression and substance use problems, particularly when provided within an integrated framework, such that both conditions can be addressed simultaneously.

INTRODUCTION

The term 'young people' in this chapter refers to those aged between 10 and 25 years and incorporates both the period of adolescence and young adulthood. These life stages encompass a period of critical development, within which a number of key tasks necessary for independent living must be accomplished. However, while this period provides an opportunity for growth, it is also a time of vulnerability, characterised by increased risk-taking and novelty-seeking, and elevated morbidity and mortality rates (Bukstein and Winters 2004).

Epidemiological surveys of youth populations report high rates of depression, anxiety and behavioural disorders, as well as substantial experimentation with drugs and alcohol (Sawyer *et al.* 2001), all of which may significantly impact on developmental processes. Young people with substance use disorders (SUD) have even higher rates of mental disorder, with community surveys suggesting they are two to three times more likely to experience anxiety, mood or disruptive behaviour disorders (Kandel *et al.* 1999; Kessler *et al.* 1997; Lewinsohn *et al.* 1993). These results are consistent with those from clinical settings, where high rates of co-existing disorders are found in adolescents seeking mental health treatment (up to 71%; Bukstein *et al.* 1992; Kramer *et al.* 2003) and those accessing youth drug services (up to 89%; Clark *et al.* 1997; DiMileo 1989).

While disruptive behaviour disorders (DBD) are the most commonly reported co-existing condition (68%), affective disorders are also highly prominent in youth populations, with 20–32% of adolescents with SUD reporting a current mood or anxiety disorder (Kandel *et al.* 1999). In one large study, young people (aged 13–15) with a combination of regular smoking, drinking and cannabis use were found to be at 27 times the risk of a depressive disorder (Boys *et al.* 2003).

While alcohol use continues to increase among young people throughout the Western world (Australian Institute of Health and Welfare 2005; Boys *et al.* 2003; Farrell *et al.* 2001), there is growing evidence of a link between problematic alcohol use and depression. For example, Rohde *et al.* (1996) found that 50% of alcohol-dependent adolescents (aged 14–18) reported a co-existing depressive disorder. Similarly, a large-scale community survey found depressed youth (aged 13–15) were twice as likely to drink regularly, while in a separate study early alcohol use significantly predicted later major depressive disorder (at age 27), even after controlling for prior episodes of depressive and substance use disorders (Boys *et al.* 2003; Brook *et al.* 2002).

In terms of illicit drug use, cannabis is the most widely used by young people within Australia and most Western countries (Australian Institute of Health and Welfare 2005; Boys *et al.* 2003; Farrell *et al.* 2001), despite increasing concerns about a link between cannabis use and psychosis (Degenhardt and Hall 2001; Regier *et al.* 1990). In fact, while there is growing evidence that cannabis use may be associated with the onset of psychosis in young people with an underlying vulnerability (Arseneault *et al.* 2004; Hides *et al.* 2006; Zammit *et al.* 2002), comparatively little attention has been paid to the relationship between cannabis use and more prevalent mental health conditions such as anxiety, depressive and behavioural disorders (Degenhardt and Hall 2003). This is especially concerning given that early cannabis use has been found to predict antisocial personality and major depressive disorder in late adolescence and adulthood (Brook *et al.* 1998, 2002; Fergusson and Horwood 1997). Furthermore, the increasingly high association between depression, cannabis use and youth suicide (e.g. Beautrais *et al.* 1999) underscores the need to address high prevalence disorders in this population, despite a lack of specific interventions and research in this area.

The consistent association between suicidality, drug and alcohol problems and depression in young people is alarming (Lewinsohn *et al.* 1995; Shafii *et al.* 1988; Wagner *et al.* 1996), especially as current models of service delivery tend to focus on low prevalence disorders and often fail to address adequately the needs of young people with high prevalence co-existing conditions (Riggs and Davies 2002). With this in mind, along with the observation that SUD and unipolar depression are two of the three most common disorders among adolescents (Curry *et al.* 2003), this chapter will specifically focus on assessment and treatment strategies for adolescents with co-existing depression and alcohol/other drug use problems. Although few studies to date have specifically applied evidence-based treatments to this population, there is a growing evidence base for the use of cognitive behaviour therapy (CBT) in the treatment of child and adolescent internalising (Compton *et al.* 2002; Lewinsohn and Clarke 1999) and externalising disorders (see Farmer *et al.* 2002 for a review). However, the majority of these studies exclude adolescents with drug and alcohol problems, despite increasing evidence for the efficacy of CBT for such problems in young people (Waldron and Kaminer 2004).

More recently, there has been an emphasis on the need for more integrated approaches (as described in Chapters 4 and 12) to the treatment of young people with co-existing depression and substance use problems, in recognition of the growing evidence that parallel or sequential treatments may be less effective (Bukstein *et al.* 1992; Riggs and Davies 2002). Positive outcomes for integrated CBT interventions for depression and alcohol dependence in young people have been reported in two studies. Sertraline (a selective serotonin reuptake inhibitor or SSRI), in combination with a group CBT intervention, resulted in significant reductions in depression scores and drinking behaviours in a 12-week, double-blind, placebo-controlled study of 10 adolescents with co-existing depression and alcohol dependence (Deas *et al.* 2000a). In addition, a randomised 12-week, placebo-controlled trial of 82 depressed, alcohol-dependent adolescents found that Sertraline with CBT focused on depression and alcohol relapse prevention resulted in fewer drinks per drinking day and reduced depression scores among female adolescents (Moak *et al.* 2003).

Thus, while large-scale randomised control trials (RCTs) of integrated CBT treatment for depression and drug and alcohol problems are yet to be conducted, preliminary evidence from a number of recently published pilot studies has demonstrated the efficacy of integrated CBT interventions in alcohol-dependent adolescents with co-existing depression. This chapter describes the application of an integrated CBT intervention for co-existing depression and substance misuse using a treatment manual developed by Kay-Lambkin *et al.* (2002). This intervention has been modified for use with young people and is currently being trialled in an effectiveness study at ORYGEN Youth Health (OYH) in Melbourne, Australia.

CONTEXT OF THERAPY

Therapist variables

Engagement is enhanced by therapists with an open, honest, non-judgemental, conversational style, as well as an optimistic, long-term and process-oriented focus. Motivational interviewing, assertive outreach, practical help with everyday tasks and assisting with the identification of goals and the steps toward achieving them are particularly useful. In addition to a treatment focus, a prevention perspective may assist in reducing the likelihood of later problematic drug and alcohol use. For example, we take the view that all young people at high risk of mental health disorders (e.g. with a family history of disorder) should receive psycho-education about the potential influence of alcohol use on their mental health, be reinforced for not using substances and be advised to avoid future use, particularly regular use.

Client variables

Consideration should be given to the young person's developmental stage, cognitive functioning, motivation to change and progress in achieving key developmental tasks (Deas *et al.* 2000b; Schulenberg and Maggs 2002; Schulenberg *et al.* 2001). Experimental substance use may be seen as normative within their social circle (Clark 2004; Schulenberg and Maggs 2002; Schulenberg *et al.* 2001), necessitating a harm reduction framework and flexibility in delivery of treatment (Colby *et al.* 2004). It is also important to consider the role of drug and alcohol use and other risk-taking behaviours in helping young people to identify with their peer group and individuate from their parents (Schulenberg and Maggs 2002).

Young people are unlikely to attend all scheduled appointments or complete all homework tasks. These issues need to be addressed early in treatment: the content of early sessions needs to be prioritised to meet the young person's immediate needs to ensure they see the value of treatment. Weekly risk assessments are a critical component of treatment due to the consistent association between suicidality, drug and alcohol use and depression in young people (Lewinsohn *et al.* 1995; Shafii *et al.* 1988; Wagner *et al.* 1996). Other important issues include legal, social, family and cultural contexts. Preservation of family and social supports and re-engagement with educational and vocational activities will enhance a sense of connectedness with the community. Further, providing family members with psycho-education regarding the young person's depression and substance misuse, and the developmental nature of adolescence, may increase their understanding of the child's experiences, and assist with adjusting their expectations of the young person's behaviour, and negotiating boundaries for its management. While some individual work with parents may be required, it is important to preserve confidentiality with the young person and collaboratively involve them in interactions with their family.

ASSESSMENT OF YOUNG PEOPLE WITH DEPRESSION AND DRUG AND ALCOHOL PROBLEMS

Phase 1: Engagement, assessment, case formulation and psycho-education

In the first phase of treatment, the therapist's task is to engage the young person, conduct a comprehensive assessment and develop a biopsychosocial formulation of the young person's presenting concerns. A well-conducted assessment can increase engagement in treatment and be a therapeutic intervention in itself. However, clinical judgement is required regarding the extent and length of the assessment process due to its potential negative impact on the engagement of the young person.

A standard clinical interview should first be conducted in order to begin developing a formulation of the young person's current presenting concerns. Young people should be interviewed both individually and with family members, and collateral information should be collected from relevant sources. Frequent reassessment and monitoring is required, especially during the first two weeks, as young people often initially present in crisis, and withdrawal symptoms may develop during this time.

While distinguishing between primary and secondary disorders may be diagnostically useful, it contributes little to the young person's understanding of their presenting concerns and is not essential for developing an integrated treatment plan for co-existing conditions. Instead, it is more useful to map relevant clinical details from the young person's history onto a lifetime timeline that includes major life events throughout development, as well as the onset and number of episodes of depression (as well as other mental health symptoms and behavioural problems) in relationship to their substance use (including onset, periods of intoxication, withdrawal and abstinence) (Riggs and Davies 2002). A medical, family, developmental and forensic history should also be taken. Premorbid personality and protective factors also need to be assessed. A mental state examination and a risk assessment should also be conducted. In addition to a clinical interview, and self-monitoring of substance use and mental health symptoms, the use of self-report measures is also recommended.

Self-report scales

Few studies have examined the reliability and validity of self-report measures of depressive disorders or other mental health disorders in young people or substance misusing populations, and caution needs to be used when interpreting their results. While the measures described in Chapter 2 may be used with young people, the following questionnaires may also be useful with this population.

Mental health measures:

- the Mood and Anxiety Symptom Questionnaire (MASQ; Watson *et al.* 1995), a 62-item measure of general distress and depressive and anxiety symptoms with good reliability and discriminant validity between anxious and depressive symptoms in adult and youth populations;
- the Kessler 10 (K10; Kessler *et al.* 2003), a 10-item measure of psychological distress associated with depressive and anxious symptoms which has been found to be valid and reliable for detecting the presence of depressive and anxiety disorders in young adult and older populations (Furukawa *et al.* 2003; Kessler *et al.* 2003); there is some preliminary evidence for its use among substance-misusing adults (Hides *et al.* 2004);
- the Hamilton Depression Rating Scale (HAM-D; Dozois 2003), a clinician-rated 17-item scale of mood and vegetative and cognitive symptoms of depression that has well-established reliability and validity in young people; it is particularly useful for treatment monitoring; and
- the Coping Inventory for Stressful Situations, a 48-item measure of emotion-, task- and avoidance-oriented coping which has demonstrated good reliability and validity in youth populations (Endler and Parker 1994).

Substance use measures:

- the timeline followback (TLFB; Sobell and Sobell 1996), which retrospectively assesses the frequency and quantity of alcohol and other substance use and has well-established reliability and validity for assessing alcohol and illicit drug use in adolescent and adult populations (Dennis *et al.* 2004; Fals Stewart *et al.* 2000);
- the Alcohol Use Disorders Identification Test (AUDIT; Saunders *et al.* 1993), a 10-item measure of harmful or problematic drinking that has well-established reliability and validity in adolescent and adult populations (Allen *et al.* 1997; Chung *et al.* 2000; Conigrave *et al.* 1995; Daeppen *et al.* 2000);
- the Alcohol, Smoking and Substance Involvement Screening Test (ASSIST; WHO ASSIST Working Group 2002), an eight-item screen for alcohol and substance use which has high levels of internal consistency and test–retest reliability in adult populations; and
- the Drinking/Drug Use Motives Measure (DMM: Cooper *et al.* 1992; DUMM: Mueser *et al.* 1995), a 20-item measure of reasons for substance

use which has demonstrated acceptable levels of internal consistency and construct validity in young people.

Once assessment data have been collected it is important to provide the young person with personalised, informal assessment feedback. This provides opportunities for psycho-education regarding the common symptoms of depression and substance misuse and the links between them. In addition, it is useful to provide them with take-home materials including handouts, details of internet sites and other self-help materials as appropriate (see Key Resources section, p. 152). This may potentially be the only chance for intervention if the young person discontinues treatment.

The provision of assessment feedback also brings important opportunities for the young person to identify a list of problems (including symptoms of depression, anxiety, substance use) they are currently experiencing and begin developing an understanding of the links between them. The therapist's role is to develop hypotheses about the factors in the young person's life that may have predisposed them to their current problems, as well as those that precipitate and maintain them. It is also important to identify protective factors (e.g. social supports) that may enhance treatment and potentially reduce the impact of current problems. For some young people, it is useful to represent the case formulation diagrammatically to help increase their understanding of their presenting problems and demonstrate the sequences and circularity of recurring problems.

TREATMENT OF YOUNG PEOPLE WITH DEPRESSION AND DRUG AND ALCOHOL PROBLEMS

The Self-Help for Alcohol/Other Drug Use and Depression (SHADE) intervention for young people at OYH in Melbourne, Australia, targets the cognitive, affective and behavioural symptoms of co-existing depression and substance misuse, and is delivered individually over 10 one-hour therapy sessions. The SHADE intervention was modified for use in a youth population to make it more developmentally appropriate; its content and language were simplified and the links between the model and the cognitive behavioural components of treatment made more explicit. The structure of the sessions was also decreased so that treatment was flexible enough to meet the young person's changing needs, and the time allocated to case management (up to 10 additional sessions) was increased to allow for the intervention to be delivered as part of an integrated treatment approach.

The overall goals of treatment are to:

- prevent relapse to an acute episode of depression;

- enhance the young person's understanding of possible interactions between their use of alcohol and/or other drugs and their mental health problems (symptomatology and treatment compliance); and
- reduce the harm (e.g. mental and physical health, financial, social, occupational) associated with problematic alcohol and other drug use and psychiatric symptomatology.

More specific goals for treatment are developed collaboratively with the young person.

Treatment proceeds in five stages:

- Phase I: engagement, assessment, case formulation and psycho-education;
- Phase II: motivational enhancement and goal-setting;
- Phase III: CBT;
- Phase IV: relapse prevention; and
- Phase V: pulling it all together.

The young person's response to treatment needs to be monitored throughout therapy. If their depressive symptoms or substance use do not significantly improve within the first two months of treatment, or if their psychosocial functioning deteriorates or suicide risk increases, the intensity of treatment may need to be increased (Riggs and Davies 2002). Pharmacotherapy may also need to be considered, particularly SSRIs, which are considered to be first-line pharmacotherapy for co-existing depression in adolescents with SUD (Cornelius *et al.* 1997; Deas and Thomas 2001; Riggs *et al.* 1997), despite recent concerns regarding their side-effect profile.

Phase II: Motivational enhancement and goal-setting

The second phase of treatment focuses on enhancing the young person's motivation and commitment to change using motivational interviewing strategies. These strategies are particularly useful for assisting them to recognise potential problems, resolve ambivalence and start addressing their issues by making a change (Miller and Rollnick 2002). These strategies are ideally suited to the treatment of substance misuse in young people due to their respectful, non-confrontational style and use of ambivalence to build motivation for change (Baer *et al.* 2001; Marlatt *et al.* 1998; Monti *et al.* 1999; Tevyaw and Monti 2004), but are readily applicable to a range of other problems, including mental health disorders (Baker and Hambridge 2002). In people with co-existing mental health and drug and alcohol problems, motivational enhancement strategies can be applied to either or both conditions. Chapter 3 describes these techniques in more detail.

When the young person has entered the late contemplation stage, motivational interviewing can then focus on setting goals that relate to both the depression and substance misuse. Goals in relation to the young person's substance use must be realistic and achievable, and life-long abstinence may be a particularly difficult goal for adolescents to achieve (Colby *et al.* 2004). As such, it may be more useful for the therapist to adopt a harm reduction framework focused on reducing the harm caused by substance use and its consequences, and to offer a range of both short- and long-term substance use options (e.g. trial period of abstinence or moderation) (Clark 2004; Schulenberg and Maggs 2002; Schulenberg *et al.* 2001). Motivation to achieve goals may also be increased by the young person clearly specifying their reasons for making a change, as well as identifying rewards for successfully accomplishing each step.

Phase III: Cognitive behaviour therapy (CBT)

In the early stages of treatment it is useful to begin identifying high-risk situations, as well as cognitive, affective and behavioural triggers for both depression and substance misuse (Graham *et al.* 2004; Monti *et al.* 1989), as described in Chapter 4. The CBT phase of treatment focuses on identifying and challenging the negative or unrealistic beliefs that underlie and maintain the young person's problematic emotions and behaviour, and replacing them with more positive or adaptive beliefs (Beck *et al.* 1979, 1993). Coping skills training is an important element of treatment, focused on helping the young person to identify and utilise cognitive, affective and behavioural skills for dealing with their symptoms of depression and substance misuse (Kadden *et al.* 1995).

Cognitive therapy

The heavy emphasis on cognitive therapy (CT) in treatment is due to its well-established evidence base in the treatment of depression (Compton *et al.* 2002; Lewinsohn and Clarke 1999). The major components of the CT intervention for co-existing depression and substance misuse are: (i) introduction to the ABC model; (ii) identifying negative thought patterns; (iii) challenging negative thoughts; and (iv) schema change. These are described in more detail in Chapter 4.

The young person is first provided with a clear, developmentally appropriate rationale for CBT treatment using the ABC model (Beck *et al.* 1979, 1993; Free 1999; Graham *et al.* 2004), and then taught how to identify negative thought patterns using thought monitoring techniques (Beck *et al.* 1979). Many young people find it difficult to identify the negative thoughts associated with their depression and substance use, and struggle to complete thought monitoring tasks. The importance of practising this skill should be highlighted, and some young people report finding it easier to identify their emotions first and work through the thought monitoring form backwards to identify their negative thought patterns. Nonetheless, thought monitoring forms may need to be completed in session during the initial stages of treatment in order to demonstrate the importance of thought monitoring to young people.

Once the young person has learnt to identify negative thought patterns, the next step is to help them to learn ways to modify and challenge their beliefs, so they can develop new, more positive or helpful ways of thinking via cognitive restructuring (Beck *et al.* 1979; Persons *et al.* 2001; Segal *et al.* 2002), as described in Chapter 4. While the therapist may already have an understanding of the young person's core beliefs based on their case formulation and thought monitoring, more complex techniques may be required to identify negative core beliefs, such as the downward arrow or vertical arrow technique (discussed in Chapter 4).

The therapist should maintain a developmental perspective when working through a cognitive therapy program with a young person. For example, for schema change, the developmental origins (described in the case study later in this chapter) of the core belief 'I'm a waste of space' could be related to physical abuse as a child, disappointment in lack of maternal protection, and the belief that one is not loved by one's parents.

Coping skills training

The coping skills component of treatment starts with an assessment of the young person's current coping skills repertoire. Coping skills are typical or habitual ways of approaching or dealing with problems or negative emotions (Carver *et al.* 1989). A distinction is made between active problem-focused coping and emotion-focused coping such as denial (ignore the problem, minimise its severity) or avoidance (divert attention away from a problem) (Carver *et al.* 1989). The experience of day-to-day life problems and emotions is normalised and the need to identify, accept, tolerate and work through them is highlighted, rather than ignoring them or dealing with them impulsively (Linehan 1993). Young people are then provided with training in a solution-orientated approach focused on increasing their capacity to cope with day-to-day life problems and the cognitive, behavioural and affective symptoms of depression and substance misuse (Kadden *et al.* 1995). There is a clear emphasis both on helping the young person to identify appropriate coping skills and on building self-efficacy in their ability to use them, as these two factors have been found to be critical in successful coping (Kadden *et al.* 1995).

The solution-focused approach to coping skills training consists of the following five steps (see Figure 8.1):

- identify and understand what the problem and/or emotion is;
- identify possible solutions to the problem/emotion and choose the best solution;

- develop an action plan and put it into action;
- use cognitive, affective and behavioural skills to cope with the problem/ emotion; and
- evaluate whether the practical solutions and coping skills have worked.

The young person is first taught to use problem-solving skills to define what the problem or emotion is and to use the ABC model to increase their understanding of it. Second, the young person is instructed to identify potential solutions to the problem/emotion and choose the best solution by identifying the pros and cons of putting each option into practice. The young person is then assisted with developing a step plan for addressing the problem/emotion in the near future and taught to use cognitive, behavioural and affective skills to cope with it in the meantime. Finally, the young person is taught to evaluate whether the practical solutions or coping skills have worked.

Coping skills

Cognitive coping skills include mood monitoring, thought monitoring, thought challenging and mindfulness skills, as described in Chapters 4 and 12. The most important behavioural coping skill for reducing vulnerability to negative thoughts, emotions and behaviours among young people is to look after themselves: trying to eat a more balanced, healthy diet, sleeping regularly, treating physical illnesses and exercising (Linehan 1993). As with adults, pleasant event scheduling (behavioural activation) is also a key focus in the early stages of treatment, as scheduling positive events helps improve the young person's mood and distracts them from drug use (Persons et al. 2001). Young people may also benefit from a specific focus on identifying and coping with cravings. A number of relaxation techniques may be useful for targeting the affective symptoms of depression, to avoid substance misuse to manage them. Mindfulness techniques such as the three-minute breathing space are particularly useful and involve teaching the young person to step out of automatic pilot and focus their awareness on their breath, as the best way to relax is to stop trying to make things different (Segal et al. 2002). Slow breathing techniques, progressive muscle relaxation and imagery techniques are also useful (see Davis et al. 1995 for a review). If the young person is still experiencing difficulties coping with painful emotions, using the above strategies then distraction techniques may be useful (Linehan 1993). This involves helping the young person reduce contact with emotional stimuli by distracting themselves with other activities, thoughts, feelings, behaviours, sensations or images (Linehan 1993).

You can use this approach for any problem or negative emotion you experience in everyday life. A solution-orientated approach consists of five steps.

STEP 1: *What is going on? How are you feeling? Use the ABC model to find out*

Define exactly what the problem is: *I'm bored and have nothing to do.*

Date and time	A Situation/trigger *Where was I?* *Who was I with?*	B Beliefs/thoughts *What did I think?*	C Feelings/ emotions *What did I feel?*	C Behaviours *What did I do?* *What did I drink/use?*
Monday 10 am	At home, bored Nothing to do all day	I've never got anything to do; I'll never amount to anything; I'm a loser	Sad, useless, worthless	Drank a bottle of bourbon Scored some speed

STEP 2: *What are the possible solutions? Brainstorm ideas for dealing with the problem and/or emotions, and choose the solution that has more positives than negatives and that you like best.*

Write each option in here	Write in the **advantages** of this option	Write in the **disadvantages** of this option
Ring my brother or go to my sister's Go and spend time with Mia Look at activity schedule	Not bored anymore; spend time with family Make my daughter happy Keep busy; do things I need to do	Have to deal with feelings Hard to do things when feeling down
Drink or use drugs	Feel better, not bored	Feel guilty about using, get nothing done

STEP 3: *Develop an ACTION plan and put it into ACTION! What are the steps to putting your plan into action?*

Pick your best idea, and break it down into small practical steps.

Step 1: Ring my sister and check if she's home
Step 2: Ask her to come pick me up or catch the bus
Step 3: Keep busy playing with the kids and make plans for tomorrow
Step 4: Try and think positively, stay focused on my goals and challenge negative thoughts

If there is something you can do about the problem right now? DO IT! If NOT, plan to deal with the problem in the near future.

STEP 4: *Use cognitive, affective and behavioural skills to COPE with the problem/emotion*

BEHAVIOURAL COPING SKILLS

1) Look after yourself:
   a) Balance eating
   b) Balance sleep
   c) Treat physical illness
   d) Get exercise

Figure 8.1 Solution-orientated approach to coping.

2) Increase positive feelings:
   a) Do things that make you feel good (positive events):
     i) Select a positive activity from your activities list.
     ii) Develop a list of small steps towards achieving them.
       Step 1: _____
       Step 2: _____
       Step 3: _____
     iii) Fill out an activity log or set a time and day to do them.
       Day/s: _____ Time/s: _____
   b) Avoid avoiding: Don't let yourself back out or give excuses.
   c) Be mindful of pleasant activities: focus on positive events while they're happening and REFOCUS on the positive when your mind wanders to the negative.

COGNITIVE COPING SKILLS

3) Thought challenging:
   Try to think more positively, and use the table below to challenge negative or unhelpful thoughts.

STOP! STEP OUT of AUTO PILOT!!	Ask yourself: Does this belief fit the facts? What is the evidence for and against this belief?		Do I hold the same rule for other people?	Is there another way of looking at it?	Feelings now
	For	Against			
FOCUS on your BREATH Tell yourself: 'This is just a thought' 'Thoughts are not facts'	No job; Dad abused me; Mum didn't protect me	Worked the last five years; I'm a good brother, father and friend	No, I wouldn't hold the same rule for others	Just because I've got nothing to do doesn't mean I'm a waste of space; I'm unemployed because of my depression	OK

4) Look over your Schema (Core Belief) Continuum and review the evidence on the 'Alternative View' worksheet for your alternative more helpful core schema.

AFFECTIVE COPING SKILLS

5) Decrease negative feelings:
   a) Observe how you are feeling and describe it. Accept the emotion and experience the emotion as waves that come and go.
   b) Belly breathing (breathe in for 3 seconds, hold for 3 seconds, breathe out for 3 seconds).
   c) Remember the best way to relax is to stop trying to makes things different. Use your mindfulness skills to step out of automatic pilot and focus on the moment instead.
   d) 3-minute breathing space: Increase current awareness of what thoughts, feelings and physical sensations you are experiencing and just notice and acknowledge them without trying to push them away, change or control them. Then bring the focus of attention to your breath and spread the focus of awareness over the whole of your body over a 3-minute period.
   e) Allowing/letting be skills: Increase current awareness of your thoughts, feelings and physical sensations and just allow them to be by saying to yourself – *this is OK, whatever this thought or feeling is, it's OK, let me feel it* – while staying with your breath in the present moment until they no longer pull your attention away.

Figure 8.1 (Continued.)

COPING WITH CRAVINGS

6) Cravings:
   a) I will leave or change the situation. Safe place I can go: _____
   b) I will put off the decision to use for 15 minutes. I'll remember that my craving usually goes away and I have dealt with cravings successfully in the past.

CRISIS SURVIVAL SKILLS

7) Talk to someone:
   Even though you may feel like there is no-one you can talk to, there usually is someone. Examples: your parents, friends, aunt, uncle, family friend, the family pet, neighbours, teachers, or call your case manager or local crisis team.
   My list of support people:
   Name: _____ Phone: _____
   Name: _____ Phone: _____
   Case manager: _____ Phone: _____
   After hours emergency contact: _____

8) Do something to distract yourself:
   a) Do activities: TV, music, computer, walk the dog, ring a friend, make plans, go and do SOMETHING.
   b) Self-soothe each of your five senses: listen to music, look at old photos, take a bath, go for a walk, eat your favourite food.
   c) Take a brief vacation: go to bed and pull the covers up over your head for 20 minutes, have breakfast in bed, read a book in bed, lie in a park.
   d) Encouragement: be your own cheerleader, talk to yourself as you would talk to someone you care about who is in crisis. Say: 'I can stand it' 'It won't last forever.'

STEP 5: **Evaluate whether the practical solutions and coping skills have worked**

The final step is to look at whether your practical solution or coping skills worked. Ask yourself the questions:

'Was the plan successful? Why or why not?'
'Did I carry out my plan as I wrote down or did I only do part of it?'
'Is there anything about my plan that I need to change to make sure this is successful?'
'Should I look at using one of the other ideas I came up with in Step 2?'

Figure 8.1 (Continued.)

Phase IV: Relapse prevention

In the initial stages and throughout treatment, young people are encouraged to avoid or reduce exposure to high-risk situations for substance misuse and depression, and to avoid making seemingly irrelevant decisions which result in an increased risk of exposure to these situations (Graham *et al.* 2004; Marlatt and Gordon 1985; Monti *et al.* 1989). A personalised relapse prevention plan for the young person should be developed, clearly identifying their relapse indicators, their plan for avoiding or reducing such exposure, the cognitive, behavioural and affective skills for coping with such situations, and rewards for managing lapses and high-risk situations effectively (Graham *et al.* 2004; Segal *et al.* 2002).

Phase V: Pulling it all together

In the final stages of treatment it is important to reiterate the links between the young person's presenting concerns, their case formulation and the treatment provided. Specifically, the need to use coping skills in problematic everyday situations and the negative thoughts, feelings and behaviours associated with depression and substance misuse should be highlighted. It is also useful to summarise the treatment process and document which coping skills the young person found most effective on a handout for future reference. Young people often set strict rules about the need to cease their drug use immediately and not feel depressed any more, and often blame themselves for any lapse that occurs. As such it is important to teach young people how to cope with this 'abstinence violation' or 'breaking the rule effect' by first acknowledging that setbacks and lapses will happen, and that one day of drug use or a depressed mood does not constitute a relapse.

Finally, it is important to begin addressing termination issues early with young people, in order to address or circumvent any issues that may arise. As part of this process it may be useful to review the client's progress in treatment, highlighting changes in their depression and substance use as well as changes in their thoughts, feelings and behaviours. The young person should be encouraged to reflect on the progress they have made towards achieving their depression and substance use goals, even if they are yet to reach them, and encouraged to provide themselves with rewards.

CASE STUDY

Peter is a 19-year-old unemployed male, referred to the OYH assessment team by his brother after he took an overdose of painkillers. He was initially admitted to the inpatient unit involuntarily, but was discharged after four days and referred to the Mood and Anxiety Disorders Clinic at OYH.

Peter initially resisted attempts to engage him in outpatient treatment and missed two appointments. However, assertive outreach indicated Peter had not attended his appointments due to concerns he would be re-admitted to hospital by the police due to his ongoing level of suicidal ideation. Peter was reassured that hospital admissions were only used if the risk of suicide was extremely high and no other options were available. A crisis plan was also developed with Peter that clearly specified the steps to be taken if his mental state deteriorated. He was also given some practical assistance with accommodation and contacting legal aid services in order to address immediate problems and to facilitate engagement.

Assessment results

Peter presented with a four-month history of a depressed/irritable mood, hopelessness, insomnia, reduced appetite, poor memory and concentration, decreased energy and motivation, and suicidal ideation, with two previous overdoses in as many months. He also reported that his substance abuse had escalated to daily amphetamine ($30/day), alcohol (approximately 12 standard drinks/day) and cannabis (3–10 cones/day) use in the past month.

Peter had experienced a number of negative life events in the past four months, including family conflict, his partner of two years leaving him, loss of access to his two-year-old daughter, unemployment, financial problems and homelessness after the lease expired on his house. Peter described a four-year history of intermittent low/irritable mood amphetamine and alcohol use (usually two to three times a week) and daily cannabis use. He first started drinking and smoking cannabis on weekends with his mates at the age of 13. Peter recalled beginning to use cannabis and alcohol weekly at the age of 15, when he was feeling bored or upset and usually alone. He first tried amphetamines at the age of 16 and began using them two to three times a week two years ago to feel 'good'.

Peter reported no previous contact with either mental health or substance use services but had taken antidepressant medication for six months, one year ago, with little effect. His parents were divorced and he was the second eldest in a sibship of five. Peter described being estranged from his parents, due to a history of physical abuse from his father from a young age and conflict about his substance use. Peter had been involved in a romantic relationship with Lisa, his ex-partner, for two years and considered his drug use to be the major reason for their break-up. He described having close supportive relationships with his siblings. Peter's father had a history of alcohol misuse and his mother and sister suffered from depression. Peter reported getting 'average' marks at school, and had worked in a variety of labouring jobs.

The following interaction illustrates assessment, feedback and hypothesis testing:

Therapist: This is a summary of your assessment results. You reported severe symptoms of depression including a low mood, a loss of interest in things, poor appetite, poor concentration and memory as well as some ongoing suicidal thoughts. You also reported an increase in your drug use over the past four months, particularly in the past month. Does that sound correct?

Peter: Yes.

Therapist: Based on what you've told me so far and what you reported in the self-report measures you seem to become upset or angry when faced with problems and tend to avoid dealing with them by using drugs.

Peter: Yeah, that's true – I mainly use drugs when I'm upset, bored or can't sleep.

Therapist: Has this always been the case?

Peter: No, originally I started drinking and smoking pot on the weekends at parties with my mates, but then I started doing it at night by myself.

Therapist: Were there times when you were more likely to use drugs?

Peter: Yeah, when I was bored or really stressed at night, or if I had a fight with my girlfriend I'd definitely use.

Therapist: Do you think the amount of stress you've been under lately might have had something to do with the amount of drugs you've been using?

Peter: Yeah, but it's just made things worse because now I have to deal with that as well as all of the other stuff.

Therapist: So, what you're saying is that while the drugs initially seemed to help you cope with things, over time they became another problem to deal with on top of the other problems you already had.

Case formulation

The following case formulation was derived collaboratively with Peter.

Problem list

Depressed mood, suicidality and amphetamine, alcohol and cannabis abuse/ dependence.

Relationship between depression and substance misuse

Peter used when feeling bored, angry, upset, worried or unable to sleep. Amphetamine use results in feelings of disappointment and guilt.

Triggers

Depression: boredom, conflict, missing daughter.
Substance misuse: boredom, stressed/worried, can't sleep.

Predisposing factors

Peter had a family history of depression and alcohol dependence, a negative early childhood environment, a history of physical abuse, poor attachment with parents and emotional neglect. He also had negative schemas about himself (e.g. 'I'm worthless').

Precipitants

Peter had experienced a number of negative life events and significant losses in the preceding four months including: family conflict, his partner of two years leaving him, loss of access to his two-year-old daughter, unemployment, financial problems and homelessness.

Perpetuating factors

Peter's difficulties with access to his daughter, unemployment, financial problems, unstable accommodation, poor affect regulation and coping skills, coping motives for substance use, and reduced social support, were all perpetuating factors.

Protective factors

Peter had social support from his siblings and a good work history; he was also seeking treatment and engaged.

Treatment

Peter engaged well in treatment. His motivation and commitment to making a change increased and he easily completed a decisional balance sheet (see Table 8.1). Peter saw his amphetamine use as problematic and set an abstinence goal, but wanted to continue using cannabis and alcohol 'socially' with his friends.

Peter responded well to the initial behavioural focus of treatment and completed most of his activity scheduling homework. However, Peter struggled to complete his thought monitoring homework tasks, requiring in-session completion of these tasks on most weeks. Nonetheless, Peter's thought monitoring revealed that he experienced negative thoughts about being unlovable and his perceived lack of achievement, triggered by boredom and conflict, which resulted in feelings of sadness, anger and worthlessness (see Figure 8.1). The vertical arrow technique (see Chapter 4 on CBT, section on integrated cognitive therapy) was then used to identify Peter's core beliefs, as illustrated below.

Therapist: We've been monitoring your thoughts for a few weeks now. You seem to experience the negative automatic thought that things aren't going to work out for you. Let's look at this thought more closely. If things are never going to work out for you, what would that mean about you?

Table 8.1 Pros and cons decisional balance sheet

Positives about continuing to drink/use	Negatives about continuing to drink/use
Feels good	Makes things worse
I like it	Makes me feel more depressed
Kills time	Never get Lisa back and won't see Mia
Spend time with friends	Family upset at me
Have fun	I'm a loser
Makes my worries go away	Costs heaps
	It takes control
	Won't get another job
	Makes me sick

Positives about changing my use	Negatives about changing my use
Improve relationships with Lisa and family	How to cope with things without it?
See Mia	Lose contact with my mates
Feel better about myself	
Better physical health	
Can get a job and house	
Make plans for the future	

Peter: That it's hopeless to try.
Therapist: If it were hopeless to try, what would that mean?
Peter: That I should just give up.
Therapist: And what would it mean if you should give up?
Peter: That I'm a waste of space.

Peter responded well to the cognitive elements of treatment, and used his thought challenging skills regularly (see Figure 8.1). He did not find relaxation or mindfulness techniques useful but found delaying the decision to use amphetamines worked well when he experienced drug cravings. On two occasions during treatment, Peter presented in crisis after making a suicide attempt via overdose. These attempts were both precipitated by situational crises (e.g. financial and accommodation problems) that could have been easily avoided. As treatment progressed, Peter began using his problem-solving skills to address stresses and use coping skills to manage them, rather than ignoring them or dealing with them impulsively (see Figure 8.1).

Overall, Peter's substance use decreased during the course of treatment but he still used amphetamines during periods of stress, which often resulted in self-blame and feelings of guilt. As such, it was important to address this abstinence violation effect during relapse prevention, as illustrated below.

Peter (at the beginning of the session): I've used five times this week, so I'm right back at step one.

Therapist:	OK, let's use your monitoring form to figure out what's been going on for you this week.
Peter:	Well, I had to go to see legal aid on Monday, I had a fight with Lisa on Wednesday and now haven't seen Mia for three weeks and my sister just told me today that she wants me to move out next week.
Therapist:	Gee, it sounds like a lot of things have been going on. Can you identify any thoughts you've been having?
Peter:	No not really.
Therapist:	What about how you've been feeling?
Peter:	Shithouse, really down, really angry.
Therapist:	What sorts of things were going through your head when you were feeling that way?
Peter:	Things like – why is it so hard, why don't things ever work out for me, why do I bother trying?
Therapist:	So what did you end up doing?
Peter:	I went and scored some speed and then I kept on doing it because I thought well I've stuffed up, I'm never going to stop using so I might as well keep using now.
Therapist:	OK, so it sounds like a lot of really stressful things have happened this week, which seemed to set off your beliefs about things not working out for you, which resulted in you using. What do you think you could have done differently?
Peter:	Well, I could have tried challenging what I was thinking and tried to get back on track rather than using more.
Therapist:	How could you have done this?

CONCLUSION

Adolescence and young adulthood is associated with a multitude of challenges, many of which increase the risk of developing affective or substance use disorders. While there is growing evidence describing a link between substance misuse, depression and suicidal behaviour in youth, evidence-based approaches to the treatment of this population are lacking. This is in part related to the segregation of drug treatment and mental health services, and the limited resources available to each service system to meet the needs of young people with co-existing problems. What is increasingly clear is the need for integrated approaches to the treatment of young people with co-existing depression and drug and alcohol problems, and the relative ineffectiveness of parallel or sequential treatments. In this regard, there is growing evidence for the effectiveness of CBT in the treatment of co-existing conditions, although few integrated treatments have been rigorously evaluated with young people.

The adapted intervention described in this chapter (Kay-Lambkin *et al.* 2002) offers a structured approach to this population. While this intervention requires further validation, it offers significant gains for young people, their families, treatment providers and policy-makers, and provides a coherent framework for the treatment of co-existing problems in young people.

KEY RESOURCES

Websites

American Academy of Child and Adolescent Psychiatry, *The American Academy of Child and Adolescent Psychiatry*. Washington: AACAP, 2005. Available at http://www.aacap.org (accessed 2 September 2005).

Australian Drug Foundation, *Australian Drug Foundation – Preventing Drug Problems*. North Melbourne: ADF, 2004. Available at http://www.adf.org.au (accessed 2 September 2005).

Beyondblue, *Beyondblue – The National Depression Initiative*. Hawthorn West, VIC: Beyondblue, 2005. Available at http://www.beyondblue.org.au (accessed 30 August 2005).

Beyondblue, *Ybblue – A Youth Depression Awareness Campaign*. Hawthorn West, VIC: Beyondblue, 2005. Available at http://www.ybblue.com.au (accessed 30 August 2005).

Centre for Mental Health Research, *The MoodGYM Training Program*. Canberra: The Australian National University, 2005. Available at http://www.moodgym.anu.edu.au (accessed 30 August 2005).

Drug Info Clearinghouse, *The Drug Prevention Network*. West Melbourne: Australian Drug Foundation, 2003. Available at http://www.druginfo.com.au/container.asp?id=571 (accessed 2 September 2005).

Inspire Foundation, *Reach Out*. Rozelle, NSW: Inspire Foundation, 2005. Available at http://www.reachout.com.au (accessed 2 September 2005).

Royal College of Psychiatry, *The Royal College of Psychiatry – Let Wisdom Guide*. London: Royal College of Psychiatrists, 2004. Available at http://www.rcpsych.ac.uk (accessed 2 September 2005).

Sciacca, K., *Dual Diagnosis Website*. New York: Sciacca Comprehensive Service Development for Mental Illness, Drug Addiction and Alcoholism, 1996. Available at http://users.erols.com/ksciacca/disclaim.htm (accessed 2 September 2005).

Substance Abuse and Mental Health Services Administration, *United States Department of Health and Human Services – Substance Abuse and Mental Health Services Administration*. Washington: United States Department of Health and Humane Services, 2005. Available at http://www.samhsa.gov/matrix/matrix_cooc.aspx (accessed 2 September 2005).

Treatment manuals

Baker, A., Kay-Lambkin, F. J., Lee, N. K., Claire, M. and Jenner, L., *A Brief Cognitive Behavioural Intervention for Regular Amphetamine Users*. Canberra: Australian

Government Department of Health and Ageing, 2003. Available at http://www.
nationaldrugstrategy.gov.au/publications/illicit.htm (accessed 2 September 2005).

Kay-Lambkin, F. J., Baker, A. L. and Bucci, S. R., *Self-Help for Alcohol/Other
Drug Use and Depression (SHADE) Intervention*. Callaghan, NSW: University of
Newcastle, 2002.

Other resources

Kaminer, Y., *Adolescent Substance Abuse: A Comprehensive Guide to Theory and Practice*. New York: Plenum, 1994.

National Drug Strategy, *National Comorbidity Project: Current Practice in the
Management of Clients with Comorbid Mental Health and Substance Use Disorders
in Tertiary Care Settings*. Canberra, 2003. Available at http://www.health.gov.au/
internet/wcms/publishing.nsf/content/health-pubhlth-strateg-comorbidity-index.
htm (accessed 2 September 2005).

Substance Use and Mental Health Administration (SAMHSA), *The Relationship
Between Mental Health and Substance Abuse Among Adolescents*. Rockville,
MD: US Department of Health and Human Services, 1999. Available at http://
www.samhsa.gov (accessed 2 September 2005).

REFERENCES

Allen, J. P., Litten, R. Z., Fertig, J. B. and Babor, T., 'A review of research on the
Alcohol Use Disorders Identification Test (AUDIT)', *Alcoholism: Clinical and
Experimental Research*, *21*, 613–9, 1997.

Arseneault, L., Cannon, M., Witton, J. and Murray, R. M., 'Causal association
between cannabis and psychosis: Examination of the evidence', *British Journal of
Psychiatry*, *184*, 110–7, 2004.

Australian Institute of Health and Welfare, *2004 National Drug Strategy Household
Survey: First Results*. Canberra AIHW, 2005.

Baer, J. S., Kivlahan, D. R., Blume, A. W., McKnight, P. and Marlatt, G. A., 'Brief
intervention for heavy drinking college students: Four-year follow up and natural
history', *American Journal of Public Health*, *91*, 1310–6, 2001.

Baker, A. and Hambridge, J., 'Motivational interviewing: Enhancing engagement in
treatment for mental health problems', *Behaviour Change*, *19*, 138–45, 2002.

Beautrais, A. L., Joyce, P. R. and Mulder, R. T., 'Cannabis abuse and serious suicide
attempts', *Addiction*, *94*, 1993–5, 1999.

Beck, A. T., Rush, A. J., Shaw, B. F. and Emery, G., *Cognitive Therapy of Depression*.
New York: Guilford Press, 1979.

Beck, A. T., Wright, F. D., Newman, C. F. and Liese, B. S., *Cognitive Therapy of
Substance Abuse*. New York: Guilford Press, 1993.

Boys, A., Farrell, M., Taylor, C., Marsden, J., Goodman, R., Brugha, T. *et al.*,
'Psychiatric morbidity and substance use in young people aged 13–15 years:
Results from the child and adolescent survey of mental health', *British Journal of
Psychiatry*, *182*, 509–17, 2003.

Brook, D. W., Brook, J. S., Zhang, C., Cohen, P. and Whiteman, M., 'Drug use and the risk of major depressive disorder, alcohol dependence and substance use disorders', *Archives of General Psychiatry*, *59*, 1039–44, 2002.

Brook, J. S., Cohen, P. and Brook, D. W., 'Longitudinal study of co-occurring psychiatric disorders and substance use', *Journal of the American Academy of Child and Adolescent Psychiatry*, *37*, 322–30, 1998.

Bukstein, O. G., Glancy, L. G. and Kaminer, Y., 'Patterns of affective comorbidity in a clinical population of dually diagnosed adolescent substance abusers', *Journal of the American Academy of Child and Adolescent Psychiatry*, *31*, 1041–5, 1992.

Bukstein, O. and Winters, K., 'Salient variables for treatment research of adolescent alcohol and other substance use disorders', *Addiction*, *99*, 23–37, 2004.

Carver, C. S., Scheier, M. R. and Weintraub, J. K., 'Assessing coping strategies: A theoretically based approach', *Journal of Personality and Social Psychology*, *56*, 267–83, 1989.

Chung, T., Colby, S. M., Barnett, N. P., Rohsenow, D. J., Spirito, A. and Monti, P. M., 'Screening adolescents for problem drinking: Performance of brief screens against DSM-IV alcohol diagnoses', *Journal of Studies on Alcohol*, *61*, 579–87, 2000.

Clark, D. A., 'The natural history of adolescent alcohol use disorders', *Addiction*, *99*, 5–22, 2004.

Clark, D. A., Pollock, N. K., Bukstein, O. G., Mezzich, A. C., Bromberger, J. and Donovan, J., 'Gender and comorbid psychopathology in adolescents with alcohol dependence', *Journal of the American Academy of Child and Adolescent Psychiatry*, *36*, 1195–203, 1997.

Colby, S. M., Lee, C. S., Lewis-Esquerre, J., Esposito-Smythers, C. and Monti, P. M., 'Adolescent alcohol misuse: Methodological issues for enhancing treatment research', *Addiction*, *99*, 47–62, 2004.

Compton, S. N., Burns, B. J., Egger, H. L. and Robertson, E., 'Review of the evidence base for treatment of childhood psychopathology: Internalising disorders', *Journal of Consulting and Clinical Psychology*, *70*, 1240–66, 2002.

Conigrave, K. M., Saunders, J. B. and Reznik, R. B., 'Predictive capacity of the AUDIT questionnaire for alcohol-related harm', *Addiction*, *90*, 1479–85, 1995.

Cooper, M. L., Russell, M., Skinner, J. B., Frone, M. R. and Mudar, P., 'Development and validation of a three-dimensional measure of drinking motives', *Psychological Assessment*, *4*, 123–32, 1992.

Cornelius, J. R., Salloum, I. M. and Ehler, J. G., 'Fluoxetine in depressed alcoholics: A double-blind, placebo controlled trial', *Archives of General Psychiatry*, *54*, 700–5, 1997.

Curry, J. F., Wells, K. C., Lochman, J. E., Craighead, W. E. and Nagy, P. D., 'Cognitive-behavioural intervention for depressed, substance-abusing adolescents: Development and pilot testing', *Journal of the American Academy of Child and Adolescent Psychiatry*, *42*, 656–65, 2003.

Daeppen, J. B., Yersin, B., Landry, U., Pecoud, A. and Decrey, H., 'Reliability and validity of the Alcohol Use Disorders Identification Test (AUDIT) embedded within a general health risk screening questionnaire: Results of a survey in 332 primary care patients', *Alcoholism: Clinical and Experimental Research*, *24*, 659–65, 2000.

Davis, M., Eshelman, E. R. and McKay, M., *The Relaxation and Stress Reduction Workbook*. Oakland, CA: New Harbinger, 1995.

Deas, D., Randall, C. L., Roberts, J. S. and Anton, R., 'A double-blind, placebo-controlled trial of sertraline in depressed adolescent alcoholics: A pilot study', *Human Psychopharmacology*, *15*, 461–9, 2000a.

Deas, D., Riggs, P., Landenbucher, J., Goldman, M. and Brown, S., 'Adolescents are not adults: Developmental considerations in alcohol users', *Alcoholism: Clinical and Experimental Research*, *24*, 232–7, 2000b.

Deas, D. and Thomas, S., 'An overview of controlled studies of adolescent substance abuse treatment', *The American Journal on Addictions*, *10*, 178–89, 2001.

Degenhardt, L. and Hall, W., 'The Association between psychosis and problematic drug use among Australian adults: Findings from the National Survey of Mental Health and Well-Being', *Psychological Medicine*, *31*, 659–68, 2001.

Degenhardt, L. and Hall, W., 'Patterns of co-morbidity between alcohol use and other substance use in the Australian population', *Drug and Alcohol Review*, *22*, 7–13, 2003.

Dennis, M. L., Funk, R., Godley, S. H., Godley, M. D. and Waldron, H., 'Cross-validation of the alcohol and cannabis use measures in the global appraisal of individual needs (GAIN) and timeline followback (TLFB; Form 90) among adolescents in substance abuse treatment', *Addiction*, *99*, 120–8, 2004.

DiMileo, L., 'Psychiatric syndromes in adolescent substance abusers', *American Journal of Psychiatry*, *146*, 1212–4, 1989.

Dozois, D. J. A., 'The psychometric characteristics of the Hamilton Depression Inventory', *Journal of Personality Assessment*, *80*, 31–40, 2003.

Endler, N. S. and Parker, J. D. A., 'Assessment of multidimensional coping: Task, emotion, and avoidance strategies', *Psychological Assessment*, *6*, 50–60, 1994.

Fals Stewart, W., O'Farrell, T. J., Freitas, T. T., McFarlin, S. K. and Rutigliano, P., 'The timeline followback reports of psychoactive substance use by drug-abusing patients: Psychometric properties', *Journal of Consulting and Clinical Psychology*, *68*, 134–44, 2000.

Farmer, E. M., Compton, S. N., Burns, B. J. and Robertson, E., 'Review of the evidence base for treatment of childhood psychopathology: Externalising disorders', *Journal of Consulting and Clinical Psychology*, *70*, 1267–302, 2002.

Farrell, M., Howes, S., Bebbington, P., Brugha, T., Jenkins, R., Lewis, G. *et al.*, 'Nicotine, alcohol and drug dependence and psychiatric comorbidity: Results of a national household survey', *British Journal of Psychiatry*, *179*, 432–7, 2001.

Fergusson, D. M. and Horwood, L. J., 'Early onset cannabis use and psychosocial adjustment in young adults', *Addiction*, *92*, 15–21, 1997.

Free, M. L., *Cognitive Therapy in Groups: Guidelines and Resources for Practice*. New York: John Wiley, 1999.

Furukawa, T. A., Kessler, R. C., Slade, T. and Andrews, G., 'The performance of the K6 and K10 screening scales for psychological distress in the Australian National Survey of Mental Health and Well-Being', *Psychological Medicine*, *33*, 357–62, 2003.

Graham, H. L., Copello, A., Birchwood, M. J., Mueser, K. T., Orford, J., McGovern, D. *et al.*, *Cognitive-Behavioural Integrated Treatment (C-BIT): A Treatment Manual for Substance Misuse in People with Severe Mental Health Problems*. Chichester: John Wiley, 2004.

Hides, L., Devlin, H., Lubman, D. I., Aitken, C., Gregson, S. and Hellard, M., 'The reliability and validity of the K10 and PHQ amongst injecting drug users', *Australian and New Zealand Journal of Psychiatry*, in press, 2006.

Hides, L., Lubman, D. I. and Dawe, S., 'Models of co-occurring substance misuse and psychosis: Are personality traits the missing link?' *Drug and Alcohol Review*, *23*, 425–32, 2004.

Kadden, R., Carroll, K., Donovan, D., Cooney, N., Monti, P., Abrams, D. L. M. and Hester, R., *Cognitive-Behavioural Coping Skills Therapy Manual*. Rockville, MD: US Department of Health and Human Services, 1995.

Kandel, D. B., Johnson, J. G., Bird, H. R., Weissman, M. M., Goodman, S. H., Lahey, B. B. *et al.*, 'Psychiatric comorbidity among adolescents with substance use disorders: Findings from the MECA study', *Journal of the American Academy of Child and Adolescent Psychiatry*, *38*, 693–9, 1999.

Kay-Lambkin, F. J., Baker, A. L. and Bucci, S. R., *Self-Help for Alcohol/Other Drug Use and Depression (SHADE) Intervention*. Callaghan, NSW: University of Newcastle, 2002.

Kessler, R., Crum, R. M., Warner, L. A., Nelson, C. B., Schulenberg, J. and Anthony, J., 'Lifetime co-occurrence of DSM-III-R alcohol abuse and dependence with other psychiatric disorders in the national comorbidity survey', *Archives of General Psychiatry*, *54*, 313–21, 1997.

Kessler, R. C., Barker, P. R., Colpe, L. J., Epstein, J. F., Gfroerer, J. C., Hiripi, E. *et al.*, 'Screening for serious mental illness in the general population', *Archives of General Psychiatry*, *60*, 184–9, 2003.

Kramer, T. L., Robbins, J. M., Phillips, S. D., Miller, T. L. and Burns, B. J., 'Detection and outcomes of substance use disorders in adolescents seeking mental health treatment', *Journal of the American Academy of Child and Adolescent Psychiatry*, *42*, 1318–26, 2003.

Lewinsohn, P. M. and Clarke, G. N., 'Psychosocial treatments for adolescent depression', *Clinical Psychology Review*, *19*, 329–42, 1999.

Lewinsohn, P. M., Hops, H., Roberts, R. E., Seeley, J. R. and Andrews, J., 'Adolescent psychopathology I. Prevalence and incidence of depression and other DSM-III-R disorders in high school students', *Journal of Abnormal Psychology*, *102*, 133–44, 1993.

Lewinsohn, P. M., Rohde, P. and Seeley, J. R., 'Adolescent psychopathology III: The clinical consequences of comorbidity', *Journal of the American Academy of Child and Adolescent Psychiatry*, *35*, 510–9, 1995.

Linehan, M. M., *Cognitive-Behavioural Treatment of Borderline Personality Disorder*. New York: Guilford Press, 1993.

Marlatt, G. and Gordon, J. R., *Relapse Prevention*. New York: Guilford Press, 1985.

Marlatt, G. A., Baer, J. S., Kivlahan, D. R., Dimeff, L. A., Larimer, M. E., Quigley, L. A. *et al.*, 'Screening and brief intervention for high-risk college student drinkers: Results from a 2-year follow up assessment', *Journal of Consulting and Clinical Psychology*, *66*, 604–15, 1998.

Miller, W. R. and Rollnick, S., *Motivational Interviewing: Preparing People for Change*, 2nd ed. New York: Guilford Press, 2002.

Moak, D. H., Anton, R. F., Latham, P. K., Voronin, K. E., Waid, R. L. and Durazo-Arvizu, R., 'Sertraline and cognitive behavioural therapy for depressed alcoholics: Results of a placebo-controlled trial', *Journal of Clinical Psychopharmacology*, *23*, 553–62, 2003.

Monti, P. M., Abrams, D. B., Kadden, R. M. and Cooney, N. L., *Treating Alcohol Dependence: A Coping Skills Training Guide*. New York: Guilford Press, 1989.

Monti, P. M., Colby, S. M., Barnett, N. P., Spirito, A., Rohsenow, D. J., Myers, M. et al., 'Brief interventions for harm reduction with alcohol-positive older adolescents in a hospital emergency department', *Journal of Consulting and Clinical Psychology*, 67, 989–94, 1999.

Mueser, K. T., Pallavi, N., Tracy, J. I., DeGirolamo, J. and Molinaro, M., 'Expectations and motives for substance use in schizophrenia', *Schizophrenia Bulletin*, 21, 367–78, 1995.

Persons, J. B., Davidson, J. and Tompkins, M. A., *Essential Components of Cognitive-Behaviour Therapy for Depression*. Washington: American Psychological Association, 2001.

Regier, D. A., Farmer, M. E., Rae, D. S., Locke, B. Z., Keith, S. J., Judd, L. L. and Goodwin, F. K., 'Comorbidity of mental disorders with alcohol and other drug abuse: Results from the epidemiological catchment area (ECA) study', *Journal of the American Medical Association*, 264, 2511–8, 1990.

Riggs, P. D. and Davies, R. D., 'A clinical approach to integrating treatment for adolescent depression and substance abuse', *Journal of the American Academy of Child and Adolescent Psychiatry*, 41, 1253–5, 2002.

Riggs, P. D., Mikulich, S. K., Coffman, L. M. and Crowley, T. J., 'Fluoxetine in drug-dependent delinquents with major depression: An open trial', *Journal of Child and Adolescent Psychopharmacology*, 7, 87–95, 1997.

Rohde, P., Lewinsohn, P. and Seeley, J., 'Psychiatric comorbidity with problematic alcohol use in high school students', *Journal of the American Academy of Child and Adolescent Psychiatry*, 35, 101–9, 1996.

Saunders, J. B., Aasland, O. G., Babor, T. F., de le Fuente, J. R. and Grant, M., 'Development of the Alcohol Use Disorders Identification Test (AUDIT): WHO collaborative project on early detection of persons with harmful alcohol consumption', *Addiction*, 88, 791–804, 1993.

Sawyer, M. G., Arney, F. M., Baghurst, P. A., Clark, J. J., Graetz, B. W., Kosky, R. J. et al., 'The mental health of young people in Australia: Key findings from the child and adolescent component of the National Survey of Mental Health and Well-Being', *Australian and New Zealand Journal of Psychiatry*, 35, 806–14, 2001.

Schulenberg, J. E. and Maggs, J. L., 'A developmental perspective on alcohol use and heavy drinking during adolescence and the transition to young adulthood', *Journal of Studies on Alcohol*, 14, 54–70, 2002.

Schulenberg, J. E., Maggs, J. L., Long, S. W., Sher, K. J., Gotham, H. J., Baer, J. S. et al., 'The problem of college drinking: Insights from a developmental perspective', *Alcoholism: Clinical and Experimental Research*, 25, 473–7, 2001.

Segal, Z. V., Williams, J. M. G. and Teasdale, J. D., *Mindfulness-Based Cognitive Therapy for Depression: A New Approach to Preventing Relapse*. New York: Guilford Press, 2002.

Shafii, M., Steltz, L. J., McCue-Derrick, A., Beckner, C. and Whittinghill, J. R., 'Comorbidity of mental disorders in the post-mortem diagnosis of completed suicide in children and adolescents', *Journal of Affective Disorders*, 15, 227–33, 1988.

Sobell, L. C. and Sobell, M. B., *Timeline Followback User's Guide: A Calendar Method for Assessing Alcohol and Drug Use.* Toronto: Addiction Research Foundation, 1996.

Tevyaw, T. O. and Monti, P. M., 'Motivational enhancement and other brief interventions for adolescent substance abuse: Foundations, applications and evaluations', *Addiction, 99*, 63–75, 2004.

Wagner, B. M., Cole, R. E. and Schwartzman, P., 'Comorbidity of symptoms among junior and senior high school student suicide attempters', *Suicide and Life Threatening Behaviour, 26*, 300–7, 1996.

Waldron, H. B. and Kaminer, Y., 'On the learning curve: The emerging evidence supporting cognitive-behavioural therapies for adolescent substance abuse', *Addiction, 99*, 93–105, 2004.

Watson, D., Clark, L. A., Weber, K., Assenheimer, J. S., Strauss, M. and McCormick, R., 'Testing a tripartite model I. Evaluating the convergent and discriminant validity of anxiety and depression symptom scales', *Journal of Abnormal Psychology, 104*, 3–14, 1995.

WHO ASSIST Working Group, 'The Alcohol, Smoking and Substance Involvement Screening Test (ASSIST): Development, reliability and feasibility', *Addiction, 97*, 1183–94, 2002.

Zammit, S., Allebeck, P., Andreasson, S., Lundberg, I. and Lewis, G., 'Self reported cannabis use as a risk factor for schizophrenia in Swedish conscripts of 1969: Historical cohort study', *British Medical Journal, 325*, 1199–204, 2002.

Chapter 9

Rurally isolated populations and co-existing mental health and drug and alcohol problems

Brian Kelly, Frances J. Kay-Lambkin and David J. Kavanagh

KEY POINTS

1 Data from epidemiological studies suggest that rates of co-existing mental health and substance use problems are similar for urban and rural areas.

2 Important barriers to mental health care exist in rural/remote communities, which often mean that residents are unable to access specialized treatment.

3 Alternatives to face-to-face interventions such as correspondence- or computer-based platforms have shown promise in bridging service gaps, with psychological assessment and treatment transferring well to these modes.

4 There is limited research testing the applications of alternative delivery modes to co-existing mental health and substance use problems. Results from pilot studies conducted by the authors are encouraging.

INTRODUCTION

Major national surveys of mental health (Judd *et al.* 2002; Somers *et al.* 2004) have found few consistent differences between rural and urban areas in prevalence rates of psychiatric and substance use disorders. However, rural communities show marked geographic and cultural diversity, and national surveys may miss specific local factors. Incidence studies are needed that can identify factors that precipitate the onset of mental health problems in rural communities, including local risk and protective factors (Somers *et al.* 2004). Proximal personal and family characteristics and their influence on patterns of drug use and mental health problems should also be encompassed (Robertson and Donnermeyer 1997).

Potential confounds influence interpretations of studies of rural mental health. In many countries, rural areas have a higher proportion of indigenous peoples, who have poorer health outcomes than other residents (Cass 2004).

While the incidence of co-existing mental health and drug and alcohol problems is often lower than that found in urban areas (Diala *et al.* 2004), this result may be affected by differences in the availability of some drugs. Substance use problems remain a significant concern of these communities (Hunter and D'Abbs 2003).

Sociodemographic factors such as employment, marital status and gender, and life events and social support, are usually more significant predictors of mental health and substance misuse than rurality (Judd *et al.* 2002; Paykel *et al.* 2000). In the UK, differences between rural and urban residents in terms of psychiatric disorder and substance use were no longer significant when key social differences were taken into consideration (Paykel *et al.* 2000). In fact, rural life may provide mental health advantages, given failures to demonstrate consistently higher rates of psychiatric disorder despite an often lower socio-economic status and the fragility of the agricultural employment base (Fraser *et al.* 2002). However, specific increased risks may be experienced by subgroups of rural populations. High prevalence rates of substance-related and mental health disorders in rural indigenous communities and poor general health outcomes require particular attention, and have challenged models of health care and social policy in many countries (Brady 2004).

Rural settings also confer disadvantages in terms of accessing treatment, because of limited services and geographical isolation (Kavanagh *et al.* 2000; Robertson and Donnermeyer 1997). Isolation from services is a particular problem in areas with very low population density, limited travel infrastructure or high travel costs. In common with urban areas, rural services are beset by problems arising from splitting the management of substance misuse and mental health disorders across service systems (Kavanagh *et al.* 2000). There are differing priorities and procedures, limited development of staff expertise in treating co-existing problems, and barriers to consultation and joint management. In some rural areas, co-location and small size of services facilitates communication, but low staff levels can undercut any advantage this brings (Kavanagh *et al.* 2000).

Barriers to care in rural areas also include social, economic and community factors (Anderson 2003; Robertson and Donnermeyer 1997). Attitudinal or cultural barriers to treatment for substance misuse or co-existing problems may be more apparent and influential in some rural communities (Booth *et al.* 2000; Robertson and Donnermeyer 1997). It is difficult to maintain anonymity of attendance at self-help meetings in very small communities, increasing vulnerability to social stigma. Methods of treatment that are well accepted by these communities and can effectively reach remote locations are required (Booth *et al.* 2000; Metsch and McCoy 1999; Paykel *et al.* 2000).

CONTEXT OF THERAPY

Therapist variables

The accessibility and acceptability of primary care means that people with co-existing mental health and substance use disorders will commonly be seen in that context, especially in the early stages or when disorders are less severe (Hickie *et al.* 2001). As a result, there is necessarily a strong reliance on primary care for both detection and management of co-existing problems. Limited access to specialist services in rural areas puts even greater reliance on primary care providers. Even when specialist services are present, unless financial or other location incentives are in place, staff are often less experienced and have less access to supervision than in urban contexts (Kavanagh *et al.* 2003). Problems are exacerbated when there is a shortage of primary care practitioners, since it becomes difficult for remaining practitioners to service complex client needs and provide extended consultations. Rural models of care require a focus on a broad health workforce and on treatment models that can be applied in the absence of specialist services.

Client variables

Adolescents in rural areas are at particularly high risk of substance use disorders and mental health problems (Spoth *et al.* 2001), and use of alcohol and other substances is probably a factor in the high rate of suicide among rural men (Caldwell *et al.* 2004). Adolescents with co-existing mental health and substance use disorders in rural areas may be particularly unlikely to receive the necessary integrated care (Anderson 2003). In some countries, solvent use is more common in remote areas (Burns *et al.* 1995), and recent reports have highlighted the multiple social and behavioural problems of children engaging in inhalant use (Wu *et al.* 2004). Use of inhalants such as petrol or gasoline is a particular problem among young indigenous people in the USA, Canada and Australia (Burns *et al.* 1995; Maruff *et al.* 1998) and poses additional challenges for treatment services in rural/remote areas.

Complex social, cultural and historical issues in many indigenous communities have necessitated the development of innovative interventions in collaboration with those communities (Brady 2004; Burns *et al.* 1995). This has highlighted the importance of social and cultural factors in interventions to address mental health and substance use in remote communities (Burns *et al.* 1995; Donnermeyer *et al.* 2002).

ASSESSMENT OF CO-EXISTING MENTAL HEALTH AND ALCOHOL/OTHER DRUG USE PROBLEMS IN RURAL OR REMOTE SETTINGS

Assessment of co-existing mental health and alcohol/other drug use problems in rural or remote settings should follow a similar process as in urban areas. However, issues with access to appropriately trained specialists in rural areas will impact on assessment and treatment provision. Individual barriers such as shame or embarrassment, and restriction of access to limited times or days, may also delay assessment and treatment-seeking in these regions (Tate and Zabinski 2004). Accordingly, this section focuses on methods to overcome these barriers.

Telephone-based interviewing is a common method of choice for social and health surveys across the world (Wilkins *et al.* 2003), and widespread use of computers now offers increasing opportunities for computer-based assessment. In 2005, an estimated 88.5 million people will use the internet to research health topics and communicate with health providers (Ball and Lillis 2001). Five years ago, over half of around 46 million adults in the UK accessed the internet, and around one in two had a personal computer at home (Saliba 2000). These percentages are now presumably even higher. The internet therefore offers a potential solution to the barriers facing rural communities in accessing psychological information and treatments (Tate and Zabinski 2004). Ease of use and availability make computers an attractive alternative to face-to-face assessments.

Computerized assessment can be integrated into services. Computers in the waiting rooms of general practices, emergency rooms or pharmacies allow patients to undertake screening immediately before an interaction with a health professional, in which test results and potential actions can be discussed. They can also be used to prompt assessments by primary care providers, potentially increasing fidelity of assessments and the confidence of non-specialist practitioners in the application of screening or assessment.

Computer-based assessment (or treatment) can take several forms:

- synchronous computer-mediated communication (videoconferencing, internet relay chat) where therapist and client communicate simultaneously as in regular face-to-face communication;
- asynchronous communication (email) where there is no 'real-time' conversation between therapist and client; and
- pre-programmed computerized modules that deliver assessment/treatment programs independently of a therapist (Castelnuovo *et al.* 2003).

Videoconferencing and telemedicine have a significant potential role in providing clinical assessment to remote areas, and have been used successfully for clinical assessment, treatment and the provision of clinical supervision across a broad range of health fields. Guidelines assist in maximizing acceptability and utility for delivery of mental health services in rural areas, and research has indicated that telemedicine compares favourably to in-person care in some circumstances (Capner 2000; Hilty *et al.* 2004), although further research is required to evaluate its effectiveness in different clinical settings (e.g. differing age groups, clinical disorders, cultural groups, types of treatments; Hilty *et al.* 2004). In addition, technical problems currently limit its utility (Smith and Kelly 2002).

Computerized interviews have been developed to screen for depression (Carr *et al.* 1981), phobias (Carr and Ghosh 1983) and substance misuse (Davis *et al.* 1992). Studies comparing computerized assessments with those completed by psychiatrists have revealed that computer-based diagnoses, for the most part, corroborate the clinical judgements and diagnoses of practising clinicians (Epstein and Klinkenberg 2001; Marks 1999). For example, a computer-administered version of the Diagnostic Interview Schedule was developed in the USA and trialled among 117 people with psychiatric conditions (Erdman *et al.* 1992). Participants received their assessment in one of three ways: entirely via the computer program, via the computer program with assistance from an interviewer or entirely via an interviewer. Results indicated that both forms of computerized assessment produced similar diagnoses to the face-to-face-delivered assessment (Erdman *et al.* 1992). Similarly, a study of the web-based delivery of alcohol assessment measures has shown a close correspondence with paper-based delivery (Miller *et al.* 2002).

Computerized/alternative modes of assessment may even be preferable for some clients. For example, lack of face-to-face interaction may reduce the influence of social desirability, and may increase the accuracy of reports of dangerous, unhealthy or stigmatising experiences (such as frequency of drug/alcohol use and presence of mental health symptoms; Tate and Zabinski 2004). In some studies of men with problematic alcohol use, levels of alcohol consumption detected via computerized assessment have been up to two times higher than those found via face-to-face approaches (e.g. Duffy and Waterton 1984).

Despite the obvious advantages of computerized approaches for rural mental health care, more needs to be done to promote their application in the field. To date, applications of remote assessment strategies for mental health or substance use have been limited outside research settings. For example, a recent survey by the American Psychological Association revealed that only 2 per cent of responding psychologists had used internet-based technologies to deliver health care (Castelnuovo *et al.* 2003).

TREATMENT OF CO-EXISTING MENTAL HEALTH AND ALCOHOL/OTHER DRUG USE PROBLEMS IN RURAL OR REMOTE SETTINGS

Specific treatments for rural clients are not discussed here, given that the issues are similar to those in other populations. This section reports on alternative modes of treatment delivery that may better meet the needs of people in rural communities.

There is evidence that alternative modes of treatment delivery can be effective. Bibliotherapy has successfully treated mild depression (Cuijpers 1997; Smith *et al.* 1997) and correspondence-based cognitive behaviour therapy (CBT) for alcohol misuse gives a 50 per cent reduction in alcohol use in people who complete the initial treatment phases, with effects being maintained over 12 months (Kavanagh *et al.* 1999; Sitharthan *et al.* 1996). A recent meta-analysis of bibliotherapy for alcohol problems (Apodaca and Miller 2003) found an average pre–post effect size of .80 for treatment seekers; comparisons with no intervention gave an effect size of .31. Comparisons of bibliotherapy with more extensive interventions had an effect size near zero, thus demonstrating similar effectiveness. The effect size for people offered intervention after screening was lower (.65), and comparisons with no treatment were more variable. Quality of trials was generally high, giving confidence in the results.

There are no published studies testing alternative treatment modes for co-existing mental health and drug and alcohol use problems. A current treatment trial (Kavanagh *et al.* in progress) examines an adaptation of a correspondence treatment for alcohol misuse (Kavanagh *et al.* 1999) for people who also have depression. Clients receive eight 'newsletters' over 12 weeks, which guide the acquisition of relevant CBT skills. Worksheets are completed, along with daily monitoring forms for mood and alcohol intake; these are returned to researchers. Participants also maintain regular contact with their general practitioner (GP). Results are compared with those from a correspondence intervention focused only on alcohol use, and with those from GP contact alone.

As in assessment, computerized treatment delivery holds great promise. The potential for increased interactivity, along with the flexibility and convenience of computerized treatments, could even see this mode of treatment delivery improve on results seen in trials of other treatment platforms (Copeland and Martin 2004). While there are few controlled trials of web-based interventions for substance misuse or mental disorders to date (Copeland and Martin 2004; Kypri *et al.* 2005), existing evidence regarding the acceptability and effects of computer-based programs appears promising. For example, a randomized controlled trial within a student health service using a web-based intervention for alcohol misuse (10–15 minutes of screening, feedback and brief advice) resulted in lower alcohol consumption and fewer alcohol problems after six weeks than did provision of an alcohol information leaflet (Kypri *et al.* 2004). Effects on alcohol problems were maintained at six months, although effects on consumption had then lost statistical significance. Given the brevity and low cost of the intervention, these results, though modest, are remarkable. A longer intervention using CD-ROM delivery (Schinke *et al.* 2004) focused on prevention of alcohol problems in 514 young people. Children aged 10–12 were randomly allocated to no intervention, 10 45-minute CD-ROM sessions or CD-ROM plus a parent intervention to support changes in behaviour. Both interventions resulted in lower alcohol, tobacco and marijuana use three years later. The parent intervention had an added effect on alcohol use.

Osgood-Hynes *et al.* (1998) used a computer-aided telephone system for people with mild–moderate depression, which taught cognitive restructuring, assertive communication and increasing pleasant activities. This was combined with videotaped psycho-education, and instruction booklets that included homework exercises. Over 12 weeks, the program produced a 40 per cent reduction in depressive symptomatology (Osgood-Hynes *et al.* 1998).

There are several other examples of computerized delivery of CBT for depression (Proudfoot *et al.* 2003; Selmi *et al.* 1990), anxiety (White *et al.* 2000), panic (Carlbring *et al.* 2001), agoraphobia (Ghosh and Marks 1987), smoking (Hilton personal communication 1999; Shiffman *et al.* 2001) and harmful drinking (Hester and Delaney 1997). Videoconferencing has been used to deliver group CBT for loneliness (Hopps *et al.* 2003) and panic disorder with agoraphobia (Bouchard *et al.* 2004). There is the potential for other psychotherapies to be adapted for alternative modes of delivery and for a wider range of conditions to be addressed.

At present, there are few computerized interventions for substances other than alcohol or nicotine (Copeland and Martin 2004), and no published studies report on computerized interventions for people with co-existing mental health and drug and alcohol use problems. One reason may be the perception that computerized therapy is only appropriate for mild problems (Tate and Zabinski 2004). In an ongoing multi-site randomized controlled trial, Kay-Lambkin *et al.* are trialling a 10-session computer-based CBT treatment program that integrates depression and substance use-focused strategies (Self-Help for Alcohol/other drug use and Depression; SHADE; Kay-Lambkin *et al.* 2002a, 2002b). On average, SHADE participants score in the severe range for depressive symptoms and smoke around nine cones of cannabis per day; 50 per cent meet criteria for alcohol dependence (Kay-Lambkin *et al.* 2004). Motivation enhancement is used throughout SHADE, which also includes mindfulness meditation, schema-focused work and relapse prevention strategies. A 5–10-minute 'check-in' occurs at the end of each SHADE module to monitor progress. Preliminary results indicate that the SHADE computer therapy has similar impact to an equivalent therapist-delivered treatment (Kay-Lambkin *et al.* 2004).

In general, the clinical outcomes of computerized CBT and motivational enhancement appear comparable to face-to-face approaches (Cavanagh and Shapiro 2004), and the community is becoming increasingly open to the use of computers for health care delivery. In a study by Graham and colleagues in the UK, 91 per cent of survey respondents wanted to access psychotherapy via computer (Graham et al. 2001).

The potential utility of computer-based therapy in rural settings is substantial. If, for example, the SHADE computer program is effective, it will be immediately available for primary care settings, with minimal training or additional resources required. This will directly impact on people with co-existing depression and substance use problems and related conditions in rural communities. However, more research is clearly required into the utility of computer-based therapies for people with severe mental health disorders such as schizophrenia; these people often have less insight into their difficulties and treatment needs.

Application of research to clinical practice

Several authors have suggested that correspondence or computerized treatment may be most useful when offered in a stepped care framework (Chapter 1), or as an adjunct to treatment by non-specialist clinicians (Castelnuovo et al. 2003; Cavanagh and Shapiro 2004; Kirkby and Lambert 1996; National Institute for Clinical Excellence 2002; Tate and Zabinski 2004). Stepped care is highly applicable to rural settings. Although the most appropriate pathways for the use of these methods are not clearly articulated, they could potentially be introduced at any stage – from psycho-education and primary and specialist care to relapse prevention. Regular computerized or telephone monitoring could allow rational decision-making regarding increased intensity of care.

Challenges to implementing alternative methods of assessment/treatment

There are several potential blocks to the acceptance of alternative delivery modes.

Computer anxiety

One major obstacle to the acceptability of computerized health care is anxiety.

Computer anxiety is positively correlated with age (Ellis and Allaire 1999). Older people are less likely to have used a computer or be interested in the technology, and this effect is especially marked in women (Irizarry and Downing 1997). This is of concern, since the population aged 75 and over is growing (Karavidas *et al.* 2005), and there are limited resources to cope with likely demands for services. The benefits of computer use by older people are not restricted to treatment delivery. The internet presents opportunities to socialize that bypass the physical barriers limiting these activities in later life (Karavidas *et al.* 2005). This can help relieve loneliness and boredom, which can influence mental health and drug/alcohol use.

After brief training, computer literacy among older adults improves, although computer anxiety remains (Ellis and Allaire 1999). To enhance engagement with computerized treatment, clinicians could encourage and help apprehensive clients to persist with the use of a program until basic strategies are learned and confidence is established. Strategies for self-defeating thoughts may also sometimes be needed.

Cognitive limitations and literacy

Even if written treatment is segmented into small units and content is tailored to people with relatively low reading ability, these programs will still be more attractive to people with higher academic skills (Kavanagh *et al.* 1999; Sitharthan *et al.* 1996). SHADE attempts to address this obstacle by using voiceover recordings that read the text. Oral sessions are conducted with people who cannot read or write, brainstorming ways to complete homework (e.g. using audio recordings). Internet programs emphasize pictures and diagrams, and where possible allow selection of alternatives rather than text entry.

Where clients have cognitive deficits, additional challenges are faced. All of these approaches rely on ability to access and apply strategies with minimal support. Many approaches rely on relatively intact attention and memory. Equivalents to assertive face-to-face care and programs that compensate for cognitive deficits may be developed. Cognitive deficits present significant challenges to effective remote treatments.

Non-completion

An ongoing issue with remote interventions is that treatment may not be completed. In alcohol correspondence studies, treatment completion rates can be as low as 50 per cent (Kavanagh *et al.* 1999; Sitharthan *et al.* 1996). Similarly, an internet-based program on smoking was only accessed once by 38 per cent of users, and six-month data were provided by just 44 per cent (Schneider *et al.* 1990). When use of internet sites is uncontrolled, users choose aspects that are most attractive or of greatest perceived relevance. Competing interests, inadequate commitment, perceived ineffectiveness and achievement of satisfactory outcomes can all result in non-completion. To ensure adequate treatment exposure, key elements need to be presented early, and made attractive and entertaining. Automated cues and progress summaries may also assist. In correspondence approaches, retention appears to improve with shorter units, less homework, material on addressing lapses and rapid response to late homework.

Financial considerations

Access to computers is higher in more affluent groups, and some people most in need of computerized intervention are also those who can least afford it. Availability through community or health facilities is only a partial answer, where these are close to users. While this issue will become less relevant as costs fall, correspondence and telephone modes may remain important for some time.

Non-specific factors

Computer programs can only detect and respond to the issues for which they have been designed (Marks 1999). We cannot isolate all factors important to therapeutic relationships, and it is unlikely that computers can emulate such interactions, although associated email, telephone or video contact may help. However, in some cases computerized interventions may be preferred by clients (Newman 2004). If alternative delivery modes are available within stepped care, face-to-face approaches can be applied when indicated.

Technical considerations

Development and evaluation of computerized programs requires substantial initial investment, but their subsequent use is cost-effective when compared with traditional approaches (National Institute for Clinical Excellence 2002; Proudfoot et al. 2003). Computer speed, image quality and delays in information transfer may influence engagement and adherence (Castelnuovo et al. 2003). Until greater bandwidth is more readily available, internet programs with only text or line drawings should be used, to minimize the time needed for upload.

Despite these limitations, alternatives to face-to-face interventions offer exciting prospects for remote communities. A key challenge is to maximize their uptake by clients and clinicians.

CASE STUDY

Mary is a 45-year-old woman who lives in a remote town of around 1,000 people. She went to see her GP for sleeping tablets, as her sleep had been disturbed over the past few months 'worrying about the farm and not being able to sell our livestock'. Mary's GP is 100 km from her home town, and it had taken several weeks to organize this appointment.

Her doctor saw that Mary's eyes were bloodshot and she had dark circles under her eyes. He was concerned about the 'worries' that were keeping her awake. He noticed that since Mary's last check-up several months ago, she had gained around 10 kg (increasing body weight by over 10 per cent). The doctor decided to screen for signs of depression. Mary completed the Beck Depression Inventory (BDI-II; Beck *et al.* 1996) and scored in the moderate range (20). The doctor noticed a slight tremor in Mary's hands, and asked if she was anxious about the consultation. Mary said she had these tremors 'every morning lately'. The doctor inquired more closely into Mary's daily activities.

Doctor: It sounds like you've had a pretty tough time of things lately, and I'm wondering if you'd mind telling me a bit more about that. . . . Can you take me through a typical day in your life, please, starting with the time you wake up and ending with your experiences with sleep. Try to include everything you can think of, no matter how unimportant you think it might be.

Mary described the stress of running a farm and the pressure her husband felt to make a success of the family business, which had been affected by recent disease outbreaks and quarantine requirements. After prompting, Mary revealed a pattern of daily drinking, commencing at lunch and lasting until bedtime. A drug and alcohol screen indicated that Mary consumed caffeine and alcohol daily, but used no other drugs. Her daily alcohol intake was about 90 gm alcohol, mainly comprising vodka or gin with mixers. A Readiness to Change Questionnaire (Rollnick *et al.* 1992) placed Mary in the contemplation stage for changing her drinking. She was alarmed to receive health warnings from the doctor about her consumption.

The doctor recommended CBT from the local community health centre plus a course of pharmacotherapy for alcohol craving. However, Mary felt unable to travel 100 km every week for treatment and, given her heightened concern about her health, felt unable to wait the three months it would take to start treatment. She did not want medication for her alcohol use or depression. Accordingly, the doctor suggested a computerized CBT treatment that she could take home that day. Although initially sceptical of the ability of the program to deliver effective treatment, Mary agreed to 'give it a try' for 10 weeks.

Mary and the GP agreed to meet in five weeks then again in 10 weeks to review progress. The practice nurse agreed to telephone Mary each week to conduct a 'check-in' session. Before Mary left the surgery, she made the follow-up appointments and met briefly with the practice nurse, who showed her how to access the program and provided the telephone numbers of crisis services in case she required emergency assistance.

At the pre-arranged time the following week, the practice nurse called Mary. She checked it was still a convenient time, and asked if Mary had had time to do the first session.

Mary: Yes I have and it was OK. It's not as hard to use as I first thought it was. I think I'll stick with it.

Practice nurse: I'm glad you had a go, especially given your initial concerns about using the computer in the first place. What sorts of things have you learned about so far?

Mary: Well, the first module was a lot of information about depression, and drinking alcohol . . . which was good, I guess, because I didn't know much about it. I guess I really do have those things after all. . . . And then I had to do this pros and cons thing – kind of weigh up the good things and bad things about my drinking and feeling this way.

Practice nurse: And how did you find that process?

Mary: Pretty good, actually. It does help to get things down on paper. I guess I really do need to do something about my drinking.

Practice nurse: So . . . how has your drinking been going over the past week? How much did you drink yesterday, for example?

The practice nurse also asked about Mary's current depressive symptoms, conducted a brief suicide risk assessment and asked about progress with homework. Satisfied with Mary's progress, the practice nurse agreed to contact Mary the following week at the same time. The interaction lasted about 15 minutes.

During a second 'check-in' session, Mary revealed to the practice nurse that she had not completed the self-monitoring and behavioural activation tasks set for homework.

Practice nurse: Well, thanks for being open and honest with me about not being able to do those take-home tasks from last week. What sorts of things happened to make them hard to complete?

Mary: Oh well . . . first of all it was really hard to get some time alone to do it . . . you know. . . . I've got my husband to look after, and the kids around, asking me what I'm doing. . . . It's hard to get it done. And then, I forgot what to do because it had been a while since I completed the module . . . so I just didn't get around to it.

Practice nurse: Oh, yes . . . sometimes things will come up during the week that do make it difficult to get these things done and that is totally understandable. I can see how not having a lot of

	privacy can make it hard to concentrate on these activities, and I also find that if I haven't written down what I'm supposed to do and I don't do it right away, I forget about it.
Mary:	Yes . . . that's pretty much what happened to me.
Practice nurse:	And that's totally understandable. On the other hand, these activities set down to do through the week are really quite important – it's one of the most important parts of cognitive behaviour therapy as it is a really good way to take all the things that you learn during these sessions, and try them out at home. What I'm wondering is if we can have a talk about some of the difficulties you've had in making time for those tasks over the past week, and see if we can come up with some ideas to make it easier for you to get this done.

They then developed ideas to maximize her chances of completing the take-home activities, including:

- summarizing the tasks and how and when she would complete them, and recording them in her diary (Mary referred to her diary several times each day);
- planning to complete homework forms before she went to bed: this ensured privacy, and prevented tasks building up over the week;
- keeping homework forms in the cover of a book she read before going to bed; and
- using the computer program to remind her of the things she had learned, and to remind her about homework.

The next few weeks passed without incident. Mary was unable to make it to her mid-treatment review with her GP. She confirmed the post-treatment appointment and commented, 'Things are going pretty well for me at the moment.' The practice nurse passed this message on to the doctor, and noted that Mary had reported significant improvements in depressive symptoms and reductions in alcohol use. The doctor sent Mary a letter confirming their next appointment and commending her on her progress.

At 10 weeks, Mary attended her appointment with the doctor. Her BDI-II score had fallen to 8, indicating only minimal symptoms of depression. She had reduced her alcohol consumption to 20 gm twice weekly, usually with friends on social occasions or on Friday afternoons with her husband. She felt able to maintain this level of intake. Mary completed all 10 sessions of the computerized program, although she admitted that she probably would not have done so without the prompting of the practice nurse ('Just knowing she was going to call made me remember to do the module for that week. . . . It helped me stick with it').

Given Mary's improvement, the doctor decided to forego referral to the community health service and 'discharged' her. She was given a copy of the computerized therapy to keep at home, and to consult as needed. Over the next three months, the practice nurse continued to telephone Mary on a monthly basis to screen for depression, alcohol use and suicidality. Mary then met with her doctor for another formal review to determine any further action. The doctor encouraged Mary to keep the crisis phone numbers, and to see him at any time if she felt her problems were returning.

CONCLUSION

Co-existing mental health and substance use problems in rural areas are not necessarily different in nature or incidence from these problems in urban areas, although specifically local problems and issues with specific groups such as indigenous populations do arise. The differential needs of these areas focus on access to appropriate services. Developing the integrated and collaborative treatments that are needed for co-existing problems is especially challenging where services are limited. There is evidence for the effectiveness and acceptability of a range of alternative modes of treatment delivery, although further controlled trials are clearly required. A stepped care approach, with inexpensive, low-intensity interventions at initial stages, is likely to work well. A key challenge remains ensuring that alternative strategies are widely and consistently used by clients and clinicians.

KEY RESOURCE

Kay-Lambkin, F. J., Baker, A. L. and Bucci, S. R., *The SHADE Computerized Treatment Protocol: Self-Help for Alcohol/other drug use problems and DEpression.* Callaghan, NSW: University of Newcastle, 2002.

REFERENCES

Anderson, R. L., 'Use of community-based services by rural adolescents with mental health and substance use disorders', *Psychiatric Services, 54*, 1339–41, 2003.

Apodaca, T. R. and Miller, W. R., 'A meta-analysis of the effectiveness of biblio-therapy for alcohol problems', *Journal of Clinical Psychology, 59*, 289–304, 2003.

Ball, M. J. and Lillis, J., 'E-health: Transforming the physician/patient relationship', *International Journal of Medical Informatics, 61*, 1–10, 2001.

Beck, A. T., Steer, R. A. and Brown, G. K., *The Beck Depression Inventory, Second Edition: Manual.* San Antonio: The Psychological Corporation, 1996.

Booth, B. M., Kirchner, J., Fortney, J., Ross, R. and Rost, K., 'Rural at-risk drinkers: Correlates and one-year use of alcoholism treatment services', *Journal of Studies on Alcohol, 61*, 267–77, 2000.

Bouchard, S., Paquin, B., Payeur, R., Allard, M., Rivard, V., Fournier, T. *et al.*, 'Delivering cognitive-behavior therapy for panic disorder with agoraphobia in videoconference', *Telemedicine Journal and E-Health, 10*, 13–25, 2004.

Brady, M., *Indigenous Australia and Alcohol Policy: Meeting Difference with Indifference*. Sydney: University of New South Wales Press, 2004.

Burns, C. B., Currie, B. J., Clough, A. B. and Wuridjal, R., 'Evaluation of strategies used by a remote aboriginal community to eliminate petrol sniffing', *Medical Journal of Australia, 163*, 82–6, 1995.

Caldwell, C. H., Kohn-Wood, L. P., Schmeelk-Cone, K. H., Chavous, T. M. and Zimmerman, M. A., 'Racial discrimination and racial identity as risk or protective factors for violent behaviors in African American young adults', *American Journal of Community Psychology, 33*, 91–105, 2004.

Capner, M., 'Videoconferencing in the provision of psychological services at a distance', *Journal of Telemedicine and Telecare, 6*, 311–9, 2000.

Carlbring, P., Westling, B., Ljungstrand, P., Ekselius, H. P. and Andersson, G., 'Treatment of panic disorder via the internet: A randomized trial of a self-help program', *Behavior Therapy, 32*, 751–64, 2001.

Carr, A., Ancill, R., Ghosh, A. and Margo, A., 'Direct assessment of depression by microcomputer: A feasibility study', *Acta Psychiatrica Scandinavica, 64*, 415–22, 1981.

Carr, A. and Ghosh, A., 'Accuracy of behavioural assessment', *British Journal of Psychiatry, 142*, 66–70, 1983.

Cass, A., 'Health outcomes in aboriginal populations', *Canadian Medical Association Journal, 171*, 597–8, 2004.

Castelnuovo, G., Gaggioli, A., Mantovani, F. and Riva, G., 'New and old tools in psychotherapy: The use of technology for the integration of traditional clinical treatments', *Psychotherapy: Theory, Research, Practice, Training, 40*, 33–44, 2003.

Cavanagh, K. and Shapiro, D. A., 'Computer treatment for common mental health problems', *Journal of Clinical Psychology, 60*, 239–51, 2004.

Copeland, J. and Martin, G., 'Web-based interventions for substance use disorder: A qualitative review', *Journal of Substance Abuse Treatment, 26*, 109–16, 2004.

Cuijpers, P., 'Bibliotherapy in unipolar depression: A meta-analysis', *Journal of Behavior Therapy and Experimental Psychiatry, 28*, 139–47, 1997.

Davis, L., Hoffman, N. G., Morse, R. and Luehr, J., 'Substance Use Disorder Diagnostic Schedule (SUDDS): The equivalence and validity of a computer-administered and interviewer-administered format', *Alcoholism: Clinical and Experimental Research, 16*, 250–4, 1992.

Diala, C. C., Muntaner, C. and Walrath, C., 'Gender, occupational, and socio-economic correlates of alcohol and drug abuse among US rural, metropolitan, and urban residents', *American Journal of Drug and Alcohol Abuse, 30*, 409–28, 2004.

Donnermeyer, J. F., Barclay, E. M. and Jobes, P. C., 'Drug-related offences and the structure of communities in rural Australia', *Substance Use and Misuse, 37*, 631–61, 2002.

Duffy, J. C. and Waterton, J. J., 'Under-reporting of alcohol consumption in sample surveys: The effect of computer interviewing in fieldwork', *British Journal of Addiction, 79*, 303–8, 1984.

Ellis, R. D. and Allaire, J., 'Modelling computer interest in older adults: The role of age, education, computer knowledge and computer anxiety', *Human Factors*, *41*, 345–55, 1999.

Epstein, J. and Klinkenberg, W. D., 'From Eliza to internet: A brief history of computerized assessment', *Computers in Human Behavior*, *17*, 295–314, 2001.

Erdman, H. P., Klein, M. H., Greist, J. H., Skare, S., Husted, J., Robins, L. *et al.*, 'A comparison of two computer-administered versions of the NIMH Diagnostic Interview Schedule', *Journal of Psychiatric Research*, *26*, 85–95, 1992.

Fraser, C., Judd, F. and Jackson, H. J., 'Does one size really fit all? Why the mental health of rural Australians requires further research', *Australian Journal of Rural Health*, *10*, 288–95, 2002.

Ghosh, A. and Marks, I. M., 'Self-treatment of agoraphobia by exposure', *Behavior Therapy*, *18*, 3–18, 1987.

Graham, C., Franses, A., Kenwright, M. and Marks, I. M., 'Problem severity in people using alternative therapies for anxiety difficulties', *Psychiatric Bulletin*, *25*, 12–4, 2001.

Hester, R. K. and Delaney, H. D., 'Behavioral self-control program for Windows: Results of a controlled clinical trial', *Journal of Consulting and Clinical Psychology*, *65*, 686–93, 1997.

Hickie, I. B., Davenport, T. A., Naismith, S. L. and Scott, E. M., 'Sphere: A national depression project', *Medical Journal of Australia*, *175*, S4–S5, 2001.

Hilty, D., Marks, S. L., Urness, D. and Yellowlees, P. M., 'Clinical and educational telepsychiatry applications: A review', *Canadian Journal of Psychiatry*, *49*, 12–23, 2004.

Hopps, S. L., Pepin, M. and Boisvert, J.-M., 'The effectiveness of cognitive-behavioral group therapy for loneliness via inter-relay-chat among people with physical disabilities', *Psychotherapy: Theory, Research, Practice, Training*, *40*, 136–47, 2003.

Hunter, E. and D'Abbs, P., 'In "modest but practical ways": Medical practitioners and substance misuse in aboriginal Australians', *Internal Medicine Journal*, *33*, 333–5, 2003.

Irizarry, C. and Downing, A., 'Computers enhancing the lives of older people', *Australian Journal on Ageing*, *16*, 161–5, 1997.

Judd, F. K., Jackson, H. J. and Komiti, A., 'High prevalence disorders in urban and rural communities', *Australian and New Zealand Journal of Psychiatry*, *36*, 104–13, 2002.

Karavidas, M., Lim, N. K. and Katsikas, S. L., 'The effects of computers on older adults', *Computers in Human Behavior*, *21*, 697–712, 2005.

Kavanagh, D. J., Greenaway, L., Jenner, L., Saunders, J. B., White, A., Sorban, J. and Hamilton, G., 'Contrasting views and experiences of health professionals on the management of comorbid substance abuse and mental disorders', *Australian and New Zealand Journal of Psychiatry*, *34*, 279–89, 2000.

Kavanagh, D. J., Sitharthan, T., Spilsbury, G. and Vignaendra, S., 'An evaluation of brief correspondence programs for problem drinkers', *Behavior Therapy*, *30*, 641–56, 1999.

Kavanagh, D. J., Spence, S. H., Strong, J., Wilson, J., Sturk, H. and Crow, N., 'Supervision practices in allied mental health: A staff survey', *Mental Health Services Research*, *5*, 187–95, 2003.

Kay-Lambkin, F. J., Baker, A. L. and Bucci, S. R., *Treatment Manual for the SHADE*

Project (Self-Help for Alcohol/other drug use problems and DEpression). Callaghan, NSW: University of Newcastle, 2002a.

Kay-Lambkin, F. J., Baker, A. L. and Bucci, S. R., *The SHADE Computerized Treatment Protocol: Self-Help for Alcohol/other drug use problems and DEpression*. Callaghan, NSW: University of Newcastle, 2002b. Available at http://www. newcastle.edu.au/centre/cmhs/

Kay-Lambkin, F. J., Baker, A., Lewin, T. Bucci, S. R. and Carr, V. J., 'Computerised cognitive behaviour therapy for co-occurring depression and alcohol/other drug use problems: Preliminary results', Poster presented at the Annual Conference of the European Association of Behavioral and Cognitive Therapy, September 2004.

Kirkby, K. C. and Lambert, T. J., 'Computer aids to treatment in psychiatry', *Australian and New Zealand Journal of Psychiatry*, *30*, 142–5, 1996.

Kypri, K., Sitharthan, T., Cunningham, J. A., Kavanagh, D. J. and Dean, J. I., 'Innovative approaches to intervention for problem drinking', *Current Opinion in Psychiatry*, *18*, 229–34, 2005.

Kypri, K. J., Saunders, J. B., Williams, S. M., McGee, R. O., Langley, J. D., Cashell-Smith, M. L. and Gallagher, S., 'Web-based screening and brief intervention for hazardous drinking: A double-blind randomized controlled trial', *Addiction*, *99*, 1410–7, 2004.

Marks, I. M., 'Computer aids to mental health care', *Canadian Journal of Psychiatry*, *44*, 548–55, 1999.

Maruff, P., Burns, C. B., Tyler, B. J. and Currie, J., 'Neurological and cognitive abnormalities associated with chronic petrol sniffing', *Brain*, *121*, 1903–17, 1998.

Metsch, L. R. and McCoy, C. B., 'Drug treatment experiences: Rural and urban comparisons', *Substance Use and Misuse*, *34*, 763–84, 1999.

Miller, E. T., Neal, D. J., Roberts, L. J., Baer, J. S., Cressler, S. O., Metrick, J. and Marlatt, G. A., 'Test–retest reliability of alcohol measures: Is there a difference between internet-based assessment and traditional methods?' *Psychology of Addictive Behaviors*, *16*, 56–63, 2002.

National Institute for Clinical Excellence, *Guidance on the Use of Computerised Cognitive Behavioural Therapy for Anxiety and Depression* (Technology Appraisal No. 51). London: NICE, 2002.

Newman, M. G., 'Technology in psychotherapy: An introduction', *Journal of Clinical Psychology*, *60*, 141–5, 2004.

Osgood-Hynes, D. J., Greist, J. H., Marks, I. M., Baer, L., Heneman, S. W., Wenzel, K. W. *et al.*, 'Self-administered psychotherapy for depression using a telephone-accessed computer system plus booklets: An open US–UK study', *Journal of Clinical Psychiatry*, *59*, 358–65, 1998.

Paykel, E. S., Abbott, R., Jenkins, R., Brugha, T. and Meltzer, H., 'Urban and rural mental health differences in Great Britain: Findings from the national morbidity survey', *Psychological Medicine*, *30*, 269–80, 2000.

Proudfoot, J., Goldberg, D., Mann, A., Everitt, B., Marks, I. M. and Gray, J., 'Computerised, interactive, multi-media cognitive behavioural program for anxiety and depression in general practice', *Psychological Medicine*, *33*, 217–27, 2003.

Robertson, E. B. and Donnermeyer, J. F., 'Illegal drug use among rural adults: Mental health consequences and treatment utilization', *American Journal of Drug and Alcohol Abuse*, *23*, 467–85, 1997.

Rollnick, S., Heather, N., Gold, R. and Hall, W., 'Development of a short "Readiness to Change Questionnaire" for use in brief, opportunistic interventions among excessive drinkers', *British Journal of Addiction*, 87, 743–54, 1992.

Saliba, C., 'Report: UK net usage surging', *E-Commerce Times*, 2000. Available at http://www.ecommercetimes.com/story/6062.html (accessed 5 January 2005).

Schinke, S. P., Schwinn, T. M., Di Nola, J. and Cole, K. C., 'Reducing the risks of alcohol use among urban youth: Three-year effects of a computer-based intervention with and without parent involvement', *Journal of Studies on Alcohol*, 65, 443–9, 2004.

Schneider, S. J., Walter, R. and O'Donnell, R., 'Computerized communication as a medium for behavioural smoking cessation: Controlled evaluation', *Computers in Human Behavior*, 6, 141–51, 1990.

Selmi, P. A., Klein, M. H., Greist, J. H., Sorrell, S. P. and Erdman, H. P., 'Computer-administered cognitive-behavioral therapy for depression', *American Journal of Psychiatry*, 147, 51–6, 1990.

Shiffman, S., Paty, J. A., Rohay, J. M., Di Marino, M. E. and Gitchell, J. G., 'The efficacy of computer-tailored smoking cessation material as a supplement to nicotine patch therapy', *Drug and Alcohol Dependence*, 64, 35–46, 2001.

Sitharthan, T., Kavanagh, D. J. and Sayer, G., 'Moderating drinking by correspondence: An evaluation of a new method of intervention', *Addiction*, 91, 345–55, 1996.

Smith, G. L. and Kelly, K. J., 'Utilizing technology: The challenges and opportunities facing "substance abuse" professionals in rural communities', *Substance Use and Misuse*, 37, 805–14, 2002.

Smith, N. M., Floyd, M. R. and Jamison, C. S., 'Three-year follow-up of bibliotherapy for depression', *Journal of Consulting and Clinical Psychology*, 65, 324–7, 1997.

Somers, J. M., Goldner, E. M., Waraich, P. and Hsu, L., 'Prevalence studies of substance-related disorders: A systematic review of the literature', *Canadian Journal of Psychiatry – Revue Canadienne de Psychiatrie*, 49, 373–84, 2004.

Spoth, R., Goldberg, C. and Neppl, T., 'Rural–urban differences in the distribution of parent-reported factors for substance use among young adolescents', *Journal of Substance Abuse*, 13, 609–23, 2001.

Tate, D. F. and Zabinski, M. F., 'Computer and internet applications for psychological treatment: Update for clinicians', *Journal of Clinical Psychology*, 60, 209–20, 2004.

White, J., Jones, R. and McGarry, E., 'Cognitive behaviour computer therapy for the anxiety disorders: A pilot study', *Journal of Mental Health*, 9, 505–16, 2000.

Wilkins, C., Casswell, S., Barnes, H. M. and Pledger, M., 'A pilot study of a computer-assisted cell-phone interview (CACI) methodology to survey respondents in households without telephones about alcohol use', *Drug and Alcohol Review*, 22, 221–5, 2003.

Wu, L.-T., Pilowsky, D. J. and Shlenger, W. E., 'Inhalant abuse and dependence among adolescents in the United States', *Journal of the American Academy of Child and Adolescent Psychiatry*, 43, 1206–14, 2004.

Chapter 10

Homelessness alongside co-existing mental health and drug and alcohol problems

Richard Velleman

KEY POINTS

1   There is convincing evidence that homeless people have higher rates of both mental health and substance misuse problems than the general population, in addition to lowered access to services and other helping resources.

2   It is proposed that a model of care which includes designated, well-trained, and well-supervised workers who can work effectively across the various domains of mental health, substance misuse, and housing will be the main future direction.

3   It is important to adopt a holistic (and pragmatic) view as to what the targets of treatment should be.

4   Therapists need very high levels of skill in engagement.

5   The assessment of co-existing mental health and alcohol/other drug use problems in people who are also homeless should follow a similar process as for other clients. However, there are important individual barriers and organizational issues that need to be addressed.

6   There are four areas from which treatment ideas can be drawn: substance misuse, mental health generally, assertive outreach in particular, and housing.

INTRODUCTION

Co-existing problems with both substance use and mental health are for many people a 'double whammy': as Chapter 1 shows, many people get little help with either problem, as they get passed from one agency (specializing in one of these problems) to another (specializing in the other problem), caught up in what to them appear arcane arguments as to 'primary diagnosis'. Unfortunately, the situation is even worse for those individuals who have these co-existing problems and who are also homeless (Nwakeze *et al.* 2003; Reed and Klee 1999).

Homelessness: some terminology[1]

In the UK, homelessness legislation in force since the 1970s includes legal definitions of homelessness and gives local authorities responsibility to house those homeless people deemed to be 'in priority need'. These definitions usually exclude most homeless people without dependents from a statutory right to be housed. The UK government only systematically collects statistics on those homeless people who have applied to local authorities for help – usually families with children and others deemed to be especially vulnerable. Government figures, therefore, do not include overall figures on the number of single homeless people.

Apart from legal definitions of homelessness, a broad general definition is often taken to include people who are either literally 'roofless' or who experience 'hidden homelessness' – that is, people who are forced to live in insecure, overcrowded, dangerous, illegal, or very temporary accommodation (e.g. bed and breakfast hotels, women's refuges, hostels, friend's/relative's floors, and squats; also women forced through lack of alternatives to remain in abusive situations).

While recent government initiatives have reduced the number of 'rough' sleepers in the UK, homelessness overall has increased significantly in recent years. This has been due to a number of economic and social factors, including a decline in the availability of rented accommodation, a lack of affordable accommodation for those on low incomes, unemployment, and the growth in single households.

Co-existing homelessness and mental health and drug and alcohol problems

Gill et al. (2003) presented a detailed examination of the prevalence of mental health and substance misuse problems among homeless adults in the UK. They presented data from four samples of such adults collected in the mid-1990s: residents of homelessness hostels; homeless people (mainly families) housed temporarily in private sector leased accommodation; people staying within night shelters; and those sleeping rough who visited day centres. Prevalence figures for these groups are given in Table 10.1.

A major study in the UK (Farrell et al. 2003) looked back at surveys in the 1990s to examine the rates of both mental health and substance use problems in the homeless population, as compared to people living in the community (National Household Survey) or in institutions for people with mental disorders. This study demonstrated that among the homeless population: rates of alcohol dependence were three to four times higher than in the other two groups; rates of moderate and heavy smoking were more than twice that of the household population; rates of 'ever' using other drugs were more than five times higher than in the community sample and almost three times higher

Table 10.1 The prevalence of psychiatric morbidity and substance misuse among homeless adults in the UK

	Mental health problems (%)		Substance misuse (%)	
	'Neurotic'	'Psychotic'	Alcohol	Drugs
Hostels (n = 530)	38	8	16	11
Private rented (n = 268)	35	2	3	7
Night shelter (n = 187)	60	_*	44	29
Rough sleepers (n = 181)	57	_*	50	24

From figures in Gill *et al.* (2003).
* Data not collected.

than in the institutional sample; and rates of drug dependence were 10–15 times higher than in the community sample.

Within the different homeless populations, there are also different prevalences: for example, co-existing mental health and substance misuse problems tend to be more prevalent among rough sleepers than among hostel dwellers (Warnes *et al.* 2003). In more recent years, the percentage of the homeless population with severe drug problems has risen. Fountain *et al.* (2002) found that 80 per cent of homeless people were regular drug users, with almost half having used heroin or crack within the previous month, and similar findings are provided by Wincup *et al.* (2003).

In addition to mental health, alcohol, and illicit drug problems, Kershaw *et al.* (2003) report that 82 per cent of a sample of 225 homeless people in Glasgow, Scotland, were current smokers and 51 per cent smoked heavily (20 or more cigarettes per day).

In sum, then, there is convincing evidence that homeless people have higher rates of both mental health and substance misuse problems than do the general population, while having lowered access to services and other helping resources.

The model(s) that guides treatment of these co-existing problems

Even when homeless people do access mainstream services, they are more likely to be discharged early and more likely to return to the streets following psychiatric inpatient treatment (Belcher and First 1988). These risks are increased if the person is discharged without having a permanent address in place; if this happens, there is also a concomitant lack of compliance with aftercare (Belcher and First 1988). An assertive outreach style of working with people who are homeless and who have severe mental health disorders has been shown to be much more effective, leading to reduced use of inpatient facilities, increased housing stability, increased life satisfaction, and better clinical outcomes (Lehman *et al.* 1997, 1999). However, often these services are denied to people who also have substance use problems. Similarly, drug use is a major factor in exclusion from social housing (Fakhoury *et al.* 2002).

For these reasons, some areas have considered developing specialist treatment services. Killaspy *et al.* (2004: 599) reported:

> The designation of a specific ward appears to have encouraged admission of a particularly difficult group of homeless mentally ill who have been able to achieve and sustain housing stability, improve their engagement with services, and reduce the factors influencing non-compliance with medication.

Similarly, Gray and Fraser (2005) assessed the impact of 'floating support' schemes in helping heroin users acquire stable housing. They concluded that such schemes can make a significant difference to people's experiences of accessing, obtaining, and then keeping stable housing, and hence provide the opportunity to address drug use.

However, given the costs of these specialist treatment services, and the growth in numbers of people with these multiple problems, it is highly unlikely that sufficient such specialist services will be developed to deal adequately with the need. It is much more likely that a model, described below and in the case study, of designated, well-trained, and well-supervised workers who can effectively work across the various domains of mental health, substance misuse, and housing will be the main future direction.

The targets of treatment

There are many who argue that clarifying a 'primary diagnosis' with respect to co-existing problems is vital. However, it is the position of this chapter that, with complex problems such as these, where people have difficulties with housing, mental health, substance use, and probably other areas such as physical health, it is important to adopt a holistic (and pragmatic) view as to what the targets of treatment should be. It is of course the case, as Haracopos *et al.* (2003) have demonstrated, that it is difficult to improve treatment outcomes unless basic needs such as accommodation are addressed. Nevertheless, the approach favoured by this author is to focus on engagement of the client, and follow that with a gentle assessment process which will allow the client to set the agenda and to decide on which problem area s/he wants to deal with first.

It is also important to focus not only on the obvious targets of treatment in such cases (mental health, substance use, accommodation) but on other important areas where there is good evidence that development of skills will assist rates of improvement. These include employment, family connectivity, and social networks with people who encourage non-problematic use (or non-use) of substances and who embrace a recovery approach to mental health difficulties.

CONTEXT OF THERAPY

Therapist variables

Dealing with homeless people with co-existing problems requires great sensitivity: they are usually very aware that they are often perceived to be at the very bottom of the social pile. They are unlikely to attend all appointments, or to complete many homework tasks. Therapists need to be engaging and take an optimistic, non-judgemental, long-term, process-oriented focus. The priority should be on meeting the client's immediate needs to ensure that they see the value of working with us on their problems. Flexibility (e.g. offering practical help) and knowledge of the welfare system are also required.

Because there is a great deal of research evidence in both the substance misuse and mental health fields demonstrating the effectiveness of working with family and other non-substance-misusing social networks (e.g. Chapter 5, this volume; Copello *et al.* 2005; Pharoah *et al.* 2003), it makes sense for therapists to be familiar with these family- and network-based approaches when working with this population. However, it is possible that making contact with family may be one of the most difficult tasks for a client with these multiple problems. Hence, contact may be made later (if at all) as opposed to earlier, as with social behaviour and network therapy (Copello *et al.* 2002) and other social context-focussed approaches.

Client variables

Clients with these multiple problems will very often have serious physical health difficulties too (e.g. Warnes *et al.* 2003). If sleeping rough they will also have nowhere to live, and they may be malnourished and hungry. Many therefore may have many immediate physical needs, and will not be able to focus on their substance misuse or their mental health problems as issues to be tackled immediately.

If they do wish to start therapeutic work, many will only want to discuss one issue – often their homelessness, sometimes their physical health problems, maybe their benefits situation, sometimes their mental health difficulties, sometimes their substance misuse. Clients will rarely wish to discuss all of these problems initially.

ASSESSMENT OF CO-EXISTING MENTAL HEALTH AND ALCOHOL/OTHER DRUG USE PROBLEMS IN PEOPLE WHO ALSO ARE HOMELESS

In general, the assessment of co-existing mental health and alcohol/other drug use problems in people who are also homeless should follow a similar process as for other clients. However, as noted above, these are often individuals who present themselves in highly chaotic and disorganized ways, and hence there are a number of issues which can get in the way of such assessments.

There are also organizational issues, such as lack of access within homelessness services to appropriately trained mental health and/or drug and alcohol clinicians, which will often mean that these clients' needs in one or both of these domains are not adequately assessed. Other organizational issues, such as requiring people to attend appointments at pre-arranged times and days and discharging them if they do not attend, will also have a large impact on this group.

Similarly, individual barriers such as shame or embarrassment concerning sensitive issues (such as mental health symptoms and/or alcohol/drug usage) may mean that people do not reveal or discuss such important areas, especially at first.

Once clients are sufficiently engaged such that an assessment can be started, a key is to ensure that the assessment is very client-centred. Clinicians will need to start by clarifying with the client what their problems are, and which problems they wish to work on first. Often this will not be best undertaken by the use of standardized questionnaires, but by careful and empathic interviewing (Velleman 2001).

Assessment will probably need to cover a wide range of domains, and will need to examine both wants and needs. Domains will include mental health issues and symptoms, and substance use and misuse (including alcohol, tobacco, and a range of other drugs). Assessment must focus on what the client's goals and aspirations are. As always, the task is to ensure engagement is retained and enhanced while conducting a comprehensive assessment, thus developing a clear formulation of the person's presenting concerns. It is well established that a well-conducted assessment can increase engagement in treatment and be a therapeutic intervention in itself. At the same time too formal an approach, or too long a session with someone whose concentration is impaired, can be very counterproductive: good clinical judgement is required!

As outlined at the start of this chapter, it is generally not useful to try to attempt to distinguish between primary and secondary disorders, and a diagnostic approach is not recommended. Rather, a 'problems' approach (Velleman 2001), which tries to clarify the range of problems which a person has or is able to reveal at this stage, and then helps the client prioritize them as targets to be worked on, is preferred.

I have usually found it beneficial to adopt a life-history approach to assessment, although this can be problematic when clients are very disorganized or have a very unclear recollection of past events. In this life-history approach, I assist the client in mapping relevant information from their past onto a lifetime timeline which includes their major life events and the onset and development of their substance use/misuse and their mental health problems and symptoms. Included in both domains are details of any problem-free periods or periods of reduced problems, and antecedent and consequential events related to these. This is also sometimes known as the 'timeline follow-back' interviewing technique (Sobell and Sobell 1992).

It can be useful to introduce clients to the idea of self-monitoring, and to suggest that ongoing and recorded self-monitoring of both substance use and problematic mental health symptoms is maintained.

Assessment has two main aims: (i) to develop a comprehensible formulation of how the client's problems in different domains developed and are being maintained (see Chapter 4 for an in-depth discussion of formulation); and (ii) to assist the client in deciding which problem areas to work on, and what is a sensible prioritization of the order with which they should be tackled (always bearing in mind that it is likely that more than one problem area will need to be tackled simultaneously).

Having said above that assessment is often not best undertaken via the use of standardized questionnaires, there are some which can be useful. The most important issue is that whatever is used needs to be kept short. It is often the case that concentration levels are impaired in this population, and reading levels may also be low.

Of the questionnaires outlined in Chapter 2, and other chapters within this volume, the ones I recommend most for this population are outlined below. For assessing substance misuse/mental health symptoms, the best short measures (all with satisfactory internal consistency and test–retest reliability) are:

- the Fast Alcohol Screening Test (FAST; Hodgson *et al.* 2002), a four-item questionnaire based on the Alcohol Use Disorders Identification Test (AUDIT; Saunders *et al.* 1993), which is slightly longer at 10 items but also a good measure of harmful or problematic drinking;
- the Alcohol, Smoking, and Substance Involvement Screening Test (ASSIST; WHO ASSIST Working Group 2002), an eight-item screen for alcohol and substance use;
- the Manchester Short Assessment of Quality of Life (MANSA; Priebe *et al.* 1999), a 25-item measure of quality of life, derived as a short-form of the Lancashire Quality of Life Profile; and
- the Social Functioning Scale (SFS; Birchwood *et al.* 1990), a relatively brief (15-minute), objectively scored self-report measure that addresses multiple facets of community adjustment, including social engagement

and withdrawal, interpersonal behaviour, prosocial activities, recreation, independence, and employment or occupation.

TREATMENT OF HOMELESS CLIENTS WITH CO-EXISTING DISORDERS

Specific treatments for homeless clients with co-existing disorders will not be discussed here, given that their co-existing mental health and drug and alcohol issues are similar to those in other populations. The motivational approach described in Chapter 3 is especially relevant for clients with these multiple problems, as is the cognitive behaviour therapy (CBT) approach described in Chapter 4.

This section will simply outline other techniques which can be used alongside these motivational and CBT approaches. In general, there are four areas from which treatment ideas can be drawn: substance misuse, mental health generally, assertive outreach in particular, and housing.

Substance misuse

A large number of social, cognitive, and behavioural interventions have been shown to be helpful and effective (Anglin *et al.* 1997; Brown 2004; Gossop *et al.* 2003; Hubbard *et al.* 1997; Miller and Wilbourne 2002; Project MATCH Research Group 1997). Among the most effective are brief interventions, motivational enhancement, social skills training, community reinforcement, behavioural contracting, behavioural marital therapy, case management, self-monitoring, cognitive therapy, and client-centred counselling. (It is also the case that some pharmacological interventions for both alcohol and drug problems are also effective, including the use of methadone, buprenorphine, naltrexone, and acamprosate).

Some common themes within these psychological interventions are:

- the provision of information: both because many people with alcohol or drug problems are actually relatively ignorant about the effects and properties of the substances they use, and because there is good evidence that simply giving people advice and information is a highly effective way of helping, even for people with very severe substance misuse problems;
- focussing on clients' goals: helping them to set goals which are manageable, realistic, and achievable, and balancing intermediate, short-term goals with aspirational goals towards which clients can work over a longer period;
- helping clients to believe they can change: using methods and techniques such as raising their awareness of the environmental forces that push them towards using substances (maybe by using self-monitoring techniques

to enable them to think more about the antecedents of their behaviour), and then using more active CBT techniques to help them to re-think what they can do instead of using;

- helping clients acquire new skills: both to deal with old problems and new strategies to overcome anticipated problems, using behavioural ideas such as practising these new skills until they become 'second nature'; both avoidance strategies (helping clients to recognize problem situations and not to get involved with them) and problem-solving strategies (helping clients to cope with problem situations once they are in them) are important; and
- helping clients to develop and then utilize their social and familial networks to assist them in the process of change.

All of these are also covered in more detail in Velleman (2001).

Mental health

The area of psychosocial interventions within mental health has grown and developed exponentially in recent years, and there are now a number of widely used and well-evaluated approaches (all covered in more detail in other chapters in this volume; see also Velleman *et al.* 2007) from which treatment ideas can be drawn to be utilized with this population. These include:

- early symptom recognition and control (Addington *et al.* 2003; Birchwood *et al.* 2000; McGorry and Warner 2002);
- medication management (Miller *et al.* 2004; Owen *et al.* 2000);
- CBT work on unhelpful thoughts (see Chapter 4 of this volume; Kingdon and Turkington 1994; National Institute for Clinical Excellence 2004a, 2004b; Williams 2001);
- thought stopping and control (Lazarus 1971); and
- relapse prevention (Geddes 2002; Segal *et al.* 2002).

Housing

Although housing interventions have not generally been thought of as 'treatments', in the case of working with people with co-existing problems who are also homeless, enabling them to access stable accommodation is a major step forward, allowing them to start to reflect on substance and mental health issues. Other than the provision of hostels, night shelters, and day/drop-in centres, and of course more suitable housing (flats, shared houses, sheltered housing), some innovative services have been developed which are all helpful possibilities. Among the more recent ideas developed in this field have been: street outreach teams (Warnes *et al.* 2003), resettlement services (Warnes *et al.* 2003), and floating support (Gray and Fraser 2005).

However, such new services are rare, and the main work of helping home-less people with co-existing problems falls on their key workers. The main tasks here are to be active in helping and supporting clients, to enable them to take action: if a client is trying to resettle into more secure accommodation, a key intervention may be to accompany him/her to the housing department to help them complete a housing application form, or to write support letters to the housing department explaining their vulnerability as a homeless person with mental health issues. A further key idea is the continuation of support even after housing is secured, because there will almost certainly be setbacks, and clients need to know that their key worker is there for them 'for the long haul'.

Assertive outreach

Assertive outreach (AO) originated in the USA in the late 1970s when multi-disciplinary teams moved into the community, providing intensive, com-prehensive services to people who were at high risk of hospital re-admission and who could not be maintained by more usual community-based treat-ments (Stein and Santos 1998). Randomized trials have consistently shown that assertive community treatment leads to a reduction in inpatient admis-sions and promotes continuity of outpatient care (Marshall and Lockwood 2002). Later studies did not demonstrate the same effect in reducing the need for hospital care as the earlier US studies, which led to considerable debate about the 'essential ingredients' for AO (Burns 2002). Nonetheless, there is substantial agreement about the nature of AO.

Many of the techniques of AO can be implemented for the homeless population with co-existing problems. Indeed, one could argue that such individuals are archetypal AO clients. AO provides high levels of input for people who tend to be difficult to engage in standard services; most will have experienced many relapses in the past. It is distinct from other mental health services in that the qualified staff members have small caseloads (10–12) and are able to maintain daily contact, if necessary, seven days a week. Other distinctive features are that the team members go out to see clients (e.g. at home, in local cafés) instead of expecting them to come in to the profes-sional's place of work, and caseloads are shared across clinicians.

CASE STUDY

Details from several cases have been blended to protect individual identities.

Gerry is a 35-year-old man, separated from and out of touch with his family. When he was first referred to Ian, the dual disorder[2] outreach worker who works out of the night shelter for homeless people, Gerry had recently been released from prison after a conviction for theft. He had already returned to being an extremely challenging and chaotic poly-drug user (dependent on heroin and using alcohol, nicotine, and a variety of other drugs, injecting where he could), was currently sleeping rough in a disused factory, and was experiencing psychotic symptoms. He was regularly begging and shoplifting for alcohol and food, and was also involved in theft and burglary to fund his other drug use.

It was very difficult at first to engage with Gerry. He was extremely distrustful, and said (in no uncertain terms!) that he was not interested in being helped. However, after much persistence, he gradually began to talk and allowed Ian to support him. Initially, this meant that Gerry began to accept Ian's presence when he 'popped round'. After some time, the rapport gradually built up and Gerry started to accept the possibility of attending the night shelter, and from that, started to accept the possibility of receiving a health care check-up with the primary health care professionals based within the night shelter.

It emerged that Gerry had a very long history of interaction with care and helping services and had experienced much rejection from them (see 'The role of the past' below). Before his last spell in prison he had found that no helping services would work with him (with substance misuse services referring him to mental health services and vice versa, and homeless services refusing to work with him due to his chaotic lifestyle and behaviours).

After many weeks, Gerry moved into the night shelter. In order to address Gerry's anxieties about explaining his health issues, Ian (with the agreement of Gerry) accompanied him to his health check-up, which covered both physical and psychological areas. As a result, he was prescribed anti-psychotic medication, the team started to work on a number of his other physical health problems, and Ian could start to undertake more overt therapeutic work with him on both his mental health difficulties and his substance misuse. It remained the case, however, that building up Gerry's trust took many months.

Prioritizing the therapeutic work

Once Gerry had engaged sufficiently with the worker and the service such that initial physical health concerns and florid psychotic symptoms could be controlled, the worker was able to start to talk in more depth with Gerry about his concerns. It must be stressed that Gerry had already made significant progress, just to get to this point. Initially, he was distrustful of all authority, rather paranoid, and unwilling to entertain the idea of entering 'the system' – the night shelter, the primary care team, and so on. Even to start to talk about his mental health issues, or his substance misuse, was a huge step for him and for the worker, who had put in much time to get to this stage.

However, following careful discussion and gentle probing, Gerry was able to start to describe his alcohol and other drug use, and his mental health experiences, and the worker was able to start to discuss with Gerry what he might want to change. Gerry said at this time:

Gerry: I'd like to be working, I would like to have contact with my children, and I would like somewhere to live, just somewhere that I'm not feeling that if I meet someone in the wrong mood around me I could be kicked out. That is what I want, that is all, I'm not asking for much. Maybe I would ask for a bit of help to maybe deal with and look into things that have gone on in my life.

Ian saw a lot of Gerry by virtue of him being based at the night shelter, but they also decided that there would be actual 'sessions' where Ian would sit with Gerry in private, without interruption, and start to work through his various issues.

The work undertaken is divided into different categories below. In reality, all proceeded in tandem, with the agenda for each session being set at the start of session. Some sessions would focus only on one of these major areas, but most looked at both substance use and mental health issues, separately but within the same session.

Drug and alcohol work

Initially, Gerry did not want to change any aspect of his substance use. However, after some time he began to accept that there might be some utility in having a methadone prescription to use instead of his illicit heroin. Helping Gerry to get to this stage took a long time. Motivators for his agreement included his lack of money, his desire not to return to prison, and his paranoia (although under check due to his anti-psychotic medication) about being caught with a dealer.

Ian supported Gerry initially by arranging his appointments at the prescribing clinic and accompanying him to them. Gerry now has the confidence to attend his appointments unaccompanied. He was initially put on an oral methadone prescription with daily supervised consumption at the clinic, moving to daily supervised consumption at a community pharmacist when he was deemed sufficiently stable.

Using a motivational interviewing approach (as did all the interactions between Ian and Gerry), Gerry's injecting behaviour was addressed next. Again, this order of priorities came from Gerry. His health check had revealed a number of infected abscesses, he was having great difficulty in finding veins which were sufficiently undamaged to inject into, and he was becoming aware that he was in danger of requiring an amputation of his leg if he continued. Gerry followed Ian's suggestion of gradually weaning himself off injecting as opposed to suddenly ceasing and, with the daily supervised methadone and many discussions with Ian over 'lapses', he successfully stopped injecting.

Work on Gerry's alcohol and cannabis use was much more difficult to start. Gerry was adamant initially that he did not wish to deal with either of these issues. However, as with the issues above, Ian found ways to open the discussion. With alcohol, the opening was provided by concerns about money, shoplifting, and returning to prison. With cannabis, concerns regarding psychotic symptoms provided the 'in'. Gerry trusted Ian sufficiently by that time to indulge in some experimentation, whereby he could see that his use of cannabis was related to an exacerbation of his symptoms.

Mental health work

Gerry had a number of major mental health problems. He was very paranoid (e.g. he had found it very difficult to have someone approach him from the side or from behind) and he suffered from severe anxiety and depression. Although his paranoia was initially quite well controlled by his medication, soon after his admission to the night shelter he developed pleurisy and was quite unwell, followed by recurring pain from abscesses on his leg. The combination of medications prescribed by his general practitioner to deal with these physical complaints increased Gerry's anxiety, associated agitation and paranoia and he became quite aggressive to others within the shelter. There was a very real danger that he would be asked to leave, even though it was clear if this happened it was almost certain that all the gains made thus far would be lost. Fortunately, his relationship with Ian was sufficiently strong by this time that Gerry was able to trust Ian to the extent of utilizing his suggestions of taking 'time out' when he felt defensively aggressive, and of asking staff for help at these times.

Ian worked with Gerry on these mental health symptoms using a number of psychosocial interventions (all covered in more detail in other chapters in this volume and in Velleman *et al.* 2007), including early symptom recognition and control, medication management, CBT work on unhelpful thoughts, thought stopping and control, and relapse prevention.

Housing work

Looking to resettle Gerry into more secure accommodation, Ian accompanied him to the housing department and helped him fill in a housing application form. Further support took the form of letters to the housing department explaining Gerry's vulnerability as a homeless man with mental health issues. Gerry and the project worker pursued his application regularly until eventually he was offered suitable accommodation.

The work with Gerry continued with help in accessing furniture for his new flat via a furniture donation service. Assistance was also given in helping

Gerry fill in a Community Care Grant form for essential items such as a fridge and a cooker. He received a £500 grant. Ian continued to support Gerry for the first few months of his tenancy, visiting him at home to ensure he was coping with the responsibilities associated with a tenancy.

The role of the past

Gerry had spent much of his first 16 years being moved from one institution to another. His father had had a severe alcohol problem and Gerry had become disruptive and difficult at a young age. His parents had found him difficult to cope with, and there were child protection concerns about domestic violence. He was repeatedly accommodated by social services with a variety of short-term foster carers, and then re-united with his mother (and often his father, when he was living in the family home). At 11 he was taken into care on a more permanent basis, where unfortunately the cycle of abuse and emotional neglect continued. He was placed in a series of children's homes, assessment centres, and secure units where his loneliness and depression became progressively worse, as did his behaviour. By the time he was 15 he was sniffing glue and stealing cars.

Gerry:　I was getting no help for the problems I was facing inside, I was very depressed, and I tried to take my life a couple of times. I was serious about it because I overdosed twice. I took them and went to bed, told no-one about it and then just got up in the morning the next day and it didn't bother me. I was just going crazy. I had this unbelievably horrible feeling, you know, anxiety. Powerful. When I'd get the anxiety and it would come on again I would break into cars, go for a drive. I did a lot of that.

His behaviour (and his underlying problems) continued to get worse. At 17 he was moved into a flat but found it impossible to cope and began staying on friends' floors and sleeping rough. His difficulties eventually led him to experience periods within both psychiatric services and prison. Gerry had received training as an electrician when institutionalized, but he had only worked infrequently in the trade. At one stage he entered into a long-term relationship and had two children, but this fell apart as his mental health deteriorated and his substance misuse increased, and he had not had any contact with his partner or children for a number of years. He had not had any contact with his family of origin since he was aged 16.

Ian spent some time with Gerry discussing these past experiences and started to help Gerry formulate some explanations for himself about why things had gone wrong in the past and how these were related to his current difficulties. It was clear that his failed family experiences, both as a child and then as an adult, weighed heavily on him, and Ian began exploring with Gerry whether he might want to try to re-make contact with either or both families, how he might do that, and what he would want to achieve by so doing.

Outcomes

At the time of writing, Gerry is still maintaining his tenancy and his mental health and substance misuse are now stable. He says that the work that Ian and others helped him with have given him 'a reason to get up in the morning'. The support that they provided has helped to ensure that he is happy and managing in his flat. He now volunteers at a related project set up to better engage people with multiple problems (homelessness, mental health issues, substance misuse, physical health concerns, serious debt, etc.). One of the things this project does is to take donations of unwanted furniture and household goods, restore them, and then give them to people on low income; it also restores antique furniture for a fee, generating funds for the project. Gerry is learning how to undertake each of these elements of the work. He has developed a lot of skills through volunteering and feels '100 per cent more confident'. Gerry is now thinking about topping up his electrician's training to take account of new regulations and starting work as an electrician. He has not yet made contact with either family, but is still actively considering this as a future possibility 'when I am a bit more sorted'.

CONCLUSION

Key factors in successfully helping Gerry

It can be seen from this case study that difficulties abound when trying to work with street homeless and vulnerable people, where statutory services are consistently over-subscribed. Clients such as Gerry are often so vulnerable that they are unable to wait for an appointment, especially once they have started the process of accepting help. They often want to start work on their other issues and problems immediately, and it becomes increasingly difficult for staff to keep up a client's morale and enthusiasm over a period of weeks or months of waiting for professional help.

Factors which eased the difficulties in this case include:

- There was liaison between Ian and other staff at the night shelter, the statutory drug and alcohol services, the statutory mental health services, primary care, community pharmacy provision, and the local authority housing department. This liaison has been strong and consistent, and has facilitated an effective multi-agency approach to service provision for Gerry.

- There was no need to refer Gerry on to other services. Having a designated 'dual disorder' worker located within the homelessness service ensured that a 'one-stop shop' could be offered, where all the therapeutic work could be undertaken by Ian, with him accessing support and training outside if needed.
- Ian received high quality and regular support and supervision from his line manager, who was a very experienced clinical psychologist in both substance misuse and mental health work.
- Ian had also received excellent training, and understood and could utilize a range of psychosocial interventions which are useful within both substance misuse and mental disorder contexts, including CBT, motivational interviewing, relapse management, medication management, etc.

Working with Gerry involved a very lengthy engagement period. Ian persevered even though Gerry was adamant that he was not interested in addressing his alcohol, tobacco, or other drug use, his injecting behaviour, his mental health issues, and his rough sleeping!

NOTES

1 Some of the text in this section is taken from the *Crisis: Homelessness* website and publications – see the 'Key Resources' section.
2 My health services organization (Avon and Wiltshire Mental Health Partnership NHS Trust) within the UK has decided to utilize this terminology for people with co-existing drug and alcohol and mental health problems.

KEY RESOURCES

Crane, M. and Warnes, A., *Wet Day Centres for Street Drinkers: A Research Report and Manual*. Sheffield: Sheffield Institute for Studies on Ageing (SISA), University of Sheffield, 2004. Available at http://www.kingsfund.org.uk/resources/publications/wet_day_centres.html (accessed 2 August 2005).

CRISIS, *CRISIS Fighting for Hope for Homeless People*. London: Crisis, 2005. Available at http://www.crisis.org.uk/ (accessed 1 August 2005).

Foord, M., Palmer, T. and Simpson, D., *Bricks without Mortar*. London: Crisis, 1998. Available at http://www.homelesspages.org.uk/subs/..%5cprods%5cproducts. asp?prid=243 (accessed 16 September 2005).

Fountain, J., Howes, S. and Baker, O., *Home and Dry? Homelessness and Substance Use in London*. London: Crisis, 2002. Available at http://www.crisis.org.uk/pdf/homeanddry.pdf (accessed 2 August 2005).

Gorton, S., *Guide to Models of Delivering Health Services to Homeless People*. London: Crisis, 2003. Available at http://www.crisis.org.uk/pdf/nhsmodels.pdf (accessed 2 August 2005).

Lownsbrough, H., *Include Me In: How Life Skills Help Homeless People Back into Work*. London: Demon and Crisis, 2005. Available at http://www.demos.co.uk/catalogue/includemein/ (accessed 2 August 2005).

Office of the Deputy Prime Minister, *Coming in from the Cold: The Government's Strategy on Rough Sleeping*. London: Office of the Deputy Prime Minister, 1999. Available at http://www.homelesspages.org.uk/index.asp (accessed 2 August 2005).

Office of the Deputy Prime Minister, *More than a Roof: A Report into Tackling Homelessness*. London: Office of the Deputy Prime Minister, 2002. Available at http://www.odpm.gov.uk/stellent/groups/odpm_homelessness/documents/sectionhomepage/odpm_homelessness_ page.hcsp (accessed 2 August 2005).

Office of the Deputy Prime Minister, *Homelessness*. London: Office of the Deputy Prime Minister, 2005. Available at http://www.odpm.gov.uk/stellent/groups/odpm_homelessness/documents/sectionhomepage/odpm_homelessness_page.hcsp (accessed 2 August 2005).

Social Exclusion Unit, *Social Exclusion Unit*. London: Office of the Deputy Prime Minister, 2005. Available at: http://www.socialexclusionunit.gov.uk/ (accessed 2 August 2005).

Stephens, J., *The Mental Health Needs of Homeless Young People*. London: The Mental Health Foundation, 2002. Available at http://www.mentalhealth.org.uk/html/content/homelessyp.pdf

Stone, E., *All About Homelessness*. London: Shelter, 2004. Available at http://www.homelesspages.org.uk/index.asp (accessed 2 August 2005).

Warnes, A., Crane, M., Whitehead N. and Fu, R., *The Homelessness Factfile*. London: Crisis, 2003. Available at http://www.crisis.org.uk/publications (accessed 2 August 2005).

Watson, P., ed., *Homelessness Pages*. London: Resource Information Service, 2003. Available at http://www.homelesspages.org.uk/index.asp (accessed 1 August 2005).

Zlonkiewicz, T. and Davis, J., *Multi-Agency Assessment Panels Toolkit: A Best Practice Manual*. London: Shelter, 2004.

Research on single homelessness

Fitzpatrick, S., Kemp, P. and Klinker, S., *Single Homelessness: An Overview of Research in Britain 1990–1999*. Bristol: Policy Press, 2000. Available at http://www.crashindex.org.uk/jr073.pdf (accessed 2 August 2005).

Klinker, S. and Fitzpatrick, S., *A Bibliography of Single Homelessness Research*. Bristol: Policy Press, 2000. Available at http://www.crashindex.org.uk/biblio.html (accessed 2 August 2005).

Sterling, R. and Fitzpatrick, S., *A Review of Single Homelessness Research: Research Summaries and Bibliography. Update: December 1999–December 2000*. London: CRASH, 2001. Available at http://www.jrf.org.uk/knowledge/findings/housing/pdf/410.pdf (accessed 2 August 2005).

Toolkits and good practice guides related to co-existing problems

Department of Health, *Dual Diagnosis Good Practice Guide*. London: HMSO, 2002. Available at http://www.dh.gov.uk/assetroot/04/06/04/35/04060435.pdf (accessed 2 August 2005).

Hawkins, C. and Gilburt, H., *Dual Diagnosis Toolkit: Mental Health and Substance Misuse*. London: Rethink and Turning Point, 2004. Available at http://www.rethink.org/dualdiagnosis/ (accessed 2 August 2005).

REFERENCES

Addington, J., Leriger, E. and Addington, D., 'Symptom outcome 1 year after admission to an early psychosis program', *Canadian Journal of Psychiatry*, *48*, 204–7, 2003.

Anglin, M., Hser, Y. and Grella, C., 'Drug addiction and treatment careers among clients in the Drug Abuse Treatment Outcome Study (DATOS)', *Psychology of Addictive Behaviours*, *11*, 308–23, 1997.

Belcher, J. and First, R., 'The homeless mentally ill: Barriers to effective service delivery', *Journal of Applied Social Sciences*, *12*, 62–78, 1988.

Birchwood, M. J., Smith, J., Cochrane, R., Wetton, S. and Copestak, S., 'The Social Functioning Scale: The development and validation of a new scale of social adjustment for use in family intervention programmes with schizophrenic patients', *British Journal of Psychiatry*, *157*, 853–9, 1990.

Birchwood, M. J., Spencer, E. and McGovern, D., 'Schizophrenia: Early warning signs', *Advances in Psychiatric Treatment*, *6*, 93–101, 2000.

Brown, J., 'The effectiveness of treatment', in Heather, N. and Stockwell, T., eds, *The Essential Handbook of Treatment and Prevention of Alcohol Problems*, pp. 9–20. Chichester: John Wiley, 2004.

Burns, T., 'The UK 700 trial of intensive case management: An overview and discussion', *World Psychiatry*, *1*, 175–8, 2002.

Copello, A., Orford, J., Hodgson, R., Tober, G. and Barrett, C., 'Social behaviour and network therapy: Basic principles and early experiences', *Addictive Behaviors*, *27*, 345–66, 2002.

Copello, A., Velleman, R. and Templeton, L., 'Family interventions in the treatment of alcohol and drug problems', *Drug and Alcohol Review*, *24*, 369–85, 2005.

Fakhoury, W., Murray, A., Shepherd, G. and Priebe, S., 'Research in supported housing', *Social Psychiatry and Psychiatric Epidemiology*, *37*, 301–15, 2002.

Farrell, M., Howes, S., Taylor, C., Lewis, G., Jenkins, R., Bebbington, P. *et al.*, 'Substance misuse and psychiatric comorbidity: An overview of the OPCS National Psychiatric Comorbidity Survey', *International Review of Psychiatry*, *15*, 43–9, 2003.

Fountain, J., Howes, S. and Baker, O., *Home and Dry? Homelessness and substance use in London*. London: Crisis, 2002. Available at http://www.crisis.org.uk/pdf/homeanddry.pdf (accessed 2 August 2005).

Geddes, J., 'Prevention of relapse in schizophrenia', *The New England Journal of Medicine*, *346*, 56–8, 2002.

Gill, B., Meltzer, H. and Hinds, K., 'The prevalence of psychiatric morbidity among homeless adults', *International Review of Psychiatry*, *15*, 134–40, 2003.

Gossop, M., Marsden, J., Stewart, D. and Kidd, T., 'The National Treatment Outcome Research Study (NTORS): 4–5 year follow-up results', *Addiction*, *98*, 291–303, 2003.

Gray, P. and Fraser, P., 'Housing and heroin use: The role of floating support', *Drugs: Education, Prevention and Policy*, *12*, 269–78, 2005.

Haracopos, A., Dennis, D., Turnbull, P., Parsons, J. and Hought, M., *On the Rocks: A Follow-up Study of Crack Users in London*. London, 2003.

Hodgson, R., Alwyn, T., John, B., Thom, E. and Smith, A., 'The FAST (Fast Alcohol Screening Test)', *Alcohol and Alcoholism*, *37*, 61–6, 2002.

Hubbard, R. L., Craddock, S. G., Flynn, P. M., Anderson, J. and Etheridge, R. M., 'Outcomes of one year follow up outcomes in the Drug Abuse Treatment Outcome Study (DATOS)', *Psychology of Addictive Behaviours*, *11*, 261–78, 1997.

Kershaw, A., Singleton, N. and Meltzer, H., 'Survey of the health and well-being of homeless people in Glasgow', *International Review of Psychiatry*, *15*, 141–3, 2003.

Killaspy, H., Ritchie, C., Greer, E. and Robertson, M., 'Treating the homeless mentally ill: Does designated inpatient facility improve outcome?' *Journal of Mental Health*, *13*, 593–9, 2004.

Kingdon, D. and Turkington, D., *Cognitive Behavioural Therapy of Schizophrenia*. New York: Guilford Press, 1994.

Lazarus, A., 'New techniques for behavior change', *Rational Living*, *6*, 1–13, 1971.

Lehman, A. F., Dixon, L. B., Hoch, J., DeForge, B., Kernan, E. and Frank, R., 'Cost-effectiveness of assertive community treatment for homeless persons with severe mental illness', *British Journal of Psychiatry*, *174*, 346–52, 1999.

Lehman, A. F., Dixon, L. B., Kernan, E., DeForge, B. and Postrado, L., 'A randomized trial of assertive community treatment for homeless persons with severe mental illness', *Archives of General Psychiatry*, *54*, 1938–43, 1997.

Marshall, M. and Lockwood, A., *Assertive Community Treatment for People with Severe Mental Disorders (Cochrane Review)*. The Cochrane Library, Issue 3. Oxford: Update Software, 2002.

McGorry, P. and Warner, R., 'Consensus on early intervention in schizophrenia', *Schizophrenia Bulletin*, *28*, 543–4, 2002.

Miller, A., Crimson, M., Rush, A. J., Chiles, J., Kashner, T. M., Toprac, M. *et al.*, 'The Texas Medication Algorithm Project: Clinical results for schizophrenia', *Schizophrenia Bulletin*, *30*, 627–47, 2004.

Miller, W. R. and Wilbourne, P. L., 'Mesa Grande: A methodological analysis of clinical trials of treatments for alcohol use disorders', *Addiction*, *97*, 265–77, 2002.

National Institute for Clinical Excellence, *Anxiety: Management of Anxiety (Panic Disorder, with or without Agoraphobia, and Generalised Anxiety Disorder) in Adults in Primary, Secondary and Community Care*. London: NICE, 2004a.

National Institute for Clinical Excellence, *Depression: Management of Depression in Primary and Secondary Care*. London: NICE, 2004b.

Nwakeze, P., Magura, S., Rosenblum, A. and Joseph, H., 'Homelessness, substance misuse, and access to public entitlements in a soup kitchen population', *Substance Use and Misuse Journal*, *38*, 645–68, 2003.

Owen, R., Thrush, C., Kirchner, J., Fischer, E. P. and Booth, B. M., 'Performance measurement for schizophrenia: Adherence to guidelines for antipsychotic dose', *International Journal of Quality in Health Care*, *12*, 475–82, 2000.

Pharoah, F. M., Rathbone, J., Mari, J. and Streiner, D., *Family Intervention for Schizophrenia (Cochrane Review)*. The Cochrane Library, Issue 2. Oxford: Update Software, 2003.

Priebe, S., Huxley, P., Knight, S. and Evans, S., 'Application and results of the Manchester Short Assessment of Quality of Life (MANSA)', *International Journal of Social Psychiatry*, *45*, 7–12, 1999.

Project MATCH Research Group, 'Matching alcoholism treatments to client heterogeneity: Project MATCH post-treatment drinking outcomes', *Journal of Studies on Alcohol*, *58*, 7–29, 1997.

Reed, P. and Klee, H., 'Young homeless people and service provision', *Health and Social Care in the Community*, *7*, 17–24, 1999.

Saunders, J. B., Aasland, O. G., Babor, T. F., de le Fuente, J. R. and Grant, M., 'Development of the Alcohol Use Disorders Identification Test (AUDIT): WHO collaborative project on early detection of persons with harmful alcohol consumption', *Addiction*, *88*, 791–804, 1993.

Segal, Z. V., Williams, J. M. G. and Teasdale, J. D., *Mindfulness-Based Cognitive Therapy for Depression: A New Approach to Preventing Relapse*. New York: Guilford Press, 2002.

Sobell, L. C. and Sobell, M. B., 'Timeline follow-back: A technique for assessing self-reported alcohol consumption', In Litten, R. and Allen, J., eds, *Measuring Alcohol Consumption: Psychosocial and Biochemical Methods*, pp. 41–72. Totoa, NJ: Humana Press, 1992.

Stein, L. and Santos, A., *Assertive Community Treatment of Persons with Severe Mental Illness*. New York: W. W. Norton, 1998.

Velleman, R., *Counselling for Alcohol Problems*, 2nd ed. London: Sage, 2001.

Velleman, R., Davis, E., Drage, M. and Smith, G., *Changing Outcomes in Psychosis: Collaborative Cases from Users, Carers, and Practitioners*. London: Blackwell, 2007.

Warnes, A., Crane, M., Whitehead, N. and Fu, R., *The Homelessness Factfile*. London: Crisis, 2003. Available at http://www.crisis.org.uk/publications (accessed 2 August 2005).

WHO ASSIST Working Group, 'The Alcohol, Smoking and Substance Involvement Screening Test (ASSIST): Development, reliability and feasibility', *Addiction*, *97*, 1183–94, 2002.

Williams, C. J., *Overcoming Depression: A Five Areas Approach*. London: Hodder Arnold, 2001.

Wincup, E., Buckland, G. and Bayliss, R., *Youth Homelessness and Substance Use: Report to the Drugs and Alcohol Research Unit*. Home Office research study 191. London: HMSO, 2003.

Chapter 11

Anxiety and drug and alcohol problems

Andrew Baillie and Claudia Sannibale

KEY POINTS

1 A period of abstinence or significantly reduced substance use is the first target of treatment for co-existing anxiety and substance use disorders. Motivational interviewing is the most useful intervention to achieve this target.
2 If anxiety persists after a period of abstinence or substantially reduced substance use, an integrated treatment should be provided. When substance use is circumscribed to phobic situations it is reasonable to target anxiety first.
3 Where the client cannot tolerate a trial of abstinence for four weeks, an intensive integrated treatment which teaches skills to reduce distress, while working towards reducing substance use, is indicated.
4 When treating clients with complex problems, the guiding principles remain flexibility, empathy and an individualized approach.

INTRODUCTION

Anxiety disorders and substance use disorders are among the most common mental disorders. Approximately one in five adults will experience a substance use disorder, predominantly with alcohol, in their lifetime, and one in ten will have experienced it in the past 12 months. Anxiety disorders affect approximately one in four people in their lifetime and one in six in the past 12 months (Andrews *et al.* 2001; Kessler *et al.* 1994; Regier *et al.* 1990).

Anxiety and substance use disorders frequently co-exist. Between 25 and 45 percent of people seeking treatment for alcohol use disorders have a current or past anxiety disorder. Conversely, between 15 and 25 percent of those seeking treatment for anxiety disorders have a current or past alcohol use disorder (Barlow 1997). Similar rates of co-existing anxiety and substance use disorders have been reported in epidemiological samples. One in three people with alcohol dependence and one in two people with other drug dependence have a co-existing anxiety disorder within the same 12-month period, and about one in five with anxiety disorders have a substance use disorder (Degenhardt *et al.* 2001; Kessler *et al.* 1996; Regier *et al.* 1990; Teesson *et al.* 2000). The co-existence of disorders means more severe problems that respond more slowly to treatment.

The focus of this chapter is on co-existing substance misuse and the anxiety disorders that most commonly present for treatment (panic disorder with and without agoraphobia, generalized anxiety disorder, social phobia or social anxiety disorder, and obsessive compulsive disorder (OCD)). Specific phobias are not covered as they are rarely the primary reason for seeking help. Co-existing post-traumatic stress disorder (PTSD) and substance use disorder have been covered by other authors (Coffey *et al.* 2005; Najavits 2001; Ouimette and Brown 2002). While the full range of substance misuse problems co-exist with anxiety disorders, we will focus on alcohol because it is more common in the literature and in our clinical experience.

Anxiety disorders can be precipitated by an aversive experience with substances (Barlow 1997). In these cases, where substance use has ceased, standard treatment for anxiety disorders is recommended.

The distinction between the emotion of anxiety and anxiety disorders (anxiety out of proportion to the situation faced) is important. Anxiety or increased autonomic arousal may be an effect of substance use (e.g. alcohol; Edwards *et al.* 2003) or a stress response to socioeconomic hardship and other chronic environmental difficulties. These difficulties and the anxious response can complicate the treatment of substance use disorders but they are unlikely to be improved by treatment for an anxiety disorder.

Our general approach

Motivational interviewing (MI; see Chapter 3) and cognitive behaviour therapy (CBT; see Chapter 4) underlie the present chapter. There is a growing body of randomized controlled trial evidence that supports the use of CBT in treating anxiety disorders (Abramowitz 1998; Fedoroff and Taylor 2001; Gould *et al.* 1995, 1997) and, to a lesser extent, substance use disorders (e.g. Monti *et al.* 2002; Project MATCH Research Group 1997, 1998).

Evidence from treatment outcome research

Six randomized controlled trials of treatment for co-existing anxiety and substance use disorders were identified from searches of PsycINFO, MEDLINE and Science Direct (Bowen *et al.* 2000; Fals-Stewart and Schafer 1992; Ormrod and Budd 1991; Otto *et al.* 1993; Randall *et al.* 2001; Toneatto 2005). These studies employed heterogeneous samples to compare different treatments for different combinations of anxiety and substance use disorders across a variety of settings. For those with more than moderate substance dependence there is remarkable consistency – standard treatment for substance use disorders leads to the best outcomes except in Fals-Stewart and Schafer (1992).

Randall *et al.* (2001) compared CBT for alcohol problems with CBT focusing on both alcohol problems and social phobia in a randomized controlled trial with people diagnosed with both alcohol dependence and social phobia. Treatment was manual-guided and provided individually in 12 weekly sessions. They report that three months after the completion of treatment those who received the dual treatment achieved significantly worse drinking outcomes but were not significantly different on social anxiety measures. They also reported no significant correlation between reductions in drinking and social anxiety measures, indicating that the processes of change for these two outcomes were unrelated. A lack of integration between the CBT for social phobia and CBT for alcohol, and resulting client confusion, may account for the lack of additional effects for additional anxiety treatment.

Ormrod and Budd (1991) compared a multi-component cognitive behavioural anxiety management program and a progressive muscle relaxation program with a health education control group for outpatients who screened positive for anxiety and alcohol problems. Both anxiety management and relaxation training reduced anxiety levels compared with the control, but there was no difference in drinking outcomes.

The best evidence for integrated treatment of anxiety and substance use comes from a randomized controlled trial of CBT in the discontinuation of benzodiazepine use (Otto *et al.* 1993). In this trial of 33 people who had been taking a benzodiazepine for panic disorder for six months or more, 13 of 17 (76 percent) who received group CBT in addition to a slow taper of benzodiazepines were abstinent compared to four of 16 (25 percent) who received the slow taper alone. The 10-week CBT intervention was an adaptation of Barlow and Craske's (1994) panic control therapy. A treatment manual is available (Otto *et al.* 1996a, 1996b). The participants in this trial had been taking benzodiazepines under medical supervision for a pre-existing anxiety disorder, and the severity of their dependence on benzodiazepines is unclear. So while the results of this trial are encouraging, they may not easily generalize to clients with co-existing anxiety and alcohol problems who use benzodiazepines outside medical supervision and/or in the context of other drugs, or who are more highly dependent on benzodiazepines. In the absence of other evidence, Otto *et al.*'s (1996a, 1996b) treatment manual remains a good starting point.

Fals-Stewart and Schafer (1992) report that adding three sessions of behaviour therapy for obsessive compulsive disorder to the usual program at a therapeutic community for substance use disorders led to better anxiety and substance use outcomes than the usual care in the therapeutic community or the usual care plus relaxation training. It is surprising that significant reductions in OCD (an otherwise chronic and difficult-to-treat disorder) could be achieved in as little as three sessions. While the authors describe the combination of therapeutic community and three sessions of behaviour therapy as 'integrated' we prefer the term 'concurrent' as there is no evidence in their paper that the behaviour therapy was integrated into the therapeutic community intervention. This strategy of providing concurrent intervention for co-existing disorders has not shown a benefit in terms of substance use outcomes in other trials.

Bowen *et al.* (2000) examined whether adding 12 hours of CBT for panic disorder to an existing inpatient treatment program targeting alcohol dependence influenced the drinking or anxiety outcomes of a group of people (CBT = 146; usual treatment = 85) with co-existing panic disorder (with or without agoraphobia) and alcohol dependence. There were no statistically significant differences between the groups on anxiety or drinking outcomes. The authors attributed the lack of treatment effect to resistance from other staff to introducing the program and the relatively brief nature of the CBT intervention. They also raise the possibility that the anxiety disorder experienced by people with co-existing substance use disorders may be different from the anxiety experienced by those who have no co-existing problems.

Toneatto (2005) compared a 10-session integrated cognitive therapy approach to co-existing alcohol dependence and agoraphobia with five sessions of alcohol-oriented behaviour therapy followed by five sessions of behaviour therapy targeting agoraphobia among 14 people. There were no statistically significant differences between integrated cognitive therapy and the sequential behaviour therapy. This study needs to be replicated with a larger sample and perhaps a 10-session behavioural treatment for alcohol as a comparison group. Broadly, this study could be seen as supporting our recommendation to treat substance dependence first.

CONTEXT OF THERAPY

Therapist variables

Empathy and a non-confrontational style of interaction in substance misuse treatment have been shown to be important therapist variables associated with better treatment outcome (Miller and Baca 1983; Miller *et al.* 1993). Such a therapist style has also been argued to be important in cognitive therapy for anxiety disorders (Wells 1997). It is important to distinguish empathy from sympathy, particularly when working with anxious clients who experience strong physical symptoms and seek emergency responses from health services. When they are told there is 'nothing wrong' with them it is common for them to feel misunderstood and frustrated. So it is important for the engagement of such clients to express empathy for their predicament ('You were certain you were about to die and then they said there was nothing wrong with you: how did you feel?'). Sympathy ('That must have been awful') runs the risk of partially validating their catastrophic fears about possible health concerns.

The structured nature of therapy sessions is a feature of CBT that has been related to positive outcomes in therapy for depression (Shaw *et al.* 1999). It may be that the structuring of therapy sessions helps clients to bring some order to their otherwise chaotic problems.

Client variables

Client motivation for change and for intervention is perhaps the single most important issue in the treatment of substance misuse. For example, client motivation and self-efficacy in Project MATCH were the most potent predictors of drinking outcome (DiClemente *et al.* 2003).

Clients may be willing to address some problems but not others. For example, many clients present using multiple substances (Shand and Mattick 2001) but they may be ready and willing to work on a single substance only. Likewise, many clients come to treatment with a belief that they can continue to use their substance. This may be unreasonable but in the interests of maintaining engagement in treatment we recommend working with the client's goals (although without colluding in their overestimation of the positive effects of use and their underestimation of the negative effects).

ASSESSMENT OF CO-EXISTING ANXIETY AND DRUG AND ALCOHOL PROBLEMS

Early meetings with the client have two aims: to find out about the client's problems and to engage or motivate them for change. The therapist's task is also to convey to the client that their distress has been heard, that their problems, at least in part, are understood and that there is hope of change. If this message is not conveyed successfully, the client may see no point in commencing or continuing therapy. We will assume that readers are familiar with active listening, reflection, Socratic questioning, periodic summaries and other counselling techniques that are used to convey to clients that they have been heard (see also Chapter 3).

The clinician needs to know why the client has presented at a treatment facility and what they want to achieve. Clients can come to therapy because of pressure from loved ones and/or the legal system. These triggers to presentation, which may be perceived as self-evident disadvantages to drinking, can be used to enhance the client's motivation for change through MI.

Our broad strategy is to recommend that multiple sources of information are used for assessment. The minimum is a clinical interview backed up with self-report measures; in some cases direct observation of target behaviour, reports from a significant other or biochemical measures may also be of use.

In addition to typical assessment, an assessment for integrated therapy of clients with co-existing conditions should include a thorough behavioural or functional assessment of recent instances of substance use and peaks of anxiety. Careful attention should be paid to the temporal sequence of triggers, beliefs, emotions and actions during these instances, as this forms the basis of a situation-level case formulation (Persons and Tompkins 1997). Because of difficulties with recalling information, it is often useful to ask the client to self-monitor their substance use and anxiety and its internal and external context. Some of these patterns may not become obvious until the acute effects of the substance have diminished.

When assessing anxiety experiences it is important to consider the physiological (physical sensations and symptoms), subjective (thoughts and emotions) and behavioural response systems. People with long histories of substance use have often experienced violence, perhaps because of their association with crime or because intoxication puts them at risk of violence. These experiences may lead to PTSD and a sensitive assessment can be required.

Assessment of substance use includes age at first use and first problem use, recency of current level of substance use, any periods of controlled substance use or abstinence and the circumstances surrounding those periods – when they happened, why they happened, how long they lasted and which events lead to relapse.

Some of the assessment questionnaires we commonly use are briefly outlined in the case study below (see Table 11.1).

TREATMENT OF CO-EXISTING ANXIETY AND DRUG AND ALCOHOL PROBLEMS

For co-existing anxiety and substance use disorders, we propose that if the client meets criteria for substance dependence the first target of treatment should be a period of abstinence or significantly reduced use. The suggested clinical pathway is shown in Figure 11.1. If there is a likelihood of moderate to serious withdrawal, clients could be referred to a general practitioner or an outpatient or residential detoxification service to assess and oversee withdrawal. The ASAM (American Society for Addiction Medicine 1991) criteria can assist with these decisions. The client's level of dependence, social supports during detoxification, previous history of withdrawal and beliefs that they will not be able to stop substance use without support, and the client's preferences, are all indicators of whether assistance will be needed during withdrawal.

Targeting substance use first makes clinical sense for several reasons. First,

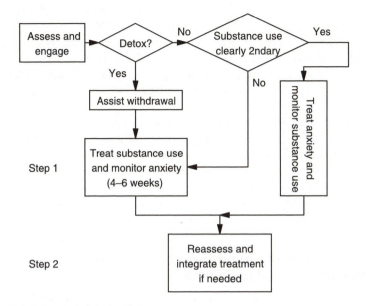

Figure 11.1 Suggested clinical pathway.

it assists the process of diagnosis and problem formulation by reducing the acute impact of substances or withdrawal on clinical presentation. Abstinence frequently improves the client's mood, anxiety, sleep, nutrition and general well-being. It also helps the client to mobilize their existing skills and resources, thereby contributing to increased confidence and self-efficacy. MI (Miller and Rollnick 2002) is a useful first step as it promotes engagement and mobilizes ambivalent clients effectively; it is supported by Project MATCH findings (Project MATCH Research Group 1997, 1998). Daily monitoring of urges, substance use, mood, anxiety, triggers and other contextual information provides important material for case formulation and intervention. Twelve-step groups may become useful for those people who are particularly isolated and may need daily reminders of their desire to change.

If the client continues to have anxiety problems after four to six weeks of abstinence or substantially reduced substance use (Schuckit and Monterio 1988; Scott *et al.* 1998), or if anxiety disorders emerge during this period, we recommend a comprehensive intervention which integrates techniques from evidence-based treatments for substance use and anxiety disorders based on an idiopathic case formulation. A Beckian-style cognitive therapy (e.g. Beck *et al.* 1993; Wells 1997) is easily integrated with MI and is empirically supported for anxiety disorders (Abramowitz 1998; Fedoroff and Taylor 2001; Gould *et al.* 1995, 1997). It also provides a framework to develop a case formulation that explains the maintenance of the client's problems (Persons and Tompkins 1997). However, this approach lacks clear empirical support over other therapies for substance use disorders in clinical trials (Crits-Christoph *et al.* 1999; Miller and Wilbourne 2002).

Only if substance dependence and consumption are relatively low, there is clear evidence that substance use is a safety behaviour, or that use is circumscribed to contact with phobic stimuli, and the anxiety disorder predates the substance use, would we recommend that treatment for anxiety disorders be the first step.

If the client does not accept or cannot tolerate a period of abstinence, or if a persistent anxiety disorder emerges during abstinence, they may require integrated treatment. Because there is little research to guide the clinician, we believe that careful assessment and an individual formulation of the factors that maintain the co-existing problems should be undertaken to guide treatment. In the following section we outline some of the mechanisms that may be maintaining factors.

Evidence about the maintenance of co-existing anxiety and alcohol problems

As clinical trial evidence is sparse and inconclusive we recommend that clinicians carefully assess each client and construct an idiopathic case formulation that hypothesizes processes that maintain the client's problems (Persons and Tompkins 1997). An individualized treatment plan that interferes with maintaining processes can then be devised. To assist the development of case formulations, we briefly review some of the processes that may maintain co-existing conditions.

Perhaps the most pervasive mechanism underlying co-existing anxiety and substance misuse is that both consumption of and withdrawal from the various psychoactive substances can increase anxiety and other negative emotional states. In contrast the widely-held belief that substance use continues because it reduces or 'self-medicates' anxiety (e.g. Khantzian 1985) is not well supported in the empirical literature (Greeley and Oei 1999).

Self-handicapping (Higgins and Harris 1988; Jones and Berglas 1978) refers to a self-serving bias by which self-esteem is protected following performance failures (and perceived negative evaluation): these failures are attributed to an external rather than internal cause ('It was the alcohol that made me do it'). Anxious clients tend to rely on almost superstitious strategies to control their anxiety. These safety behaviours are strategies which reduce the danger clients perceive themselves to be facing in the short term, but in the longer term increase their certainty that they do in fact face that threat (Kamphuis and Telch 1998; Salkovskis *et al.* 1999). Thus, a careful assessment of what the client does to control their anxiety, and what they believe it is doing, can also be useful in understanding why a client remains anxious.

Impairments in cognitive functioning may help to maintain substance use and anxiety by decreasing awareness and/or salience of longer-term consequences. Thus, the client may find it more difficult to balance the salient short-term effects of substance use against the longer-term consequences.

For those with co-existing anxiety and substance use disorders, unhelpful thoughts can range from unreasonably low estimates of ability to resist urges and cravings to the more familiar low confidence in ability to change and/or the successfulness of treatment. The clinician should be alert to all of these as they can undermine motivation and inhibit change. In addition, the beliefs that are proposed to be at the centre of anxiety disorders (e.g. 'I will die/go crazy/lose control of myself/be unable to cope/make a fool of myself') are likely to be present.

Some clients with anxiety disorders are highly motivated to seek treatment, particularly when they believe their anxiety places them in imminent physical or mental danger. Others may be shy and believe that their problems are character flaws ('It's just the way I am') and hence tend not to seek treatment. It is useful to find out the beliefs that are behind a seeming lack of motivation. Some clients may also lack the specific social skills (ability and/or confidence) required to interact successfully with others and to refuse substances when offered.

Anxiety sensitivity (AS) refers to a trait like perturbation with physical manifestations of anxiety. While it is clear that AS is related to anxiety disorders, Stewart et al. (1999) conclude that there is likely to be a two-way relationship between AS and substance misuse: AS may predispose towards and promote substance use (as a strategy to avoid feared sensations) while continued substance use may maintain AS. There is some evidence that the link between AS and substance use may be stronger for women.

Hierarchy of target behaviours

Sometimes the client's problems seem too complex for the therapist to see a clear starting point for therapy. In these instances we have found Linehan's (1993) hierarchies of target behaviours in outpatient therapy for borderline personality disorder to be a useful heuristic (see also Chapter 16). Linehan recommends giving priority to suicidal behaviours and therapy-interfering behaviours and quality of life-interfering behaviours, and then increasing behavioural skills. Client motivation can drive therapy-interfering behaviours and so is an early priority. Both MI (Miller and Rollnick 2002) and the early stages of Beck's cognitive therapy for depression (Beck et al. 1979; see also chapter 12), which focuses on activating immobile and withdrawn clients, can provide some assistance.

CASE STUDY

The following case material has been constructed from the file notes of a number of our clients and identifying information has been removed to protect confidentiality.

Pat was a 44-year-old single mother of two who worked as a part-time sales assistant. She presented for help with her drinking to an outpatient drug and alcohol service on a friend's recommendation. Pat drank about seven standard drinks of wine per day and up to 14 on weekends twice a month. Her preferred goal was 'a drink with friends on social occasions'. Liver function tests were normal. She felt embarrassed about drinking and tried to hide it from her children and friends and minimize it to the therapist. Pat's ex-husband was a heavy drinker who was at times verbally abusive. During their relationship Pat's drinking increased to current levels. The relationship was relatively short-lived – after the birth of their second daughter they separated.

Before presenting for treatment she was prescribed antidepressants by her general practitioner but did not complete a full course. She had had no previous treatment for drinking.

Pat reported lifelong anxiety attacks and said she drank because it helped her relax, especially in social situations. Her drinking, anxiety and dysphoria had worsened 18 months before, when her grandmother, with whom she was living, passed away. Since then, Pat had moved house several times, was struggling with finances, and had frequent arguments with her ex-husband over maintenance payments. These stressors increased the likelihood of panic attacks. Pat's attacks involved sweats, difficulty breathing, burning in her stomach, hot/cold flushes, tingling in her fingers and body, a feeling of unreality, dizziness and fear of losing control. These attacks were unexpected and happened in a variety of situations. She feared their recurrence but did not avoid situations for fear of an attack. Pat was most concerned that she would lose control of her mind and be unable to care for herself and her daughters. She also worried about her financial problems, her social isolation and loneliness. She felt trapped, hopeless about the future and guilty about 'being a bad parent'. She was frequently tearful, found it difficult to get out of bed in the morning, seemed to have lost enjoyment of her normal activities and fell asleep after drinking at night. Her weight and appetite were normal and, although she had some transient suicidal thoughts, there was no specific plan or intention.

Pat's results from various questionnaires are summarized in Table 11.1. These measures indicate severe anxiety and depression, severe impairment in day-to-day functioning and low alcohol dependence, but substantial alcohol cravings and low self-efficacy for abstinence.

Pat was diagnosed with mild alcohol dependence, major depressive episode (possibly secondary to alcohol) and panic disorder without agoraphobia: a formulation is summarized in Table 11.2.

Table 11.1 Summary of Pat's baseline questionnaire scores

Measure	Raw score	Scaled score	Brief interpretation
Depression Anxiety Stress Scales 21 item (Lovibond and Lovibond 1993)		(a)	
Depression subscale	22	2.3	Severe
Anxiety subscale	18	2.7	Severe
Stress subscale	24	1.8	Moderate
12-item Short Form Health Questionnaire (Ware *et al.* 1995)		(b)	
Mental component summary score		33.0	Severe
Physical component summary score		60.4	Above average
Alcohol Dependence Scale (Skinner and Horn 1984)	9		Low
Penn Alcohol Craving Scale (Flannery *et al.* 1999)	23		High
Alcohol Abstinence Self-efficacy Scale (DiClemente *et al.* 1994)	30		Low

Notes: (a) Scaled as z scores with mean 0 and standard deviation 1; (b) Scaled as T scores with mean 50 and standard deviation 10.

In addition to the treatment described below, Pat reluctantly began a course of antidepressant medication and diazepam to assist with withdrawal.

Sessions 1–2: Assessment and engagement

During the early stages of Pat's treatment, the therapist's principal focus was on monitoring her depression and withdrawal, and achieving a period of abstinence. Pat's experiences were described in normalizing terms, so that she could see the relationship between financial pressures and conflict with her ex-husband and her anxiety and substance use as understandable, but unhelpful, reactions. As her distress subsided, educational material was used to help Pat understand her panic attacks and reduce her fear of their consequences.

Pat's reasons for wanting to reduce her drinking were elicited using MI and Socratic questioning. She described drinking as 'comforting', as time to herself and time when she did not worry. On the other hand, she disliked drinking alone, falling asleep in her chair after drinking, missing meals, going to bed in the early hours of the morning, going to work late and leaving her daughters to fend for themselves. Although Pat's goal was controlled drinking, a period of abstinence was negotiated to achieve a more rapid improvement in mood, anxiety and general well-being. Pat agreed to abstain in the short term. (Her preferred goal of reduced drinking was reasonable

Table 11.2 Outline of case formulation for Pat

Identifying information	Pat, 44-year-old female
Problem list	1 Harmful alcohol consumption (seven standard drinks/day) 2 Depressed mood (DASS depression score of 22) 3 Low activity level – staying in bed until 11am on four or five week days 4 Panic attacks (four per day) 5 Financial pressures and worry about these 6 Verbal abuse from ex-husband 7 Difficulty finding suitable accommodation
Core beliefs	I can't cope Anxiety will overwhelm me and I'll lose control of myself and end up dependent on others for my daily needs I'll be unable to care for my daughters and I'll be a bad mother Drinking reduces my anxiety
Precipitants and activating situations	
1 Case-level precipitants	Relationship with ex-husband Financial pressure of being single mother Death of grandmother
2 Situation-level activating situations	Verbal abuse from ex-husband Awareness of sensations of unreality and disorientation Reminders of chronic financial and housing problems
Working hypothesis	Use of alcohol – believed to reduce worries and give a rest from troubles – instead reduces time for productive problem-solving and otherwise reduces capacity to solve problems, and increases anxiety and depression Hopelessness about situation leads to withdrawal and reduction in active problem-solving, leading to chronic financial and housing problems which in turn increase hopelessness and belief in inability to cope Hyper-vigilance for sensations consistent with losing control (unreality and disorientation) leading to beliefs of loss of control and hence panic attacks; these attacks in turn increase belief in inability to cope
Origins	High trait anxiety, perhaps anxiety sensitivity, but otherwise unclear

Treatment plan

1 Goals	Reduce drinking to less than three standard drinks on social occasions Improve mood Reduce panic attacks
2 Interventions	1 Reduce depressed mood with antidepressants 2 Increase active problem-solving with structured problem-solving, which will in turn provide evidence that can cope 3 Monitor withdrawal symptoms 4 Substitute slow breathing technique for alcohol when feeling overwhelmed 5 Psycho-education about anxiety and panic attacks, and thought challenging to reduce belief in inability to cope and that will lose control of mind
Predicted obstacles to treatment	Likely that ex-husband will continue verbal abuse during inevitable contact relating to care of children Severity of cravings and low confidence in ability to resist them

given her mild alcohol dependence.) She was asked to keep a daily diary of her mood, the number of drinks she consumed, her craving for alcohol and her experiences of panic and anxiety.

By the second week, Pat reported having reduced her drinking rather than withdrawing from alcohol altogether: she was now drinking three to four standard drinks per day, and was satisfied with this achievement. Without jeopardizing this early mastery, Pat was reminded that continued drinking could slow down her improvement and that it may be unsafe to drink while taking antidepressant medication. However Pat gently insisted on a drinking goal of three drinks per day with two alcohol-free days per week. The therapist accepted this goal to maintain engagement without agreeing with her inflated beliefs about the benefits of drinking.

Sessions 3–5: Psycho-education and anxiety management

Pat completed a daily diary which revealed that she was having four moderately intense panic attacks per day, each lasting between 15 seconds and two minutes, either when working alone at home or when with others. The attacks usually began with feelings of unreality and disorientation and were followed by feeling unsteady, dizzy or faint, with a racing and pounding heart, trembling, shaking and fear of losing control. When with others, Pat's attacks were more intense and lasted longer, because she felt embarrassed, went 'blank' and feared that people thought she was 'weird'. Fear of negative evaluation was secondary to Pat's main concern that she would lose control of her mind and be unable to care for herself and her daughters. When alone, attacks were triggered by thoughts about her inability to cope, entrapment and hopelessness.

Pat was given some psycho-educational material which defined anxiety and panic attacks, and explained the 'fight or flight' response, the sympathetic nervous system and the cognitive, behavioural and physiological components of anxiety and their interaction (Baillie and Rapee 2001; Craske and Barlow 2001). Her attacks usually began with an awareness of increasing sensations of unreality and disorientation. On one occasion when she was with other people, when she began to feel unreal she thought that they could see what she was experiencing and would think that she was 'weird'. This increased her fear and anxiety, which focused her attention more on her bodily sensations, thus enhancing them, which in turn made her more worried about 'making a total fool' of herself. Pat then escaped to the bathroom (when at home she would pour herself a drink) and tried to calm down. On another occasion, when she was alone, a panic attack was triggered by sensations of unreality and she thought that she was losing her mind. The meaning of this thought, using the downward arrow technique, was found to be that ultimately she would 'lose her mind completely (and irreversibly) and have to be admitted to a nursing home'. The therapist worked with Pat to devise her own cognitive model of panic using this example (Clark 1999).

Pat was taught a slow breathing technique to increase her confidence that she could resist strong cravings for alcohol. Slow breathing has become less widely used in cognitive therapy for anxiety disorders (Baillie and Rapee 2001; Clark 1999; Wells 1997), but it remains a useful alternative for those who use substances to control unwanted emotions.

Sessions 6–9: Cognitive restructuring

Over the following four sessions, Pat's mood continued to improve. At times she was still tearful and anxious and felt hopeless about the future, but crucially she was less certain that she would lose control of her mind in a panic attack. Her panic attacks became fewer, shorter and less frightening. She was practising slow breathing and finding it helpful.

She had been able to maintain her drinking at three to four drinks a day and had introduced two alcohol-free days per week. Her cravings were still moderate but manageable. She was more alert and able to grasp new concepts. However Pat was not monitoring her drinking and tended to change the subject when it was raised. The therapist reflected this back to Pat, which led to a discussion about her embarrassment about drinking. Pat was introduced to more formal thought challenging. The antecedents, beliefs and consequences (ABC) model, the relationship between thoughts, feelings and actions, and erroneous or unhelpful thoughts were reiterated. Challenging unhelpful thoughts and developing counter-statements was demonstrated in session. She was given a form to use to record 'dysfunctional' thoughts. The belief that she could lose control of her mind in the panic cycle was reviewed with examples from her recent episodes of anxiety. Pat estimated that she had had over 1,000 panic attacks and yet had not lost control of her mind.

Pat was also introduced to problem-solving strategies to address her day-to-day problems (parenting, dealing with an abusive ex-husband, problems at work and finding suitable accommodation).

Sessions 10–12: Dealing with lapses

Following a spate of unpleasant exchanges with her ex-husband, Pat became more stressed. She returned to drinking seven standard drinks per day, with no abstinent days. She felt 'very down most of the time', but had stopped taking her antidepressants because she believed they reduced her control over her mind. Her catastrophic beliefs had somewhat altered to a fear that not coping with stress would lead to her losing control of her mind. Her medical practitioner suggested a different antidepressant but reiterated that abstinence would do more to improve her mood. Through three weeks of relapse Pat attended every appointment and applied herself to addressing her immediate concerns. This was noted and reflected back to Pat.

The circumstances leading to this relapse were carefully analysed, leading to a greater realization that her drinking did affect her anxiety, mood and ability to think her way through problems. Her drinking reduced to five standard drinks per day with two abstinent days.

Sessions 13–16: Cognitive restructuring

The focus of this phase of treatment was improving recognition of unhelpful cognitions, challenging them and replacing them with more functional statements. Pat still practised the slow breathing exercises and problem-solving strategies. In treatment sessions, Pat learned that all her panic attacks occurred in the context of cognitive distortions (i.e. 'mind-reading' in social settings, 'all or nothing' thinking, 'shoulds' and 'fortune-telling'). She developed skills to deal with panic attacks in social situations (e.g. challenging her beliefs about how obvious her attacks were to others and having coping statements ready). Panic attacks were reduced to between one and two a day, with lower intensity and fear. However, Pat did not complete her 'take home tasks'. This potentially therapy-interfering behaviour may have indicated low self-mastery and was discussed with Pat.

Mood was now moderate to good most days, and Pat's drinking reduced to three standard drinks per day with two alcohol-free days. Pat was becoming more positive in her outlook, had introduced exercise twice a week and scheduled time for herself when her daughters were with their father. Pat dealt better with her day-to-day demands, which in turn increased her confidence and sense of mastery. She learned more self-protecting ways of interacting with her ex-husband and sought legal advice.

Maintenance

Pat continued to participate in therapy for 12 months, during which time there were many stressful life events, lapses to heavier drinking and episodes of low mood and anxiety. Her drinking stabilized to two to three standard drinks per day with two alcohol-free days. Her Depression and Anxiety Stress Scales scores (DASS; Lovibond and Lovibond 1993) were now within the normal range and her general mental health functioning (SF12-MCS; Ware et al. 1995) was in the mild range.

Pat's case illustrates how engagement is enhanced when there is flexibility about substance use goals, lapses are dealt with and information gained through therapy is used to refine the formulation. There was no breakthrough, but a slow and sustained improvement in all areas of functioning.

CONCLUSION

In the absence of strong evidence from clinical trials, we suggest that substance use be targeted as the first step, using MI. If this is insufficient, we recommend careful assessment to develop a case formulation and individual treatment plan with integrated treatment of anxiety and substance use.

KEY RESOURCES

Beck, A. T., Wright, F. D., Newman, C. F. and Liese, B. S., *Cognitive Therapy of Substance Abuse*. New York: Guilford Press, 1993.

Bishop, F. M., *Managing Addictions: Cognitive, Emotive, and Behavioural Techniques*. New York: Jason Aronson Inc., 2001.

Linehan, M. M., *Cognitive-Behavioral Treatment of Borderline Personality Disorder*. New York: Guilford Press, 1993.

Otto, M. W., Jones, J. C., Barlow, D. H. and Craske, M. G., *Stopping Anxiety Medication: Panic Control Therapy for Benzodiazepine Discontinuation, Therapist Guide*. New York: Oxford University Press, 1996.

Cognitive therapy

Andrews, G., Creamer, M., Crino, R., Hunt, C., Lampe, L. and Page, A., *The Treatment of Anxiety Disorders: Clinician's Guide and Patient Manuals*, 2nd ed. New York: Cambridge University Press, 2002.

Baillie, A. and Rapee, R., 'Panic and agoraphobia', in Hersen, M. and Porzelius, L. K., eds, *Diagnosis, Conceptualisation, and Treatment Planning for Adults: A Textbook*, pp. 113–32. Mahwah: Lawrence Erlbaum Associates, 2001.

Wells, A., *Cognitive Therapy of Anxiety Disorders: A Practice and Conceptual Guide*. Chichester: John Wiley, 1997.

Treatment of substance use disorders

Higgins, R. L., Budney, A. J. and Sigmon, S. C., 'Cocaine dependence', in Barlow, D. H., ed., *Clinical Handbook of Psychological Disorders*, 3rd ed, pp. 434–69. New York: Guilford Press, 2001.

McCrady, B. S., 'Alcohol use disorders', in Barlow, D. H., ed., *Clinical Handbook of Psychological Disorders*, 3rd ed, pp. 376–433. New York: Guilford Press, 2001.

Miller, W. R. and Rollnick, S., *Motivational Interviewing: Preparing People for Change*, 2nd ed. New York: Guilford Press, 2002.

Monti, P. E., Kadden, R. M., Rohsenow, D. J., Abrams, D. B. and Cooney, N. L., *Treating Alcohol Dependence: A Coping Skills Training Guide*, 2nd ed. New York: Guilford Press, 2002.

Websites

Carroll, K. M., *A Cognitive-Behavioral Approach: Treating Cocaine Addiction*. National Institute on Drug Abuse, 1998. Available at http://www.drugabuse.gov/txmanuals/cbt/cbt1.html (accessed 16 September 2005).

Miller, W. R., *Motivational Enhancement Therapy with Drug Abusers*. The University of New Mexico, 1995. Available at http://motivationalinterview.org/clinical/metdrugabuse.pdf (accessed 16 September 2005).

REFERENCES

Abramowitz, J. S., 'Does cognitive-behavioral therapy cure obsessive-compulsive disorder? A meta-analytic evaluation of clinical significance', *Behavior Therapy*, *29*, 339–55, 1998.

American Society for Addiction Medicine, *Patient Placement Criteria for the Treatment of Psychoactive Substance Use Disorders*. Washington: American Society for Addiction Medicine, 1991.

Andrews, G., Henderson, S. and Hall, W., 'Overview of the Australian national mental health survey', *British Journal of Psychiatry*, *178*, 145–53, 2001.

Baillie, A. and Rapee, R., 'Panic and agoraphobia', in Hersen, M. and Porzelius, L. K. eds, *Diagnosis, Conceptualisation, and Treatment Planning for Adults: A Textbook*, pp. 113–32. Mahwah: Lawrence Erlbaum Associates, 2001.

Barlow, D. H., 'Anxiety disorders, comorbid substance abuse, and benzodiazepine discontinuation: Implications for treatment', in Onken, L. S., Blaine, J. D., Genser, S. and Horton, A. M. J., eds, *Treatment of Drug-dependent Individuals with Comorbid Mental Disorders* (NIDA Research Monograph 172), pp. 33–50. Rockville: National Institute on Drug Abuse, 1997.

Barlow, D. H. and Craske, M. G., *Mastery of Anxiety and Panic – II*. Albany: Graywind Publications, 1994.

Beck, A. T., Rush, A. J., Shaw, B. F. and Emery, G., *Cognitive Therapy for Depression*. New York: Guilford Press, 1979.

Beck, A. T., Wright, F. D., Newman, C. F. and Liese, B. S., *Cognitive Therapy of Substance Abuse*. New York: Guilford Press, 1993.

Bowen, R. C., D'Arcy, C., Keegan, D. and Senthilselvan, A., 'A controlled trial of cognitive behavioral treatment of panic in alcoholic inpatients with comorbid panic disorder', *Addictive Behaviors*, *25*, 593–7, 2000.

Clark, D. M., 'Anxiety disorders: Why they persist and how to treat them', *Behaviour Research and Therapy*, *37*, S5–27, 1999.

Coffey, S. F., Schumacher, J. A., Brimo, M. L. and Brady, K. T., 'Exposure therapy for substance abusers with PTSD: Translating research into practice', *Behavior Modification*, *29*, 10–38, 2005.

Craske, M. G. and Barlow, D. H., 'Panic disorder and agoraphobia', in Barlow, D. H., ed., *Clinical Handbook of Psychological Disorders*, 3rd ed, pp. 1–59. New York: Guilford Press, 2001.

Crits-Christoph, P., Siqueland, L., Blaine, J. D., Frank, A., Luborsky, L., Onken, L. S. *et al.*, 'Psychosocial treatments for cocaine dependence: National Institute on Drug Abuse collaborative cocaine treatment study', *Archives of General Psychiatry*, *56*, 493–502, 1999.

Degenhardt, L., Hall, W. and Lynskey, M., 'Alcohol, cannabis and tobacco use among Australians: A comparison of their associations with other drug use and use disorders, affective and anxiety disorders, and psychosis', *Addiction*, *96*, 1603–14, 2001.

DiClemente, C. C., Carbonari, J., Montgomery, R. and Hughes, S., 'The Alcohol Abstinence Self-Efficacy Scale', *Journal of Studies on Alcohol*, *55*, 141–8, 1994.

DiClemente, C. C., Carroll, K. M., Miller, W. R., Connors, G. J. and Donovan, D. M., 'A look inside treatment: Therapist effects, the therapeutic alliance, and the process of intentional behaviour change', in Babor, T. F., and DelBoca, F. K., eds, *Treatment Matching in Alcoholism*, pp. 166–83. Cambridge: Cambridge University Press, 2003.

Edwards, G., Marshall, E. J. and Cook, C. C. H., *The Treatment of Drinking Problems: A Guide for the Helping Professions*, 4th ed. Cambridge: Cambridge University Press, 2003.

Fals-Stewart, W. and Schafer, J., 'The treatment of substance abusers diagnosed with obsessive-compulsive disorder: An outcome study', *Journal of Substance Abuse Treatment*, *9*, 365–70, 1992.

Fedoroff, I. C. and Taylor, S., 'Psychological and pharmacological treatments of social phobia: A meta-analysis', *Journal of Clinical Psychopharmacology*, *21*, 311–24, 2001.

Flannery, B., Volpicelli, J. and Pettinati, H., 'Psychometric properties of the Penn Alcohol Craving Scale', *Alcoholism: Clinical and Experimental Research*, *23*, 1289–95, 1999.

Gould, R. A., Otto, M. W. and Pollack, M. H., 'A meta-analysis of treatment outcome for panic disorder', *Clinical Psychology Review*, *15*, 819–44, 1995.

Gould, R. A., Otto, M. W., Pollack, M. H. and Yap, L., 'Cognitive behavioral and pharmacological treatment of generalized anxiety disorder: A preliminary meta-analysis', *Behavior Therapy*, *28*, 285–305, 1997.

Greeley, J. and Oei, T., 'Alcohol and tension reduction', in Leonard, K. E. and Blane, H. T., eds, *Psychological Theories of Drinking and Alcoholism. The Guilford Substance Abuse Series*, 2nd ed, pp. 14–53. New York: Guilford Press, 1999.

Higgins, R. L. and Harris, R. N., 'Strategic "alcohol" use: Drinking to self-handicap', *Journal of Social and Clinical Psychology*, 6, 191–202, 1988.

Jones, E. E. and Berglas, S., 'Control of attributions about the self through self-handicapping strategies: The appeal of alcohol and the role of underachievement', *Personality and Social Psychology Bulletin*, 4, 200–6, 1978.

Kamphuis, J. H. and Telch, M. J., 'Assessment of strategies to manage or avoid perceived threats among panic disorder patients: The Texas Safety Manoeuvre Scale (TSMS)', *Clinical Psychology and Psychotherapy*, 5, 177–86, 1998.

Kessler, R. C., McGonagle, K. A., Zhao, S., Nelson, C. B., Hughes, M., Eshleman, S. et al., 'Lifetime and 12-month prevalence of DSM-III-R psychiatric disorders in the United States: Results of the national comorbidity survey', *Archives of General Psychiatry*, 51, 8–19, 1994.

Kessler, R. C., Nelson, C. B., McGonagle, K. A., Edlund, M. J., Frank, R. G. and Leaf, P. J., 'The epidemiology of co-occurring addictive and mental disorders: Implications for prevention and service utilisation', *American Journal of Orthopsychiatry*, 66, 17–31, 1996.

Khantzian, E. J., 'The self-medication hypothesis of addictive disorders: Focus on heroin and cocaine dependence', *American Journal of Psychiatry*, 142, 1259–64, 1985.

Linehan, M. M., *Cognitive-Behavioral Treatment of Borderline Personality Disorder*. New York: Guilford Press, 1993.

Lovibond, S. H. and Lovibond, P. F., *Manual for the Depression, Anxiety and Stress Scales (DASS)*. Sydney: Psychology Foundation Monograph, 1993.

Miller, W. R. and Baca, L. M., 'Two-year follow-up of bibliotherapy and therapist directed controlled drinking training for problem drinkers', *Behavior Therapy*, 14, 441–8, 1983.

Miller, W. R., Benefield, R. G. and Tonigan, J. S., 'Enhancing motivation for change in problem drinking: A controlled comparison of two therapist styles', *Journal of Consulting and Clinical Psychology*, 61, 455–61, 1993.

Miller, W. R. and Rollnick, S., *Motivational Interviewing: Preparing People for Change*, 2nd ed. New York: Guilford Press, 2002.

Miller, W. and Wilbourne, P., 'Mesa Grande: A methodological analysis of clinical trials of treatments for alcohol use disorders', *Addiction*, 97, 265–77, 2002.

Monti, P. E., Kadden, R. M., Rohsenow, D. J., Abrams, D. B. and Cooney, N. L., *Treating Alcohol Dependence: A Coping Skills Training Guide*, 2nd ed. New York: Guilford Press, 2002.

Najavits, L. M., *Seeking Safety: A Treatment Manual for PTSD and Substance Abuse*. New York: Guilford Press, 2001.

Ormrod, J. and Budd, R., 'A comparison of two treatment interventions aimed at lowering anxiety levels and alcohol consumption amongst alcohol abusers', *Drug and Alcohol Dependence*, 27, 233–43, 1991.

Otto, M. W., Jones, J. C., Barlow, D. H. and Craske, M. G., *Stopping Anxiety Medication: Panic Control Therapy for Benzodiazepine Discontinuation, Therapist Guide*. New York: Oxford University Press, 1996a.

Otto, M. W., Pollack, M. H. and Barlow, D. H., *Stopping Anxiety Medication: Panic*

Control Therapy for Benzodiazepine Discontinuation, Patient Workbook. Albany: Graywind, 1996b.

Otto, M. W., Pollack, M. H., Sachs, G. S., Reiter, S. R., Meltzer-Brody, S. and Rosenbaum, J. F., 'Discontinuation of benzodiazepine treatment: Efficacy of cognitive-behavioral therapy for patients with panic disorder', *American Journal of Psychiatry, 150*, 1485–90, 1993.

Ouimette, P. C. and Brown, P., *Trauma and Substance Abuse: Causes, Consequences, and Treatment of Comorbid Disorders.* Washington: American Psychological Association, 2002.

Persons, J. B. and Tompkins, M. A., 'Cognitive-behavioural case formulation', in Eells, T. D., ed., *Handbook of Psychotherapy Case Formulation*, pp. 314–39. New York: Guilford Press, 1997.

Project MATCH Research Group, 'Matching alcoholism treatments to client heterogeneity: Project MATCH post-treatment drinking outcomes', *Journal of Studies on Alcohol, 58*, 7–29, 1997.

Project MATCH Research Group, 'Matching alcoholism treatments to client heterogeneity: Project MATCH three-year drinking outcomes', *Alcoholism: Clinical and Experimental Research, 22*, 1300–11, 1998.

Randall, C. L., Thomas, S. and Thevos, A. K., 'Concurrent alcoholism and social anxiety disorder: A first step toward developing effective treatments', *Alcoholism: Clinical and Experimental Research, 25*, 210–20, 2001.

Regier, D. A., Farmer, M. F., Rae, D. S., Locke, B. Z., Keith, S. J., Judd, L. L. and Goodwin, F. K., 'Comorbidity of mental disorders with alcohol and other drug abuse: Results from the epidemiologic catchment area (ECA) study', *The Journal of the American Medical Association, 264*, 2511–18, 1990.

Salkovskis, P. M., Clark, D. M., Hackmann, A., Wells, A. and Gelder, M. G., 'An experimental investigation of the role of safety-seeking behaviours in the maintenance of panic disorder with agoraphobia', *Behaviour Research and Therapy, 37*, 559–74, 1999.

Schuckit, M. A. and Monterio, M. G., 'Alcoholism, anxiety and depression', *British Journal of Addiction, 83*, 1373–80, 1988.

Scott, J., Gilvarry, E. and Farrell, M., 'Managing anxiety and depression in alcohol and drug dependence', *Addictive Behaviors, 23*, 919–31, 1998.

Shand, F. L. and Mattick, R. P., *Clients of Treatment Service Agencies: May 2001 Census Findings* (National Drug Strategy Monograph No. 47). Canberra: Commonwealth Department of Health and Ageing, 2001.

Shaw, B. F., Elkin, I., Yamaguchi, J., Olmstead, M., Vallis, T. M., Dobson, K. *et al.*, 'Therapist competence ratings in relation to clinical outcome in cognitive therapy of depression', *Journal of Consulting and Clinical Psychology, 67*, 837–46, 1999.

Skinner, H. A. and Horn, J. L., *Alcohol Dependence Scale: Users Guide.* Toronto: Addiction Research Foundation, 1984.

Stewart, S. H., Samoluk, S. B. and MacDonald, A. B., 'Anxiety sensitivity and substance use and abuse', In Taylor, S., ed., *Anxiety Sensitivity: Theory, Research, and Treatment of the Fear of Anxiety*, pp. 287–319. Mahwah: Lawrence Erlbaum Associates, 1999.

Teesson, M., Hall, W., Lynskey, M. and Degenhardt, L., 'Alcohol and drug use disorders in Australia: Implications of the national survey of mental health and well being', *Australia and New Zealand Journal of Psychiatry, 34*, 206–13, 2000.

Toneatto, T., 'Cognitive versus behavioral treatment of concurrent alcohol dependence and agoraphobia: A pilot study', *Addictive Behaviors*, *30*, 115–25, 2005.

Ware, J. E., Kosinski, M. and Keller, S. D., *SF-12: How to Score the SF-12 Physical and Mental Health Summary Scales*. Boston: The Health Institute, 1995.

Wells, A., *Cognitive Therapy of Anxiety Disorders: A Practice and Conceptual Guide*. Chichester: John Wiley, 1997.

Chapter 12

Depression and drug and alcohol problems

Frances J. Kay-Lambkin, Amanda Baker and Vaughan J. Carr

KEY POINTS

1 Depression and co-existing substance use problems present a unique set of complications for treatment providers and individuals experiencing these conditions.
2 Treatment has typically been based on the temporal relationship between the depressive and substance use disorders. However, there are practical difficulties in reliably diagnosing primary and secondary conditions. This often means that treatment is suspended pending a firm diagnosis.
3 Recently, researchers have suggested that a better approach is to focus on the distress and symptoms associated with depression and co-existing alcohol/other drug use problems, rather than on diagnostic categories. This potentially facilitates earlier entry into treatment.
4 Comprehensive screening for and assessment of the symptoms and distress of co-existing depression and substance use problems are essential to effective treatment planning and delivery. Specific approaches are described within this chapter.
5 Several pharmacological and non-pharmacological treatment approaches can be readily incorporated into a treatment plan that focuses on both depressive symptoms and problematic substance use, most notably case formulation, motivational enhancement and cognitive behaviour therapy. These approaches, as they apply to depression and co-existing substance use problems, are described.

INTRODUCTION

Co-existing depression and drug and alcohol problems are associated with premature treatment dropout, more frequent relapses and subsequent treatment for substance dependence if left unaddressed (Brown *et al.* 1997). Although various environmental, genetic and neurobiological factors are involved in depression and drug and alcohol problems occurring separately, the mechanisms underlying these conditions as they co-occur are not well understood (Volkow 2004). While determining the aetiology of these problems arguably impacts on the course of the conditions and optimal treatment approaches (Pettinati 2004), others have suggested that the primary/secondary distinction is immaterial once depression and alcohol/other drug use have surfaced (Powell *et al.* 1992). Indeed, the primary/secondary distinction, at least for alcohol use problems and depression, is not predictive of treatment outcomes (e.g. Hasin *et al.* 1996), and indeed the relationship between drug and alcohol use and depression may change over time (e.g. Crum *et al.* 2001).

Schuckit and colleagues suggest that the focus of treatment should be on the impairment and distress caused by symptoms, as opposed to diagnostic subtype, classification or model of aetiology (Schuckit *et al.* 1997). Westermeyer (2003) has proposed that treatment can commence even when clients continue to use drugs/alcohol and can proceed when a clear or formal diagnosis has not been established.

The complex nature of co-existing mental health and drug and alcohol problems suggests it is likely that a range of treatment strategies will be needed to assist clients in meeting their goals (Kavanagh *et al.* 2003). Moreover, the treatment program used for one person may not necessarily be the optimal combination of strategies to use with another (Kavanagh *et al.* 2003). Kay-Lambkin *et al.* (2004b) have recently reviewed the evidence for motivational and cognitive behaviour therapy (CBT) programs for co-existing mental health and substance use problems and noted that depression improves among a proportion of people following only minimal intervention for the drug or alcohol problem. In addition, CBT for problematic drug use can also significantly improve depression, at least for some people in the short-term. However, many still report clinical levels of depression even following intervention for problematic drug use. As such, a stepped care approach to intervention, as described in Chapter 1, may be more appropriate for this population (Kay-Lambkin *et al.* 2004b). Recommendations for stepped care approaches to treatment have been made for depression (Scogin *et al.* 2003); anxiety (Baillie and Rapee 2003); alcohol problems (Sobell and Sobell 2000); smoking (Smith *et al.* 2003) and in the treatment of heroin dependence with methadone maintenance (King *et al.* 2002).

Within a stepped care framework, all clients would be screened for both depression and alcohol/other drug use, provided with further assessment if indicated, and regularly monitored over time. Depending on the results of assessment, and considering the history of the problems and their severity, the therapist may implement a brief intervention for one or other of the problems (e.g. motivational intervention for hazardous drinking, psychoeducation for depression) and monitor outcome across several domains of change. Alternatively, the therapist may implement an integrated treatment (e.g. CBT for co-existing depression and regular cannabis use), targeting co-existing problems simultaneously with a more intensive treatment.

CONTEXT OF THERAPY

Therapist variables

Therapists may not be able to identify from the outset which clients have a depression that will persist beyond abstinence from substances (Schuckit *et al.* 1997) and they should not base treatment on primary/secondary models. Therapists should be trained in the assessment of risk for suicide and feel confident in assessing and monitoring suicide risk in all clients presenting with depression. Regular clinical supervision or peer review is recommended for therapists using the psychotherapy skills described in this chapter, and should especially be available following cases of attempted or completed suicide.

Client variables

As epidemiological studies suggest possible under-reporting of affective states in men and substance use in women, screening for both conditions in every presentation is important (Andrews *et al.* 2001). In addition, screening for other co-existing problems such as anxiety, personality and medical problems, and occupational and lifestyle difficulties, is recommended as these are common among this client group (Brown *et al.* 1995). As depression induces feelings of fatigue, loss of energy, problems with decision-making and concentration and an inability to enjoy activities, motivational enhancement (see Chapter 3) and assertive strategies such as following up missed appointments or flexible appointment scheduling may improve treatment attendance (Herman *et al.* 2004).

ASSESSMENT

Chapter 2 describes the general processes involved in the detection of mental health and drug and alcohol problems. In addition to these processes, the following procedures may be useful.

Assessing depressive symptoms via clinical interview

According to the *Diagnostic and Statistical Manual of the Mental Disorders* (DSM-IV-TR) the key features of a depressive disorder are (APA 2000):

*   low mood for most of the day, nearly every day; and/or
*   loss of interest or pleasure in almost all activities.

In addition, several of the following symptoms may also be present (APA 2000):

- significant weight change (loss or gain of more than five per cent body weight in one month);
- changes in sleep;
- feelings of restlessness or feeling slowed down in movements;
- fatigue or loss of energy;
- feelings of worthlessness or excessive/inappropriate guilt;
- problems with thinking, concentrating and/or decision-making; and
- recurrent thoughts of death and/or suicidal thoughts/behaviours.

These symptoms should be sought and discussed where present to identify characteristics such as frequency, intensity, duration and degree of distress. Clinical assessment may be supplemented with appropriate questionnaires (see below) to measure the severity of symptoms at baseline and to monitor the progress of treatment. Diagnosis of major depressive disorder should only be made by a suitably qualified therapist.

The age at, and context of, the first experience of depressive symptoms, and similarly the occasions of subsequent episodes, should also be established. This will provide important insights into the client's high-risk situations for relapse and also help to establish the temporal relationship between the first appearance of depression and the onset of problematic drug and alcohol use.

All clients presenting with depression should be screened for suicide risk, using the questions listed in Table 12.1 as a guide. Each clinical service should have a suicide risk assessment and intervention policy in place, to which therapists are expected to adhere. In general, if a client expresses the intent to take their life in the near future and/or has a defined plan of suicide, the assessment should cease and crisis intervention should immediately be arranged.

Questionnaires measuring severity of depression

Evidence for the reliability and validity of screening for mental health problems among people with drug and alcohol problems is sparse. Myrick and Brady (2003) suggest that the overlap between symptoms, particularly between depression and withdrawal from substances, makes the conditions difficult to disentangle. Several self-report instruments are available for use among people who may be experiencing both depression and drug and alcohol use problems.

The Beck Depression Inventory (second edition, BDI-II; Beck et al. 1996) is a 21-item questionnaire that has been validated among adult and adolescent populations (Beck et al. 1996), and widely used among people with drug and alcohol problems (Dawe et al. 2002). Beck et al. (2000) developed a

Table 12.1 Questions for assessing suicide risk, adapted from the Treatment Protocol Project (TPP 2000)

Previous attempts

1 Have you ever tried to harm yourself in the past? If so, how long ago?

2 What were the circumstances? [Prompt: what did the person do, how lethal was the attempt, what was the outcome?]

3 Have you tried to harm yourself more than once? [Prompt: dates and any help received]

Suicidal thoughts and plans

1 Recently, what specifically have you thought of doing to yourself?

2 Have you taken any steps toward doing this (e.g. getting pills/buying a gun)?

3 Have you thought about when and where you would do this?

4 Have you made any plans for your possessions or left any instructions for people for after your death, such as a note or a will?

Mental health concerns

1 Have you been feeling depressed for several days at a time?

2 When you feel this way, have you ever had thoughts of killing yourself?

3 When did these thoughts occur?

4 What did you think you might do to yourself?

5 Did you act on these thoughts in any way?

6 How often do these thoughts occur?

7 When was the last time you had these thoughts?

8 Have your thoughts ever included harming someone else as well as yourself?

Protective factors

1 Have you thought about the effect your death would have on your family and friends?

2 What has stopped you from acting on your thoughts so far?

3 What are your thoughts about staying alive?

4 What help could make it easier to cope with your problems at the moment?

5 How does talking about all of this make you feel?

---

seven-item version, the BDI-Fast Screen, which excludes the somatic symptoms of depression on the BDI-II that may overlap with substance use and/or withdrawal symptoms. As such, the BDI-Fast Screen may provide a more accurate view of depressive symptoms among this population.

The 20-item Centre for Epidemiologic Studies Depression Scale–Revised (CESDR; Eaton *et al.* 2003) provides the therapist with a probability that the respondent meets DSM-IV criteria for major depressive disorder. A major advantage of the CESDR is the minimal symptom overlap with other confounding medical and substance use conditions. The CESDR has successfully identified depressive disorder among people with drug and alcohol use disorders. However, detection rates may be better among alcohol users than among users of other substances (Eaton *et al.* 2003).

History of drug and alcohol problems and possible association with depressive symptoms

A brief discussion about patterns of drug and alcohol use over the client's lifetime will yield relevant information about progression to regular use, heaviest use, previous periods of abstinence or reduced use and situations that led to slips and relapses. A timeline corresponding to the history of depression may provide insights into the relationship between drug use and the development and maintenance of depressive symptoms, and vice versa. If the person does not volunteer information about substance use, ask the following: 'Can you tell me where your drinking/using/smoking fits in?' Explore the person's beliefs about their use in the following way: 'How does your use of [substances] affect your mood?' This information will be invaluable in arriving at a case formulation that addresses the co-existing problems.

More detailed assessment via self-report questionnaires may be useful, as described in Chapter 2, and should include drugs used problematically in the past and present, including nicotine. Table 12.2 lists the drug types commonly used by clients, and can be used as a guide when screening for the use of specific substances. Substances currently being used (i.e. within the past month) may be a focus for treatment.

In addition, the following instruments are useful in examining the quantity, frequency and severity of alcohol/other drug use: the Opiate Treatment Index (OTI; Darke *et al.* 1991), the Alcohol Use Disorders Identification Test (AUDIT; Saunders *et al.* 1993), the Fagerstrom Test for Nicotine Dependence (Heatherton *et al.* 1991), the Cannabis Use Disorders Identification Test (CUDIT; Adamson and Sellman 2003), the Severity of Dependence Scale (SDS; Gossop *et al.* 1995) and the Readiness to Change Scale (Rollnick *et al.* 1992).

Assessment of multiple domains

Clients with co-existing depression and substance use problems often experience deficits in multiple areas, and therapists should therefore consider the relevance of measures of functioning, quality of life, anxiety, personality disorder and general health in their assessment. These additional problems may influence the client's ability to attend appointments and the scope of the treatment plan. Information about previous treatments for depression and drug and alcohol use will give the therapist insight into previous successes and potential obstacles to treatment. Medication adherence, if applicable, should also be assessed and discussed with the client.

Table 12.2 Drug and alcohol use screen

Drug class	Ever used?	When was the last time you used?
Tobacco	❑ Yes ❑ No	❑ Past week ❑ Past month ❑ <12 months ❑ >12 months ❑ Never
Caffeine	❑ Yes ❑ No	❑ Past week ❑ Past month ❑ <12 months ❑ >12 months ❑ Never
Alcohol	❑ Yes ❑ No	❑ Past week ❑ Past month ❑ <12 months ❑ >12 months ❑ Never
Cannabis	❑ Yes ❑ No	❑ Past week ❑ Past month ❑ <12 months ❑ >12 months ❑ Never
Ecstasy	❑ Yes ❑ No	❑ Past week ❑ Past month ❑ <12 months ❑ >12 months ❑ Never
Other party drugs	❑ Yes ❑ No	❑ Past week ❑ Past month ❑ <12 months ❑ >12 months ❑ Never
Heroin	❑ Yes ❑ No	❑ Past week ❑ Past month ❑ <12 months ❑ >12 months ❑ Never
Other Opiates	❑ Yes ❑ No	❑ Past week ❑ Past month ❑ <12 months ❑ >12 months ❑ Never
Amphetamines	❑ Yes ❑ No	❑ Past week ❑ Past month ❑ <12 months ❑ >12 months ❑ Never
Cocaine	❑ Yes ❑ No	❑ Past week ❑ Past month ❑ <12 months ❑ >12 months ❑ Never
'Crack'	❑ Yes ❑ No	❑ Past week ❑ Past month ❑ <12 months ❑ >12 months ❑ Never
Tranquillizers	❑ Yes ❑ No	❑ Past week ❑ Past month ❑ <12 months ❑ >12 months ❑ Never
Barbiturates	❑ Yes ❑ No	❑ Past week ❑ Past month ❑ <12 months ❑ >12 months ❑ Never
Hallucinogens	❑ Yes ❑ No	❑ Past week ❑ Past month ❑ <12 months ❑ >12 months ❑ Never
Inhalants	❑ Yes ❑ No	❑ Past week ❑ Past month ❑ <12 months ❑ >12 months ❑ Never

TREATMENT

There is a paucity of research examining the use of pharmacotherapy among people with co-existing depression and drug and alcohol problems (Pettinati 2004). In the few studies that have compared active medication to placebo among this group, psychological treatment, most notably CBT, has always been provided across treatment conditions (Kosten and Kosten 2004). Although pharmacotherapy may be considered at any point within a stepped care framework, it is usually reserved for severe symptoms and/or in the withdrawal phase of substance use treatment (APA 1995; Shand *et al.* 2003). Should clients be non-responsive to psychological treatment, their suitability for medication should be assessed. As with all medication, pharmacotherapy is most successful when people are motivated to change and willing to comply with the medication regime. As such, psychological therapies can continue to be beneficial in this phase of treatment to encourage compliance and commitment to the treatment plan. To guide therapist decision-making, Kosten and Kosten (2004) suggest that a medication regimen should aim to treat the depression effectively, provide some relief for withdrawal symptoms, prevent relapse to substances, have a low abuse potential, have a low dose frequency and have minimal side effects to maximize compliance.

Pharmacotherapy for substance dependence has been well researched for three drug types – alcohol, opiates and nicotine – but not among large samples of people presenting with major depression. Given that the focus of this book is on psychological treatments, readers are referred to the following recent papers on the pharmacological management of co-existing depression and alcohol dependence (Shand *et al.* 2003), cocaine dependence (Rounsaville 2004), opiate dependence (Nunes *et al.* 2004) and nicotine dependence (Wilhelm *et al.* 2003). These preliminary studies may guide the therapist's decision-making.

Carroll (2004) has reviewed the evidence for the psychological treatments that have been developed/adapted for people with co-existing depression and drug and alcohol problems. While few well-controlled clinical studies exist, the evidence suggests that motivational interviewing can improve treatment engagement and that CBT is associated with moderate but durable effects on depressive symptoms and drug and alcohol use (Carroll 2004).

The following section describes motivational interviewing and CBT treatment strategies offered within an integrated approach to treatment, where both depression and drug and alcohol treatment strategies are introduced to the client simultaneously. Such an approach permits exploration of the relationship between the two conditions and builds on this with the simultaneous application of CBT strategies for both problems. Preliminary results using a manualized version of this approach are promising (Kay-Lambkin *et al.* 2002, 2004a). Integration occurs from the outset with assessment and continues through the phases of treatment.

The therapist can select from the strategies described here and tailor an individual treatment plan for the client based on a detailed case formulation (see Chapter 4) and the time and resources available. Chapter 4 also describes many CBT strategies that may be employed among this population. The strategies described here illustrate ways in which therapists may skilfully integrate approaches to improve depression and influence the behaviours and cognitions associated with drug and alcohol problems. Chapter 8 describes the application of this treatment to young people with co-existing depression and drug and alcohol problems.

Early sessions: setting the scene for change

Initially, therapy focuses on symptom relief, building rapport and engagement with the therapeutic process and enhancing motivation to change. Therapists may also need to seek additional support for the client by making appropriate mental health (e.g. crisis team support for suicidality) or drug and alcohol referrals (e.g. detoxification in the case of severe alcohol dependence, maintenance pharmacotherapy for opiate dependence) and addressing other crises (e.g. homelessness).

In the early stages of CBT the focus of therapy should be on behavioural activities and restoring client functioning to appropriate levels, including symptom relief (Beck *et al.* 1979; Lewis 2004). This includes increasing the client's daily activity levels and self-monitoring of mood fluctuations and drug and alcohol use. For many clients, the act of self-monitoring will result in some improvement in both of these domains, and will permit better understanding of the cognitive-based strategies introduced in later sessions.

Increasing activity levels (behavioural activation)

When people are depressed it is rare for them to recall participation in enjoyable activities (Beck *et al.* 1979). It is very important that clients continue to give themselves opportunities for rewarding experience, even if initially this is just for the purposes of distraction and increase in physical activity. This is the first step in recovery from low mood and a lack of energy and motivation.

People with co-existing drug and alcohol problems often narrow their behavioural repertoire to activities associated with drinking or using drugs. As such, they tend to over-emphasize the importance of using or drinking in their day. An activity schedule broadens the selection of activities in which they can be involved. Creating a diary of activities, identifying enjoyment and achievement tasks and planning time for these activities to occur should be the focus of the first few sessions.

Self-monitoring

Monitoring mood fluctuations and drug and alcohol use on a daily basis is an important early step in helping the client to recognize the associations between their mood and drug and alcohol use. It also addresses negative thoughts and feelings, including those that lead to using. Monitoring helps the client to identify the situations in which thoughts/feelings/cravings occur. In particular, clients need to pay close attention to those times of the day when they are feeling at their worst, or experiencing the strongest urges to drink or use drugs, and also those times when they are feeling at their best.

Once the client has grown accustomed to self-monitoring, the therapist can expand this activity and introduce the cognitive strategies outlined below in the later sessions of therapy. Clients can continue to monitor levels of depression and drug and alcohol use, at least on a weekly basis.

Setting goals

Any discussion about modifying drug and alcohol use in these early stages is likely to provoke some resistance and defensiveness from the client. As such, motivation enhancement strategies (see Chapter 3) are integral to treatment sessions. Ideally, the client will recognize that their depression and drug and alcohol use can be addressed simultaneously, with individualized goals established for these and other problems.

Later sessions: enhancing ability to change

Once the client has experienced some symptom relief, and/or has expressed a desire to work on their substance use, therapists can incorporate more cognitively-focused strategies to supplement those already learned. Such strategies include cognitive restructuring, mindfulness meditation, problem-solving, coping with cravings, improving communication skills and planning for emergencies (all described in Chapter 4). These can be introduced as needed over the course of therapy.

Cognitive strategies

When demonstrating the cognitive model, the 'ABCs' (see Chapter 4) are best illustrated separately for depression (when irrational thinking has led to negative mood) and drug/alcohol use (when irrational thinking unrelated to mood has led to drinking or drug use), and also combined (when negative mood has led to cravings or drug use has been followed by negative mood). The client is asked to describe their reaction in personal examples of each of these situations.

When monitoring ABCs, the client uses a monitoring form as in single-focus CBT but also describes the feelings or symptoms experienced (e.g. craving in response to negative mood or negative mood following a binge) and their resultant behaviours (e.g. whether they used, continued to drink, went for a walk, tried to 'switch off', etc.). Clients then identify patterns of problematic thinking and challenge negative automatic thought patterns and schemas (see Chapter 4).

Mindfulness meditation

Negative thoughts are automatically triggered whenever clients are depressed, often without any awareness that this has occurred (Beck et al. 1979). When people are caught up in this automatic, negative mode, additional situations will trigger additional negative thoughts about the past and the future. As Segal et al. (2002) explain, this 'mind wandering' allows negative thoughts/feelings to run through the client's mind, feeding a depressed mood and locking them in a cycle of feeling bad and craving substances to help them cope. However, by learning how to step out of 'automatic pilot' clients can learn to break this cycle.

Mindfulness teaches people to pay attention in a particular way to what is happening in the present moment, without judgement (Segal et al. 2002). This is in contrast to the usual patterns of thinking characterized by judgements and evaluations (e.g. 'Am I doing well enough?' 'Is my mood better today?' 'I think I'm feeling worse today, it's happening again'). Such thoughts/worries/ judgements consume time and energy and keep feeding into the cycle of depression and substance use (Segal *et al.* 2002).

For a full description of mindfulness strategies as they apply to cognitive therapy for depression, readers are referred to *Mindfulness-based Cognitive Therapy for Depression: A New Approach to Preventing Relapse* (Segal *et al.* 2002). However, in general, mindfulness meditation involves a deliberate focus on the physical sensations associated with everyday, routine activities that are often carried out on 'automatic pilot'. Such activities include walking, eating, breathing etc. Clients practising mindfulness meditation are asked to carry out these routine activities with a renewed focus on all the small sensations that make up that activity.

For example, in mindful walking practice (Segal *et al.* 2002), clients practise walking like it is the first time they have ever walked, focusing first on the soles of their feet, noticing what it feels like where their feet and ground make contact. Next, clients shift their weight onto their right foot, noticing the change in physical sensations in their legs and feet as their left leg 'empties' of weight and their right leg takes over support for the body (Segal *et al.* 2002). Clients then go through the process of taking a first step, and noticing all the changes in sensations that occur with that movement. Then, they practise mindful walking using many steps, keeping their focus on the sensations associated with walking that they would not normally attend to.

As described in Chapter 4, various other strategies may be helpful to the individual, including strategies for coping with cravings and enhanced problem-solving and communication skills.

Maintaining change

The final sessions should focus on anticipating situations in the future that pose risks to the client in terms of relapsing into depression and/or problematic drug and alcohol use. This can help increase their self-efficacy about how to cope in these high-risk situations, perhaps circumventing a relapse in the process (Wilson 1992). Part of preventing a relapse to depression and/or drug and alcohol use is for clients gradually to learn ways to take care of themselves. They need to learn that despite a busy schedule, it is essential to prioritize activities that they enjoy, as well as those which provide a sense of achievement (Segal *et al.* 2002). A discussion of the following will prepare the client well for coping with the daily pace of life:

- What am I doing in my daily life that I enjoy or that gives me a sense of achievement?
- How can I make sure that I continue to do these things or become more aware of them?

- What am I doing in my daily life (or what have I done before) that drains my energy and lowers my mood?
- How can I make sure that these activities are done less often?

Clients will benefit from developing a relapse management/prevention plan in advance of problematic situations, as it is much easier to recognize warning signs while mood and substance use is stable (Segal *et al.* 2002). The key elements that make up a relapse prevention plan are: anticipating difficult situations; regulating thoughts and feelings ('What might be an unreasonable thought in response to a lapse?' 'What can I do to deal more effectively with this situation?'); identifying necessary support; and regulating consequences ('How will I know that I am maintaining my behaviour/thoughts?' 'How can I reward myself for a job well done?').

CASE STUDY

Kel is a 26-year-old man who was referred to a community-based drug and alcohol service from a university counselling service. He self-referred to the university counselling service asking for special consideration for the upcoming examination period, following a distressing relationship breakdown with his girlfriend of six months, who stipulated she would not consider resuming the relationship until Kel stopped using cannabis. The university therapist agreed to provide the requested special consideration letter for Kel and referred him to the drug and alcohol service.

Assessment

Kel attended the drug and alcohol service for an assessment looking slightly dishevelled and unshaven, and in a dirty T-shirt. He presented as a shy person, and was clearly embarrassed about the appointment. A therapist commenced a general assessment of his current drug and alcohol use, mental health, general quality of life etc.

The main aim of the therapist's first session with Kel was to build rapport and engage him with the service. This was somewhat difficult as Kel was resistant to the idea that his cannabis use was a problem, and resented the referral to the service. After spending the first few minutes introducing herself, and discussing the nature of Kel's referral, the therapist commenced an assessment of other areas of Kel's life that were causing him distress. They discussed his low mood and feelings of inadequacy that had been present for a couple of months. Kel completed the BDI-II and scored in the moderate range (score = 25). When the therapist totalled the BDI-II-Fast Screen items, Kel still scored in the moderate range (score = 8), indicating his symptoms were probably related to a depressive condition. In particular, Kel endorsed the following items on the BDI-II: sadness, pessimism, past failure, guilt, self-dislike, worthlessness and loss of interest in other people and activities. He had no current thoughts of suicide. Kel had not previously received an assessment or treatment for depression or any other mental health problem. He admitted that his feelings had existed for some time prior to the relationship breakdown ('probably back at school . . . I dunno . . . maybe since I was about 14 or so').

After this discussion, the therapist had a reasonable idea of the type of symptoms currently worrying Kel, and so commenced a drug and alcohol assessment as follows:

Therapist: Well, it really does sound like things are pretty tough for you at the moment, Kel, and maybe they've been that way for some time now. What sorts of things help you cope with all this stress?

Kel: I dunno. . . . I just keep to myself, really, try to deal with it myself.

Therapist: What sorts of things help you deal with it yourself?

Kel: I used to play soccer with a group of mates, you know, a Uni team, but I've stopped that now.

Therapist: Any reasons for stopping?

Kel: Oh, I just didn't fit in, really. And I was unfit – couldn't keep up with the game . . . didn't want to let the team down.

Therapist: So, you were feeling like you didn't belong and had begun to question your physical condition. . . . I wonder, did the cannabis use fit in here?

Kel: Well, it didn't, my team mates didn't touch it and I was smoking more and getting more unfit . . .

Therapist: So, smoking began to change from an occasional thing to something that set you apart from your team mates and affected your fitness . . . and being fit had previously been helpful in dealing with stress.

Kel: Yeah, I guess so, but lots of other mates use it . . .

Therapist: So, on one hand, some of your mates use cannabis and on the other, your team mates don't and you feel like you don't belong with them anymore and also feel really unfit . . .

Kel: Yeah . . . kinda . . . yeah.

Therapist: I'd like to talk with you more about how you handle stress and how the cannabis use has changed over time . . . also how your mood has also changed. . . . I'd like to see whether we might make some sense from these changes, to see if they are linked in any way . . .

The drug and alcohol use inventory of the OTI indicated that Kel was currently using tobacco, caffeine, alcohol and cannabis, with the occasional ecstasy tablet taken at parties. Tobacco, caffeine and cannabis were used in the few days prior to assessment, and alcohol had been used in the previous month.

Kel revealed a steady increase in his use of cannabis from his first smoke at age 14 through to regular daily use. His level of use varied between 10 and 20 units per day, depending on whether he was alone or at a party/with friends.

Kel completed the SDS and the Readiness to Change Scale for cannabis use. The results indicated dependence on cannabis and placed him in the contemplation stage of change for his cannabis use. Further discussion about Kel's cannabis use indicated his primary reasons for use were to forget worries, to improve self-confidence, to relax and to help with his moods/feelings.

Given Kel's admission that he believed smoking cannabis relieved his low mood, the therapist decided to explore his beliefs about the relationship between his symptoms of depression and his use of cannabis and summarized thus:

Therapist: So there's kind of a cycle going on then. . . . You feeling pretty low or bored . . . then using pot to cope with those feelings . . . but then sometimes that adds to your low mood the next day . . . so perhaps you feel like you need pot even more for a break.

Throughout the discussion, Kel mentioned additional problems with finances, as he felt unable to hold down a job, and particularly guilty for relying on his parents to support him. He still lived at home with his parents who 'constantly tell me to move out and get a life . . . like my brother.' He reported being compared to his 'perfect' older brother and feeling inadequate in the outcome of that comparison. This depleted his energy and motivation further.

The therapist concluded the assessment session with Kel. She decided at this point that it was premature to provide educational material on cannabis use or depression at the risk of affecting engagement. The therapist formally terminated the session and Kel agreed to attend another session the following week to receive some feedback from the therapist's assessment.

Treatment

The initial session

Having processed the information collected from the assessment, Kel's therapist developed a formulation that focused on Kel's current symptoms of depression, his use of cannabis and how they interrelate. Given that Kel had been regularly smoking cannabis at high levels over the previous six-month period, in which he also reported several symptoms of a major depressive episode, it was difficult for the therapist to determine whether Kel met the criteria for a primary depressive condition. As such, the specific aims of this session were:

- to provide Kel with feedback from the assessment, including the impressions gained about his depressive symptoms and cannabis use;
- to share the draft case formulation with Kel, and work together to develop a comprehensive problem list and working hypothesis of how his current situation came about; and
- to decide on an appropriate course of treatment, including the establishment of some initial goals for change.

Kel's therapist began the session in a non-threatening way, talking through the main problems she identified from the assessment that relate to Kel's current distress, as opposed to discussing diagnoses of abuse, dependence and/or major depressive disorder. To facilitate this process, Kel's therapist prepared a case formulation sheet (see Table 12.3) listing these main problems.

The therapist provided advice on Kel's current levels of cannabis use, and explained that the drug could be contributing to and perpetuating his low mood. She explained Kel's scores on the BDI-II and her concerns about the severity of his mood problems. Using the information in Table 12.3, the therapist described the pattern of beliefs that she thought were keeping Kel in the cycle of using and feeling depressed, including the permissive beliefs of his social group towards using cannabis. The therapist finished this discussion by explaining the working hypothesis she had developed to summarize all the information collected thus far, and sought Kel's permission to write to his general practitioner. After the provision of each new piece of information, the therapist sought Kel's thoughts on what this information meant to him.

Therapist: I realize that this is a lot of information to take on in the one session, particularly when we've been talking about some pretty personal information. How are you travelling at the moment?

Kel: Oh . . . I'm all right I guess. It's stuff that I've known about for a while, my girlfriend . . . I mean my ex went on about it all the time. . . . I just haven't thought about it all as related to each other.

Therapist: Actually, in my experience, that's true of a lot of people. That's sometimes why it is good to have someone to talk to about these thoughts and feelings. . . . Sometimes just having that extra perspective can help link a few things together that are hard to see when you are in the thick of it all. . . . I'm wondering where all this information, and these new links you've made, leaves you. . . . What are your thoughts about a way through this?

Kel: Well . . . obviously I need help . . . that's what you want me to say, isn't it?

Table 12.3 Kel's case formulation summary worksheet

Problem list

1 Frequent feelings of sadness, low mood, guilt

2 Problems with concentration and motivation for university

3 Finances – no job

4 Boredom

5 Daily use of cannabis

Working hypothesis

Beliefs: 'I don't fit in at uni – I'm not smart and I'm not good enough to pass'; 'Pot helps me relax and chill out from my thoughts – plus lots of my uni friends do it.'

High-risk situations: Parties, sitting at home, exam time, going to uni each day, relationships.

Origins: School – use of cannabis as part of social group; pressure from parents to be as good as brother.

Summary of the working hypothesis:

Growing up, Kel felt he was constantly being compared by his parents to his older brother, and could never measure up. As such, he developed the belief that he was 'not good enough' academically, socially or at work. This made school a difficult experience for Kel, who fell in with a crowd who encouraged deviant-type behaviour (e.g. missing school, tests and assignments, acting out in class etc.). However, he didn't feel that he ever truly fitted in with this crowd and felt increasingly socially isolated as the years progressed. These experiences and beliefs have given rise to problems in later life, as Kel continues to experience difficulties with relationships, and is plagued by feelings of inadequacy. In addition, during his school career Kel started experimenting with alcohol and cannabis, and found that these substances helped him to feel more at ease in social situations, and worry less about pressures at school and from his parents. As a result, with increasing pressure in his current life Kel's use of cannabis has increased to daily use, as he believes he requires it to 'feel normal'. However, this has led to further problems as his girlfriend disapproves of his lifestyle and has recently split up with Kel over his lack of drive and use of cannabis. These additional problems feed back into Kel's problematic cycle of feeling worthless and using cannabis as a way to cope with these feelings. This has led to Kel believing more strongly that he needs cannabis to help cope with this situation. In addition, Kel's social circle reinforces the use of cannabis at parties; however, Kel feels increasingly unable to attend such social functions given his current relationship loss, and he continues to fall behind at uni from lack of attendance. As a result, Kel's problems have continued to worsen.

Therapist: Well, it is true that I have some ideas about how you might be able to reduce some of the stress you are feeling at the moment. . . . But the truth is that I'm not here to change you. I couldn't change you if I wanted to. I hope that I can help you think about your present situation and consider what, if anything, you might want to do, but if there is any changing, you will be the one who does it. I've given you a lot of information about yourself, but what you do with all of that after our session together is completely up to you. The only person who can decide whether and how you change is you. How does that sound to you?

Kel: Fine, I guess. . . . I guess I would like to start feeling a bit better about things, I mean that's what started all this.

Therapist: Well . . . where would you like to go from here?

Kel: I dunno. . . . You're the expert in that, aren't you . . .

Therapist: Well, I think that it would be beneficial to have a few more sessions together to talk some more about some of the things we've already mentioned today. In particular, I'd like to try a particular kind of counselling with you called cognitive behaviour therapy, which targets the way people think about themselves and their surroundings, and teaches them a more balanced way of coping with what goes on in their lives. How does that sound?

Kel: Yep, that's fine with me. . . . I could do that.

Introduction to CBT for depression

Over the next three sessions, the therapist decided to focus on behavioural activation strategies to address Kel's problems of boredom, low motivation and lack of direction. The therapist introduced regular self-monitoring for both depressive symptoms and cannabis use to assist Kel in identifying problem times of day and situations that exacerbate his distress.

Motivational enhancement strategies for cannabis use

While using depression as a focus for skill building, the therapist implemented motivational enhancement techniques to shift Kel from contemplating his current cannabis use patterns to making a decision to take action. By re-introducing pleasant/achievement tasks into Kel's everyday life, it was hoped that his reliance on cannabis to achieve these ends instead would diminish.

Potential barriers to treatment

Finally, the therapist highlighted issues that might pose difficulties in the treatment process. She perceived a real need to work hard on rapport-building and engagement strategies with Kel, given his reluctance to generate discussion and express a real commitment to treatment. In addition, the therapist was concerned that Kel's belief 'I'm not good enough' might undermine his progress in therapy should he experience difficulties in achieving goals: she was concerned that he might give up on set tasks should he experience 'failure' in the early stages. This was discussed in any rationale provided for take-home and other tasks.

Early sessions

Over the next three sessions, Kel and his therapist worked together on the treatment strategies outlined above. Each session was structured in the same way:

- review the previous week and set the agenda for the session:

Therapist: Let's start with a brief check-in: I want to hear about your week and how you are feeling. Then, we'll set an agenda for the session, and start going through those agenda items from there.

- review any take-home activities;
- address any agenda items requested by Kel;
- focus on skill building/motivation enhancement; then
- conclusion and take-home activity.

By the end of three sessions, Kel had noticed some improvements in his mood and had also experimented with reducing his cannabis use, restricting it to after 5pm. He had reduced the number of cones per day by half but continued to use on four or five days per week. The therapist decided to review Kel's progress formally during the third session, and asked him to complete another BDI-II. While his score on the BDI-II had reduced (score = 20), it was still in the moderate range. Kel and his therapist agreed to meet for a further 10 sessions of CBT, with a review session at the conclusion of this treatment period.

The therapist covered the following strategies over the sessions, and reserved the final session for review and termination: goal-setting for cannabis use; cognitive restructuring; mindfulness meditation; coping with cravings; and problem-solving and communication skills (cannabis refusal). The therapist also used motivational enhancement techniques throughout each session. Kel maintained regular fortnightly contact with his general practitioner, who monitored him for withdrawal symptoms from cannabis.

Termination

The last session of this phase of treatment was a summary session for Kel, who had managed to reduce his use of cannabis to several cones on weekends. His depressive symptoms had improved considerably; he now scored 10 on the BDI-II (indicating that some mild symptoms are still present). In addition, Kel was attending university lectures once again and was feeling more comfortable with the pressures associated with studying, given his improved problem-solving skills. The therapist suggested tapering treatment to monthly check-ins for several months to monitor progress.

The therapist spent the last part of the session discussing the importance of looking after oneself even at times of high stress, and developed with Kel a relapse plan to manage his early warning signs and high-risk situations for smoking/feeling depressed. In addition, she pointed out that time management skills may also help Kel keep on top of his studies.

The therapist identified further goals to work on. These include focusing on his cannabis use more closely, discussing healthy sleeping habits and reinforcing the cognitive restructuring skills Kel has already learned.

CONCLUSION

Given the significant impact that major depression and co-existing drug and alcohol problems can have on the individual, these conditions should be treated in a comprehensive, integrated way. This is particularly important as untreated symptoms of depression are often linked to relapse to substance use among this group (Brown *et al.* 1997; Crum *et al.* 2001; Hasin *et al.* 1996).

The recommended strategies allow for flexibility in the intensity of treatments offered. Individuals with co-existing depression and drug and alcohol problems are a heterogeneous group in terms of type, severity and readiness to address their various problems in treatment. As such, this chapter provides the therapist with a basic structure with which to guide decision-making and tailor treatment plans to individual clients, in order to meet their individual needs. This structure dovetails well with a stepped care approach, and could be implemented by virtually any health care professional, regardless of the context in which they work.

Integrated treatment for co-existing depression and drug and alcohol problems offers clients simultaneous treatment for both conditions, with treatment provided by the same therapist. This method allows the client to explore for themselves the relationship between their depressive and drug and alcohol problems and examine the links to current distress and impairment from both perspectives. Where CBT is implemented, it can address the behavioural, cognitive and affective features of depression and drug and alcohol problems at the same time.

KEY RESOURCES

Assessment instruments

Babor, T. F., Higgin-Biddle, J. C., Saunders, J. B. and Monteiro, M. G., *Alcohol Use Disorders Identification Test (AUDIT) Guidelines for Use in Primary Care*. Geneva: World Health Organization, 2001. Available at http://www.who.int/substance_abuse/docs/audit2.pdf (accessed 2 September 2005).

Beck, A. T., Steer, R. A. and Brown, G. K., *Beck Depression Inventory – Second Edition (BDI-II)*. San Antonio: The Psychological Corporation, Harcourt Brace, 1996. Available at http://www.harcourt-uk.com (accessed 2 September 2005).

Darke, S., Ward, J., Hall, W., Heather, N. and Wodak, A., *The Opiate Treatment Index (OTI) Researcher's Manual*. Sydney: National Drug and Alcohol Research Centre, 1991. Available at http://www.med.unsw.edu.au/ndarc/ (accessed 2 September 2005).

Dawe, S., Loxton, N., Hides, L., Kavanagh, D. and Mattick, R., *Review of Diagnostic and Screening Instruments for Alcohol and Other Drug Use and Other Psychiatric Disorders*, 2nd ed. Brisbane, 2002. Available at http://www.nationaldrugstrategy. gov.au/publications/monographs.htm (accessed 2 September 2005).

Medical Decision Logic, *CESD-R*. Towson, MD: Medical Decision Logic Inc., 2005. Available at http://www.mdlogix.com (accessed 2 September 2005).

Treatment manuals

Baker, A., Kay-Lambkin, F. J., Lee, N. K., Claire, M. and Jenner, L., *A Brief Cognitive Behavioural Intervention for Regular Amphetamine Users*. Canberra: Australian Government Department of Health and Ageing, 2003. Available at http://www. nationaldrugstrategy.gov.au/publications/illicit.htm (accessed 2 September 2005).

Kay-Lambkin, F. J., Baker, A. L. and Bucci, S. R., *Self-Help for Alcohol/Other Drug Use and Depression (SHADE) Intervention*. Callaghan, NSW: University of Newcastle, 2002.

Website

The Royal Australian and New Zealand College of Psychiatrists, *The Royal Australian and New Zealand College of Psychiatrists Clinical Practice Guidelines*. Melbourne, 2005. Available at http://www.ranzcp.org (accessed 2 September 2005).

REFERENCES

Adamson, S. J. and Sellman, J. D., 'A prototype screening instrument for cannabis use disorder: The Cannabis Use Disorder Identification Test (CUDIT) in an alcohol-dependent sample', *Drug and Alcohol Review*, *22*, 309–15, 2003.

American Psychiatric Association (APA), 'Practice guideline for the treatment of patients with substance use disorders: Alcohol, cocaine, opioids', *American Journal of Psychiatry*, *152*, 1–59, 1995.

American Psychiatric Association (APA), *Diagnostic and Statistical Manual of the Mental Disorders, Fourth Edition, Text Revision*. Washington: APA, 2000.

Andrews, G., Henderson, S. and Hall, W., 'Prevalence, comorbidity, disability and service utilisation: Overview of the Australian National Mental Health Survey', *British Journal of Psychiatry*, *178*, 145–53, 2001.

Baillie, A. J. and Rapee, R. M., 'Predicting who benefits from psychoeducation and self help for panic attacks', *Behavior Research and Therapy*, *42*, 513–27, 2003.

Beck, A. T., Rush, A. J., Shaw, B. F. and Emery, G., *Cognitive Therapy of Depression*. New York: Guilford Press, 1979.

Beck, A. T., Steer, R. A. and Brown, G. K., *The Beck Depression Inventory, Second Edition: Manual*. San Antonio: The Psychological Corporation, 1996.

Beck, A. T., Steer, R. A. and Brown, G. K., *The Beck Depression Inventory – Fast Screen Manual*. San Antonio: The Psychological Corporation, 2000.

Brown, R. A., Evans, D. M., Miller, I. W., Burgess, E. S. and Mueller, T. I., 'Cognitive-behavioural treatment for depression in alcoholism', *Journal of Consulting and Clinical Psychology*, 65, 715–26, 1997.

Brown, R. A., Inaba, R. K., Christian, G. J., Schuckit, M. A., Stewart, M. A. and Irwin, M. R., 'Alcoholism and affective disorder: Clinical course of depressive symptoms', *American Journal of Psychiatry*, 152, 45–52, 1995.

Carroll, K. M., 'Behavioural therapies for co-occurring substance use and mood disorders', *Biological Psychiatry*, 56, 778–84, 2004.

Crum, R. M., Brown, C., Liang, K.-Y. and Eaton, W. W., 'The association of depression and problem drinking: The results of the Baltimore ECA follow-up study', *Addictive Behaviors*, 26, 773–6, 2001.

Darke, S., Ward, J., Hall, W., Heather, N. and Wodak, A., *The Opiate Treatment Index (OTI) Manual*. Sydney: National Drug and Alcohol Research Centre, 1991.

Dawe, S., Loxton, N., Hides, L., Kavanagh, D. and Mattick, R., *Review of Diagnostic and Screening Instruments for Alcohol and Other Drug Use and Other Psychiatric Disorders*, 2nd ed. Brisbane: Commonwealth of Australia, 2002.

Eaton, W. W., Muntaner, C., Smith, C., Tien, A. and Ybarra, M., 'Centre for Epidemiologic Studies Depression Scale: Review and revision (CES-D and CESDR)', in Maruish, M. E., ed., *The Use of Psychological Testing for Treatment Planning and Outcomes Assessment*, 3rd ed. Mahwah: Lawrence Erlbaum Associates, 2003.

Gossop, M., Darke, S., Griffiths, P., Hando, J., Powis, B., Hall, W. and Strang, J., 'The Severity of Dependence Scale (SDS): Psychometric properties of the SDS in Australian and English samples of heroin, cocaine and amphetamine users', *Addiction*, 90, 607–14, 1995.

Hasin, D. S., Tsai, W.-Y., Endicott, J., Mueller, T. I., Coryell, W. and Keller, M., 'Five-year course of major depression: Effects of comorbid alcoholism', *Journal of Affective Disorders*, 41, 63–70, 1996.

Heatherton, T. F., Kozlowski, L. T., Frecker, R. C. and Fagerstrom, K. O., 'The Fagerstrom Test for Nicotine Dependence: A revision of the Fagerstrom Tolerance Questionnaire', *British Journal of Addiction*, 86, 1119–27, 1991.

Herman, D. S., Solomon, D. A., Anthony, J. L., Anderson, B. J., Ramsey, S. E. and Miller, I. W., 'Adherence to treatment of depression in active injection drug users. The Minerva study', *Journal of Substance Abuse Treatment*, 26, 87–93, 2004.

Kavanagh, D. J., Mueser, K. and Baker, A., 'Management of co-morbidity', in Teesson, M., ed., *Co-morbid Mental Disorders and Substance Use Disorders: Epidemiology, Prevention and Treatment*, pp. 78–107. Canberra: Commonwealth of Australia, 2003.

Kay-Lambkin, F. J., Baker, A. L. and Bucci, S. R., *Treatment Manual for the SHADE Project (Self-Help for Alcohol/Other Drug Use Problems and DEpression)*. Callaghan, NSW: University of Newcastle, 2002.

Kay-Lambkin, F. J., Baker, A. L., Kelly, B., Lewin, T., Underwood, L. and Carr, V. J., 'Computerised integrated cognitive behaviour therapy for coexisting depression and alcohol/other drug use problems: Preliminary results', paper presented at the Annual Conference of the Australasian Society for Psychiatric Research, Fremantle, Western Australia, 2004a.

Kay-Lambkin, F. J., Baker, A. and Lewin, T., 'The "co-morbidity roundabout": A framework to guide assessment and intervention strategies and engineer change among people with co-morbid problems', *Drug and Alcohol Review*, *23*, 407–24, 2004b.

King, V. L., Stoller, K. B., Hayes, M., Umbricht, A., Currens, M., Kidorf, M. S. *et al.*, 'A multicentre randomized evaluation of methadone medical maintenance', *Drug and Alcohol Dependence*, *65*, 137–48, 2002.

Kosten, T. R. and Kosten, T. A., 'New medication strategies for comorbid substance use and bipolar affective disorders', *Biological Psychiatry*, *56*, 771–7, 2004.

Lewis, L., 'Dual diagnosis: The Depression and Bipolar Support Alliance's patient perspective', *Biological Psychiatry*, *56*, 728–9, 2004.

Myrick, H. and Brady, K. T., 'Current review of the comorbidity of affective, anxiety, and substance use disorders', *Current Opinion in Psychiatry*, *16*, 261–70, 2003.

Nunes, E. V., Sullivan, M. A. and Levin, F. R., 'Treatment of depression in patients with opiate dependence', *Biological Psychiatry*, *56*, 793–802, 2004.

Pettinati, H. M., 'Antidepressant treatment of co-occurring depression and alcohol dependence', *Biological Psychiatry*, *56*, 785–92, 2004.

Powell, B. J., Penick, E. C., Nickel, E. J., Liskow, B. I., Riesenmy, K. D., Campion, S. L. and Brown, E. F., 'Outcomes of co-morbid alcoholic men: A 1-year follow-up', *Alcoholism: Clinical and Experimental Research*, *16*, 131–8, 1992.

Rollnick, S., Heather, N., Gold, R. and Hall, W., 'Development of a short "readiness to change" questionnaire for use in brief, opportunistic interventions among excessive drinkers', *British Journal of Addiction*, *87*, 743–54, 1992.

Rounsaville, B. J., 'Treatment of cocaine dependence and depression', *Biological Psychiatry*, *56*, 803–9, 2004.

Saunders, J. B., Aasland, O. G., Babor, T. F., de le Fuente, J. R. and Grant, M., 'Development of the Alcohol Use Disorders Identification Test (AUDIT): WHO collaborative project on the early detection of persons with harmful alcohol consumption', *Addiction*, *88*, 791–804, 1993.

Schuckit, M. A., Tipp, J. E., Bergman, M., Reich, W., Hesselbrock, V. M. and Smith, T. L., 'Comparison of induced and independent major depressive disorders in 2,945 alcoholics', *American Journal of Psychiatry*, *154*, 948–57, 1997.

Scogin, F. R., Hanson, A. and Welsh, D., 'Self-administered treatment in stepped-care models of depression treatment', *Journal of Clinical Psychology*, *59*, 341–9, 2003.

Segal, Z. V., Williams, J. M. G. and Teasdale, J. D., *Mindfulness-Based Cognitive Therapy for Depression: A New Approach to Preventing Relapse*. New York: Guilford Press, 2002.

Shand, F., Gates, J., Fawcett, J. and Mattick, R., *The Treatment of Alcohol Problems: A Review of the Evidence*. Canberra: Australian Commonwealth Department of Health and Ageing, 2003.

Smith, S. S., Jorenby, D. E., Fiore, M. C., Anderson, J. E., Mielke, M. M., Beach, K. E. *et al.*, 'Strike while the iron is hot: Can stepped care treatments resurrect relapsing smokers?' *Journal of Consulting and Clinical Psychology*, *69*, 429–39, 2003.

Sobell, M. B. and Sobell, L. C., 'Stepped care as a heuristic approach to the treatment of alcohol problems', *Journal of Consulting and Clinical Psychology*, *68*, 573–9, 2000.

Treatment Protocol Project (TPP), *Management of Mental Disorders*, 3rd ed. Sydney: World Health Organization Collaborating Centre for Mental Health and Substance Abuse, 2000.

Volkow, N. D., 'The reality of comorbidity: Depression and drug abuse', *Biological Psychiatry*, *56*, 714–17, 2004.

Westermeyer, J. J., *Addressing Co-occurring Mood and Substance Use Disorders*. London: Johns Hopkins University Press, 2003.

Wilhelm, K., Mitchell, P., Slade, T., Brownhill, S. and Andrews, G., 'Prevalence and correlates of DSM-IV major depression in an Australian national survey', *Journal of Affective Disorders*, *75*, 155–62, 2003.

Wilson, P. H., 'Depression', in Wilson, P. H., ed., *Principles and Practice of Relapse Prevention*, pp. 15–32. New York: Guilford Press, 1992.

Chapter 13

Psychosis and drug and alcohol problems

*Christine Barrowclough, Gillian Haddock, Ian Lowens,
Rory Allott, Paul Earnshaw, Mike Fitzsimmons and
Sarah Nothard*[1]

KEY POINTS

1   Substance misuse is very common in people with psychosis and is associated with many problems including suicide, more inpatient stays, violence and poorer overall prognosis. However, despite the size and impact of the problem, research into treatment development is very limited.
2   The psychological processes determining and maintaining substance use in clients with psychosis seem to be similar to those found in all substance users.
3   However, in the case of psychosis it is likely that social, biological and psychological vulnerabilities associated with psychosis increase the likelihood of people getting locked into a cycle of substance use. These factors need to be considered in treatment.
4   Motivation to reduce substance use in clients with psychosis is usually low, and helping the client to make links between their key problems or life goals and substance use issues is important in developing motivation.
5   Motivational interviewing can be successfully employed with people with psychosis, although some of the strategies may have to be adapted.
6   The treatment approach we have employed is formulation-driven, integrates motivational interviewing and cognitive behaviour therapy and is built around two phases: 'motivation building' and an 'action' phase. The intervention is sufficiently flexible to work with other client-led problems if the initial attempts to increase the client's motivation for change in substance use are unsuccessful.

INTRODUCTION

Substance misuse is common in people with psychosis. Estimates of lifetime prevalence of drug misuse, harmful alcohol drinking or substance dependence for this client group are around 50 per cent (Mueser *et al.* 1995a; Regier *et al.* 1990). People with psychosis and substance use problems are at high risk for a number of associated problems including suicide, poorer compliance with treatment, more inpatient stays, violence and poorer overall prognosis (Maslin 2003). However, despite the size and impact of the problem, research into treatment development is very limited.

Published accounts of treatment for this client group can broadly be divided into evaluations of service delivery models and individual client therapy approaches.

The former were developed in the United States, where elements of mental health and substance misuse approaches have been integrated and treatment delivered by a dedicated team. The ingredients of such integrated programmes have included motivational interventions, assertive outreach, intensive case management, group and individual counselling and family interventions (see Mueser and Drake 2003 for descriptions). Despite the optimism of the proponents of this approach (e.g. Drake *et al.* 2001), as yet there is no evidence for the superiority of such intensive and integrated care over routine treatment (Drake *et al.* 1998; Ley and Jeffery 2003). However, these programmes have drawn attention to the importance of providing substance use treatment within mental health services rather than having geographically and organizationally separate services, and there have been recent promising developments in the integrated approach (e.g. Addington 2003; Graham *et al.* 2003).

As regards client therapy approaches, there have been very few studies. The indications are that short-term interventions have a very limited effect (e.g. Baker *et al.* 2002). However, in recent years cognitive behaviour therapy (CBT) has been recognized as effective in reducing the symptoms of psychosis (see Pilling *et al.* 2002 for a review), and there are some indications that motivational interviewing (MI) can be successfully used with people with psychosis and substance misuse (e.g. Graeber *et al.* 2003). Moreover, there are encouraging results from an approach combining both MI and CBT. The one published randomized controlled trial of an individual client care intervention for clients with schizophrenia and co-existing drug or alcohol problems found superior outcomes for a treatment that combined three intervention components – MI, CBT and a family intervention – over a nine-month period, when compared with standard psychiatric care (Barrowclough *et al.* 2001; Haddock *et al.* 2003). The client interventions from this study have been further developed and are currently being evaluated in a larger randomized controlled trial in the UK (Barrowclough and Haddock 2004).

The main focus of this chapter is on this client therapy approach to psychosis and substance misuse. To this end, we will first briefly describe the model of substance use in psychosis which underpins the therapeutic approach. This model has been adapted from the addiction literature to take account of factors pertinent to psychosis and the interactive nature of the dual problems of psychosis and substance misuse. Issues contributing to difficulties in the engagement and treatment process for clients with psychosis and co-existing substance misuse will then be considered, and then the process of therapy will be outlined and illustrated with a case example.

Understanding the interactive nature of the dual problems

Psychosis and vulnerability to substance use

Clearly, effective treatment would be greatly helped by a theoretical model of the association between psychosis, substance use and adverse outcomes. However, limited progress has been made towards understanding the linkage of the dual problems (Blanchard *et al.* 2000). Although there is recent evidence that cannabis may act as a specific trigger for psychosis in some vulnerable individuals (Arsenault *et al.* 2004), simple broad models of either substance use causing schizophrenia or schizophrenia causing substance use have been largely discredited. Consistency in the pattern of substance use in psychosis, with alcohol being the most common substance, cannabis the most common illicit drug and polysubstance use being common, has been established in the UK (Weaver *et al.* 2003), the US (see Blanchard *et al.*'s 2000 review of studies) and Australia (Kavanagh *et al.* 2004). This pattern seems to be largely unrelated to clients' symptomatology (Brunette *et al.* 1997) but is rather associated with the same demographic correlates as for the general population (Teesson *et al.* 2000). This suggests that it is the social context and availability of substances that most often dictates substance choices in psychosis (Kavanagh *et al.* 2004; Patkar *et al.* 1999), and indicates that the psychological processes determining and maintaining use may be similar to those found in all substance users.

Hence, it seems appropriate that the starting point for a model for substance use maintenance in psychosis (Figure 13.1) incorporates the key features of Marlatt and Gordon's (1985) social-cognitive model of addiction, whereby certain situations and cues trigger drug- or alcohol-related thoughts, which, in the absence of alternative strategies and in the context of low self-efficacy for resisting use, and positive expectations of use, make the person vulnerable and more likely to use. This interaction between situations and cognitive/emotional reactions becomes the basis of a repeated cycle which maintains drug or alcohol use.

In the case of psychosis it seems likely that social, biological and psychological vulnerabilities associated with psychosis increase the likelihood of people remaining locked in the cycle. For example, client reports indicate that situations and cues triggering use may be related if not directly to psychotic symptoms then to some of the negative consequences of the disorder, particularly dysphoria and distress (Blanchard *et al.* 2000). Some individuals describe using substances to try and counteract the side effects of antipsychotic medication, or as a preferred alternative to taking prescribed

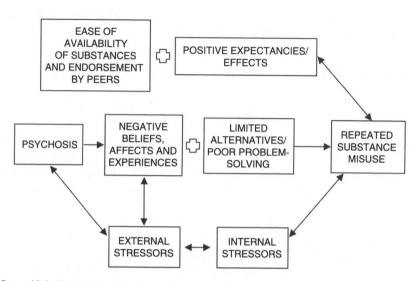

Figure 13.1 Model of maintenance of substance use in schizophrenia (adapted from Marlatt and Gordon 1985 and Blanchard *et al.* 2000).

medications (Schneier and Siris 1987). Coping motives (Mueser *et al.* 1995b), the poor problem-solving abilities of this client group (Carey and Carey 1995) and limitations to obtaining pleasure in other ways may then reinforce learned expectations of the positive benefits of use. Such perceived positive benefits may include, for example, mood enhancement, relief from boredom, anxiety reduction, opportunities for social interaction with substance-using peers, 'time out' from problems, general feelings of well-being, release from unpleasant self-consciousness and performance enhancement through physiological effects on arousal or other mechanisms.

Substance use in psychosis and adverse outcomes

Unfortunately, as noted earlier, the longer-term consequences of substance use can be very adverse in the context of psychosis. Why do drugs and alcohol have such a significant impact on people with psychosis? It has been argued that people with psychosis are particularly sensitive to the negative effects of certain substances (Chambers *et al.* 2001; Verdoux *et al.* 2003), and that negative consequences result from lower levels of use than in the general population (Drake *et al.* 1989). Negative impacts on a person's internal state which are likely to exacerbate psychotic symptoms include unpleasant withdrawal symptoms, depressed mood, increased perceptual and cognitive anomalies and increased arousal. Additionally, increased problems may arise from external stressors, such as interpersonal conflicts associated with the substance use (for example, with relatives, partners and service providers who disapprove of substance use and blame clients for worsening their situation) or financial and accommodation issues arising from drinking or drug-taking.

Thus, a vicious feed-forward cycle of maintenance and escalating problems may develop, as summarized in Figure 13.1. A common example would be a client with persistent unpleasant voices triggering distress and feelings of hopelessness, who drinks to improve his mood and to drown out the voices, only to wake the next day feeling hungover and depressed. This depression feeds into the depressive and self-derogating voice content, contributing to the voices becoming more persistent and distressing. Financial problems result from the cost of the alcohol binges, and arguments with his landlady about his drunken behaviour follow, thus further increasing stress and his 'need' to drink, leading to further exacerbation of the psychosis and the voices.

CONTEXT OF TREATMENT

Implications of the model and the psychosis for therapy

'[F]ailure to agree on a problem list dooms the treatment' (Persons 1989: 24).

The model outlined highlights a number of factors which increase the vulnerability of clients with psychosis to remaining locked in a cycle of use. These factors, along with other issues pertinent to the psychosis context, are often inter-related and may present considerable challenges for therapy.

Therapist variables

Therapist expectations regarding engagement and rate of progress need to be appropriate for this client group. Hence, the therapeutic approach we have developed is designed for working with clients for whom building alliance and then motivation for change is often a long, slow process. Therapy requires an assertive outreach approach, readiness to see clients at home, tolerance of missed appointments, flexibility in rescheduling sessions and a commitment to maintain contact with clients over an extended time period.

Client variables

Engagement may be difficult. Contributing factors include: a history of poor relationships with service providers; a reluctance to discuss substance use issues in anticipation of being criticized and lectured on the harmful consequences; a bias towards suspiciousness or paranoid interpretation of relationships, arising from the psychotic symptoms and exacerbated by substance use; and a chaotic lifestyle along with concurrent problems making appointment scheduling and engaging in structured work more difficult.

Motivation for reduction of substance use in clients with psychosis is usually low (Baker *et al.* 2002; Barrowclough *et al.* 2001). In our experience in the UK, rarely does the client come to therapy asking for help with reducing alcohol consumption or drug-taking. Rather, the therapist approaches the client and works towards getting substance use on a shared agenda for change. In terms of the model outlined, from the client's perspective substances may be perceived to offer many benefits and serve a number of functions, while any disadvantages (the negative feedback loop in Figure 13.1) are less salient to them. Psychosis is often associated with a range of complex problems and, within this context, the contributing role of substance use may not be salient to the client. A related issue may be that the levels of substance use may not be excessive in comparison to the person's peer group, making it less likely that the person will regard their substance use as problematic.

Further, clients with psychosis often suffer from low self-esteem (Barrowclough *et al.* 2003). Thus, self-efficacy may be low, which may further decrease motivation since people may feel unable to undertake change.

ASSESSMENT OF CO-EXISTING PSYCHOSIS AND DRUG AND ALCOHOL PROBLEMS

For clients who are not yet at an action phase, too much emphasis on substance use issues when establishing a therapeutic alliance is likely to be unhelpful: such a 'premature focus' may well contribute to the probability of increased resistance. Hence it is not usually appropriate for the therapist to begin by conducting a comprehensive assessment of the client's substance use. Rather, the assessment process attempts to match the client's motivational stage of change and is performed in the collaborative spirit of the MI approach. Prior to the action phase, the therapist may seek permission to collect more information in order to test out issues the client raises (e.g. How does their drinking fit with safe limits? What is the relationship between getting more paranoid and smoking cannabis? How does amphetamine use relate to their mood?). Once the client has made a firm commitment to reducing substance use, a more comprehensive assessment will be appropriate (see below in 'Phase 1').

We have discussed above how substance use and aspects of psychosis are frequently linked, and it will therefore be important that the therapist has a comprehensive assessment of the client's current mental health problems, including positive symptoms (such as hallucinations and delusional beliefs), negative symptoms (such as social withdrawal and motivational problems) and affective problems (mood and anxiety), and the change and impact of symptoms and contacts with mental health services over time. This information will be necessary to understand the context of the use of drugs and alcohol and to feed this back to the client in the shared understanding (see below). While some of the information may be obtained from client records, more detailed assessments derived from interviews and questionnaires will often be necessary to gain an understanding of the nature, development and maintenance of the symptoms associated with the psychosis, and to see how the symptoms relate to substance use and other current life concerns. Maintaining the spirit of the intervention, the therapist would ask permission to conduct such detailed assessments. The reader is referred to other specialist texts for details of assessment and problem formulation in psychosis (e.g. Haddock and Tarrier 1998).

There is also a case for including an assessment of cigarette smoking where appropriate. There is a higher than average prevalence of cigarette smoking in people diagnosed with and treated for schizophrenia (Ziedonis and George 1997). While there is some evidence that smoking tobacco can compromise the effectiveness of psychiatric medication, and in turn exacerbate psychosis (Kavanagh *et al.* 2002), there is little evidence that it has a direct effect on psychosis. Nevertheless, in our experience, smoking tobacco can act as a high-risk factor for the consumption of other substances (e.g. cannabis), or can actually act as a motivator to cease that substance (e.g. alcohol being a high-risk situation for cigarette smoking). It is clearly useful to be mindful of how a person's views of their tobacco smoking might relate to the wider formulation.

TREATMENT OF CO-EXISTING PSYCHOSIS AND DRUG AND ALCOHOL PROBLEMS

Adapting motivational interviewing for clients with psychosis

Since the early days of developing approaches for working with clients with psychosis and co-existing drug and alcohol problems, the need to enhance motivation and the value of MI (see also Chapter 3) has been emphasized. Our experience of using MI (Miller and Rollnick 2002) with clients with a schizophrenia diagnosis is that the approach can successfully be employed, although some of the strategies may have to be adapted to respond to the specific challenges faced by people experiencing psychosis (for discussions see Handmaker *et al.* 2002; Martino *et al.* 2002). Thought disorder can present challenges to understanding what the client is trying to say – a particular problem for MI where the core practice is reflective listening. In addition, people with a host of psychotic symptoms (e.g. hearing voices and/or delusional interpretations), along with concurrent substance use as well as heavy medication regimes, can experience impaired cognitive ability. For this reason it may be important to:

- make use of more frequent and short reflections to clarify meaning;

- use frequent and concise summaries to draw together information;
- detour emotionally salient material which is likely to increase thought disorder;
- provide sufficient time for the client to respond to reflections and summaries; and
- ask simple open questions and avoid multiple choices or complicated language.

Additionally, when a client has marked negative symptoms and paucity of speech, emphasis on a mainly conversationally-based approach can be uncomfortable for both client and therapist. Placing more emphasis on written concrete activities to structure the session (such as the use of balance sheets for exploring the pros and cons of substances, or ruler scales of importance and confidence for change) may be necessary. Also, increasing the ratio of questions to reflections may be necessary, while ensuring that the interviewing style remains evocative and in keeping with the spirit of motivational interviewing.

While MI places emphasis on the use of affirmations and confidence building, often with psychosis a good deal of attention needs to be paid to building and supporting the client's self-efficacy. As noted above, the person may well have a history (or a perceived history) of failures and losses, and low self-esteem is common. Symptom-related issues may also increase the likelihood of low self-efficacy, including depressed mood. This highlights the need to elicit confidence talk as well as change talk.

Finally, in our experience it is wise to avoid moving forward with action plans around substance reduction too quickly. Clients may have expectations about therapist views of themselves and their lifestyles, having heard the arguments for stopping drinking and taking drugs many times before, and have a tendency to say what others want to hear. A conservative approach, with lots of time for consolidation of motivation before moving into an action phase, is advisable.

Process of treatment: an outline of the therapeutic approach

As noted above, our research and clinical experience indicates that the majority of clients will not identify substance use as a problem, particularly in the early stages of engagement. We therefore attempt to structure the intervention so as to help clients make links between the problems or life goals that *are* important to them and substance use issues, and hence increase their awareness that they need to make changes in substance use if they are to make progress in the areas of their life they value. The intervention is sufficiently flexible to allow the therapist to work with other client-led problems if the initial attempts to increase the client's motivation for change are unsuccessful. In such cases, this client-led change area becomes a context for further motivational work for substance use reduction.

The treatment approach is built around two integrated phases. Phase 1, 'motivation building', concerns engaging the client, exploring and resolving ambivalence so as to build motivation for change, and formulating a shared understanding of factors that need to be changed if the client is to achieve the things important to them in life. The building of this shared understanding is assisted by the model of substance use in psychosis outlined above. Phase 2, the 'action' phase, develops from the case formulation: the client is helped to make changes using CBT approaches drawn from both the psychosis and substance use evidence base. The therapeutic approach is an integration of MI and CBT: in the early stages of phase 1 a strictly motivational interviewing approach is used, with CBT assessment and formulation techniques introduced alongside MI in the later stages of this phase. In phase 2, the emphasis is on CBT techniques for planning and implementing change, but the MI is integrated – it continues to permeate therapy, and is a fall-back style when motivational issues emerge (see Miller and Rollnick 2002: 27 for a discussion of integrating MI with different forms of therapy).

Integrating cognitive behaviour therapy and motivational interviewing

CBT and MI share similar approaches to working with clinical problems. Most importantly, both are rooted in the Socratic method, which emphasizes the advantages of eliciting information from the client. Significant overlap also exists between the spirit of MI and the central values of CBT. Each approach is client-centred and emphasizes the need to respect the client's autonomy. Moving between CBT and MI therefore involves a change of emphasis in the process of therapy, rather than a radical switch. Specifically, this means altering the ratio between Socratic questions and direct questions on the one hand (more of these in CBT) and reflective statements and open questions on the other (more of these in MI); the overall effect is that the client and therapist usually have equal talk time in CBT, whereas in MI the client is encouraged to do more of the talking to increase their exploration of their problems.

A brief description of the two phases of therapy is given in the following sections, and then the therapy process will be illustrated with a case example. It should be emphasized that this client group is characterized by a great deal of variability in terms of substances used (type, amount, single or multiple substances), symptomatology (persistent voices, delusions, high levels of anxiety and/or depression etc.) and lifestyle (ranging from fairly settled lives in a family home to extremely chaotic lives). These factors, along with variation in motivation for change, will influence the shape of the intervention in terms of number and duration of sessions. However, the aim in all cases is to work through all the stages described below, albeit at different rates or in a different order or with different emphases. With the client with complex problems and initial low motivation for change in mind, we would recommend therapeutic contact is maintained for at least nine to 12 months. The usual number of sessions needed to complete phase 1, and before moving to an action phase, would be from four to 12, but there are no fixed limits.

Phase I: building motivation and establishing a shared understanding

Building engagement then helping the client talk about concerns, values and life satisfactions

For reasons noted above, many clients may at first be reluctant to engage in a meaningful dialogue about their lives. In such cases a slow pace is required, with brief but frequent visits and conversation led by the client's interests. Ignoring the client's perspective and trying to push through the therapist's agenda to reduce substances will probably result in increased resistance on the client's part. Thus, therapists may have to work hard at providing the client with what may be a new experience: that of the therapist viewing the client as the expert in connection with their substance use and the therapist being interested in wider themes regarding the client's life and values. The therapist should attempt to build up a picture of key current issues for the client (negative/positive things in life that they feel strongly about). The issue of substance use should not be introduced until the client's wider concerns have been fully explored, so as to gain a thorough understanding of the context in which substance use occurs.

Identification of how substance use fits into concerns, values and life satisfactions

Initially, the therapist aims to help the client establish links, however tentative, between their substance use and key concerns, moving on to help them reflect on the positive and negative aspects of substance use in order to increase ambivalence. This is a critical aspect of developing intrinsic motivation to change.

Identification of how psychosis fits into this picture

Clients often link their substance use to attempts to reduce problems related to their psychotic disorder. Eliciting the links and/or strengthening the client's awareness of these connections is important for providing motivation to change substance use (e.g. 'The voices are upsetting; I smoke cannabis to reduce them, but in the long term it seems to make them worse. I guess it may not help in the long term'), and for boosting the client's self-efficacy for change (e.g. 'There may be other ways of coping with the voices that would be more effective. If I stop smoking cannabis, the voices might not necessarily get worse'). At this stage, where at least some ambivalence about substance use is expressed, it may be appropriate to provide information to help the client examine how substance use fits in with concerns regarding mental health, for example by completing a diary of symptoms in relation to substance use, or consulting an expert source such as a journal, book, pamphlet or website.

Establishing a shared understanding of the links between concerns, values, psychosis and substance misuse

Once the client has progressed through the above stages, it is helpful for the therapist to feed back the information gathered in earlier sessions and to present a shared understanding or formulation of the links between life concerns, values, psychosis and substance use. In this process it is helpful to use as a guide or template the model of substance use and psychosis outlined in earlier sections.

There will be a great deal of variation in the nature of this formulation for different clients. For those clients who were contemplative or have moved to contemplation then it may have been relevant to carry out quite a bit of detailed questioning and assessment of substance use and mental health issues. This might include obtaining details about:

- the client's current pattern of substance use: frequency, quantity, pattern and route of drug and alcohol use, and access to drugs/availability;
- the context of substance use: high-risk situations including symptom-related situations;
- the perceived positive impact of substance use on their life (beliefs about positive outcome expectancies);
- the perceived negative impact of substance use on their life (lifestyle problems or external stressors);
- the impact on symptom-related problems in the short and longer term (internal stressors);
- cherished values and goals;
- support structures and social environment, e.g. important others; and
- beliefs regarding self-efficacy, areas of competence and any past experiences of substance reduction.

For others, particularly those who do not see substance use as problematic, the links may be quite tentative or not established. The purpose of the shared understanding is to take stock of therapy to date, and to assess and try and consolidate the client's motivation for change in substance use – or, where the client is not motivated (i.e. not ready, willing and able to contemplate change; Miller and Rollnick 2002), to refocus on problem areas of key importance to the client which can then be used as a context for re-evaluating the function of substance use and possibly increasing motivation for reduction (see the case study below).

Phase 2: action

Where the client has made a commitment to reduce substance use, the intervention may then move towards planning, implementation and a maintenance/relapse prevention plan. While at this stage the therapist moves into a CBT style of therapy, it is extremely likely that motivation will wax and wane. Lapses are to be expected, and the therapist should be prepared for MI to regain centre stage from time to time.

A written change plan summarizing agreed goals and strategies is useful at this point. The first element of this plan (where the client is using more than one substance at a harmful level) is which substances to take action with and whether the best goal is one of reduction or abstinence. As always, the key factors are the client's motivation and choice. It is important to spend time thinking through the pros and cons of the client's options with an emphasis on what is realistic and most likely to result in a successful outcome. For example, the client may at first express a wish simply to cut down on cannabis, but on reflection decide that this would be very difficult to achieve, and feel that they would likely have more success if they opted for abstinence and a plan that involved initially staying away from places and people where they would probably be tempted.

A CBT approach for individuals with psychosis and substance use problems will be guided by individual formulations developed from the model outlined, but components are likely to include:

- identifying and increasing awareness of high-risk situations/warning signs which might make lapse/relapse more likely to occur;
- developing new coping skills for handling such high-risk situations/ warning signs, with particular attention to symptom- and mental health-related problems highlighted in the formulation (e.g. strategies for dealing with distressing voices or with depressed mood);
- coping with cravings and urges;
- making lifestyle changes so as to decrease need/urges for drugs and/or alcohol or to increase healthy activities/alternative options to substance use (e.g. activity planning where boredom or lack of social contact have been identified as key issues, avoiding or limiting contact with substance-using friends and planning alternatives);
- normalizing lapses and preparing for responding to lapses so that they do not result in full-blown relapse;

- developing strategies and plans for acting in the event of lapse/relapse so that adverse consequences may be minimized; and
- cognitive restructuring around alcohol and drug expectations.

It is beyond the scope of this chapter to provide details of such interventions. The reader might find it helpful to consult further texts, such as Tarrier and Haddock (2002) for detailed accounts of CBT approaches to psychosis and Marlatt and Gordon (1985) for CBT for substance misuse.

CASE STUDY

Jack is a 30-year-old man with a six-year history of schizophrenia. He currently lives alone, his wife having separated from him early in the psychosis. He has weekly access to the two young children from that marriage. He has had repeated hospital admissions over the years and two serious suicide attempts. He has been using alcohol heavily and regularly; he suggests his intake is around 50 units per week, with his preferred drinks being cans of strong lager. He is also a regular cannabis user, smoking most days, with his average use being 12 to 20 joints per week.

He has persistent unpleasant positive symptoms. He believes that the police are after him because they believe he has committed a murder. He does not believe he committed the murder, just that the police think he did and therefore subject him to continuous surveillance (e.g. by following him and putting bugging devices in his TV and elsewhere in the house). He also hears voices telling him he will be punished. He is extremely distressed by the voices and is very fearful of the police. He gets frightened when out due to his fear of surveillance. He has a few local contacts with whom he smokes cannabis, but spends most of his days alone in the house. However, he does attempt to go out with his children during his weekly access time. He also has a sister who is quite supportive and she visits him regularly.

Phase I: building motivation

Jack elects to see the therapist at home and is initially ambivalent about the contact. He expresses a desire to 'work on his problems' but has some fears that the therapist is connected to the police. The therapist makes several short visits initially and takes a low-key approach, talking to him about his interests (such as football and music) until Jack is happy to begin to talk about his personal concerns.

Over a period of three further visits the therapist elicits the things that Jack sees as problems and the things of value to him.

Jack: I'd like to get out when I want to. I get so bored at home all day. . . . I want to take the children places and not get scared. They don't understand why I don't want to go out and why sometimes I have to rush home. . . . I hate living in constant fear of the police. It's all I can think about some days. . . . I really, really don't want to go back in hospital. . . . I get very low. Everything gets on top of me and I feel life's not worth living.

During the first session, Jack spontaneously mentions his drinking and his cannabis use and queries its association with his problems. The therapist decides not to focus exclusively on substance use issues too early in building the collaboration, and before the client's wider concerns and the context of substance use are explored. At the third session the therapist picks up on the substance use issues again:

Therapist: You mentioned that your doctor tells you that your drinking and the smoking [cannabis] are making you worse.

The therapist makes it clear that it is the client's perspective he seeks and encourages the client to elaborate on this:

Therapist: I wondered what your thoughts are. . . . It sounds as though that's not the way you see things. Why do you think your psychiatrist sees your drinking and smoking that way? . . . Tell me from your point of view, what are the good things about drinking and smoking?

Jack begins to describe a good deal of ambivalence about smoking cannabis. On the one hand:

Jack: I don't know many people and most of the people I do know smoke. I like the feeling of sharing a joint, and a couple of smokes makes me feel more at ease.

However, on the other hand:

Jack: After about three or four joints I start getting paranoid, especially if I go out afterwards. I'm on the look out for him [the man Jack believes follows him]. I worry about attracting police attention. . . . My wife threatens to stop my access to the kids if I keep on smoking dope.

But as regards the drink, Jack is clear that he finds it a useful tool for coping with his fears:

Jack: I can't imagine what I'd do without drink when I get bad [i.e. paranoid, frightened] and the voices are really loud. . . . I can't go out, can't see anyone, can't watch TV or listen to music [he feels at these times that he is being surveyed through the TV and radio] so I just drink then go to bed and sleep to get away from it all.

Jack identifies a downside to drinking in its cost: 'I spend too much on drink so I don't have enough to spend on the kids.'

In subsequent sessions the therapist seeks the client's permission to explore further the links between substance use and psychosis symptoms. He first focuses on the cannabis, since the client has already suggested a link between this and paranoid feelings:

Therapist: You've mentioned that sometimes when you smoke, it's a pleas-urable experience that you enjoy with friends and it makes you feel at ease. However, you've heard from your psychiatrist that it will make your psychosis worse, and you've noticed that you become a bit more paranoid when you smoke a lot. I wondered if you might find it useful to have a look at that in a bit more detail – the good things and the bad things about smoking. Is that OK with you?

Having received the client's permission to look at his cannabis use in more detail, the therapist suggests one way to do this is to keep a simple record or diary of his good and bad feelings and also when and how much he smokes. Jack suggests that he might also do this with his alcohol. A very simple diary is drawn up by the therapist, charting mood and voices on scales of 0 to 100 (0 = worst ever, 100 = best ever), activity and substance use and Jack has a go at completing it retrospectively for the last three days.

At the next session, Jack has not completed the diary but says he did take more notice of how drinking and smoking affected him, and with Jack's permission they use the diary structure to look back over the week. The diary shows a temporal link between smoking and more paranoia, and also between heavy drinking in the evening and some mood relief followed by depression and voices the next day. However, the therapist encourages Jack to draw his own conclusions, rather than imposing them on him.

Therapist: Do you see any links between your mood and the smoking or drinking? . . . What do you make of this information?

Jack: It's as I thought, too much dope and I get paranoid. I suppose people might say I'm making myself worse and more depressed with the drink.

Therapist: So it sounds as though from your point of view, you still enjoy some aspects of smoking and provided you stick to one joint you're OK, but you feel that sometimes smoking cannabis can make your paranoia worse.

Jack: That's about it. Maybe I should just cut down on the smokes, but it's tricky when everyone else is smoking away.

Therapist: What do you think about the drink?

Jack: It's my choice. I might suffer from it the next day but I feel so bad the night before that I have no choice but to drink myself into a stupor.

During the eighth session the therapist seeks permission to feed back all the information discussed in earlier sessions, incorporating issues relating to life concerns, values, mental health and substance use into a shared understanding or formulation. The therapist draws these links out in the form of a diagram (see Figure 13.2). He takes care not to go beyond the links already established in previous sessions, to check out the accuracy of all the information from Jack's viewpoint and to respond to all the additions and changes Jack wishes to make.

The therapist then attempts to help Jack reflect on aspects of the shared understanding through the use of evocative questions:

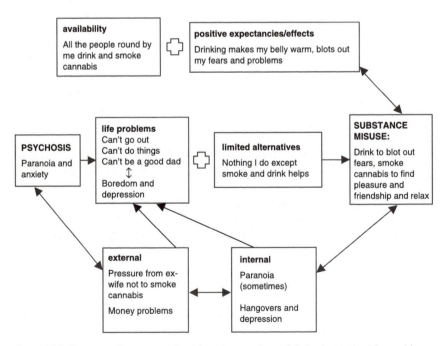

Figure 13.2 Diagram illustrating shared understanding of links between life problems, mental health issues and substance use for Jack.

Therapist: What do you make of this picture, Jack?

Jack expresses a high level of ambivalence about the use of both substances.

Jack: I can see that in the long run smoking and drinking may be making things worse for me, but for the time I'd rather stay as I am. I've got too many problems . . . and I can't see any way to change. I'm not good at change, I'm not good at anything, and maybe that's my biggest problem.

In order to get a better indication of the importance of substance use change and Jack's confidence in achieving this, the therapist uses a scaling method (see Miller and Rollnick 2002: 53). This tool helps elicit more talk from Jack concerning the importance of change for him and his confidence in making change.

Therapist: How important is it for you to reduce your cannabis use? If we look at this ruler, here, with a scale of '0' to '10', where '0' is not at all important and '10' is extremely important, where would you say you were now?

The therapist then looks at confidence using the same ruler and asks about Jack's confidence for change in the same way ('How confident would you say you are, that if you decided to reduce your cannabis use, you could do it?'). Then the therapist asks about importance of and confidence in reducing drinking using the same rulers.

Jack rates importance as '6' for cannabis ('I can see it's not worth the extra paranoia and the hassle from my ex') but his confidence is low ('3'; 'I've tried before, but seeing my friends means smoking, and I have to have some social life'). His motivation for reducing drink is much lower with an importance of '3' ('There's no way I really want to give up my escape from the bad thoughts I have') and confidence only at '2' ('I couldn't survive without drink when things are bad'). In other words, the rulers indicate that Jack has some willingness to change, especially for cannabis, but feels he isn't ready and certainly not able to initiate change.

The therapist helps Jack to reflect on the links between his use of cannabis and his experience of paranoia, using an evocative style of questioning and reflecting. For example, he asks Jack to elaborate on the paranoid con-sequences by asking him to describe how he felt on a recent occasion where he smoked 'too much'. At the same time he attempts to enhance Jack's confidence through appropriate affirmations.

Therapist: You say you're not good at change, but it seems you've given me a lot of examples of how you've managed to make changes in your life . . . for example, coping with the split from your wife and keeping in contact with your children. Many people in your position would have given up, yet you still manage to see your kids nearly every week, no matter how unwell you feel.

Although Jack continues to recognize and expand on the relationship between the intensity of his paranoia and his smoking cannabis, and his rating of the importance of reducing his cannabis rises to '7', his confidence for change stays low.

Phase 2

After 10 sessions of MI Jack's ambivalence about change has increased, especially for cannabis, but he still feels both unready for and unable to reduce his cannabis or his drinking. The therapist feels that at this stage it is best to focus on what Jack wants to achieve now. This doesn't mean abandoning the issue of substance use, but rather using the context of working on an agreed goal to build Jack's confidence for change and to re-examine the relevance of reducing substances.

Jack is clear that the most important goal for him is to be able to take his children out, and with Jack's agreement this becomes the topic of the next sessions. This necessitates a shift from the more reflective MI style to an increase in therapist questioning while the therapist makes a detailed assessment of Jack's difficulties in taking his children out. In this process it soon becomes apparent that his paranoid fears are the main obstacle, so the assessment focuses on these fears. A detailed cognitive behavioural assessment helps Jack to see the relationship between his thoughts, feelings and behaviour (see Figure 13.3). The therapist is able to use this context to help Jack to see that substance use is contributing to what he sees as his biggest problem. The therapist summarizes the picture as follows, breaking the narrative below into small chunks and checking Jack's understanding and agreement along the way:

Therapist: You can get bad thoughts and hear voices when you're out and believe that people may do terrible things to you. This is very scary, so naturally you do whatever you can to escape the situation and protect yourself. You make sure you keep a look-out for people who might watch and harm you and you get home as fast as possible. At home you escape by drinking to blot out your thoughts. A key factor triggering the bad thoughts is *how you feel*: feeling tired or depressed or paranoid after cannabis makes it more likely you get the thoughts. Because the drink and also the staying home makes you feel more depressed and lethargic, you find yourself in a sort of vicious circle: the very things you

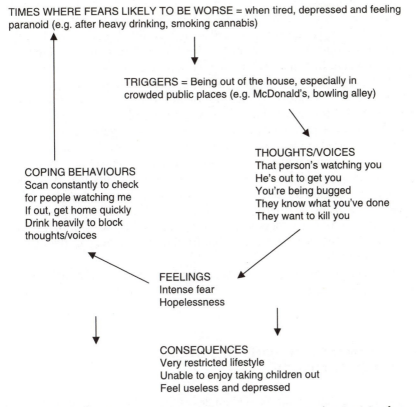

TIMES WHERE FEARS LIKELY TO BE WORSE = when tired, depressed and feeling paranoid (e.g. after heavy drinking, smoking cannabis)

TRIGGERS = Being out of the house, especially in crowded public places (e.g. McDonald's, bowling alley)

THOUGHTS/VOICES
That person's watching you
He's out to get you
You're being bugged
They know what you've done
They want to kill you

COPING BEHAVIOURS
Scan constantly to check
for people watching me
If out, get home quickly
Drink heavily to block
thoughts/voices

FEELINGS
Intense fear
Hopelessness

CONSEQUENCES
Very restricted lifestyle
Unable to enjoy taking children out
Feel useless and depressed

Figure 13.3 Shared understanding of antecedents, consequences and maintaining factors for Jack's fears.

do to try and make things better in the short term can actually make things worse. It's the same pattern with cannabis – it's something different you enjoy and it gets you out of the depression for a while, but you've noticed that smoking also brings on the fears.

You've clearly got a lot of insight into how your fears arise and how your thinking and the things that you do when you're frightened can make the situation more scary. It may seem quite complicated with a lot of factors involved, and it's no wonder you felt overwhelmed and a bit hopeless. But now we've mapped out the problem we can see there are a number of entry points to doing something about it – the thoughts themselves, the strategies you have for dealing with the thoughts, or maybe before the fears start, with the things that trigger your mood.

What do you think? Where would be a good place to start?

From this point, Jack elects to change his cannabis use on the basis that it is a lot easier to tackle the problem at the start rather than when the fears get a real hold. He identifies a need to reduce the drinking, but still feels unable to do this. After some further discussion of how much reduction of cannabis would be sufficient and how he would limit his cannabis use, Jack elects to abstain from smoking. He also identifies some alternatives to seeing his usual group of cannabis-smoking friends. This action plan is combined with strategies for fear reduction, agreed in a collaborative manner. Jack has tended either to stay home or go to very crowded public places; now, he works out a graded hierarchy of situations he might work through to build up his confidence in going out, beginning with quiet places near home with his sister to support him at first, then alone with his children. With Jack's permission, he and the therapist also look at other more benign explanations for the signs he interprets as people watching and wanting to harm him, and do some behavioural experiments challenging the value of his hypervigilance. He completes a written change plan with help from the therapist (see Figure 13.4).

After several months and some reduction in his level of fear, Jack commits himself to reducing his alcohol and this is incorporated in a new change plan.

FAMILY INTERVENTION FOR PSYCHOSIS AND SUBSTANCE MISUSE

Although this chapter has focused on describing a client-centred approach, it is important to emphasize the social context of clients' problems and it is often appropriate and advisable to include significant others in intervention strategies. It is beyond the scope of this chapter to review such family-based interventions: the reader is referred to the work of Barrowclough *et al.* (2001) and Barrowclough (2003) for descriptions of family work for clients with psychosis and substance misuse.

CONCLUSIONS

Psychosis is associated with a wide range of long-term psychological and social problems. It is unsurprising that clinicians are struggling to find effective approaches for clients where there is the additional and significant complication of substance misuse, particularly when aspects of the psychosis and the substance use are locked into a mutually reinforcing pattern. While significant progress has been made in developing approaches to working with clients with substance misuse and psychosis, there is clearly a need for further research and clinical development. Meanwhile, there is cautious

The changes I want to make are
1 Stop smoking cannabis
2 Take my kids out more
3 Be less frightened by thoughts about the police

The most important reasons I want to make these changes are
1 To be a better dad
2 To feel less depressed
3 To do more with my life

The steps I plan to take in changing are
1 Keep seeing my therapist
2 Stop smoking cannabis
3 Work on a plan of gradually increasing my confidence getting out of the house
4 Avoid spending time with people who smoke
5 Find new things and people to occupy my time

The ways other people can help me are
1 My sister can have me round
2 My sister can escort me going out at first
3 My therapist can share ideas on how to manage my fears
4 My key worker will have some ideas on safe places I can go to occupy my time

I will know that my plan is working if
1 I am not smoking cannabis
2 I do more activities
3 I spend more time out with my children
4 I feel less fearful

Some things that can interfere with my plan are
1 If I continue to see the friends who smoke cannabis
2 If I stop seeing my therapist
3 If I don't try out new activities
4 If I drink too much alcohol

What I will do if the plan isn't working
1 Ask for more help from the people supporting me
2 Look over the plan and see what extra help I need. Make another plan with smaller steps and more help
3 Resist blaming myself. Remind myself that change is difficult and lapses are very likely to happen. Remind myself that I can learn from lapses

Figure 13.4 Example of first written change plan for Jack.

optimism that clients may benefit from interventions that are available over extended time periods, place a strong emphasis on client autonomy and motivational issues and are based in the context of a mental health service with the flexibility to offer help with symptom- or other psychosis-related issues.

NOTE

1 The authors acknowledge the contributions of all the members of the MIDAS team, especially Nick Tarrier, Jan Moring, Til Wykes and Patricia Conrod. The current work associated with this chapter is funded by the UK's Medical Research Council and Department of Health.

KEY RESOURCES

Kadden, R. M., Carroll, K., Donovan, D. M., Cooney, N. L., Monti, P. E., Abrams, D. B. *et al.*, *Cognitive Behavioral Coping Skills Therapy Manual*. Rockville, MD: US Department of Health and Human Sciences, 2003.

Miller W. R. and Rollnick, S., *Motivational Interviewing: Preparing People for Change*, 2nd ed. New York: Guilford Press, 2002.

Miller W. R., Zweben, A., DiClemente, C. C. and Rychtarik, R. G., *Motivational Enhancement Therapy Manual*. Rockville, MD: US Department of Health and Human Sciences, 2003.

Tarrier, N. and Haddock, G., 'Cognitive-behavioural therapy for schizophrenia: A case formulation approach', in Hoffman, S. G. and Tompson, M. C., eds, *Treating Chronic and Severe Mental Disorders: A Handbook of Empirically Supported Interventions*. New York: Guilford Press, 2002.

REFERENCES

Addington, J., 'An integrated treatment approach to substance use in an early psychosis programme', in Graham, H. L., Copello, A., Birchwood, M. J. and Mueser, K. T., eds, *Substance Misuse in Psychosis: Approaches to Treatment and Service Delivery*, pp. 121–35. Chichester: John Wiley, 2003.

Arsenault, L., Cannon, M., Witton, J. and Murray, R. M., 'Causal examination between cannabis and psychosis: Examination of the evidence', *British Journal of Psychiatry*, *184*, 110–7, 2004.

Baker, A., Lewin, T., Reichler, H., Clancy, R., Carr, V., Garrett, R. *et al.*, 'Evaluation of a motivational interview for substance use within psychiatric in-patient services', *Addiction*, *97*, 1329–37, 2002.

Barrowclough, C., 'Family intervention for substance misuse in psychosis', in Graham, H. L., Copello, A., Birchwood, M. J. and Mueser, K. T., eds, *Substance Misuse in Psychosis: Approaches to Treatment and Service Delivery*, pp. 227–43. Chichester: John Wiley, 2003.

Barrowclough, C. and Haddock, G., *Motivational Interventions for Drugs and Alcohol Misuse in Schizophrenia*. University of Manchester, 2004. Available at http://www.midastrial.man.ac.uk (accessed 16 August 2005).

Barrowclough, C., Haddock, G., Tarrier, N., Lewis, S., Moring, J., O'Brien, R., *et al.*, 'Randomised controlled trial of cognitive behavioural therapy plus motivational intervention for schizophrenia and substance use', *American Journal of Psychiatry*, *158*, 1706–13, 2001.

Barrowclough, C., Tarrier, N., Humphreys, L., Ward, J., Gregg, L. and Andrews, B., 'Self esteem in schizophrenia: The relationship between self evaluation, family attitudes and symptomatology', *Journal of Abnormal Psychology*, *112*, 92–9, 2003.

Blanchard, J. J., Brown, S. A., Horan, W. P. and Sherwood, A., 'Substance use disorders in schizophrenia: Review, integration and a proposed model', *Clinical Psychology Review*, *20*, 207–34, 2000.

Brunette, M., Mueser, K. T., Xie, H. and Drake, R., 'Relationships between symptoms of schizophrenia and substance abuse', *Journal of Nervous and Mental Disease*, *185*, 251–7, 1997.

Carey, K. B. and Carey, M. P., 'Reasons for drinking among psychiatric outpatients: Relationship to drinking patterns', *Psychology of Addictive Behaviours*, *9*, 251–7, 1995.

Chambers, R. A., Krystal, J. H. and Self, D. W., 'A neurobiological basis for substance abuse comorbidity in schizophrenia', *Biological Psychiatry*, *50*, 71–83, 2001.

Drake, R. E., Essock, S. M., Shaner, A., Carey, K. B., Minkoff, K., Kola, L. *et al.*, 'Implementing dual diagnosis services for clients with severe mental illness', *Psychiatric Services*, *52*, 469–76, 2001.

Drake, R. E., Mercer-McFadden, C., Mueser, K. T., McHugo, G. J. and Bond, G. R., 'Review of integrated mental health and substance abuse treatment for patients with dual disorders', *Schizophrenia Bulletin*, *24*, 589–608, 1998.

Drake, R., Osher, F. C. and Wallach, M. A., 'Alcohol use and abuse in schizophrenia: A prospective community study', *Journal of Nervous and Mental Disease*, *177*, 408–14, 1989.

Graeber, D. A., Moyers, T. B., Griffith, G., Guajardo, E. and Tonigan, S., 'A pilot study comparing motivational interviewing and an educational intervention in patients with schizophrenia and alcohol use disorders', *Community Mental Health Journal*, *39*, 189–202, 2003.

Graham, H. L., Copello, A., Birchwood, M. J., Maslin, J., McGovern, D., Orford, J. and Gerorgiou, G., 'The combined psychosis and substance use (compass) programme: An integrated, shared care approach', in Graham, H. L., Copello, A., Birchwood, M. J. and Mueser, K. T., eds, *Substance Misuse in Psychosis: Approaches to Treatment and Service Delivery*, pp. 106–20. Chichester: John Wiley, 2003.

Haddock, G., Barrowclough, C., Tarrier, N., Moring, J., O'Brien, R., Schofield, N. *et al.*, 'Randomised controlled trial of cognitive-behaviour therapy and motivational intervention for schizophrenia and substance use: 18 month, carer and economic outcomes', *British Journal of Psychiatry*, *183*, 418–26, 2003.

Haddock, G. and Tarrier, N., 'Assessment and formulation in the cognitive behavioural treatment of psychosis', in Tarrier, N., Wells, A. and Haddock, G., eds, *Treating Complex Cases: The Cognitive Behavioural Approach*, pp. 155–75. Chichester: John Wiley, 1998.

Handmaker, N., Packard, M. and Conforti, K., 'Motivational interviewing in the treatment of dual disorders', in Miller, W. R. and Rollnick, S., eds, *Motivational Interviewing: Preparing People for Change*, 2nd ed, pp. 362–76. New York: Guilford Press, 2002.

Kavanagh, D., McGrath, J., Saunders, J., Dore, G. and Clarke, D., 'Substance misuse in patients with schizophrenia', *Drugs*, *62*, 743–55, 2002.

Kavanagh, D. J., Waghorn, G., Jenner, L., Chant, D. C., Carr, V., Evans, M. *et al.*,

'Demographic and clinical correlates of comorbid substance use disorders in psychosis: Multivariate analyses from an epidemiological sample', *Schizophrenia Research, 66,* 115–24, 2004.

Ley, A. and Jeffery, D., 'Cochrane Review of treatment outcome studies and its implications for future development', in Graham, H. L., Copello, A., Birchwood, M. J. and Mueser, K. T., eds, *Substance Misuse in Psychosis: Approaches to Treatment and Service Delivery*, pp. 349–66. Chichester: John Wiley, 2003.

Marlatt, G. A. and Gordon, J. R., *Relapse Prevention: Maintenance Strategies in the Treatment of Addictive Behaviours*. New York: Guilford Press, 1985.

Martino, S., Carroll, K. M., Kostas, D., Perkins, J. and Rounsaville, B. J., 'Dual diagnosis motivational interviewing: A modification of motivational interviewing for substance-abusing patients with psychotic disorders', *Journal of Substance Abuse Treatment, 23,* 297–308, 2002.

Maslin, J., 'Substance misuse in psychosis: Contextual issues', in Graham, H. L., Copello, A., Birchwood, M. J. and Mueser, K. T., eds, *Substance Misuse in Psychosis: Approaches to Treatment and Service Delivery*, pp. 3–23. Chichester: John Wiley, 2003.

Miller, W. R. and Rollnick, S., *Motivational Interviewing: Preparing People for Change*, 2nd ed. New York: Guilford Press, 2002.

Mueser, K. T., Bennet, M. and Kushner, M. G., 'Epidemiology of substance use disorders among persons with chronic mental illnesses', in Lehman, A. F. and Dixon, L. B., eds, *Double-jeopardy: Chronic Mental Illness and Substance Use Disorders*, pp. 9–26. Philadelphia: Harwood, 1995a.

Mueser, K. T. and Drake, R., 'Integrated dual diagnosis treatment in New Hampshire (USA)', in Graham, H. L., Copello, A., Birchwood, M. J. and Mueser, K. T., eds, *Substance Misuse in Psychosis: Approaches to Treatment and Service Delivery*, pp. 93–105. Chichester: John Wiley, 2003.

Mueser, K. T., Nishith, P., Tracy, J. I., DeGirolamo, J. and Molinaro, M., 'Expectations and motives for substance use in schizophrenia', *Schizophrenia Bulletin, 21,* 367–78, 1995b.

Patkar, A. A., Alexander, R. C., Lundy, A. and Certa, K. M., 'Changing patterns of illicit substance use among schizophrenic patients', *American Journal of Addiction, 8,* 65–71, 1999.

Persons, J. B., *Cognitive Therapy in Practice: A Case Formulation Approach*. New York: W. W. Norton, 1989.

Pilling, S., Bebbington, P., Kuipers, E., Garety, P., Geddes, J., Orbach, G. and Morgan, C., 'Psychological treatments in schizophrenia: I. Meta-analysis of family intervention and cognitive behaviour therapy', *Psychological Medicine, 32,* 763–82, 2002.

Regier, D. A., Farmer, M. F., Rae, D. S., Locke, B. Z., Keith, S. J., Judd, L. L. and Goodwin, F. K., 'Comorbidity of mental disorders with alcohol and other drug abuse: Results from the Epidemiologic Catchment Area (ECA) study', *Journal of the American Medical Association, 264,* 2511–8, 1990.

Schneier, F. R. and Siris, S. G., 'A review of psychoactive substance use and abuse in schizophrenia: Patterns of drug choice', *Journal of Nervous and Mental Disease, 175,* 641–52, 1987.

Tarrier, N. and Haddock, G., 'Cognitive-behavioural therapy for schizophrenia: A case formulation approach', in Hofmann, S. G. and Tompson, M. C., eds, *Treating*

Chronic and Severe Mental Disorders: A Handbook of Empirically Supported Interventions, pp. 69–95. New York: Guilford Press, 2002.

Teesson, M., Hall, W., Lynskey, M. and Degenhardt, L., 'Alcohol and drug use disorders in Australia: Implications of the national survey of mental health and well being', *Australia and New Zealand Journal of Psychiatry, 34*, 206–13, 2000.

Verdoux, H., Gindre, C., Sorbara, F., Tournier, M. and Swendsen, J. D., 'Effects of cannabis psychosis vulnerability in daily life: An experience sampling test study', *Psychological Medicine, 33*, 23–32, 2003.

Weaver, T., Madden, P., Charles, V., Stimson, G., Renton, A., Tyrer, P. *et al.*, 'Comorbidity of substance misuse and mental illness in community mental health and substance misuse services', *British Journal of Psychiatry, 183*, 304–13, 2003.

Ziedonis, D. and George, T. P., 'Schizophrenia and nicotine use: Report of a pilot smoking cessation programme and review of neurobiological and clinical issues', *Schizophrenia Bulletin, 23*, 247–54, 1997.

Chapter 14

Bipolar affective disorder and drug and alcohol problems

Emma Whicher and Mohammed Abou-Saleh

KEY POINTS

1 The treatment of people with co-existing bipolar disorder and drug and alcohol problems is often difficult, especially as these particular clients often have poorer outcomes and lower compliance than people with a single disorder.
2 Integrated care in a supportive environment with a named key worker addressing both drug and alcohol use and psychiatric disorder is the most effective.
3 Psychological therapies can be helpful, but may need an unconfrontational approach with an emphasis on reducing anxiety and improving engagement.
4 There is increasing evidence for the benefits of mood stabilizers and quetiapine in the treatment of both mood disorder and drug and alcohol problems.
5 It is important that mood symptoms and drug and alcohol use are addressed concurrently as this increases the likelihood of improvement.

INTRODUCTION

Bipolar affective disorder is a syndrome of affective disturbance comprising episodes of depression and mania or hypomania. In DSM-IV (American Psychiatric Association 1994) the disorder is divided into Bipolar I and II. Bipolar I is made up of major depressive and manic episodes or manic episodes alone. Bipolar II also comprises major depressive episodes, but manic or hypo-manic episodes are only attributable to treatment.

The Epidemiological Catchment Area survey found a 1.2 per cent lifetime prevalence for bipolar affective disorder (Reiger *et al.* 1984). The same survey also found that, compared with other specific mental disorders, bipolar affective disorder had the highest level of association with substance misuse. A person with bipolar disorder was almost five times more likely to suffer from an alcohol misuse disorder and 11 times more likely to suffer from a drug misuse disorder than the general population. Other surveys of clients being treated for bipolar disorder have found a prevalence of 21–31 per cent for co-existing substance misuse disorders (Brady *et al.* 1991; Miller *et al.* 1989). Elevated rates of smoking have also been reported among people with bipolar disorder (Farrell *et al.* 1998; Itkin *et al.* 2001). Co-existing drug and alcohol problems are also associated with an increased rate of suicide, an increased risk of mixed mania and a raised likelihood of medication non-compliance in people with bipolar affective disorder (Comtois *et al.* 2004; Goldberg *et al.* 1999; Keck *et al.* 1998; Keller *et al.* 1986).

Three hypothetical models proposed by Mueser *et al.* (1998) to explain the link between a severe mental disorder and drug and alcohol problems may be relevant to co-existing bipolar affective disorder and drug and alcohol problems. The first is the common factor model, which explains the high rates of co-existing problems in terms of shared vulnerabilities towards both disorders. These could be genetic or due to an underlying antisocial personality disorder. However, studies have found that a genetic risk of bipolar disorder is not associated with an increased risk of a substance misuse disorder in first-degree relatives (Bidaut-Russell *et al.* 1994). Second, psychological risk factor models postulate that drug and alcohol problems are secondary to severe mental illness. This is because drugs and/or alcohol are often used either as self-medication, to alleviate dysphoria (Addington and Duchak 1997), or in the context of multiple risk factors such as poor social status. Finally, the super sensitivity model hypothesizes that psychological vulnerabilities combined with genetic and environmental factors mean that drugs and alcohol act as a biological stressor precipitating the onset and relapse of severe mental illness. This is supported by the fact that people with severe mental disorders appear to have lower levels of psychological dependence than those without severe mental disorders. Overall, however, there is a lack of research into possible models of co-existing bipolar affective disorder and drug and alcohol problems.

The models of treatment for bipolar disorder and co-existing drug and alcohol problems are the same as those for people with other severe mental disorders. As a consequence, an integrated model of treatment incorporating both mental health services and addiction services is optimal (Lowe and Abou-Saleh 2004). Ideally this should be delivered within an assertive outreach model, in order to facilitate engagement and treatment (Drake and Mueser 2000).

CONTEXT OF THERAPY

Therapist variables

Most models of treatment for people with co-existing major mental disorder and drug and alcohol problems advocate a trusting supportive relationship with a named therapist. Repeated change of therapist and a confrontational or judgmental approach are liable to reduce the likelihood of engagement in treatment and adversely affect its outcome.

Any previous experience of people with bipolar disorder or substance misuse in the therapist's private or work life, may mean that the therapist can commence treatment with a set of expectations about a client. In particular, personal experience of mental illness or substance misuse could adversely affect the relationship between a client and therapist. As a consequence, supervision of the therapist is a fundamental component of treatment.

Client variables

Clients suffering from bipolar disorder have almost triple the risk of aggression compared to the normal population (Barlow *et al.* 2000). Violence has been linked with medication non-compliance (Swartz *et al.* 1998) and can impact on the therapeutic relationship, reducing the effectiveness of treatment.

Client characteristics such as rapid cycling of mood, impulsivity or additional anxiety disorders will have a negative impact on the success of treatment. Clients with rapid cycling of mood have been demonstrated to have more severe illness, poorer functioning and a lower chance of recovery than people without (Schneck *et al.* 2004). People with bipolar disorder and concomitant anxiety disorders have been shown to have higher rates of substance misuse and suicide attempts (Simon *et al.* 2004). Finally, impulsivity is associated with a greater risk of attempted suicide in people with bipolar disorder (Michaelis *et al.* 2004).

ASSESSMENT OF CO-EXISTING BIPOLAR AFFECTIVE DISORDER AND DRUG AND ALCOHOL PROBLEMS

It is vital that people presenting to psychiatric services are routinely screened for drug and alcohol use (including tobacco) and vice versa for those presenting to drug and alcohol services. The detection and assessment of drug and alcohol use is based on self-report, collateral information, screening tests and laboratory tests such as urine screening and hair testing. Assessment is best conducted when the client's symptoms are stable and the client is not intoxicated. Manic episodes and acute intoxication may present with similar symptoms, such as hallucinations and thought disorder (Harrison and Abou-Saleh 2002). The starting point of any assessment is a full history and mental state examination. A detailed exploration of mental health problems (including depression, mania and anxiety) and any drug and alcohol use is crucial, to see in particular whether there is any interaction between the two – does heavy drinking precede an episode of mania, or during an episode of depression does cannabis use become heavier? Interdependence between the two problems does not necessarily imply a causal link.

It may not be possible to distinguish between a primary and secondary disorder during a period of assessment. Bipolar affective disorder usually starts in an individual's 20s or 30s, but problematic drug and alcohol use may precede this. However, the chronological sequence of progression should not be taken to imply cause or effect between different disorders. By the time a client is assessed it is often the case that mental disorder and drug and alcohol problems have been concurrent for many years.

The second stage of an assessment is a functional evaluation, to determine the impact of drug and alcohol use on relationships, housing, work, criminal activity and personal goals. Third, a risk assessment is important to characterize any risks of self-harm, harm to others (particularly children), self-neglect and infection. The final stage of the assessment process is to evaluate the level of motivation for change and develop a treatment plan incorporating the client's wishes and goals.

There are, however, specific problems involved in assessing drug and alcohol use in people with severe mental disorder. There can be significant under-reporting of drug and alcohol use by both clients and informants. This may be compounded by the fact that even clients who have engaged well with psychiatric services are often in a pre-contemplative stage (Prochaska and DiClemente 1992) regarding their substance misuse, and hence are unwilling to undergo this assessment.

Another important factor is that people with co-existing bipolar disorder and drug and alcohol problems may have different patterns of drug and alcohol use to people without severe mental disorder. In particular, those with co-existing disorders may experience drug- and alcohol-related problems at lower levels of drugs or alcohol, but still not fulfil the criteria for a dependence syndrome. Conversely, they may have more severe consequences in relation to financial issues, housing needs and compliance with other treatment. Therefore, standard addiction severity instruments can be insensitive to levels of problematic drug and alcohol use among people with severe mental disorder.

Diagnostic instruments

Multiple diagnostic instruments have been used to screen, diagnose and differentiate between primary mental and substance use disorders. These are mostly used in the context of research trials and their use with people with bipolar affective disorder is limited (Abou-Saleh 2004). The Psychiatric Research Interview for Substance and Mental Disorders (PRISM), which is based on DSM-IV (American Psychiatric Association 1994), has been found to have good reliability in diagnosing primary depression, psychosis and bipolar affective disorder in clients with co-existing drug and alcohol problems (Hasin *et al.* 1996).

Clinically, assessment over time can enable the therapist to decide which diagnosis is primary and what kind (if any) of interdependence is involved. This is often better after a detoxification or in the inpatient setting, when the level of drug and alcohol use misuse can be minimized.

Screening and assessment of drug and alcohol problems

Screening instruments are generally short questionnaires which are either interviewer-administered or self-report. Rapid scales such as the CAGE questionnaire can be useful to gauge initially the extent of any alcohol use and dependence, if time is limited (Rydon *et al.* 1992; the acronym 'CAGE' comes from the capitalized letters in each of the four items: Have you ever thought you should Cut down on your drinking? Felt Annoyed by others criticizing your drinking? Felt bad or Guilty about your drinking? Had a drink first thing in the morning to steady your nerves or get not of a hangover (Eye-opener)?). The Dartmouth Assessment of Life Instrument (DALI) is a general screening tool for drug and alcohol use that can be used with people with mental health problems (Rosenberg *et al.* 1998). The Alcohol Use Disorders Identification Test (AUDIT; Babor *et al.* 1989) and the Drug Abuse Screening Test (DAST-10; Skinner 1982) are self-report instruments specifically designed to screen for drug and alcohol problems and can be employed among people with severe and enduring mental disorders. All clients should be screened for smoking and the Fagerstrom Test for Nicotine Dependence may be useful (Heatherton *et al.* 1991). Screening tools are useful to identify drug and alcohol use, but further questionnaires may be needed to determine problem severity and to identify primary and secondary disorders.

Finally, the Addiction Severity Index (ASI; McLellan *et al.* 1992) is widely used to assess drug and alcohol use but may not be reliable in the severely mentally disordered population. The Chemical Use, Abuse and Dependence Scale (CUAD; Appleby *et al.* 1996) is reliable in assessing the severity of drug and alcohol problems in people with severe mental disorder. These instruments have mainly been used to assess drug and alcohol misuse in people with major depression or schizophrenia, so it is difficult to assess their reliability when diagnosing drug and alcohol misuse in people with bipolar affective disorder.

Other scales involved in assessment are the Substance Abuse Treatment Scale (SATS; McHugo *et al.* 1995), which measures stage of change for treatment, and the Stages of Change Readiness and Treatment Eagerness Scale (SOCRATES; Carey and Correia 1998), which measures readiness to change. Both of these can be used to develop a treatment plan while assessment is ongoing. Table 14.1 summarizes the typical assessment process for clients with co-existing bipolar affective disorder and drug and alcohol problems.

TREATMENT OF CO-EXISTING BIPOLAR AFFECTIVE DISORDER AND DRUG AND ALCOHOL PROBLEMS

Useful models of treatment

Several different models of treatment are helpful for treating clients with severe mental disorder and co-existing drug and alcohol problems; these are pertinent for people with bipolar disorder.

Client matching

This involves matching an individual client to a specific treatment depending on their personal characteristics and situation. Although there is little evidence to support this as a basis of treatment (Ouimette *et al.* 1999), in

Table 14.1 Typical assessment process for co-existing bipolar affective disorder and drug and alcohol problems

- Detection by self-report or collateral information
- History and mental state examination incorporating a detailed assessment of drug and alcohol use and any interaction with bipolar affective disorder
- Functional assessment of impact of both disorders on relationships and social situation
- Assessment of risks to self or others, with evaluation of any child protection concerns
- Use of structured interviews, e.g. PRISM to aid with diagnosis
- Assessment of motivation to change and treatment preferences
- Physical examination
- Laboratory tests such as urine screening and hair testing for drug and alcohol use
- Assessment after period of abstinence from drugs and alcohol
- Treatment planning to take into account levels of motivation and treatment preferences

practice a treatment plan for any client is likely to be more successful if it incorporates their wishes and needs.

Inpatient treatment

This may occur in the context of either psychiatric or addiction inpatient services. Treatment in a psychiatric ward may become necessary if clients with bipolar affective disorder become acutely psychotic or present a risk to themselves or others. As a consequence, treating the acute mental illness becomes a priority, and, where drug and alcohol problems are severe, inpatient detoxification may also be indicated. If drug and alcohol problems are not addressed, they may interfere with any acute treatment (e.g. the client may leave the ward in search of alcohol or drugs to alleviate withdrawal symptoms). Inpatient psychiatric admissions provide an excellent opportunity for addressing drug and alcohol problems. It is often the case, however, that the treatment of substance misuse disorders takes second place to that of the acute psychiatric disorder. As a consequence, specially designated dual diagnosis wards have been trialled and shown to be effective in the treatment of both major mental illness and substance misuse (Galanter *et al.* 1994). However, these have only been run in limited centres, particularly in the US, and are not practicable for most psychiatric services.

Integrated treatment

Ideally, treatment for people with co-existing severe mental illness and drug and alcohol problems should take an integrated approach (Drake *et al.* 1998; Mueser *et al.* 2003). Integrated care in a supportive environment with a named key worker addressing both drug and alcohol use and psychiatric disorder is the most effective. Parallel and sequential approaches to treatment by different services can produce mistrust between health professionals and allow clients to fall between the cracks. Furthermore, it has become clear that traditional methods of treating drug and alcohol problems are far less effective if people also have a severe mental disorder. Figure 14.1 illustrates some recommended principles of integrated treatment.

Integrated treatment involves the concurrent treatment of both the severe mental disorder and the drug and alcohol problems by the same team or organization. The principles of this model of treatment are as follows. First, there must be an assertive outreach approach to facilitate engagement and address social problems. It is especially important to provide a supportive, non-confrontational treatment approach with emphasis on engagement, improving functioning and reducing hospital inpatient treatment. Second, the integrated approach places emphasis on close monitoring of clients to provide structure and access to a wide range of treatments. Negotiating stable living conditions is also instrumental in the effectiveness of an integrated

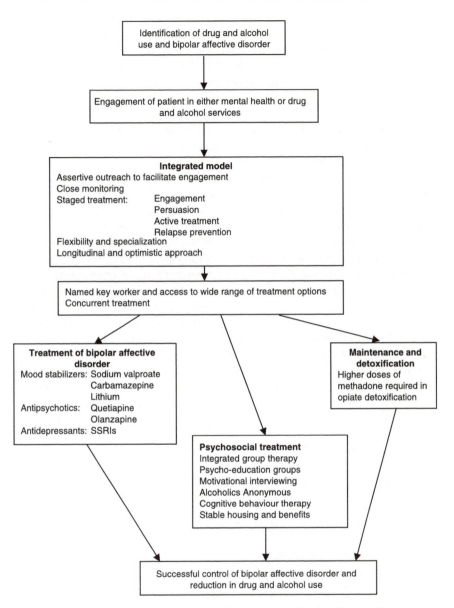

Figure 14.1 Principles of integrated treatment for co-existing bipolar affective disorder and drug and alcohol problems.

approach. Any interventions are designed to be flexible and specialized. Finally, a longitudinal perspective towards care and an optimistic attitude to instill hope are integral to this model.

Other core components are group interventions – which focus on peer support, addressing drug and alcohol problems and the promotion of coping strategies – and education about possible interactions between drug and alcohol use and mental disorder, especially the detrimental effects of alcohol and drugs on mental health. Finally, motivational techniques (Miller and Rollnick 1991, 2002) are important in working towards reduction and abstinence.

Some integrated models posit specific stages of recovery. The New Hampshire Model uses engagement, persuasion, active treatment and relapse prevention (Osher and Kofoed 1989), described in Chapter 6. The integrated model emphasizes the reduction of anxiety, empathy, harm reduction rather than abstinence, and long-term management. It provides a framework within which clinicians and clients can undertake treatment, and it can incorporate both psychological and pharmacological interventions. Recent follow-up studies of integrated treatment for people with bipolar disorder and co-existing substance misuse found a modest improvement in mental health symptoms, but a greater improvement in substance misuse, with 61 per cent achieving abstinence in three years. Furthermore, those in integrated treatment achieved significantly greater levels of independent living and employment than those not in integrated treatment programmes (Drake *et al.* 2004).

Although the integrated approach was developed in the US, many of the principles have been adopted by services in the UK. Drug services in the UK have traditionally emphasized a harm reduction approach. Shared care models, where both psychiatric and substance misuse teams work together when treating a client with co-existing mental disorder and substance misuse, are increasingly used. In some areas, specific teams specializing in substance misuse work alongside assertive outreach teams. This has been pioneered by initiatives such as the COMPASS project (Combined Psychosis and Substance Use Programme, see Chapter 7) in Birmingham in the UK, where a designated substance misuse team works with the assertive outreach team to provide integrated care (Graham *et al.* 2003).

Psychological interventions

Motivational interviewing

Motivational interviewing (Miller and Rollnick 1991) has been expanded for use with people with co-existing severe mental disorders, with specific emphasis on developing and achieving personal goals (Mueser *et al.* 2003). It often needs to be carried out at a slower pace than with people without co-existing mental disorders (see Chapters 3 and 13).

Cognitive behaviour therapy

Cognitive behaviour therapy (CBT) is usually centred on relapse prevention skills and helping people learn more effective strategies for coping with emotions, behaviours and situations associated with their drug and alcohol problems (see Chapter 4). CBT is increasingly being used as a therapy of choice with people with a range of severe mental disorders (Perry *et al.* 1999; Pilling *et al.* 2002; Tarrier *et al.* 2004). Studies have found that CBT reduces levels of substance misuse and improves psychiatric symptoms more than treatment based on 12-step programmes (Jerrell and Ridgely 1995).

More recently, cognitive behavioural integrated treatment (C-BIT; see Chapter 7) has been developed to treat substance misuse among people with severe mental illness. It is based on a CBT model and emphasizes the links between a person's beliefs about their mental illness and substance misuse. It includes motivational, social and behavioural components (Graham *et al.* 2004).

Group therapies

Group therapies are especially popular for the treatment of drug and alcohol problems and are described more fully in Chapter 6. There have been several studies based in the US examining the effectiveness of specific group therapies for people with bipolar affective disorder and drug and alcohol problems. Psycho-education group therapy for inpatients with bipolar disorder reduced co-existing drug and alcohol use (Galanter *et al.* 1994). Integrated group therapy (IGT) comprising a manualized cognitive-behavioural-based relapse prevention programme showed greater efficacy in improving manic symptoms, drug use and medication compliance than non-integrated group therapy in people with bipolar disorder (Weiss *et al.* 2000).

Self-help groups such as Alcoholics Anonymous and Narcotics Anonymous have been an important component in the treatment of drug and alcohol problems for the last 50 years. However, people with severe mental health problems may feel uncomfortable attending 12-step programmes due to their mental disorder; they are less likely to attend, and when they do they are less likely to find it effective (e.g. Kelly *et al.* 2003, although see also Laudet *et al.* 2004 for the usefulness of specialized 12-step groups specifically for people with co-existing alcohol and drug and serious mental health problems; and also see Chapter 6, this volume).

Pharmacotherapy

Psychological therapies should not be used to the exclusion of pharmacological treatment in people with bipolar disorder and co-existing drug and alcohol problems. There is increasing evidence for the use of medication when treating these disorders together, although most studies have been open rather than controlled (Levin and Hennessy 2004).

The mainstays of treatment for bipolar affective disorder are mood stabilizers, specifically lithium, sodium valproate and carbamazepine. Antipsychotics and antidepressants are also prescribed, particularly in the acute phases of the disorder.

Sodium valproate appears to be especially effective in people with co-existing bipolar affective disorder and drug and alcohol problems. In one retrospective study, 50 per cent of those on sodium valproate reduced their drug and alcohol use (Hertzman 2000). It has also been shown to be effective in maintaining abstinence in clients with mania and alcohol problems (Drake *et al.* 1998) and reducing cocaine use in people with bipolar affective disorder (Brown *et al.* 2002; Halikas *et al.* 2001). Divalpoex, a better-tolerated formulation of sodium valproate, has also been found to be effective in reducing cocaine use (Myrick *et al.* 2001). In addition, both sodium valproate and carbamazepine have been shown to have greater efficacy than lithium in treating mixed manic states in people with co-existing bipolar disorder and drug and alcohol problems (Brady and Sonne 1995; Goldberg *et al.* 1999). Carbamazepine also reduced the number of cocaine-positive urine tests in cocaine-dependent people with bipolar affective disorder, as compared to placebo (Brady *et al.* 2002).

Historically, lithium has been advocated as a treatment for alcohol misuse, independent of its mood-stabilizing effects. However, numerous trials over the 1980s brought into dispute its alleged anti-dependence properties and it is no longer used as a treatment for alcohol misuse alone (Abou-Saleh 1992). More recent research has shown that lithium can reduce opioid-like withdrawal signs in mice (Dehpour *et al.* 2002) and diminish physical dependence on morphine in mice (Dehpour *et al.* 1995). Trials have also shown that lithium can reduce both substance use and mood symptoms in adolescents with co-existing bipolar affective disorder and substance misuse (Geller *et al.* 1992).

As there is evidence supporting the efficacy of sodium valproate in treating both bipolar affective disorder and drug and alcohol problems, it is probably the first choice when treating such clients. Furthermore, sodium valproate may be more acceptable to the client as regular blood monitoring is not required (unlike lithium). Attendance for regular blood tests may be difficult for someone who has a chaotic lifestyle, and taking blood may be complicated by damaged veins in an intravenous drug user. On the other hand, stability of mood is likely to have a direct effect upon treatment compliance, so if lithium is the most effective mood stabilizer for a particular individual it should be continued.

Antipsychotic medication is also efficacious in the treatment of bipolar affective disorder. There is increasing evidence that atypical antipsychotics are successful in treating severe mental illness and co-existing drug and alcohol problems, including smoking (Keck *et al.* 1996; Sernjak *et al.* 1997;

Vartian *et al.* 2004). Most research has been done on the treatment of schizophrenia. However, some open trials and case reports have evaluated the use of antipsychotics in the treatment of people with bipolar affective disorder and drug and alcohol problems. Quetiapine appears to improve psychiatric symptoms and reduce cravings in people with bipolar affective disorder who are also dependent on cocaine (Brown *et al.* 2002). Quetiapine also appears to reduce alcohol craving in the same population (Longoria *et al.* 2004). Other case series have indicated that olanzapine may be useful in reducing anxiety and craving in alcohol-dependent people with bipolar affective disorder (Sattar *et al.* 2003). There appears to be little evidence regarding the use of risperidone and clozapine in people with co-existing bipolar disorder and substance misuse (Kosten and Kosten 2004).

Imipramine and selective serotonin re-uptake inhibitors (SSRIs) have been shown to improve depression and reduce drug and alcohol use in trials of people with depression and co-existing substance misuse (Abou-Saleh 2004; Crome and Myton 2004). However, there are no trials evaluating their use in people with bipolar disorder.

There is a lack of evidence regarding the treatment of co-existing opioid dependence and bipolar disorder. It is reasonable to evaluate each individual and, if opioid-dependent, commence on maintenance and withdrawal treatment using methadone or buprenorphine where necessary. However, anticonvulsants, particularly carbamazepine, induce the P-450 liver enzyme system, enhancing the metabolism of methadone. This may result in higher doses of methadone being required to combat opioid withdrawal symptoms. There is some indication that naltrexone may produce severe side effects in alcohol-misusing clients with bipolar affective disorder (Sonne and Brady 2000).

CASE STUDY

Susan is a 29-year-old woman with a severe and complex history of co-existing bipolar affective disorder and drug and alcohol problems. Her mother suffered from bipolar affective disorder and her father from major depression. Her parents' marriage was unhappy and they divorced when she was aged 12. Subsequently, she went to live with her father. However, he found her behaviour difficult to manage and as a result she was in local authority care from the age of 14, where she remained until she moved to independent living at the age of 18.

Susan was considered a bright pupil at school. Unfortunately, her teachers did not feel she fulfilled her full potential, due to truancy. She stayed on to finish school, gaining her A-levels at 18, and started a three-year college course. However, Susan dropped out of her course in the first year. After this she had several very short-term jobs in offices and shops, but has not worked since her early 20s.

Susan's drug use started at the age of 12 when she began to experiment with LSD. At 14 she intermittently began to smoke crack cocaine. She began to use heavily at the age of 22, after she was raped and underwent an unrelated termination of pregnancy. Subsequent to this she started injecting crack cocaine. From the ages of 15 to 21 she used ecstasy, though her use tailed off when she started injecting crack. At the age of 24 she began injecting heroin. Furthermore, since her early teens Susan has been a heavy user of amphetamines, especially smoking 'freebase'. Finally, she has also intermittently used benzodiazepines.

Although Susan had previously suffered episodes of depression, her first admission to an acute psychiatric ward at the age of 18 occurred during a manic episode. She was detained by the police for behaving bizarrely, and diagnosed as having bipolar affective disorder.

Over the next five years Susan had numerous admissions to acute psychiatric wards. She would usually present in an extremely disturbed state with psychotic features which resulted in detention under the UK Mental Health Act. Her symptoms would include elevated affect and a preoccupation with witches, as well as auditory hallucinations. Susan's behaviour would often be extremely disinhibited, manifested in high-risk situations such as prostitution and sharing of needles. Most of her admissions were complicated by intoxication and, although a diagnosis of bipolar disorder had been given at the age of 18, subsequent diagnoses fluctuated between bipolar disorder and drug-induced psychosis. On other occasions she would attend an Accident and Emergency Department (A&E) expressing suicidal thoughts. Her lifestyle became increasingly chaotic, with periods of homelessness in the context of rent arrears and prostitution.

Susan was convicted on several occasions for theft, for which she served short prison sentences. Her behaviour became more aggressive and violent and she often assaulted staff in A&E and on the ward. This culminated in Susan serving a four-month sentence following an assault on a police officer and a member of the A&E nursing staff.

During this period Susan was under her local community mental health team (CMHT). However, they found it exceptionally difficult to engage with her when she was in the community. While in hospital she was treated with antipsychotics and mood stabilizers; however, she did not remain compliant when discharged. Carbamazepine was found to be the most successful mood stabilizer, but even this had only limited effect.

Even though Susan's drug use was recognized as the major factor contributing to her mental illness, between the ages of 18 and 26 she had only limited contact with drug and alcohol services. This involved a brief contact with the local community drug team and an inpatient admission for detoxification. However, she did not complete the detoxification, discharged herself and subsequently did not continue contact with the drug services.

Susan's behaviour and symptoms escalated and at the age of 26 she was discharged from the CMHT due to non-compliance with treatment. The consultant also questioned her diagnosis of bipolar disorder, stating that he felt she suffered from a mental and behavioural disorder secondary to polysubstance misuse. For the next three months there was no contact with any health services and Susan remained homeless.

At this point Susan discovered she was pregnant. An emergency social services meeting was called because of high concerns around the safety of her unborn child. As a consequence of this meeting, she was referred to the regional tertiary drug services, which are designed for people with complex mental health and behavioural problems.

At the point of engagement with tertiary drug services Susan was three months pregnant and injecting crack cocaine and heroin. She was also using benzodiazepines and amphetamines. Susan attended her early antenatal appointments and was diagnosed with hepatitis C after routine screening.

Susan's sessions with her key worker at the drug service centred on her fears about her pregnancy. Education about the harm caused by crack cocaine and heroin to both herself and her baby provided the starting point. Initially Susan was very ambivalent about treatment. However, she began to recognize that treatment might be beneficial for her pregnancy. Unfortunately, Susan continued to deny a link between her drug use and her mental disorder.

When Susan was four months pregnant she agreed to admission for methadone stabilization and withdrawal on the inpatient detoxification ward. During the course of the detoxification, she became elated and disturbed. Subsequently, she was referred to the secure psychiatric ward under the UK Mental Health Act. When her presentation improved she was transferred to a general adult psychiatric ward. She was then discharged after using drugs.

This pattern of seeking admission to the drug detoxification ward, and deterioration in her mental state during detoxification resulting in transfer to psychiatric services, repeated itself during her pregnancy. Susan maintained contact with drug services during her pregnancy and the CMHT became involved again.

Her child was delivered by caesarean section, immediately taken into care due to risk of neglect and subsequently adopted. She ceased contact with drug services and after no contact for six months she was discharged. However, there were repeated admissions under psychiatric services.

A month after her discharge Susan was referred by the CMHT back to tertiary drug services. She was still using heroin and crack, and experiencing auditory hallucinations, presenting in an extremely disturbed manner and assaulting staff. Methadone stabilization was commenced and she attended daily for two weeks, but then she disappeared for two weeks, subsequently reappearing intoxicated and talking about bizarre encounters with strangers on trains. Further methadone stabilization was offered but the only subsequent contact was by telephone.

At this point there were several meetings between the CMHT and tertiary drug services. A plan was devised whereby there would be continued liaison between the two services regarding Susan and the tertiary drug service would continue to keep her on their books as well as offering further appointments.

In the subsequent year Susan had continued psychiatric admissions but did not attend drug appointments, until she turned up unannounced at the drug clinic and demanded immediate inpatient detoxification. When this was not forthcoming she was violent towards staff. Subsequently she was sentenced for assaulting a police officer and sent to prison. In prison she was admitted to the forensic drug unit and continued to have contact with the CMHT. Figure 14.2 illustrates the timeline for Susan's drug and alcohol use, presentation with bipolar affective disorder, and treatment.

Susan's case raises several issues. The first relates to the diagnostic uncertainty surrounding her serious mental disorder and her co-existing drug and alcohol problems. Susan appears to suffer from bipolar affective disorder. She has episodes of both mania and depression, there is a strong family history and she has been successfully treated on occasion with carbamazepine. Unfortunately, her severe polysubstance use has resulted in multiple admissions, often complicated by intoxication, violent assaultative behaviour and non-compliance with treatment when in the community.

It has also been very difficult to assess her during a period of abstinence from drugs, so it has not been possible to make a statement about which disorder is primary. Chronologically, Susan's drug use started prior to her diagnosis of bipolar disorder, but this does not mean her bipolar disorder is a result of her drug use, although it may have increased her vulnerability to developing the disorder. This has led to some specialists stating that her symptoms are drug-induced, which resulted in the CMHT withdrawing their care at one point. This exemplifies the difficulties that occur when services are designated according to a specific diagnosis.

Initially Susan's treatment was managed by psychiatric services and an integrated approach was not used. Any contact with drug services was brief and not actively followed up.

The catalyst for a more integrated approach was Susan's pregnancy. The child protection issues resulted in tertiary drug service involvement and resumed CMHT involvement. This integrated approach enabled the concerns about Susan's care to be shared across services and an action plan to be instigated to support both Susan and her unborn child. Furthermore, this approach allowed a more seamless transfer between psychiatric and drug misuse services and resulted in her longest period of contact with drug services. Finally, it resulted in the healthy delivery of her child, even though her lifestyle remained high-risk.

The integrated approach continued. A willing liaison between services meant that the CMHT could rapidly refer to drug services when she made contact. The drug service was more flexible towards Susan than toward solely drug-misusing clients. This illustrates the importance of an empathic approach that is not just driven by the motivation of the client to continue in treatment. Even though it was very clear that Susan was not highly motivated to address her drug and alcohol problems, the drug service could attempt to work with her to reduce any harm around her drug use and try to stabilize her on methadone. This was of particular importance when she was pregnant.

The final elements of this case were the violence and assaults perpetrated by Susan. Ultimately the repeated violence did result in discharge from drug services as staff safety was paramount. Sentencing to prison resulted in detoxification and attempts to address her drug issues in a secure environment. This treatment for her drug misuse was coercive, but may lead to subsequent community treatment. Furthermore, the CMHT continued their input while Susan was in prison. Finally, liaison with forensic services and continued input while in prison improved the care received by Susan.

Susan is extremely high-risk and vulnerable due to her mental illness and drug use. In addition, her levels of violence present a risk to others. Although her drug misuse has yet to be successfully addressed and her bipolar affective disorder is uncontrolled, Susan's case emphasizes the importance of an integrated approach across services, increased flexibility in accessing drug treatment and seamless transfer between services. This is all vital in managing such high-risk clients. However, even in cases such as this one, where services do try to work together flexibly, issues arise regarding the balance to be struck between different needs: Susan has repeatedly been discharged for demonstrating the very problems (irregular attendance at services, mania, drug misuse, disturbed behaviour and violence) which brought her to the attention of services in the first place. Until services find ways of continuing to work with such difficult-to-manage clients, while still addressing the safety of staff, Susan's and other similar cases will not be manageable outside of forensic or secure facilities.

CONCLUSION

Bipolar affective disorder is the mental illness with the highest risk of co-existing substance misuse. There is significant evidence linking co-existing drug and alcohol use to poorer outcomes, particularly increased risk of suicide, poorer functioning and non-compliance. There is limited research into the treatment of this particular group and most of the evidence for the efficacy of particular interventions has been extrapolated from studies of people with schizophrenia or other severe mental disorders. The foundation of treatment is a detailed assessment of both mood symptoms and drug and

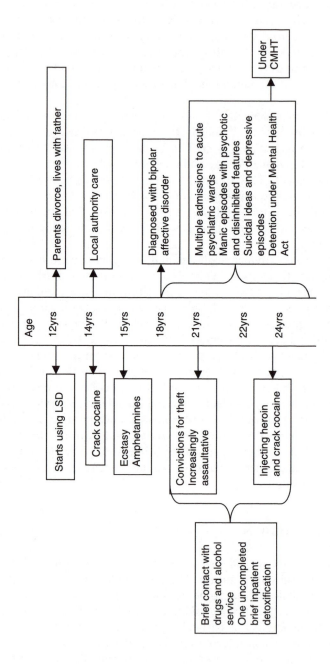

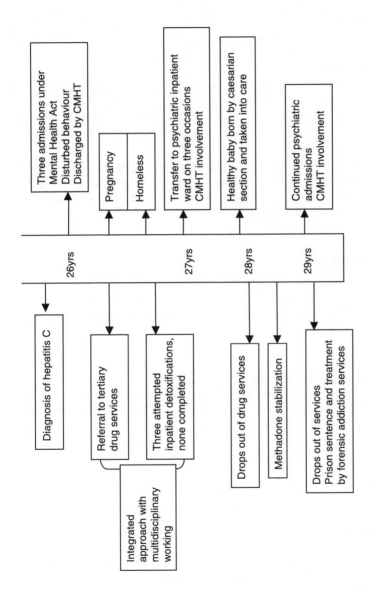

Figure 14.2 Timeline for case study of Susan.

alcohol use and any related problems. This often needs to take place over a period of time, as acute mood symptoms, and manic symptoms in particular, can make assessment of any substance misuse very difficult.

Treatment following an integrated model, in a supportive environment with a named key worker addressing both drug and alcohol use and psychiatric disorder, is likely to lead to the most successful outcomes. Psychological treatment may also be useful, but has not been evaluated by randomized controlled trials in clients with bipolar disorder. In particular, people with severe mental disorders may find group therapy for substance misuse intimidating and uncomfortable.

There is accumulating evidence to support the use of mood stabilizers and antipsychotics, especially sodium valproate and quetiapine. However, it does not appear that routine pharmacological treatment for substance misuse, such as methadone maintenance and withdrawal, has been fully evaluated in people with bipolar disorder.

Bipolar disorder can be a chronic disorder and it is likely that any co-existing drug and alcohol problems are also longstanding. As a consequence, treatment is usually long-term with integrated pharmacotherapy, psychological and social interventions.

KEY RESOURCES

Video

MIND, *Pillar to Post*, Croydon, 2003. Available at http://www.mindincroydon.org.uk

Organizations

The Depression and Bipolar Support Alliance, 730 North Franklin Street, #501, Chicago, IL 60610–7224, USA. Available at http://www.dbsalliance.org
The Manic Depression Fellowship, Castle Works, 21 Georges Road, London SE1 6ES, UK. Available at http://www.mdf.org.uk

Website

Hannant, M., *Bipolar Aware*, 2001. Available at http://www.bipolaraware.co.uk

REFERENCES

Abou-Saleh, M. T., 'Lithium', in Paykel, E. S., ed., *Handbook of Affective Disorders*, pp. 369–85. Edinburgh: Churchill Livingstone, 1992.
Abou-Saleh, M. T., 'The psychopharmacology of substance misuse and comorbid psychiatric disorders', *Acta Neuropsychiatrica*, *16*, 19–25, 2004.

Addington, J. and Duchak, V., 'Reasons for substance misuse in schizophrenia', *Acta Psychiatrica Scandinavica*, *96*, 329–33, 1997.

American Psychiatric Association, *Diagnostic and Statistical Manual of Mental Disorders*, 4th ed. Washington: APA, 1994.

Appleby, L., Dyson, V., Altman, E., McGovern, M. P. and Luchins, D. J., 'Utility of the Chemical Use, Abuse and Dependence Scale in screening patients with severe mental illness', *Psychiatric Services*, *47*, 647–9, 1996.

Babor, T. F., de la Fuente, J. R. and Saunders, J., *AUDIT: The Alcohol Use Disorders Identification Test: Guidelines for use in primary care*. Geneva: World Health Organization, 1989.

Barlow, K., Grenyer, B. and Ilkiw-Lavalle, O., 'Prevalence and precipitants of aggression in psychiatric inpatient units', *Australian and New Zealand Journal of Psychiatry*, *34*, 967–74, 2000.

Bidaut-Russell, M., Bradford, S. E. and Smith, E. M., 'Prevalence of mental illnesses in adult offspring of alcoholic mothers', *Drug and Alcohol Dependence*, *35*, 81–90, 1994.

Brady, K. T., Casto, S., Lydiard, R. B., Malcolm, R. and Arana, G., 'Substance misuse in an inpatient psychiatric sample', *American Journal of Drug and Alcohol Abuse*, *17*, 389–97, 1991.

Brady, K. T. and Sonne, S. C., 'The relationship between substance misuse and bipolar disorder', *Journal of Clinical Psychiatry*, *56*, 19–24, 1995.

Brady, K. T., Sonne, S. C., Malcolm, R., Randall, C. L., Simpson, K., Danskey, B. S. *et al.*, 'Carbamazepine in the treatment of cocaine dependence: Subtyping by affective disorder', *Experimental Clinical Psychopharmacology*, *10*, 276–85, 2002.

Brown, E. S., Nejtek, V. A., Perantie, D. C. and Bobadilla, L., 'Quetiapine in bipolar disorder and cocaine dependence', *Bipolar Disorders*, *4*, 406–11, 2002.

Carey, K. B. and Correia, C. J., 'Severe mental illness and addictions: Assessment considerations', *Addictive Behaviors*, *23*, 735–48, 1998.

Comtois, K. A., Russo, J., Roy-Byrne, P. and Ries, R. K., 'Clinicians' assessments of bipolar disorder and substance abuse as predictors of suicidal behaviour in acutely hospitalized psychiatric inpatients', *Biological Psychiatry*, *56*, 757–63, 2004.

Crome, I. B. and Myton, T., 'Pharmacotherapy in dual diagnosis', *Advances in Psychiatric Treatment*, *10*, 413–24, 2004.

Dehpour, A. R., Farsam, H. and Azizabadi-Farahani, M., 'Inhibition of morphine withdrawal syndrome and the development of physical dependence by lithium in mice', *Neuropharmacology*, *34*, 115–21, 1995.

Dehpour, A. R., Sadr, S. S., Azizi, M. R., Namiranian, K., Farahani, M. and Javidan, A. N., 'Lithium inhibits the development of physical dependence to clonidine in mice', *Pharmacology and Toxicology*, *90*, 89–93, 2002.

Drake, R. and Mueser, K. T., 'Psychosocial approaches to dual diagnosis', *Schizophrenia Bulletin*, *26*, 105–11, 2000.

Drake, R., Xie, H., McHugo, G. J. and Shumway, M., 'Three-year outcomes of long-term patients with co-occurring bipolar and substance use disorders', *Biological Psychiatry*, *56*, 749–56, 2004.

Drake, R. E., Mercer-McFadden, C., Mueser, K. T., McHugo, G. J. and Bond, G. R., 'Review of integrated mental health and substance abuse treatment for patients with dual disorders', *Schizophrenia Bulletin*, *24*, 589–608, 1998.

Farrell, M., Howes, S., Taylor, C., Lewis, G., Jenkins, R., Bebbington, P. *et al.*, 'Substance misuse and psychiatric comorbidity: An overview of the OPCS National Psychiatric Morbidity Survey', *Addictive Behaviors, 23*, 909–18, 1998.

Galanter, M., Egelko, S., Edwards, H. and Vergaray, M., 'A treatment system for combined psychiatric and addictive illness', *Addiction, 89*, 1227–35, 1994.

Geller, B., Cooper, T. B., Watts, H. E., Cosby, C. M. and Fox, L. W., 'Early findings from a pharmokinetically designed double blind and placebo controlled study of lithium for adolescents comorbid with bipolar and substance dependency disorders', *Progress in Neuro-Psychopharmacology and Biological Psychiatry, 16*, 281–99, 1992.

Goldberg, J. F., Garno, J. L., Leon, A. C., Kocsis, J. H. and Portera, L., 'A history of substance misuse complicates remission from acute mania in bipolar disorder', *Journal of Clinical Psychiatry, 60*, 733–40, 1999.

Graham, H. L., Copello, A., Birchwood, M. J., Maslin, J., McGovern, D., Orford, J. and Gerorgiou, G., 'The Combined Psychosis and Substance Use Programme (COMPASS): An integrated, shared care approach', in Graham, H. L., Copello, A., Birchwood, M. J. and Mueser, K. T., eds, *Substance Misuse in Psychosis: Approaches to Treatment and Service Delivery*, pp. 106–20. Chichester: John Wiley, 2003.

Graham, H. L., Copello, A., Birchwood, M. J., Mueser, K. T., Orford, J., McGovern, D. *et al.*, *Cognitive Behavioural Integrated Treatment (C-BIT)*. Chichester: John Wiley, 2004.

Halikas, J. A., Centre, B. A., Pearson, V. L., Carlson, G. A. and Crea, F., 'A pilot, open clinical study of depakote in the treatment of cocaine abuse', *Human Psychopharmacology, 16*, 257–64, 2001.

Harrison, C. and Abou-Saleh, M. T., 'Psychiatric disorders and substance misuse psychopathology in dual diagnosis', in Rassool, H., ed., *Substance Misuse and Psychiatric Disorders*. Oxford: Blackwell, 2002.

Hasin, D., Trautman, K., Miele, G., Samet, S., Smith, M. and Endicott, J., 'Psychiatric Research Interview for Substance Misuse and Mental Disorders (PRISM): Reliability for substance abusers', *American Journal of Psychiatry, 153*, 1195–201, 1996.

Heatherton, T. F., Kozlowski, L. T., Frecker, R. C. and Fagerstrom, K. O., 'The Fagerstrom Test for Nicotine Dependence: A revision of the Fagerstrom Tolerance Questionnaire', *British Journal of Addiction, 86*, 1119–27, 1991.

Hertzman, M., 'Divalproex sodium used to treat concomitant substance abuse and mood disorders', *Journal of Substance Abuse Treatment, 18*, 371–2, 2000.

Itkin, O., Nemets, B. and Einat, H., 'Smoking habits in bipolar and schizophrenic outpatients in southern Israel', *Journal of Clinical Psychiatry, 62*, 269–72, 2001.

Jerrell, J. and Ridgely, M. S., 'Comparative effectiveness of three approaches to serving people with severe mental illness and substance abuse disorders', *Journal of Nervous and Mental Disease, 183*, 566–76, 1995.

Keck, P. E., McElroy, S. L., Strkowski, S. M., Balistreri, T. M., Kizer, D. L. and West, S. A., 'Factors associated with maintenance antipsychotic treatment of patients with bipolar disorder', *Journal of Clinical Psychiatry, 57*, 147–51, 1996.

Keck, P. E., McElroy, S. L., Strkowski, S. M., West, S. A., Sax, K. W., Hawkins, J. M., *et al.*, '12 month outcome of patients with bipolar disorder following hospitalization for a manic or mixed episode', *American Journal of Psychiatry, 155*, 646–52, 1998.

Keller, M. B., Lavori, P. W., Coryell, W., Andreason, N. C., Endicott, J., *et al.*, 'Differential outcome of pure manic, mixed/cycling, and pure depressive episodes in patients with bipolar illness', *Journal of the American Medical Association, 255,* 3138–42, 1986.

Kelly, J. F., McKeller, J. D. and Moos, R., 'Major depression in patients with substance use disorders: Relationship to 12-step self-help involvement and substance use outcomes', *Addiction, 98,* 499–508, 2003.

Kosten, T. R. and Kosten, T. A., 'New medication strategies for comorbid substance use and bipolar affective disorders', *Journal of Biological Psychiatry, 56,* 771–7, 2004.

Laudet, A. B., Magura, S., Cleland, C. M., Vogel, H. S., Knight, E. L. and Rosenblum, A., 'The effect of 12-step based fellowship participation on abstinence among dually diagnosed persons: A two-year longitudinal study', *Journal of Psychoactive Drugs, 36,* 207–16, 2004.

Levin, F. R. and Hennessy, G., 'Bipolar disorder and substance abuse', *Journal of Biological Psychiatry, 56,* 738–48, 2004.

Longoria, J., Brown, E. S., Perantie, D. C., Bobadilla, L. and Nejtek, V. A., 'Quetiapine for alcohol use and craving in bipolar disorder', *Journal of Clinical Psychopharmacology, 24,* 101–2, 2004.

Lowe, A. L. and Abou-Saleh, M. T., 'The British experience of dual diagnosis in the National Health Service', *Acta Neuropsychiatrica, 16,* 41–6, 2004.

McHugo, G. J., Drake, R., Burton, H. L. and Ackerson, T. H., 'A scale for assessing the stage of substance abuse treatment in persons with severe mental illness', *Journal of Nervous and Mental Disease, 183,* 762–7, 1995.

McLellan, A. T., Kushner, H., Metzger, D., Peters, R., Smith, I. Grissom, G. *et al.*, 'The fifth edition of the addiction severity index', *Journal of Substance Abuse Treatment, 9,* 199–213, 1992.

Michaelis, B. H., Goldberg, J. F., Davis, G. P., Singer, T. M., Garno, J. L. and Wenze, S. J., 'Dimensions of impulsivity and aggression associated with suicide attempts among bipolar patients: A preliminary study', *Suicide and Life-Threatening Behaviour, 34,* 172–7, 2004.

Miller, F. T., Busch, F. and Tanenbaum, J. H., 'Drug abuse in schizophrenia and bipolar disorder', *American Journal of Drug and Alcohol Abuse, 15,* 291–5, 1989.

Miller, W. and Rollnick, S., *Motivational Interviewing: Preparing People for Change.* New York: Guilford Press, 1991.

Miller, W. and Rollnick, S., *Motivational Interviewing: Preparing People for Change,* 2nd ed. New York: Guilford Press, 2002.

Mueser, K. T., Drake, R. and Wallach, M. A., 'Dual diagnosis: A review of aetiological theories', *Addictive Behaviors, 23,* 717–34, 1998.

Mueser, K. T., Noordsy, D. L., Drake, R. and Fox, L. W., *Integrated Treatment for Dual Disorders: A Guide to Effective Practice.* New York: Guilford Publications, 2003.

Myrick, H., Henderson, S., Brady, K. T., Malcolm, R. and Measom, M., 'Divalproex loading in the treatment of cocaine dependence', *Journal of Psychoactive Drugs, 33,* 283–7, 2001.

Osher, F. C. and Kofoed, L. L., 'Treatment of patients with psychiatric and psychoactive substance use disorders', *Hospital and Community Psychiatry, 40,* 1025–30, 1989.

Ouimette, P. C., Finney, J. W., Gima, K. and Moos, R. H., 'A comparative evaluation of substance abuse treatment III. Examining mechanisms underlying patient treatment matching hypotheses for 12 step and cognitive behavioural treatments for substance abuse', *Alcoholism: Clinical and Experimental Research*, 23, 545–51, 1999.

Perry, A., Tarrier, N., Morriss, R., McCarthy, E. and Limb, K., 'Randomised controlled trial of efficacy of teaching patients with bipolar disorder to identify early symptoms of relapse and obtain treatment', *British Medical Journal*, 318, 149–53, 1999.

Pilling, S., Bebbington, P., Kuipers, E., Garety, P., Geddes, J., Orbach, G. and Morgan, C., 'Psychological treatments in schizophrenia: I. Meta-analysis of family intervention and cognitive behaviour therapy', *Psychological Medicine*, 32, 763–82, 2002.

Prochaska, J. O. and DiClemente, C. C., 'Stages of change in the modification of problem behaviours', in Hersen, M., Eisler, R. and Miller, P., eds, *Progress in Behavior Modification*, 28, pp. 184–214. Sycamore: Sycamore Publications, 1992.

Reiger, D. A., Myers, J. K., Krammer, M., Robins, L. M., Blazer, D. G., Hough, R. L. *et al.*, 'Epidemiological catchment area program: Historical context, major objectives, and study population characteristics', *Archives of General Psychiatry*, 41, 934–41, 1984.

Rosenberg, S. D., Drake, R., Wolford, G. L., Mueser, K. T., Oxman, T. E., Vidaver, R. M. *et al.*, 'Dartmouth Assessment of Lifestyle Instrument (DALI): A substance use disorder screen for people with severe mental illness', *American Journal of Psychiatry*, 155, 232–8, 1998.

Rydon, P., Redman, S., Sanson-Fisher, R. W. and Reid, A. L., 'Detection of alcohol-related problems in general practice', *Journal of Studies on Alcohol*, 50, 197–202, 1992.

Sattar, S. P., Grant, K., Bhatia, S. and Petty, F., 'Potential use of olanzapine in treatment of substance dependence disorders', *Journal of Clinical Psychopharmacology*, 23, 413–5, 2003.

Schneck, C. D., Miklowitz, D. J., Calabrese, J. R., Allen, M. H., Thomas, M. R., Wisniewski, S. R. *et al.*, 'Phenomenology of rapid-cycling bipolar disorder: Data from the first 500 participants in the systematic treatment enhancement program', *American Journal of Psychiatry*, 161, 1902–9, 2004.

Sernjak, M. J., Godleski, L. S., Griffin, R. A., Mazure, C. M. and Woods, S. W., 'Chronic neuroleptic exposure in bipolar patients', *Journal of Clinical Psychiatry*, 58, 193–5, 1997.

Simon, N. W., Otto, M. W., Wisniewski, S. R., Fossey, M., Sagduyu, K., Frank, E. *et al.*, 'Anxiety disorder comorbidity in bipolar disorder patients: Data from the first 500 participants in the systematic treatment enhancement program for bipolar disorder (STEP-BD)', *American Journal of Psychiatry*, 161, 222–9, 2004.

Skinner, H., 'The drug abuse screening test', *Addictive Behaviors*, 7, 363–71, 1982.

Sonne, S. C. and Brady, K. T., 'Naltrexone for individuals with co-morbid bipolar disorder and alcohol dependence', *Journal of Clinical Psychopharmacology*, 20, 114–5, 2000.

Swartz, M. S., Swanson, J. W., Hiday, V. A., Borum, R., Wagner, H. R. and Burns, B. J., 'Violence and severe mental illness: The effects of substance misuse and non-adherence to medication', *American Journal of Psychiatry*, 155, 226–31, 1998.

Tarrier, N., Lewis, S., Haddock, G., Bentall, R., Drake, R., Kinderman, P. *et al.*, 'Cognitive-behavioural therapy in first-episode and early schizophrenia: 18-month follow-up of a randomised controlled trial', *British Journal of Psychiatry, 184*, 231–9, 2004.

Vartian, B. A., Hawken, E. R. and Delva, N. J., 'Spontaneous long-term smoking cessation in a patient with schizophrenia after treatment with Ziprasidone', *Addictive Disorders and Their Treatment, 3*, 138–43, 2004.

Weiss, R. D., Griffin, M. L., Greenfield, S. F., Najavits, L. M., Wyner, D., Soto, J. A. and Hennen, J. A., 'Group therapy for patients with bipolar disorder and substance dependence: Results of a pilot study', *Journal of Clinical Psychiatry, 61*, 361–7, 2000.

Chapter 15

Eating disorders and drug and alcohol problems

*Jennifer S. Coelho, Christopher Thornton,
Stephen W. Touyz, J. Hubert Lacey and Sarah Corfe*

KEY POINTS

1   There are relatively high rates of co-existing substance misuse and
    dependence in individuals with eating disorders, in particular in those
    with bulimia nervosa or the binge/purge subtype of anorexia nervosa.
2   Clients with co-existing eating disorders and drug and alcohol problems
    are generally regarded as problematic to manage, and may exhibit a range
    of impulsive behaviours in addition to drug and alcohol use, including
    self-harm and sexual impulsivity.
3   During assessment of clients with co-existing eating disorders and drug
    and alcohol problems, the therapist's tone is important. This is because
    clients are often hesitant to discuss their problems with eating, and may
    also exhibit ambivalence about discussing their problems with drug or
    alcohol use.
4   Clients with co-existing eating disorders and drug and alcohol problems
    are often hesitant to relinquish their behaviour because of the function
    that it performs (e.g. affect regulation). Taking a motivational stance may
    help to engage clients in therapy, and serve to increase their motivation to
    change.
5   A treatment model is advocated in which an integrated approach is
    used by one primary therapist treating clients with co-existing eating
    disorders and drug and alcohol problems. In this model, therapists draw
    from a combination of strategies, including motivational enhancement,
    cognitive behavioural therapy, schema-focused therapy and dialectical
    behaviour therapy.

INTRODUCTION

Eating disorders can be viewed as extending across a wide spectrum from
disordered eating to the most serious of the eating disorders, anorexia nervosa. Across the spectrum lie eating disorders not otherwise specified and

bulimia nervosa. Eating disorders primarily affect young women. The lifetime prevalence of anorexia nervosa in women is 0.2–0.5 per cent, while that of bulimia nervosa is closer to 1 per cent (Hoek and van Hoeken 2003). The DSM IV (American Psychiatric Association 2000) diagnostic criteria for anorexia nervosa and bulimia nervosa are outlined in Table 15.1. The seriousness of these conditions is often underestimated. Anorexia nervosa, for example, has a higher mortality rate than any other psychiatric condition and a suicide rate higher than that of major depression. Early intervention is linked to more favourable outcome (Thornton *et al.* 2005).

Historically, the high rates of co-existing substance misuse and dependence in clients with bulimia nervosa, as well as in clients with a binge/purge subtype of anorexia nervosa, have been recognized (Mitchell *et al.* 1997; Wilson

Table 15.1 DSM IV diagnosis of anorexia nervosa and bulimia nervosa (APA 2000)

Anorexia nervosa	Bulimia nervosa
1 Refusal to maintain body weight at or above a minimally normal weight for age and height (e.g. weight loss leading to maintenance of body weight less than 85% of that expected, or failure to make expected weight gain during periods of growth, leading to body weight less than 85% of that expected)	1 Recurrent episodes of binge eating
	2 Recurrent inappropriate compensatory behaviours in order to prevent weight gain, such as self-induced vomiting; misuse of laxatives, diuretics, enemas or other medications; fasting; or excessive exercise
2 Intense fear of gaining weight or becoming fat, even though underweight	3 The binge eating and inappropriate compensatory behaviour both occur, on average, at least twice a week for three months
3 Disturbance in the way in which one's body weight or shape is experienced; undue influence of body weight or shape on self-evaluation; or denial of the seriousness of the current low body weight	
	4 Self-evaluation is unduly influenced by body shape and weight
4 In postmenarcheal females, amenorrhea (i.e. the absence of at least three consecutive cycles): a woman is considered to have amenorrhea if her periods occur only following hormone (e.g. oestrogen) administration	5 The disturbance does not occur exclusively during episodes of anorexia nervosa

Subtypes
1 Restricting type: during the current episode of anorexia nervosa, the person has not regularly engaged in binge eating or purging behaviour (i.e. self-induced vomiting or the misuse of laxatives, diuretics or enemas)
2 Binge eating/purging type: during the current episode of anorexia nervosa, the person has regularly engaged in binge eating or purging behaviour (i.e. self-induced vomiting or the misuse of laxatives, diuretics or enemas)

1993). It is interesting to note that Russell (1979), who provided the initial description of bulimia nervosa, drew attention to the fact that many clients with eating disorders also misused drugs and alcohol. This observation has been confirmed in many subsequent studies (e.g. Lacey 1995; Mitchell *et al.* 1985).

It may be that clients with co-existing drug and alcohol problems are over-represented in samples drawn from specialist treatment services. However, community studies also replicate the association between hazardous alcohol use and bulimia nervosa (Kozyk *et al.* 1998). On the other hand, more recent studies with both clinical (Grilo *et al.* 1995; Wilfley *et al.* 2000) and community (von Ranson *et al.* 2002) populations have compared the rates of co-existing drug and alcohol problems in eating disorders with the rates of co-existing drug and alcohol problems in other psychiatric disorders. In general, these studies indicate that the rate of co-existing drug and alcohol problems in eating disorders is no greater than the rate of co-existing drug and alcohol problems in other psychiatric conditions.

Similarly, women with drug and alcohol problems are as likely to have a co-existing eating disorder as any other psychiatric condition (Grilo *et al.* 1995). Some studies have investigated the presence of eating disorders among alcohol-dependent and drug-misusing women. Corrigan *et al.* (1990) reported rates of 8 per cent, whereas Lacey and Moureli (1986) indicated that the rates were probably a lot higher, in the order of some 41 per cent. Women with substance use problems may be more likely to present with sub-clinical eating disorders than eating problems that meet full diagnostic criteria (Grilo *et al.* 1995). Clinicians working with this population need to be aware of the need to screen for sub-clinical presentations of eating disorders, in the hope that early detection and treatment may prevent the development of clinical conditions.

There is a general consensus that the rates of alcohol and drug misuse are substantially lower in clients with restrictive anorexia nervosa (e.g. O'Brien and Vincent 2003). However, despite these lower levels of co-existing drug and alcohol problems, the rates are significant enough not to be ignored. Indeed, a number of substances, such as nicotine or amphetamines, may be used by individuals with anorexia regardless of their subtype (e.g. Wiederman and Pryor 1996). These substances may be used to increase activity levels and decrease hunger as a method of enhancing weight loss.

It is important to be aware that many clients with eating disorders will be using substances not commonly used by other populations – for example, laxatives, diuretics, diet pills and over-the-counter emetics such as Ipecac. The treatment of the misuse of these substances is described in the available eating disorders treatment literature (Harper *et al.* 2004), and will not be the focus of this chapter.

In both eating disorders and drug and alcohol misuse, the symptoms are to some extent ego-syntonic. In other words, the symptoms of these disorders may form part of clients' personalities or self-concepts. We feel that this results from the psychological function that the eating and other impulsive symptoms perform in helping clients cope with their view of the world (George *et al.* 2004; Thornton and Touyz 2004; Thornton *et al.* 2005). In clients presenting with multi-impulsive symptoms, binge-purge behaviour will often play a role in affect regulation and will provide a way of escaping from distressing thoughts about the self – for example, 'I am worthless' (Heatherton and Baumeister 1991; Waller in press; Waller and Kennerley 2003). Given that the symptoms perform a psychological function for the client, there is a reluctance to relinquish the symptom and, consequently, under-reporting or denial of the behaviour is common. In this chapter, we will elaborate on this model, and focus on ways in which therapists can address co-existing eating disorders and drug and alcohol problems.

CONTEXT OF THERAPY

Therapist variables

Specialist expertise is often needed in the treatment of clients with eating disorders. Those clients with co-existing eating disorders and drug and alcohol problems are generally regarded as more problematic to manage. The crucial question regards the competence of the therapist in treating such clients. Not all therapists skilled in the treatment of eating disorders have experience in treating drug and alcohol issues and vice versa. Should the same therapist provide treatment for both disorders, or would two therapists each with their own expertise be better suited to undertake such a therapeutic intervention? There is little research to suggest the optimum way to treat clients with co-existing eating disorders and drug and alcohol problems. Our experience suggests a model in which both disorders be treated by one treatment team. Indeed, given that these disorders are, from our perspective, serving the same underlying psychological function, we feel that treatment is best conducted by one therapist taking the stance advocated in this chapter.

Client variables

The link between eating disorders and drug and alcohol problems may not be direct, but rather related to client variables. The findings of Kozyk *et al.* (1998) suggest that an association exists between hazardous alcohol consumption and personality disorders. However, Kozyk *et al.*'s data did not indicate an association between bulimia nervosa and alcohol misuse. Hence, the presence of a personality disorder appears to be an important factor to assess when considering co-existing eating disorders and substance misuse. Such clients, with co-existing eating disorders and substance misuse, have often been referred to as having multi-impulsive bulimia nervosa (Lacey and Evans 1986) and have been well described in the literature (Lacey 1995). Around 8–10 per cent of clients with bulimia nervosa presenting to an inpatient clinic can be described as multi-impulsive. This was defined by Lacey (1995) as including at least three of the following behaviours: drinking at least 36 units of alcohol a week; using street drugs on at least four occasions in the previous 12 months; at least one overdose in the previous year; regular severe self-harm; and sexual impulsivity. Each behaviour is associated with a feeling of being out of control and seems to be interchangeable with another.

Setting

Therapy for individuals with co-existing eating disorders and substance misuse may occur in a variety of settings. There are inpatient programs in hospitals which are often designed for individuals with anorexia nervosa who are at a critically low body weight (although people with other eating disorders may also be admitted). Day programs are becoming increasingly prevalent; clients attend a treatment program during the day several times per week (Thornton *et al.* 2002; Touyz *et al.* 2003; Zipfel *et al.* 2002). Finally, clients are also seen as outpatients by therapists, often in collaboration with a medical professional whose role is to oversee medical issues and medications.

ASSESSMENT OF CO-EXISTING EATING DISORDERS AND DRUG AND ALCOHOL PROBLEMS

The clinical interview

Given the ego-syntonic nature of eating disorders, evaluating a client's motivation to change (Prochaska and DiClemente 1983) can help with the overall assessment. Clinical experience suggests that individuals with eating disorders are often hesitant to discuss their issues concerning eating, and may also hesitate to discuss possible misuse of drugs and alcohol (Mitchell *et al.* 1997). Mitchell and colleagues recommend including information provided by close friends and family members as part of the assessment. If a suspicion regarding co-existing drug or alcohol use arises, Mitchell *et al.* (1997) suggest that a urine toxicology screen or liver function tests should be considered.

As many clients presenting with an eating disorder deny the severity of their problem, or deny the problem itself, one would expect similar denials regarding problematic drug and alcohol use. The clinical interview is likely to yield much more relevant clinical information if the clinician approaches the task in a tactful indirect manner, rather than using direct questioning. An interview tone, previously described as 'rolling with resistance' when working with clients with eating disorders is especially indicated for clients with co-existing eating and substance issues (Geller *et al.* 2001; George *et al.* 2004). For example, rather than asking, 'Do you take drugs?' it would be better to say something like, 'Many young people these days experiment with drugs and alcohol. Is this something relevant to you or something you may have considered at any stage?' Such an approach is likely to yield more informative material. If a client with bulimia nervosa describes an additional impulsive feature, such as problematic alcohol use, it is important to enquire about other areas of impulsivity (Lacey 1995).

As with all clients with eating disorders, height and weight should be measured and a body mass index (weight/height × height) calculated. A series of medical investigations should also be undertaken (Thornton and Touyz 2004; Thornton *et al.* 2005).

Self-report questionnaires

There are now many questionnaires, including self-report questionnaires and structured interviews, to assist in the assessment of an individual with an eating disorder. Instruments such as the Eating Disorders Inventory 3 (Garner 2004), the Eating Attitudes Test (Garner and Garfinkel 1979), the Eating Disorders Examination (Fairburn and Cooper 1993) or the self-report version the Eating Disorders Examination Questionnaire (EDE-Q) (Fairburn and Beglin 1994) are commonly used to assess behavioural and cognitive manifestations of the eating disorders. The SCOFF questionnaire (Morgan *et al.* 1999) is a brief (five-item) interview that has been reported to be an adequate and effective brief screening tool for eating disorders. The Anorexia Nervosa Stages of Change Questionnaire (Reiger *et al.* 2000) may also be useful in estimating the client's current stage of change, although this questionnaire focuses on anorexic rather than bulimic symptoms.

Finally, the Shorter PROMIS Questionnaire (Christo *et al.* 2003) is a useful self-report instrument which assesses multiple addictive behaviours, including nicotine use, drug and alcohol use, and problematic eating behaviours. The authors of this instrument suggest that it is useful for clinicians to identify all the potentially addictive tendencies of their clients, in order to allow for the range of behaviours to be targeted during treatment.

Self-monitoring

Self-monitoring is a frequently used behavioural assessment procedure that can prove extremely useful in eliciting information about eating behaviour. Such monitoring may provide information regarding the frequency and timing of meals and snacks, binge episodes and compensatory behaviours such as exercise and vomiting, as well as the types and quantities of food consumed and the nutritional composition of the diet. If co-existing drug and alcohol problems are considered to be an issue, frequency and type of drug and alcohol use could be monitored in addition. Self-monitoring may provide valuable stimulus response information, by indicating triggers to bingeing or substance use, and may prove invaluable in assessing response to treatment interventions.

TREATMENT OF CO-EXISTING EATING DISORDERS AND DRUG AND ALCOHOL PROBLEMS

There is a dearth of literature about how clients with co-existing eating disorders and drug and alcohol problems should be treated. Many treatment studies have excluded people with co-existing drug and alcohol problems. As is often the case with the eating disorders, in the absence of such data we will describe our consensus about possible treatment methods and processes in these challenging presentations.

The primary dilemma for the clinician is whether the client with co-existing drug and alcohol problems should be engaged in a sequential treatment process whereby, typically, the substance problem is treated first and then the eating disorder is addressed (Wilson 1993). It is often the case that the substance and eating issues are treated by independent teams. Another approach is where both disorders are formulated as being a product of an underlying psychological process, such as maladaptive schemas (Waller in press; Waller and Kennerley 2003; Waller *et al.* 2000) or a personality disorder (Carroll *et al.* 1996; Kozyk *et al.* 1998). Treatment then aims not only to address the symptoms as they occur, but also to modify the underlying psychological process. Unfortunately, there is no empirical literature to guide us in making a choice between these approaches. In practice, if the substance misuse is severe, then this will usually need to be addressed first, in the knowledge that a subsequent exacerbation in the eating disordered symptoms is likely.

Our experience indicates that there are usually problems in the sequential treatment approach (whereby the client's case is divided into a series of symptoms and referred on to separate specialist services). The most common difficulty arising from this approach is 'symptom substitution' – the 'primary' symptom (i.e. the one currently the focus of treatment) responds to treatment, but the 'secondary' symptom worsens. This usually results in a referral to a specialist service for the 'secondary' symptom (which then becomes the 'primary' symptom), leading to a series of referrals and re-referrals between services. This is often seen, erroneously in our view, as a symptom of the client's resistance to treatment, or the client's attempts to deflect treatment from their 'real' issue back to the other symptom.

We feel that an integrated treatment approach, in which the treating team addresses all the presenting problems, is more respectful of the client, in that they are treated as a whole person with complex and interrelated issues. In addition to providing greater continuity of care, it also seems to be a more realistic way of treating co-existing problems. For example, it is common for clients with eating disorders to have multiple co-existing conditions in addition to drug and alcohol problems, including anxiety disorders, depression, personality disorder or post traumatic stress disorder. It is also likely that these clients present with a series of other impulsive behaviours such as self-mutilation, stealing, shopping and impulsive sexual behaviour. It is unrealistic to expect that the client should see numerous different specialists for treatment of each issue. Thus, an integrated approach with one primary therapist can be beneficial when treating clients with co-existing eating disorders and drug and alcohol problems.

A number of treatment programs for co-existing eating disorders and other problems, including drug and alcohol problems, have been described, rather than evaluated, in the literature. Mitchell *et al.* (1997) have outlined the group program they run from the University of Minnesota, USA, which meets for three hours every weekday evening. This group-based program integrates cognitive behaviour therapy (CBT) with a 12-step program that focuses on substance use. The program format comprises: one hour of check-in and review of self-monitoring and homework; another hour for a group meal; and lastly an hour-long skills-based session, where clients are taught cognitive and behavioural strategies such as thought challenging, assertiveness and problem-solving. There is an emphasis on spirituality and a 'higher power' that is not typically found in cognitive behavioural programs. However, there are difficulties with treating a binge-purge disorder from an abstinence-based addiction model (Wilson 1993). In fact, the abstinence-based approach is contraindicated in clients with eating disorders. That is, abstinence from certain food types (e.g. sugars) will lead to increased craving for those food types and act to increase the likelihood of binge eating (Polivy and Herman 1985).

A second integrated program described in the literature runs from St George's Hospital in London in the UK (Lacey 1995). This program also follows the model whereby all impulsive behaviours need to be tackled simultaneously. The program starts with a two-week assessment period during which the client's level of motivation is assessed by the team, and a choice is then offered to clients as to whether or not they feel ready and willing to engage in the treatment program. Should the client and the treatment team agree to engage in the program, the client enters into a verbal agreement with the team to take part in the full inpatient program. In the verbal contract, the client agrees: not to binge eat, vomit or attempt to lose weight; not to engage in self (or other) harm; not to use unprescribed drugs; not to drink alcohol; not to form any sexual relationship on or off the unit; and to be actively engaged in the treatment program. The inpatient program runs for 16 weeks and involves the client in CBT to help normalize eating patterns and stabilize weight. A range of group therapy activities is undertaken, focusing on shopping, cooking, communication, assertion, leisure, movement and exercise. A psychodynamically-based psychotherapy program occurs both in group and individual therapy modes. This is designed to help clients address the emotional issues that will inevitably arise when their impulsive behaviours are contained by the ward program. The inpatient phase is followed by a day treatment phase and the client attends at least four days a week for about 15 weeks. Clients continue in individual therapy during this time. Outpatient follow-up is provided by regular, but infrequent, contact with the team. Some clients continue in outpatient therapy, but are usually discharged after a number of months.

Lacey (1993) reported a long-term follow-up from the St George's multi-impulsive program and found that most clients significantly reduced their impulsive behaviours. Where impulsive behaviours continued, they largely took the form of alcohol use, but with episodes being more circumscribed.

In a 10-year retrospective follow-up study of 35 multi-impulsive bulimia nervosa clients completing this program (Corfe and Lacey, to be submitted), 31 per cent had no significant eating disorder using the EDE-Q (Fairburn and Beglin 1994), 57 per cent reported themselves to be entirely free of substance misuse, cutting and overdoses and 20 per cent reported the absence of both eating and other self-damaging behaviours.

CASE STUDY

Ann is an 18-year-old woman who lives with her parents, older sister and younger brother in a large regional town. She initially presented with bulimia nervosa to a specialist unit dealing with eating disorders at 17 years of age. At presentation, she was bingeing and purging five times per day and was within a normal weight range. Her purging behaviours included laxative misuse (10 times per day) and vomiting.

During assessment for the inpatient unit, Ann was asked about drug and alcohol use. She acknowledged social use of alcohol, but denied any drug use. As the inpatient unit program progressed, Ann's bingeing and vomiting decreased. However, it became clear that Ann had started to self-harm by cutting and burning. The issue was raised among the team that Ann was presenting with more multi-impulsive features than had initially been disclosed. With the client's consent, a meeting was arranged with Ann's parents to gain a corroborating history. Ann's mother and father reported that Ann would frequently engage in binge drinking, stay out late and occasionally not come home at all at night. Her parents also indicated that Ann's maternal grandparents had problems with substance use, but that they themselves were social drinkers only, with no history of substance problems. Ann's father reported that he was away frequently on business and there was a suggestion of some underlying marital strain.

Unable to desist from her self-harm and purging behaviour, Ann was discharged from the inpatient unit after a six-week stay. She was referred back to her general practitioner (GP) with a recommendation that she engage in long-term psychotherapy. She was referred to a clinical psychologist for individual outpatient therapy, but did not follow up this referral. Ann's bulimic symptoms returned to their initial levels. Ann acknowledged drinking a minimum of four to five glasses of wine per night and began to acknowledge that she was binge drinking on Thursday, Friday and Saturday nights, sometimes to the point of passing out. Ann was unable to report the amount of alcohol that she consumed during her binge episodes, but estimated it to be about 15 drinks per episode. Ann disclosed that she had engaged in unprotected sex on one occasion while binge drinking and presented to her GP with fears that she may have contracted HIV. The GP decided that her alcohol problem was the primary presenting issue and referred her to a drug and alcohol program.

During a four-week inpatient stay in this program, it appeared that Ann had managed to abstain from alcohol. However, it later emerged that she had continued to binge and purge throughout the program, had occasionally engaged in self-harm and had entered into inappropriate impulsive sexual relationships. Ann returned back to her GP after completing the program. Ann's drinking was more contained and she continued to meet with a drug and alcohol counsellor for follow-up once a week. However, her bulimic symptoms worsened to the point where she was bingeing and purging on average eight times a day. The drug and alcohol counsellor viewed the eating disorder symptoms as primary and referred her to another specialist eating disorder unit.

Ann initially denied the presence of alcohol use or other impulsive symptoms. One of the striking similarities between the presentation of clients with eating disorders and those with substance use disorders is their marked ambivalence about change. As we have highlighted in this chapter, this ambivalence about change may stem from the ego-syntonic nature of the symptoms. Ann may have been under-reporting her behaviours because of the psychological function that they were serving.

One problem with Ann's management was that her symptoms were seen as separate problems, treated by a distinct drug and alcohol team and a distinct eating disorder team. This illustrates that, in multi-impulsive clients with eating disorders, a sequential model of treatment where only one symptom is treated may result in the emergence or exacerbation of other impulsive areas.

Assessment

Before admitting Ann, the new eating disorders team obtained the previous treatment history from her GP and drug and alcohol counsellor, and with the client's consent conducted another family assessment.

At 12 months after the initial consultation and admission, Ann was more clearly presenting as an individual with multi-impulsive features and a possible borderline personality disorder. Armed with this collaborative information, a clinical psychologist on the eating disorders team met with Ann to discuss the treatment of her eating disorder symptoms in a day program that specializes in the treatment of eating disorders. The treatment team suggested that Ann might benefit from an admission to the inpatient unit initially, to help contain her behaviours. However, Ann was resistant to this and the team felt that a trial in the day program was warranted. In addition, the team felt that since Ann's drinking and bingeing was occurring in the evenings, a day program would allow her exposure to her psychosocial triggers, thus giving her the opportunity to practise the skills she would be learning in the program.

The treatment team understood that Ann did not present with a unitary diagnosis of eating disorder and was therefore prepared to modify the treatment contract to suit Ann's co-existing problems and stage of change for each presenting symptom (Touyz et al. 2003).

The following transcript illustrates the tone of therapy that was undertaken with Ann:

Therapist: It seems from your previous experiences of treatment that others have tried to treat either the bulimia or the alcohol and when one is treated the other gets worse. It's like it's really hard to change both behaviours at the same time. Why do you think that is?

Ann: I don't know. . . . I guess that they both help me to block the world out, sometimes I've just got to get a little oblivion.

Therapist: The binge eating and drinking help you feel better? Maybe help you to not feel?

Ann: Yes. It takes the pain away.

Therapist: Do the other behaviours [sexual activity/self-harm] also do that?

Ann: Yes.

Therapist: Ann, what strikes me is that in a way that must be very helpful. You have found a way to cope with the distress that you feel. Does that feel like I am getting that right? [A nod from Ann] It makes sense that when you give up one, the other gets worse, maybe you start to feel the pain and you need to get some oblivion any way you can.

Ann outlined some examples of how her symptoms help her to regulate her affect.

Therapist: Ann, I guess what's a bit confusing for me is that, in a way, you have found a way to cope with how you feel, to stop your suffering, and yet you are here in my office asking me to admit you to a program to take both these ways of coping away. Can you help me understand why?

Here the therapist works to validate the function of Ann's impulsivity (emotional regulation). He then plays 'devil's advocate' and highlights the advantages of the impulsive behaviours, then asks why Ann is seeking treatment. This allows Ann to tell him the disadvantages of her behaviour and elicits her motivation for change.

Ann: I just can't live like this any more. Everyone is angry with me, my friends won't go out with me because I get so trashed and they need to take care of me. I keep having sex with people I don't know, people just approach me to have sex with them because people know I'm easy. I tried to drink to cope to have sex. I need to starve to feel attractive but then I binge to stop feeling. My life is crap.

By now Ann was in floods of tears.

Therapist: I can see how the behaviours help you not feel and also make you feel that life is crap. That sounded like a horrible cycle where you feel you are so crap that you starve to be attractive, people that you don't know approach you just to have sex, you binge drink to cope with the sex, you feel like crap after the sex, you binge to cope with that feeling and that undoes all the starving. Going through that just feels endless. It feels like that the solution [impulsive behaviours] to the problem [feeling crap] is now creating the problem itself [feeling crap].

In his reflection of her response, the therapist emphasizes the reasons to change Ann has provided. He has effectively engaged her in therapy using an empathic tone and taking a motivational stance. Ann is now presenting in a contemplative stage of change. He is now in a position to outline a treatment program that will target Ann's behavioural symptoms.

It was highlighted that, although the program was focused on the treatment of the eating disorder, Ann's presentation was complex and multifactorial and staying in the program would require Ann to work with the team on her multi-impulsive behaviours. A goal of abstinence was agreed as Ann was able to see the self-reinforcing nature of her problems (i.e. her solutions were maintaining the problem). The interview went on to outline the 'non-negotiables' of the treatment program. Ann agreed to target her binge eating, binge drinking and sexual behaviours. She agreed that if her behaviours were difficult for her to change she could leave the program and continue working as an outpatient or accept an admission to the inpatient unit. The tone or spirit of the treatment contract offered the program as a choice, ensuring that change was not forced upon her.

As Ann cycled through the stages of change her ambivalence was a constant focus of treatment. She was able to consider the advantages and disadvantages of normalizing eating while containing her other impulsive behaviours (as listed in Table 15.2).

Ann's therapist validated her reasons not to change and emphasized how difficult it is to contemplate addressing these issues. The therapists in the team consistently asserted that they were impressed by Ann's ability to reduce her individual symptoms when targeted (in order to increase self-efficacy), as this indicated that Ann did possess some skills for change. The therapist reminded Ann that she would need to stay within the guidelines of the program in order to remain within it (constant reminders of the 'non-negotiables').

When Ann initially began the program she managed to reduce her bulimic symptoms. However, somewhat predictably, her levels of emotional distress increased, as did her urges to engage in binge drinking and self-harm behaviours. Ann agreed to self-monitor the triggers, cognitions and emotions around each of these behaviours. Over time a schema-based formulation was derived (George et al. 2004; Young et al. 2003). Self-monitoring was difficult for Ann and became an initial target of treatment. Ann was engaged in the 'mindfulness' module of a dialectical behaviour therapy (DBT) program at the same hospital and learnt skills such as observation, description and participation in the moment (Linehan 1993; Segal et al. 2002). As a result of this she was more able to observe the changes in her emotional state, and the triggers to her emotions. As part of the day therapy group program she was taught strategies from the 'distress tolerance' module of DBT (Linehan 1993; Safer et al. 2001; Telch et al. 2001; Thornton et al. 2002).

An example of Ann's self-monitoring is outlined in Table 15.3.

Self-monitoring allowed Ann and her therapist to develop a schema-based formulation, and she was able to understand that 'I don't matter' was a core belief. She was further able to understand that her efforts to be thin and her general perfectionism were attempts to compensate for this core belief (Waller in press). That is, to avoid the distress associated with this belief, Ann would focus on a more acceptable schema – that of unrelenting standards. Ann described how, over time, the schema compensation was less and less successful, and she became increasingly aware of her core belief that she didn't

Table 15.2 The advantages and disadvantages to Ann of changing to normalizing eating

Advantages of change	Reasons not to change
Normalize eating	Weight gain
Think less about food, weight and shape	No knowledge of how to cope without this
Get along better with family and friends	Start to remember how much I hate myself
Like myself more	Start to 'feel' again (bingeing and drinking
Long-term health issues (e.g. dental	helps avoid feelings)
decay, HIV)	
Reduce stress on family	

Table 15.3 An example of Ann's self-monitoring

Urge	To binge drink
Trigger	Returned home to an empty house
Emotions	Sadness and anger
Automatic thought(s)	– If my parents cared about me they would be here to support me – Nobody cares about me – I don't matter
Urge	Self-harm, drink
Trigger	Approached for sex in a club because of 'reputation'
Emotions	Anxiety, anger
Automatic thought(s)	– I have ruined my life – All people want from me is sex – I don't really matter

matter. In order to dissociate and disengage from the painful affect generated by her core beliefs, she increasingly engaged in impulsive behaviours in order to decrease awareness of her cognitions and affect. For example, Ann would go into a club knowing that her weight was normal and that her attempts to restrict had failed (i.e. she had failed to keep up her unrelenting standards). This in turn would lead to thoughts of 'I can't even control my weight, at a normal weight people can see that I don't matter and have nothing to offer.' This served to activate her core schema, leading to an intense and painful affect. In order to block this out, Ann would binge drink. Ann's drinking would increase the likelihood that she would engage in impulsive sexual relationships, which maintained the drinking (she used alcohol to deal with the sexual relationships). Ann described that after the sexual act, she often developed a sense of closeness with her partner, resulting in short-lived thoughts of 'I do matter' that would therefore act as a positive reinforcement to her behaviour. However, that in turn activated 'All I have to give to anybody is sex,' which reinforced her core belief of 'I don't matter.'

Minor lapses in Ann's behaviours were a constant focus of treatment. These were always used to refine the schema formulation. The emotional distress that triggered the lapse was validated and Ann was always reminded by the team that they understood (as much as they could) how difficult it was for her to reduce her impulsive behaviours and normalize her eating. Within the motivational enhancement tone it was consistently reinforced that Ann could leave the program if containing her behaviours was too difficult, and that she would be free to return to the program at any time if she were willing to continue working on her co-existing impulsive behaviours.

After two months in the program, Ann experienced a particularly difficult weekend, following her therapist changing her appointment time to accommodate the needs of another client. This clearly activated her belief that she didn't matter. She engaged in binge drinking and self-harm behaviour over a number of days. She was reviewed on the Monday, and was informed that she would need to use the skills that she had been acquiring from groups in order to contain the behaviour. The team believed that her motivation to change her behaviours was decreasing as her need to block the pain was increasing. Ann was reminded of the 'non-negotiables' of the program and was informed that if she continued to choose not to use the skills that she had gained from the groups, she would be given a time-out from the program. She actively informed the therapeutic team that she had no intention of stopping these behaviours.

A similar pattern occurred the following week, resulting in Ann being given a two-week time-out from the program, with a view to increasing her motivation. Ann continued to see the clinical psychologist during that time-out; the focus of therapy was on her motivation to change her multi-impulsive behaviours and on working to reframe the time-out in a schema-incongruent way. At the end of the time-out, Ann did not return to the program and continued to work with her outpatient therapist for another month on these themes. At this time, Ann agreed to be re-assessed for the program (using a similar motivational tone), having agreed to work to regain control over her symptoms, and agreed again to the 'non-negotiable' terms of the program for a structured six-week admission. Ann's therapy consisted of the following elements: continuing to build up coping strategies (emotional regulation/ distress tolerance); ongoing schema-focused work with attempts to understand the origins of schemas; the reframing of historical experiences; the gathering and recording of information incongruent with schemas; and further work on symptom reduction (Cooper *et al.* 2000; Young *et al.* 2003). During this admission Ann was more able to observe that when she engaged in all her symptomatic behaviours, her schemas were being maintained and reinforced. This increased her motivation to improve her eating behaviour and to reduce her drive for thinness.

Although it is traditional when writing a case history to present a client who does well in a short-term therapy and whose symptoms resolve, this was not the case for Ann. After the six-week admission, Ann continues to work in schema-focused therapy. At times, her behaviours re-emerge, but she is more able to look at these in a schema-focused way and more actively challenge her core beliefs. Work with Ann is expected to continue on an ongoing outpatient basis over the long term.

CONCLUSION

Clinicians working in the fields of substance use and eating disorders need to be cognisant of the co-existence of these and other disorders. Clinicians need to be further aware that clients with eating disorders will often use specific substances, such as emetics, laxatives and diuretics. Clients with eating disorders may also use substances such as nicotine or amphetamines for the purposes of weight loss or hunger control. The presence of co-existing drug and alcohol problems has important implications for treatment. There is little research to suggest the optimum way to treat such clients. Our experience suggests a model in which both disorders should be treated by one treatment team with one primary individual therapist. Our treatment involves using a motivational tone at all times, focusing on the treatment of the eating disorder in a group setting while working on other impulsive behaviours in parallel. When treating co-existing eating disorders and drug and alcohol problems, it can be beneficial for therapists to use a combination of strategies drawn from CBT, schema-focused therapy and DBT in order to treat both the eating and drug and alcohol problems, with the understanding that this is not an exhaustive list of treatment options. We feel that there are further significant advantages if this treatment is supplied by a specialist team in either an inpatient or day setting. Little is known of the longer-term outcome of clients with co-existing eating and substance use disorders. This research is needed as a matter of some urgency.

KEY RESOURCES

Treatment manuals

Garner, D. M. and Garfinkel, P. E., *Handbook of Treatment for Eating Disorders*, 2nd ed. New York: Guilford Press, 1997.

Assessment instruments

Christo, G., Jones, S. L., Haylett, S., Stephenson, G. M., Lefever, R. M. and Lefever, R., 'The shorter PROMIS questionnaire: Further validation of a tool for simultaneous assessment of multiple addictive behaviours', *Addictive Behaviours*, 28, 225–48, 2003.

Fairburn, C. G. and Beglin, S. J., 'Assessment of eating disorders: Interview or self report questionnaire?' *International Journal of Eating Disorders*, 16, 363–70, 1994.

Fairburn, C. G. and Cooper, Z., 'The Eating Disorders Examination', in Fairburn, C. G. and Wilson, G. T., eds, *Binge Eating: Nature, Assessment and Treatment*, pp. 317–60. New York: Guilford Press, 1993.

Garner, D. M., *Eating Disorders Inventory 3*. Odessa, FL: Psychological Assessment Resources, 2004.

Garner, D. M. and Garfinkel, P. E., 'The Eating Attitudes Test: An index of the symptoms of anorexia nervosa', *Psychological Medicine*, 12, 871–8, 1979.

Websites

Academy for Eating Disorders, *AED*. Northbrook, IL: Academy for Eating Disorders, 2005. Available at http://www.aedweb.org (accessed 12 August 2005).

Paxton, S., *Australian and New Zealand Academy for Eating Disorders.* Wahroonga, NSW: The Centre for Eating and Dieting Disorders, 2003. Available at http:// www.cedd.org.au/anzaed/anzaed.html (accessed 12 August 2005).

REFERENCES

American Psychiatric Association (APA), *Diagnostic and Statistical Manual of Mental Disorders,* 4th ed. Washington: APA, 2000.

Carroll, J. M., Touyz, S. W. and Beumont, P. J. V., 'Specific comorbidity between bulimia nervosa and personality disorders', *International Journal of Eating Disorders, 19,* 159–70, 1996.

Christo, G., Jones, S. L., Haylett, S., Stephenson, G. M., Lefever, R. M. and Lefever, R., 'The shorter PROMIS questionnaire: Further validation of a tool for simultaneous assessment of multiple addictive behaviours', *Addictive Behaviours, 28,* 225–48, 2003.

Cooper, M. J., Todd, G. and Wells, A., *Bulimia Nervosa: A Cognitive Therapy Programme for Clients.* London: Jessica Kingsley, 2000.

Corfe, S. E. and Lacey, J. H., 'Disordered eating, self-damaging and addictive behaviour in patients treated for multi-impulsive anorexia nervosa and bulimia nervosa: A long-term follow-up study'. To be submitted.

Corrigan, S. A., Johnson, W. G., Alford, G. S., Bergeron, K. C. and Lemmon, C. R., 'Prevalence of bulimia among patients in a chemical dependency treatment program', *Addictive Behaviours, 15,* 581–5, 1990.

Fairburn, C. G. and Beglin, S. J., 'Assessment of eating disorders: Interview or self report questionnaire?' *International Journal of Eating Disorders, 16,* 363–70, 1994.

Fairburn, C. G. and Cooper, Z., 'The Eating Disorders Examination', in Fairburn, C. G. and Wilson, G. T., eds, *Binge Eating: Nature, Assessment and Treatment,* pp. 317–60. New York: Guilford Press, 1993.

Garner, D. M., *Eating Disorders Inventory 3.* Odessa, FL: Psychological Assessment Resources, 2004.

Garner, D. M. and Garfinkel, P. E., 'The Eating Attitudes Test: An index of the symptoms of anorexia nervosa', *Psychological Medicine, 12,* 871–8, 1979.

Geller, J., Williams, K. D. and Srikameswaran, S., 'Clinician stance in the treatment of chronic eating disorders', *European Eating Disorders Review, 9,* 365–73, 2001.

George, L., Thornton, C. E., Touyz, S. W., Waller, G. and Beumont, P. J. V., 'Motivational enhancement and schema-focused cognitive behavioural therapy in the treatment of chronic eating disorders', *Clinical Psychologist, 8,* 81–5, 2004.

Grilo, C. M., Levy, K. N., Becker, D. F., Edell, W. S. and McGlashan, T. H., 'Eating disorders in female inpatients with versus without substance use disorders', *Addictive Behaviours, 20,* 255–60, 1995.

Harper, J., Leung, M. and Birmingham, C. L., 'A blinded laxative taper for patients with eating disorders', *Eating and Weight Disorders, 9,* 147–50, 2004.

Heatherton, T. F. and Baumeister, R. F., 'Binge eating as an escape from self awareness', *Psychological Bulletin, 110,* 86–108, 1991.

Hoek, H. W. and van Hoeken, D., 'Review of the prevalence and incidence of eating disorders', *International Journal of Eating Disorders, 34,* 383–96, 2003.

Kozyk, J. C., Touyz, S. W. and Beumont, P. J. V., 'Is there a relationship between bulimia nervosa and hazardous alcohol use?' *International Journal of Eating Disorders*, *24*, 95–9, 1998.

Lacey, J. H., 'Self damaging and addictive behaviours in bulimia nervosa: A catchment area study', *British Journal of Psychiatry*, *163*, 190–4, 1993.

Lacey, J. H., 'Inpatient treatment of multi-impulsive bulimia nervosa', in Brownell, K. D. and Fairburn, C. G., eds, *Eating Disorders and Obesity: A Comprehensive Handbook*, pp. 361–8. New York: Guilford Press, 1995.

Lacey, J. H. and Evans, C. D. H., 'The impulsivist: A multi-impulsive personality disorder', *British Journal of Addiction*, *81*, 641–9, 1986.

Lacey, J. H. and Moureli, E., 'Bulimic alcoholics: Some findings of a clinical subgroup', *British Journal of Addiction*, *81*, 389–93, 1986.

Linehan, M. M., *Skills Training Manual for Treating Borderline Personality Disorder*. New York: Guilford Press, 1993.

Mitchell, J. E., Hatsukami, D., Eckert, E. D. and Pyle, R. L., 'Characteristics of 275 patients with bulimia', *American Journal of Psychiatry*, *142*, 482–5, 1985.

Mitchell, J. E., Speckler, S. and Edmonson, K., 'Management of substance abuse and dependence', in Garner, D. M. and Garfinkel, P. E., eds, *Handbook of Treatment for Eating Disorders*, pp. 415–23. New York: Guilford Press, 1997.

Morgan, J. F., Reid, F. and Lacey, J. H., 'The SCOFF questionnaire: Assessment of a new screening tool for eating disorders', *British Medical Journal*, *319*, 1467–8, 1999.

O'Brien, K. M. and Vincent, N. K., 'Psychiatric comorbidity in anorexia and bulimia nervosa: Nature, prevalence and causal relationships', *Clinical Psychology Review*, *23*, 57–74, 2003.

Polivy, J. and Herman, C. P., 'Dieting and bingeing: A causal analysis', *American Psychologist*, *40*, 193–201, 1985.

Prochaska, J. O. and DiClemente, C. C., 'Stages and processes of self change in smoking: Towards an integrative model of change', *Journal of Consulting and Clinical Psychology*, *5*, 390–5, 1983.

Reiger, E., Touyz, S. W., Schotte, D., Beumont, P. J. V., Russell, J., Clarke, S., *et al.*, 'Development of an instrument to assess readiness to recover in anorexia nervosa', *International Journal of Eating Disorders*, *28*, 387–96, 2000.

Russell, G., 'Bulimia nervosa: An ominous variant of anorexia nervosa', *Psychological Medicine*, *9*, 429–48, 1979.

Safer, D. L., Telch, C. F. and Agras, W. S., 'Dialectical behaviour therapy for bulimia nervosa', *American Journal of Psychiatry*, *158*, 632–4, 2001.

Segal, Z. V., Williams, J. M. G. and Teasdale, J. D., *Mindfulness-based Cognitive Therapy for Depression: A New Approach to Preventing Relapse*. New York: Guilford Press, 2002.

Telch, C. F., Agras, W. S. and Linehan, M. M., 'Dialectical behaviour therapy for binge eating disorder', *Journal of Consulting and Clinical Psychology*, *69*, 1061–5, 2001.

Thornton, C. E., Beumont, P. J. V. and Touyz, S. W., 'The Australian experience of day programmes for patients with eating disorders', *International Journal of Eating Disorders*, *32*, 1–10, 2002.

Thornton, C. E. and Touyz, S. W., 'Eating disorders', in Andrews, G., Erskine, A. and Gee, H., eds, *Management of Mental Disorders*, pp. 317–414. Sydney: World Health Organization, 2004.

Thornton, C., Touyz, S. and Birmingham, L., 'Eating disorders: Management in general practice', *Medicine Today*, 6(10), 29–34, 2005.

Touyz, S. W., Thornton, C. E., Rieger, E., George, L. and Beumont, P., 'The incorporation of the stages of change model in the day hospital treatment of patients with anorexia nervosa', *European Child and Adolescent Psychiatry*, *12*, 65–71, 2003.

von Ranson, K. M., Iacono, W. G. and McGue, M., 'Disordered eating and substance use in an epidemiological sample', *International Journal of Eating Disorders*, *31*, 389–403, 2002.

Waller, G., 'A schema based cognitive behavioural model of the aetiology and maintenance of restrictive and bulimic pathology in the eating disorders', *Journal of Abnormal Psychology*. In press.

Waller, G. and Kennerley, H., 'Cognitive behavioural treatments: Current status and future directions', in Treasure, J., Schmidt, U., Dare, C. and van Furth, E., eds, *Handbook of Eating Disorders: Theory, Treatment and Research*, pp. 233–51. Chichester: Wiley, 2003.

Waller, G., Ohanian, V., Meyer, C. and Osman, S., 'Cognitive content among bulimic women: The role of core beliefs', *International Journal of Eating Disorders*, *28*, 235–41, 2000.

Wiederman, M. W. and Pryor, T., 'Substance use among women with eating disorders', *International Journal of Eating Disorders*, *20*, 163–8, 1996.

Wilfley, D. E., Friedman, M. A., Dounchis, J. Z., Stein, R. I., Welch, R. R. and Ball, S. A., 'Comorbid psychopathology in binge eating disorder: Relation to eating disorder severity at baseline and following treatment', *Journal of Consulting and Clinical Psychology*, *68*, 641–9, 2000.

Wilson, G. T., 'Binge eating and addictive disorders', in Fairburn, C. G. F. and Wilson, G. T., eds, *Binge Eating: Nature, Assessment and Treatment*, pp. 97–120. New York: Guilford Press, 1993.

Young, J., Klosko, J. and Weishaar, M., *Schema Therapy: A Practitioner's Guide*. New York: Guilford Press, 2003.

Zipfel, S., Reas, D. L., Thornton, C. E., Olmsted, M. P., Williamson, D., Gerlinghof, M. *et al.*, 'Day hospitalization: A systematic review of the literature', *International Journal of Eating Disorders*, *31*, 105–17, 2002.

Chapter 16

Personality disorders and drug and alcohol problems

Ellen M. Crouse, Keith M. Drake and Mark P. McGovern

KEY POINTS

1 Personality disorders are common in addiction treatment settings, and substance use disorders are prevalent in settings that focus on treating personality disorders. Clinicians must be prepared to address both disorders.

2 Research indicates that individuals with co-existing personality and substance use disorders are less responsive to traditional treatment, require more intensive therapeutic interventions and have poorer long-term prognoses than individuals with other disorders.

3 Dialectical behaviour therapy (DBT) has been shown to be effective in managing distress, reducing substance use and decreasing negative life outcomes for individuals with co-existing borderline personality and substance use disorders.

4 Accumulating research into medications, particularly atypical anti-psychotics, suggests that pharmacologic interventions may play a valuable adjunctive role in effective treatment.

5 Intervention research is in an early phase but is welcomed by clinicians, who seek evidence-based practices.

INTRODUCTION

Co-existing personality and substance use disorders present special challenges for treatment. Substance use can fuel or obscure personality disorder behaviours such as impulsivity, dysphoria, aggressiveness and self-destructiveness, yielding relationship problems, work dysfunction, illegal activity and dysregulated emotions and behaviour. Paradoxically, personality disordered individuals may regulate affect, avoid discomfort or alter sense of self by using substances. Indeed, the two disorders appear to self-synergize and reverberate, similar to M. C. Escher's depiction of two recursive hands drawing one another. In contending with these co-existing conditions, clinicians may experience feelings of confusion, frustration and anger. They may feel in-effective and avoid working with this population. Similarly, researchers have been perplexed by and avoided addressing these co-existing conditions. This chapter offers an overview of current research and empirically based models for treating co-existing personality and substance use disorders, providing detailed information about one approach that has accumulated evidence for effectiveness.

Prevalence of co-existing personality disorders and substance use

Considerable variability has been found in prevalence rates for co-existing substance use and personality disorders (see Table 16.1). Such variability may be due to changes in diagnostic criteria over time, as well as differences in assessment methodology and sample selection. Grant and colleagues (2004) examined prevalence rates of personality disorders in addiction treatment settings over a 12-month period in the United States; almost half of those with any type of lifetime substance use disorder also met criteria for at least one personality disorder. Prevalence rates varied depending on the sub-stances involved. Among individuals with a current alcohol use disorder, almost 29 per cent had at least one personality disorder; among those with a current (non-alcohol) substance use disorder, 48 per cent had at least one personality disorder (Grant *et al.* 2004). Individuals with an alcohol use disorder were 2.2 to 7.5 times more likely to have a personality disorder than individuals without an alcohol use disorder. When any type of substance use disorder was included in the analysis, odds ratios for having a co-existing personality disorder increased to between 4.8 and 26.0, depending on gender and the specific personality disorder (Grant *et al.* 2004). Antisocial and borderline personality disorders were the most common personality dis-orders among substance users across studies. Research suggests that rates of antisocial personality disorder among substance use disorder populations range from 25 to 50 per cent, while rates of borderline personality disorder range from 10 to 30 per cent (Brooner *et al.* 1997; de Groot *et al.* 2003; DeJong *et al.* 1993; Nadeau *et al.* 1999; Ross *et al.* 1988; Rounsaville *et al.* 1991).

Similarly, rates of substance use are considerably elevated in the personal-ity disordered population, compared to the general population. Skodol and colleagues (1999) found that over half of their clients being treated for any personality disorder also reported a lifetime diagnosis of a substance use disorder. However, Cacciola and colleagues (2001) caution that rates of substance use and other disorders vary markedly depending on the index population or subgroup being studied. Estimates of substance use disorder within the borderline personality disorder population range from 25 to 57 per cent (Dulit *et al.* 1990; Miller *et al.* 1993), although estimated rates of

Table 16.1 Prevalence of personality disorders (PD) in the general population and in individuals with co-existing substance use disorders

Country	Torgerson et al. (2001) Norway (n = 2,053)	Jackson and Burgess (2000) Australia (n = 10,461)	Grant et al. (2004) United States (n = 43,093)	
Population	General	General	General	Individuals with any substance use disorder
Paranoid PD	2.2%	1.3%	4.4%	18.6%
Schizoid PD	1.6%	1.9%	3.1%	12.3%
Borderline PD	0.7%	1.0%	(Not included)	(Not included)
Histrionic PD	1.9%	0.5%	1.8%	11.8%
Obsessive compulsive PD	1.9%	3.1%	7.9%	16.9%
Dependent PD	1.5%	2.3%	0.5%	4.6%
Antisocial PD	0.6%	0%	3.6%	27.7%
Any PD	13.4%	6.6%	14.8%	47.7%

Note: Prevalence rates for the general population are based on the past five years in the study by Torgerson *et al.* and on lifetime prevalence in the studies by Jackson *et al.* and Grant *et al.* Grant *et al.*'s subgroup analysis included individuals who reported receiving addiction treatment during the previous 12 months.

borderline personality disorder among substance use-disordered clients are somewhat lower, as noted above (Brooner *et al.* 1997; Cacciola *et al.* 2001; de Groot *et al.* 2003; Rounsaville *et al.* 1991). A similar trend has been observed for antisocial personality disorder (Cacciola *et al.* 2001; Regier *et al.* 1990). This pattern suggests that clinicians should be vigilant for substance use disorders among those with personality disorders, but conservative in diagnosing Axis II disorders in substance-using populations.

Course and treatment outcomes

Psychiatric intervention research typically excludes individuals with personality disorders from randomized controlled trials but, when included, this subgroup typically has poorer outcomes than those without personality disorders (Pettinati *et al.* 1999). Addiction treatment research reveals that clients with personality disorders present with more difficulties, fare worse during treatment, have higher rates of relapse and exhibit worse functional outcomes following treatment than individuals without personality disorders (Drake and Vaillant 1985; Goldstein *et al.* 1998; Haro *et al.* 2004; Moos *et al.* 2001; Skodol *et al.* 1999). Recent data indicate that although individuals with personality disorders may actually improve at the same rate in addiction treatment, they often leave treatment worse off than peers without personality disorders, due to lower baseline levels of functioning (Ross *et al.* 2003). Other research suggests that characteristics common to individuals with personality disorders, such as impulsivity and extreme dysphoria, are central factors in relapse (Pettinati *et al.* 1999). Borderline personality disorder in particular presents special challenges in addiction treatment. Individuals diagnosed with borderline personality disorder are more likely than those with other personality disorders to use multiple substances, seek medical treatment, see more therapists in their lifetime, engage in suicidal and parasuicidal behaviour and experience repeated hospitalizations (Dimeff *et al.* 2000). Despite these obvious clinical complexities, studies of innovative treatment approaches hold promise for clients with co-existing personality and substance use disorders.

Research-based psychosocial treatments

We have identified three different treatment models, with varying degrees of evidence for effectiveness:

- the therapeutic communities (TC) approach, used primarily with individuals with antisocial, borderline, histrionic or narcissistic (i.e. DSM-IV Cluster B) personality disorders (First *et al.* 1996; Messina *et al.* 2002; Rutter and Tyrer 2003);
- cognitive analytic therapy (CAT), which has been used in individuals with borderline and narcissistic personality disorders (Ryle 2004; Wildgoose *et al.* 2001); and
- dialectical behaviour therapy (DBT), designed for borderline personality disorder (Linehan 1993a) and recently adapted for clients with co-existing substance use disorders (Dimeff *et al.* 2000; Linehan *et al.* 1999, 2002).

Although both TC and CAT offer promising reports of efficacy, only DBT has undergone evaluation through randomized controlled trials. As such, DBT will be the central focus of the current chapter.

Dialectical behaviour therapy (DBT)

DBT was developed for borderline personality disorder, and clinical research indicates that it is effective in reducing the extreme dysphoria and suicidal/ parasuicidal behaviours associated with the disorder (Bohus *et al.* 2004; Dimeff *et al.* 2000; Linehan 1993a; Linehan *et al.* 1999). In DBT, the concept of dialectics is based on the following principles: an emphasis on wholeness and interrelatedness; the idea that all reality is composed of opposing forces, or 'all propositions contain within them their own oppositions'; and the proposal that it is the combined oppositional and interconnected nature of existence that leads to wholeness, change and growth (Bohus *et al.* 2004; Dimeff *et al.* 2000; Linehan *et al.* 1999; Miller *et al.* 1993).

Linehan's (1993a) biosocial model posits that the combination of some degree of physiological predisposition toward emotional vulnerability and an invalidating environment gives rise to the symptoms of borderline personality disorder (McMain *et al.* 2001). Biological components may include 'genetic, intrauterine, and developmental factors affecting physiological development' (Wagner 1995). The prototypical behaviours of the disorder are conceptualized as attempts to modulate extreme emotions or as direct results of emotion dysregulation (Linehan 1993a).

DBT has recently been adapted to address the high level of substance use in this population. Although initial research using DBT in substance use treatment among borderline populations met with mixed results (van den Bosch *et al.* 2002), new modifications targeting substance use appear to be effective (Dimeff *et al.* 2000; Linehan *et al.* 1999, 2002).

DBT was originally designed for outpatient settings, due in large part to one of its central goals being a decrease in inpatient hospital admissions. However, standard DBT has also been effective in partial hospitalization programs and inpatient units, including high security forensic settings (Bohus *et al.* 2004; Low *et al.* 2001; Robins and Chapman 2004). The variety of settings in which DBT has been successful suggests that the treatment environment may be less critical than inclusion of the four primary components of DBT: individual therapy; group skills training; client access to the therapist for 'skills coaching' between sessions as needed; and the availability and support of a DBT consultation team for the therapist. These components are intended to address five different targets of treatment: developing new skills; identifying motivational obstacles to implementing new skills; generalizing skills into daily life; teaching clients to structure the environment to reinforce new behaviours; and maintaining therapists' motivation and skill in DBT techniques (Linehan 1993a; Linehan *et al.* 2002; Robins and Chapman 2004).

Pharmacological treatments

A complete review of the pharmacotherapy of personality disorders exceeds the scope of the present chapter. However, neuroleptics (Frankenburg and Zanarini 1993), antidepressants (Rivas-Vazquez and Blais 2002) and mood stabilizers (Hollander *et al.* 2005) appear to be effective in treating many of the symptoms associated with personality disorders. For a current review of the evidence from trials of medication in borderline samples, see Zanarini (2004a). The reader is also referred to reviews by Soloff (1998, 2000) for further analysis of the efficacy of various medications in the treatment of personality disorder.

CONTEXT OF THERAPY

Therapist variables

DBT therapists genuinely believe in clients' ability to effect change, maintain a non-judgmental stance, are open to input from others and require in-depth training (Linehan 1993a; Trupin and Richards 2003). Therapists can unknowingly enter into dialectical binds with clients by engaging in subtle 'either/or' stand-offs regarding the client's view of the world. This is a natural phenomenon because, as the therapist empathizes with the client's world view, he or she is easily pulled into the client's dichotomous perspective. Often the therapist is unaware of the polarity; thus, the consulting team provides a sounding board, offering insight into dialectical dilemmas and new ways of viewing them (Linehan 1993a). Finally, the therapist must be committed to helping clients generalize newly-acquired skills into their daily lives. One means of assisting in the generalization of skills is the telephone 'coaching' session. Although the therapist is not required to be available for coaching on an unlimited basis, no therapist should enter into DBT without recognizing the demands of the approach. Another central DBT component is the skills training group. Pairs of therapists typically co-lead weekly skills groups. Successful leaders are adept at recognizing behaviours that are outside the group rules, reminding members of the group's function and moving the topic back to the skills being taught in a warm yet firm manner (Linehan 1993a).

Client variables

Emotional lability, impulsivity, low self-esteem, chaotic lifestyle, sudden hostility and self-harming behaviours are common features of borderline personality disorder (American Psychiatric Association 2000). In addition, this population is prone to having legal issues, poor social supports and high rates of social anxiety (Comtois *et al.* 1999, 2003). When these factors are exacerbated by substance use, individuals with borderline personality disorder are even more prone to suicidality, aggressive or socially unacceptable behaviour, social alienation, legal involvement and financial chaos. All of these variables affect clients' motivation and ability to engage in therapy.

ASSESSMENT OF CO-EXISTING PERSONALITY AND SUBSTANCE USE DISORDERS

Features of substance use disorders, such as relational disturbances, poor self-regulation, work dysfunction, mood swings, externalizing defences and isolation, are also criteria for a variety of personality disorders, creating parallel problems for clinicians and researchers. Although the American Psychiatric Association (APA 2000) has increasingly refined its definitions of substance-induced and independent disorders, much of the focus to date has been on Axis I categories such as mood, anxiety, sleep and psychotic disorders. Just as differential diagnosis of these Axis I disorders must be handled with deliberation and care, distinguishing typical personality disorder characteristics from the powerful cravings, intoxication, withdrawal and consequences of substance misuse requires a methodical analysis of each client's presentation and history. Important considerations include the chronology of onset (i.e. do personality features pre-date the use of substances and the development of the substance use disorder or vice versa?) and the level of functioning during periods of abstinence (i.e. are personality characteristics robust during substance-free periods, or do they attenuate?). Differential diagnosis may be complicated by several factors: onset for both disorders may occur during adolescence; clients may not be accurate historians at initial assessment; the period of abstinence required to determine an Axis II disorder accurately is longer than that needed to assess an Axis I disorder; and many clients have never had a period of sustained abstinence. Therefore, a personality disorder diagnosis for a person with a current (or recently active) substance use disorder must frequently be a provisional or 'rule out' diagnosis at best. In summary, it is a challenge to disentangle personality disorders, relatively common in individuals with substance use disorders, from the effects of substance misuse. In the absence of clear evidence to the contrary, a conservative rendering (or a 'rule out') of personality disorder diagnosis, with allowance for observation over time, is recommended.

Among several useful assessment tools for evaluating personality disorders is the Structural Clinical Interview for the DSM-IV for Axis I (SCID-I; Spitzer *et al.* 1994) and Axis II disorders (SCID-II; First *et al.* 1996). Given the high rates of co-existing Axis I and Axis II disorders, a complete SCID is ideal and provides the most thorough diagnostic picture. The Millon Clinical Multiaxial Inventory-III (MCMI-III; Millon 1994) is a useful self-report index of personality dimensions often employed in addiction treatment (Ball *et al.* 2004). When the primary concern is borderline personality disorder, a clinician-administered interview such as the Zanarini Rating Scale for Borderline Personality Disorder (ZAN-BPD; Zanarini 2004b) provides a more focused assessment. In addition, clinicians may find self-report instruments such as the Borderline Personality Inventory (BPI; Leichsenring 1999) helpful in providing information regarding specific symptoms or tracking change across time.

According to the APA's (2000) *Diagnostic and Statistical Manual* fourth edition text revision (DSM-IV-TR), the descriptive criteria for borderline personality disorder include nine possible symptoms, only five of which must be exhibited for diagnosis, yielding a wide variety of manifestations. In addition, the disorder is notable for its high level of co-existence with a number of other disorders besides substance use, including depression and other mood disturbances (Comtois *et al.* 1999; Joyce *et al.* 2003; Shea *et al.* 2004; Zanarini *et al.* 1989), social phobia (Comtois *et al.* 2003), post traumatic stress disorder (Comtois *et al.* 2003; McGlashan *et al.* 2000; Zlotnick *et al.* 2002) and other anxiety disorders (Shea *et al.* 2004; Zanarini *et al.* 1989). Linehan (1993a) proposes an alternative to the DSM-IV-TR criteria and posits that the disorder can best be understood as one of dysregulation across five different spheres of functioning: emotional, interpersonal, behavioural, cognitive and self-image (see Table 16.2). Although there is considerable overlap between the two models, a key difference lies in Linehan's overarching concept of dysregulation as a central feature that alters level of functioning. Within this paradigm, each of the areas of dysregulation interacts with the others, but affective dysregulation is viewed as being at the centre of the model (Linehan 1993a).

TREATMENT OF CO-EXISTING PERSONALITY AND SUBSTANCE USE DISORDERS

An overview of dialectical behaviour therapy techniques

Linehan (1993a, 1993b) developed DBT following several years of witnessing the seemingly endless distress exhibited by individuals with borderline personality disorder, combined with their tendency to view the world in 'black or white' terms. Drawing from prior training in Zen Buddhism, Linehan proposed openly acknowledging this 'all or nothing' thinking style as an

Table 16.2 Linehan's (1993a) model of dysregulation in borderline personality disorder

Sphere of function/dysregulation	Possible behaviours/symptoms/effects
Emotional dysregulation	Chronic dysphoria; anger; hostility; irritability; emotional lability
Interpersonal dysregulation	Unstable, conflictual relationships; efforts to avoid interpersonal loss; poor social support; passive approach to solving interpersonal problems
Behavioural dysregulation	Suicidal/parasuicidal behaviour; impulsive, self-damaging behaviours, such as alcohol and drug use or promiscuity; dysregulated self-care, such as erratic sleep and nutrition patterns
Cognitive dysregulation	Cognitive disturbances, such as transient dissociation or paranoia; cognitive rigidity; dichotomous thinking
Self dysregulation	Unstable self-image; feelings of chronic emptiness; poor self-esteem

important aspect of working with individuals with borderline personality disorder, and helping clients negotiate the 'middle ground' as a means of managing distress. The central dialectic in the therapeutic framework of DBT is unwavering acceptance of the client, combined with a persistent push toward change. The therapist must genuinely be able to view the client as doing the very best that she or he is able to do in the moment, offer support and validation for the client's experience and insistently nudge the client toward learning new behaviour (Linehan 1993a). This dialectic of acceptance and change is a pervasive thread throughout each component of DBT. In individual sessions, therapists balance genuine warmth and validation with techniques to evoke change. In skills groups, leaders welcome and encourage members' participation even as they work to teach and 'drag out' new behaviours. In telephone coaching sessions, therapists validate clients' emotional distress as they simultaneously define the limits of coaching sessions and push clients to generate ideas for distress tolerance. Finally, during team consultations, teams act to validate therapists' experiences and reactions to the client, simultaneously providing feedback on alternative ways of viewing problems.

However, the dialectical approach is more than mere balancing of opposites. A central goal in DBT is to help clients develop the ability to synthesize two equally valid but apparently contradictory ways of viewing problems into new perspectives that account for both views. This is accomplished both through modelling and through open discussion in therapy. In substance-misusing clients, this may develop from a conversation regarding the concept of 'dialectical abstinence'. Dialectical abstinence consists of the synthesis of two components: (1) expecting abstinence (a change strategy), and (2) practising self-acceptance and conducting a chain analysis of antecedent behaviour during episodes of relapse (Dimeff et al. 2000). Emphasis is placed on building a close bond with the therapist through validation and acceptance, so the relationship can bear the consistent push toward change.

Standard DBT includes the following, hierarchically arranged treatment targets: decreasing life-threatening and self-harming behaviours; reducing therapy-interfering behaviours; decreasing behaviours that are detrimental to quality of life; and encouraging new skills (Linehan 1993a). Treatment targets have been adapted for work with substance use-disordered populations by adding the following five sub-targets, under the rubric of 'quality of life': reducing or eliminating substance use; decreasing urges for substance use; reducing physical discomfort that accompanies withdrawal or abstinence; reducing apparently unimportant behaviours, such as keeping paraphernalia associated with substance use; and encouraging clients to close the door to drug use (e.g. getting rid of contact information for drug suppliers) (Dimeff et al. 2000; Linehan and Dimeff 1997; Linehan et al. 1999, 2002). Finally, building the therapeutic alliance is a primary focus when working with individuals with co-existing borderline personality and substance use disorders (Dimeff et al. 2000).

A few DBT techniques bear further discussion, including commitment strategies, validation, problem-solving techniques and behavioural analysis.

The DBT therapist views the client's commitment to therapy and the development of new skills as a dynamic process. Although obtaining a commitment from the client at the beginning of therapy is critical, the therapist is vigilant for changes in the client's degree of allegiance to therapy over time. Wavering commitment may be manifest in failure to complete diary cards, failure to attend individual therapy or skills groups, statements regarding distrust of the therapeutic process and other behaviours that interfere with therapy. These behaviours are addressed openly with clients in individual therapy. Adopting an 'I wonder' approach to the question of why the client is engaging in these behaviours serves to re-engage the client in therapy. In addition, it addresses a common issue in clients with borderline personality disorder – a tendency toward passive problem-solving. A second way of eliciting commitment is to adopt a paradoxical, 'irreverent' or 'devil's advocate' attitude (Linehan 1993a). The use of irreverence/paradox is a powerful strategy for change with a borderline client, that is most effective in an established, aligned therapeutic relationship. Through paradox, the therapist's role is to throw light on the innate contradictions in the client's behaviour or in the world of reality outside therapy, so the client is put in the position of finding the solution, the synthesis of the opposites (Linehan 1993a). When the client arrives at therapy without diary cards, for example, the therapist might state, 'You know, maybe you're right. Maybe we don't need to track your behaviour and urges. Should we just ditch this diary card thing and talk about the weather?' Irreverence can be powerful but must be used carefully. Individuals with borderline personality disorder are typically very sensitive to emotional tone. Without the supporting context of a strong therapeutic alliance, irreverence may come across as sarcastic or flippant, undermining its purpose (Linehan 1993a).

Validation is a powerful acceptance strategy used in standard DBT and in work with individuals with co-existing borderline personality and substance use disorders. Linehan (1993a) believes that most individuals with borderline personality disorder grew up in an environment in which they experienced some degree of invalidation of their emotions or experiences. Because it is a core acceptance strategy in DBT, validation is covered in detail in Linehan's original text (1993a), and the reader is referred to that source for elaboration of this concept. In brief, validation 'communicates to the client in a non-ambiguous way that her behaviour makes sense and is understandable in the current context' (Linehan 1993a: 221). Validation does not equate to agreeing that clients are 'right' or are making good decisions; rather, it simply conveys understanding of how individuals come to behave, think or perceive things in the context of their own lives. A central aspect of validation is being able to observe non-judgmentally the way in which the client experiences the world. Validation derives its power from the fact that many individuals with borderline personality disorder feel they have gone through life with no-one recognizing their perspective. As such, it serves as a potent bonding factor with clients with borderline characteristics.

The reciprocal strategy to validation (acceptance) in DBT is problem-solving (change). Problem-solving occurs through many avenues in DBT, but its basic premise is actively to engage clients in finding solutions to their problems, with consultation from the therapist as needed. A major problem-solving technique is the behavioural chain analysis. Using a behavioural chain analysis serves several purposes that are directly linked to the principles of DBT. First, it encourages clients to be active participants in therapy, acting as 'detectives' regarding the links between emotions and behaviour that they previously viewed as mysterious and enigmatic. Chain analysis supports the DBT principle of the therapist as a 'consultant to the client', who is viewed as being the driving force in therapy. The technique also helps clients to see the connection between behaviours and emotions, encouraging them to find appropriate points at which different courses of action create different results. In addition, during the analysis the client is encouraged to use what Linehan (1993a) describes as 'wise mind', a balance of emotional and rational thought that is often difficult to achieve for individuals with borderline personality disorder. Finally, chain analyses can serve as aversive stimuli that clients come to associate with the behaviour being analyzed, especially when the same type of event is reviewed every week in excruciating detail. Typical targets for such detailed analyses include behaviours that interfere with therapy or diminish quality of life. Chain analyses are conducted with a frank discussion of their purpose and with continual validation of the client's emotional responses to the process, as well as an attitude of genuine acceptance from the therapist.

CASE STUDY

Jason was a 36-year-old divorced male with an extensive history of childhood abuse and neglect. He had engaged in a variety of self-harm behaviours over the previous two decades and experimented with a wide spectrum of substances. His primary drugs of choice were opiates and alcohol. In his late 20s, Jason attended Narcotics Anonymous (NA) meetings. He maintained abstinence from opiates but continued to misuse alcohol intermittently, abstaining for months at a time but then in times of high stress, such as the end of the semester, bingeing on about 10 beers in a night. He felt remorseful, guilty and angry with himself the following day but had difficulty avoiding alcohol until the external stress was reduced. Poor impulse control, excessive anger and depression complicated Jason's diagnostic picture. His tendency to engage in high-risk activities contributed to two minor head injuries. Poor anger control interacted with an underlying social anxiety, causing him to withdraw from most intimate relationships and exacerbating his depression. Over the years,

Jason stated, he has 'been called everything from irresponsible, to sociopathic, to head injured, to just plain crazy'.

Jason held a variety of beliefs about his problems. He stated that 'something's just wrong with my brain'. He said that he used alcohol because it helped him feel calmer in social situations. Conversely, he reported that alcohol often 'makes me act crazy and run people off'. He added that his mother and maternal grandfather, his primary caregivers throughout childhood, 'pretty much told me I was worthless and treated me the same'. Not surprisingly, he had difficulty believing that he could do anything well.

Jason was receiving disability benefits and attending some university courses. He was overwhelmed by taking more than one or two courses per semester but had to maintain a full course load to avoid repayment of a large financial aid debt. Due to his social anxiety, he had difficulty participating in class and approaching professors with questions. As each semester progressed, Jason became more anxious, his sleep became dysregulated and his drinking increased. Bingeing on alcohol further disrupted his sleep, resulting in increased difficulty modulating emotions, cognitions and interpersonal relationships. He erratically attended Alcoholics Anonymous (AA) meetings on campus but withdrew when he was most stressed. He had difficulty with self-help groups because he felt anxious speaking about personal issues in front of strangers. In spite of Jason's articulate and somewhat intellectual presentation, his grades suffered with his inability to modulate his emotions and alcohol consumption. Over the years, Jason had seen a number of therapists. He had managed to build a good relationship recently with an occupational therapist who helped him with school-related skills. He was referred by the occupational therapist to an outpatient DBT program targeting individuals with drug or alcohol problems.

One of the early targets in DBT is obtaining a commitment to participate in therapy. The value of obtaining this original commitment cannot be overstated, as it provides groundwork for seeking renewed commitment when clients experience a sense of failure due to relapse (Linehan 1993a). As such, after initial assessment, Jason's therapist spent a session explaining the components of the program to Jason, including weekly individual therapy, completion of daily diary cards, participation in a weekly DBT skills training group for substance-related problems and telephone coaching on an as-needed basis. Additional participation in self-help programs was encouraged but not required as part of the program. Jason initially balked at the program's expectation of a year-long commitment and the DBT rule that missing four consecutive weeks of either skills group or individual therapy would mean that he was out of the program:

Jason: It just doesn't seem reasonable. I mean, what if it's the end of the semester, and I can't get my work done? Do I still have to come to group? I'd flunk out of class!

Therapist: This is a hard decision, I know. It feels like an enormous commitment. You're scared that it might make your life even harder. *[Validation of the client's perspective and emotions.]* From what you've said, it sounds like you've never done anything like this before. In spite of that, I am completely confident that you can do it. Maybe you'll need some extra coaching when things get stressful, and that's exactly the time when the skills you'll learn are most helpful. *[Using the dialectic of accepting the client where he is and simultaneously expressing belief in his ability to change.]*

Jason: I'm not sure. It's a lot to ask, especially if I am agreeing not to drink on top of that.

Therapist: You look worried. I can see that this is really tough. Maybe it's better not to do it and just keep living your life as you are now. *[The 'devil's advocate' technique can be especially effective in obtaining a commitment early in therapy.]*

Jason: [Shrugs shoulders]

Therapist: [After a pause] At the same time, you managed to quit using heroin several years ago. You had courage to make many changes to improve your life. Right now, I also am making a commitment to help you get through this year. I wouldn't agree to help you if I didn't truly believe you are capable of doing it. *[Validation, seeking commitment to therapy, conveying genuine acceptance of the client where he is and a belief in his ability to change.]*

Jason agreed at the end of the first session to commit to a year-long DBT plan. He chose to attend a campus AA group on at least a weekly basis. He attended therapy and groups regularly at first, but after a few months of continuous abstinence, Jason experienced a relapse. It was a few weeks before the end of the school semester, and he felt overwhelmed by the pressure of due dates for papers and major exams. He missed two weeks of both skills group and individual therapy. After he missed the second session of therapy, his therapist left a brief message on his answering machine stating that she has missed seeing him (*genuineness and acceptance*), describing what she imagines he may be feeling as the semester draws to a close (*validation*) and reminding him of the rules regarding missed groups and sessions (*push toward change in an old pattern of social withdrawal when stressed*). Jason arrived at the next individual therapy session looking haggard and discouraged. He had no diary cards for the previous two weeks.

Therapist: I am really happy you're here, Jason. You look tired. It's that time of the semester, huh? *[Acceptance and validation.]* I notice that you didn't bring your diary cards today. That makes it hard

	for us to figure out what's happened over the past two weeks. It gets in the way of what we're trying to do here. *[Direct description of a therapy-interfering behaviour.]* How did that happen?
Jason:	[Hangs his head] I don't know.
Therapist:	If we take a look at it, I'm sure we can figure this out. *[Conveys belief in Jason's ability to solve the problem.]* The first thing is to figure out what happened, and then we can figure out how it happened. *[Initiating a chain analysis of therapy-interfering behaviour.]* Did you not fill out the cards, or did you fill them out and leave them at home?
Jason:	I started filling them out, but then I had to say I was drinking. I didn't want to write that down and have to talk about it.
Therapist:	Let's start at the beginning, Jason. It's important for us to figure out how you got from drinking to not filling out cards and not coming to therapy. I am sure there were steps in between.

From this point, the therapist conducted a behavioural analysis, helping Jason to identify in minute detail the chain of events that led to him 'forgetting' his diary cards, followed by a second analysis of steps that led to drinking. For Jason, typical targets for analysis centred on relapse and failure to attend sessions or groups.

In the last month of the DBT skills group, Jason began to binge again and began experiencing urges to self-harm he had not felt in several years. He had called his therapist only on rare occasions for coaching; the last time he called was several months previously. Although limited phone calls might be viewed as a positive indicator, his diary cards told another story, reflecting increased depression and frequent urges to drink and cut. His therapist wisely targeted his lack of requests for coaching as therapy-interfering behaviour, as well as a quality of life issue, akin to social withdrawal when he is most in need of support. She addressed the issue openly and somewhat irreverently, in keeping with the DBT principle of moving the client toward change through paradox/irreverence.

Therapist:	Jason, I have this strange sense of déjà vu [smiles]. I am noticing the same pattern again. When you are distressed, you pull away from other people. At the same time, this is the exact moment when other people can be of the most help to you. *[Pointing out a dialectic.]*
Jason:	I knew you were going to say that [looks away from therapist]. You're always saying stuff like that to me.
Therapist:	You're absolutely right. I am like a broken record. I am always telling you to reach out to other people when you're upset. At the same time, when you are upset, you want to pull away from me and ignore what I am saying [with a small grin].

Jason: [Glares at therapist] You *are* like a broken record! You are so irritating! [Pauses, then smiles] At the same time, you are irritatingly right! And for some reason, I like the song you keep playing over and over and over . . . [laughs].

Therapist: Congratulations, Jason. You just entered the paradox! [smiles]

Not all clients have Jason's verbal skills, and not every DBT therapist would speak these same words. DBT encourages flexibility as therapist and client connect through the language that makes sense for the client. What does not change is the continual, dialectical focus on acceptance and change. The interaction above led to a serious discussion of the value of 'and' in place of the words 'but' and 'or', helping Jason recognize that he can feel miserable and still engage with another person, that he can have an urge to withdraw and still approach, that he may experience a desire to drink and still abstain. It also led to a frank discussion of his mixed emotions regarding termination of therapy.

During the final months of treatment, Jason remained abstinent from alcohol. He terminated individual therapy three months after the end of group, then returned for a six-month follow-up session with his therapist. At that session, he talked about his ongoing struggle to abstain from alcohol, his pride in his ability to do so most of the time, and his ability to practise acceptance and conduct his own chain analysis on one occasion when he drank. He stated that he used DBT techniques such as managing nutrition and sleep patterns to help himself return to abstinence when he relapsed. He made a plan with his therapist to continue AA and to leave open the option of returning to therapy in the future, to refine his DBT skills and work on issues related to his childhood history.

During the course of therapy, Jason learned to recognize and modulate his emotions and behaviour, reducing many of the symptoms of borderline personality disorder. He significantly reduced his alcohol use, as well as the destructive behaviours associated with drinking. He learned new ways of caring for his needs and gained a fresh perspective on his personality and behaviours. Finally, he strengthened his interpersonal skills, which helped his affiliation with self-help groups. Due to these changes, he appears to have a better chance at complete abstinence and long-term recovery.

CONCLUSION

DBT addresses both substance use and borderline personality disorder within the same therapeutic framework, providing an integrated and seamless means of working with individuals with these co-existing issues. Therapists who work with clients with these co-existing issues should feel encouraged that DBT is effective, but also should be aware that the approach requires training and the commitment of a group of therapists willing to work as consultants, therapists and group leaders. Nevertheless, we are still on the frontier of developing and implementing research-supported interventions for co-existing personality and substance use disorders. Researchers who develop and study interventions for these co-existing disorders are likely to find strong community treatment provider motivation and receptiveness towards evidence-based approaches for this challenging population.

KEY RESOURCES

DBT

Linehan, M. M., *Cognitive-behavioral Treatment of Borderline Personality Disorder*. New York: Guilford Press, 1993a.

Linehan, M. M., *Skills Training Manual for Treating Borderline Personality Disorder*. New York: Guilford Press, 1993b.

Therapy techniques, videotapes for clients, mindfulness and therapist training

http://faculty.washington.edu/linehan (accessed 12 August 2005).

Behavioral Tech Research, Inc., article on mindfulness practice for clients. Available at http://behavioraltech.org/mindfulness/mindfulnessForClients.cfm (accessed 1 August 2006).

Behavioral Tech Research, Inc.'s store for videos and DVDs on DBT and mindfulness practice. Available at http://behavioraltech.org/store/products.cfm (accessed 1 August 2006).

ToDo Institute's resource library for Japanese psychology and purposeful living. Available at http://www.todoinstitute.com/attn.html (accessed 1 August 2006).

Plum Village Meditation Center. Available at http://www.plumvillage.org (accessed 1 August 2006).

Adaptations of DBT for individuals with substance use disorders

Dimeff, L. A., Rizvi, S. L., Brown, M. and Linehan, M. M., 'Dialectical behavior therapy for substance abuse: A pilot application to methamphetamine-dependent women with borderline personality disorder', *Cognitive and Behavioral Practice*, 7, 457–68, 2000.

REFERENCES

American Psychiatric Association APA, *Diagnostic and Statistical Manual of Mental Disorders*, 4th ed, text revision. Washington: (APA), 2000.

Ball, S. A., Nich, C., Rounsaville, B. J., Eagan, D. and Carroll, K. M., 'Millon Clinical Multiaxial Inventory-III subtypes of opioid dependence: Validity and matching to behavioral therapies', *Journal of Consulting and Clinical Psychology*, 72, 698–711, 2004.

Bohus, M., Haaf, B., Simms, T., Limberger, M. F., Schmahl, C., Unckel, C. *et al.*, 'Effectiveness of inpatient dialectical behavioural therapy for borderline personality disorder: A controlled trial', *Behaviour Research and Therapy*, 42, 487–99, 2004.

Brooner, R. K., King, V. L., Schmidt, C. W. and Bigelow, G. E., 'Psychiatric and substance abuse comorbidity among treatment-seeking opioid abusers', *Archives of General Psychiatry*, 54, 71–80, 1997.

Cacciola, J. S., Alterman, A. I., McKay, J. R. and Rutherford, M. J., 'Psychiatric comorbidity in patients with substance use disorders: Do not forget Axis II', *Psychiatric Annals*, 31, 321–31, 2001.

Comtois, K. A., Cowley, D. S., Dunner, D. L. and Roy-Byrne, P., 'Relationship between borderline personality disorder and Axis I diagnosis in severity of depression and anxiety', *Journal of Clinical Psychiatry*, 60, 752–8, 1999.

Comtois, K. A., Russo, J., Snowden, M., Srebnik, D., Ries, R. and Roy-Byrne, P., 'Factors associated with high use of public mental health services by persons with borderline personality disorder', *Psychiatric Services*, 54, 1149–54, 2003.

de Groot, M. H., Franken, I. H. A., van der Meer, C. W. and Hendriks, V. M., 'Stability and change in dimensional ratings of personality disorders in drug abuse patients during treatment', *Journal of Substance Abuse Treatment*, 24, 115–20, 2003.

DeJong, C. A., van den Brink, W., Harteveld, F. M. and van der Wielen, E. G., 'Personality disorders in alcoholics and drug addicts', *Comprehensive Psychiatry*, 34, 87–94, 1993.

Dimeff, L. A., Rizvi, S. L., Brown, M. and Linehan, M. M., 'Dialectical behaviour therapy for substance abuse: A pilot application to methamphetamine-dependent women with borderline personality disorder', *Cognitive and Behavioural Practice*, 7, 457–68, 2000.

Drake, R. E. and Vaillant, G. E., 'A validity study of Axis II of DSM-III', *American Journal of Psychiatry*, 142, 553–8, 1985.

Dulit, R. A., Fyer, M. R., Haas, G. L., Sullivan, T. and Frances, A. J., 'Substance use in borderline personality disorder', *American Journal of Psychiatry*, 147, 1002–7, 1990.

First, M. B., Spitzer, R. L., Gibbon, M. and Williams, J. B. W., *User's Guide for the Structured Clinical Interview for Personality Disorders (SCID-III)*. Washington: American Psychiatric Press, 1996.

Frankenburg, F. R. and Zanarini, M. C., 'Clozapine treatment of borderline patients', *Comprehensive Psychiatry*, 34, 402–5, 1993.

Goldstein, R. B., Powers, S. I., McCusker, J., Lewis, B. F., Bigelow, C. and Mundt, K. A., 'Antisocial behavioural syndromes among residential drug abuse treatment clients', *Drug and Alcohol Dependence*, 49, 201–16, 1998.

Grant, B. F., Stinson, F. S., Dawson, D. A., Chou, S. P., Ruan, W. J. and Pickering, R. P., 'Co-occurrence of 12-month alcohol and drug use disorders and personality disorders in the United States', *Archives of General Psychiatry*, 61, 361–8, 2004.

Haro, G., Mateu, C., Martinez-Raga, J., Valderrama, J. C., Castellano, M. and

Cervera, G., 'The role of personality disorders on drug dependence outcomes following patient detoxification', *European Psychiatry*, *19*, 187–92, 2004.

Hollander, E., Swann, A. C., Coccaro, E. F., Jiang, P. and Smith, T. B., 'Impact of trait impulsivity and state aggression on Divalproex versus placebo response in borderline personality disorder', *American Journal of Psychiatry*, *162*, 621–4, 2005.

Jackson, H. J. and Burgess, P. M., 'Personality disorders in the community: A report from the Australian National Survey of Mental Health and Well-Being', *Social Psychiatry and Psychiatric Epidemiology*, *35*, 531–8, 2000.

Joyce, P. R., Mulder, R. T., Luty, S. E., McKenzie, J. M., Sullivan, P. F. and Cloninger, R. C., 'Borderline personality disorder in major depression: Symptomatology, temperament, character, differential drug response, and 6 month outcome', *Comprehensive Psychiatry*, *44*, 25–43, 2003.

Leichsenring, F., 'Development and first results of the Borderline Personality Inventory: A self-report instrument for assessing borderline personality disorder', *Journal of Personality Assessment*, *73*, 45–63, 1999.

Linehan, M. M., *Cognitive-Behavioral Treatment of Borderline Personality Disorder*. New York: Guilford Press, 1993a.

Linehan, M. M., *Skills Training Manual for Treating Borderline Personality Disorder*. New York: Guilford Press, 1993b.

Linehan, M. M. and Dimeff, L. A., *Dialectical Behavior Therapy Manual of Treatment Interventions for Drug Abusers with Borderline Personality Disorder*. Seattle, WA: University of Washington, 1997.

Linehan, M. M., Dimeff, L. A., Reynolds, S. K., Comtois, K. A., Welch, S. S., Heagerty, P. and Kivlahan, D. R., 'Dialectical behavior therapy versus comprehensive validation therapy for the treatment of opioid dependent women meeting criteria for borderline personality disorder', *Drug and Alcohol Dependence*, *67*, 13–26, 2002.

Linehan, M. M., Schmidt, H., Dimeff, L. A., Craft, C., Kanter, J. and Comtois, K. A., 'Dialectical behavior therapy for patients with borderline personality disorder and drug-dependence', *The American Journal on Addictions*, *8*, 279–92, 1999.

Low, G., Jones, D., Duggan, C., Power, M. and MacLeod, A., 'The treatment of deliberate self-harm in borderline personality disorder using dialectical behavior therapy: A pilot study in a high-security hospital', *Behavioural and Cognitive Psychotherapy*, *29*, 85–92, 2001.

McGlashan, T. H., Grilo, C. M., Skodol, A. E., Gunderson, J. G., Shea, M. T., Morey, L. C. *et al.*, 'The collaborative longitudinal personality disorders study: Baseline Axis I/II and II/III diagnostic co-occurrence', *Acta Psychiatrica Scandinavica*, *102*, 256–64, 2000.

McMain, S., Korman, L. M. and Dimeff, L., 'Dialectical behavior therapy and the treatment of emotion dysregulation', *Journal of Clinical Psychology*, *57*, 183–96, 2001.

Messina, N. P., Wish, E. D., Hoffman, J. A. and Nemes, S., 'Antisocial personality disorder and TC treatment outcomes'. *American Journal of Drug and Alcohol Abuse*, *28*, 197–212, 2002.

Miller, F. T., Abrams, T., Dulit, R. A. and Fyer, M. R., 'Substance abuse in borderline personality disorder', *American Journal of Drug and Alcohol Abuse*, *19*, 491–7, 1993.

Millon, T., *The Millon Clinical Multiaxial Inventory*, 3rd ed. New York: Wiley, 1994.

Moos, R. H., Moos, B. S. and Finney, J. W., 'Predictors of deterioration among patients with substance-use disorders', *Journal of Clinical Psychology*, *57*, 1403–19, 2001.

Nadeau, L., Landry, M. and Racine, S., 'Prevalence of personality disorders among clients in treatment for addiction', *Canadian Journal of Psychiatry*, *44*, 592–6, 1999.

Pettinati, H. M., Pierce, J. D., Belden, P. P. and Meyers, K., 'The relationship of Axis II personality disorders to other known predictors of addiction treatment outcome', *The American Journal on Addictions*, *8*, 136–47, 1999.

Regier, D. A., Farmer, M. E., Rae, D. S., Locke, B. Z., Keith, S. J., Judd, L. L. and Goodwin, F. K., 'Comorbidity of mental disorders with alcohol and other drug misuse: Results from the Epidemiologic Catchment Area study', *Journal of the American Medical Association*, *264*, 2511–8, 1990.

Rivas-Vazquez, R. A. and Blais, M. A., 'Pharmacologic treatment of personality disorder', *Professional Psychology: Research and Practice*, *33*, 104–7, 2002.

Robins, C. J. and Chapman, A. L., 'Dialectical behavior therapy: Current status, recent developments, and future directions', *Journal of Personality Disorders*, *18*, 73–89, 2004.

Ross, H. E., Glaser, F. B. and Germanson, T., 'The prevalence of psychiatric disorders in patients with alcohol and other drug problems', *Archives of General Psychiatry*, *45*, 1023–31, 1988.

Ross, S., Dermatis, H., Levounis, P. and Galanter, M., 'A comparison between dually diagnosed inpatients with and without Axis II comorbidity and the relationship to treatment outcome', *American Journal of Drug and Alcohol Abuse*, *29*, 263–79, 2003.

Rounsaville, B. J., Anton, S. F., Carroll, K., Budde, D. and Prusoff, B. A. G., 'Psychiatric diagnoses of treatment-seeking cocaine abusers', *Archives of General Psychiatry*, *48*, 43–51, 1991.

Rutter, D. and Tyrer, P., 'The value of therapeutic communities in the treatment of personality disorder: A suitable place for treatment?' *Journal of Psychiatric Practice*, *9*, 291–302, 2003.

Ryle, A., 'The contribution of cognitive analytic therapy to the treatment of borderline personality disorder', *Journal of Personality Disorders*, *18*, 3–35, 2004.

Shea, M. T., Stout, R. L., Yen, S., Pagano, M. E., Skodol, A. E., Morey, L. C. *et al.*, 'Associations in the course of personality disorders and Axis I disorders over time', *Journal of Abnormal Psychology*, *113*, 499–508, 2004.

Skodol, A. E., Oldham, J. M. and Gallaher, P. E., 'Axis II comorbidity of substance use disorders among patients referred for treatment of personality disorders', *American Journal of Psychiatry*, *156*, 733–8, 1999.

Soloff, P. H., 'Algorithms for pharmacological treatment of personality dimensions: Symptom-specific treatments for cognitive-perceptual, affective, and impulsive-behavioral dysregulation', *Bulletin of the Menninger Clinic*, *62*, 195–205, 1998.

Soloff, P. H., 'Psychopharmacology of borderline personality disorder', *Psychiatric Clinics of North America*, *23*, 169–92, 2000.

Spitzer, R. L., Williams, J. B., Gibbon, M. and First, M. B., *Structured Clinical Interview for DSM-IV*. New York: New York State Psychiatric Institute, 1994.

Torgerson, S., Kringlen, E. and Cramer, V., 'The prevalence of personality disorders in a community sample', *Archives of General Psychiatry*, *58*, 590–6, 2001.

Trupin, E. W. and Richards, H., 'Seattle's mental health courts: Early indicators of effectiveness', *International Journal of Law and Psychiatry*, *26*, 33–53, 2003.

van den Bosch, L. M. C., Verheul, R., Schippers, G. M. and van den Brink, W., 'Dialectical behaviour therapy of borderline patients with and without substance use problems: Implementation and long-term effects', *Addictive Behaviors*, *27*, 911–23, 2002.

Wagner, A., *Relationship Between Emotion Knowledge and Reports of Childhood Sexual Abuse Among Women With and Without Diagnoses of Borderline Personality Disorder*. Dissertation, University of Washington, 1995.

Wildgoose, A., Clarke, S. and Waller, G., 'Treating personality fragmentation and dissociation in borderline personality disorder: A pilot study of the impact of cognitive analytic therapy', *British Journal of Medical Psychology*, *74*, 47–55, 2001.

Zanarini, M. C., 'Update on pharmacotherapy of borderline personality disorder', *Current Psychiatry Reports*, *6*, 66–70, 2004a.

Zanarini, M. C., 'Zanarini rating scale for borderline personality disorder (ZAN-BPD): A continuous measure of DSM-IV borderline pathology', *Journal of Personality Disorders*, *17*, 233–42, 2004b.

Zanarini, M. C., Gunderson, J. G. and Frankenburg, F. R., 'Axis I phenomenology of borderline personality disorder', *Comprehensive Psychiatry*, *30*, 149–56, 1989.

Zlotnick, C., Franklin, C. L. and Zimmerman, M., 'Is comorbidity of posttraumatic stress disorder and borderline personality disorder related to greater pathology and impairment?' *American Journal of Psychiatry*, *159*, 1940–3, 2002.

Chapter 17

Learning disability and co-existing drug and alcohol problems

Gabrielle Barter

KEY POINTS

1   The empirical literature regarding people with learning disabilities and alcohol/drug problems is limited.
2   What little research there is has many methodological problems, and is weighted toward people with borderline and mild learning disabilities. Findings are tentative.
3   Although this population appears to have a low prevalence of alcohol/ drug use, a significant minority do use alcohol/drugs problematically and have increased vulnerability to the negative consequences of alcohol/drug use, possibly at relatively low doses.
4   Problematic alcohol/drug use by people with learning disabilities can go undetected, delaying access to appropriate treatments.
5   A number of factors can make assessment and treatment of this client group difficult, which therapists and service providers need to be aware of and make appropriate modifications for.
6   People with learning disabilities who have alcohol/drug problems are likely to have many problems (e.g. economic, social, forensic, health, mental health), suggesting a multi-modal treatment approach.
7   There are many questions about how services can configure to best serve this population's needs.

INTRODUCTION

Learning disability is defined by impairment of intellectual (intelligence quotient below 70) and adaptive functioning and onset of these problems before adulthood (Professional Affairs Board of the British Psychological Society 2001). The empirical literature regarding this population and co-existing alcohol/drug problems is sparse. What little there is in relation to assessment and treatment places greater emphasis on alcohol than drug problems. Even here there are a variety of methodological problems; for example, many studies do not state the level of learning disability of their samples. Furthermore, the definition of learning disability has changed over the years, with (more latterly) people needing a lower intelligent quotient to be defined as being part of this population. It is probable that the literature is weighted towards the borderline to mild learning disability range of functioning.

Studies have generally found lower prevalence of drug use in the learning disability population than in the general population. For example, a study of 329 people with learning disabilities found that less than 5 per cent used alcohol (Rimmer *et al.* 1995). However, given the little empirical attention this area has received and the various methodological problems, findings are tentative.

Nevertheless, despite this relatively low reported prevalence, a significant minority of people with learning disabilities are using alcohol/drugs problematically (Krishef and DiNitto 1981). Within this minority there is some evidence to suggest that the pattern of use may be different compared to the general population – less frequent, fewer substances used in a lifetime, later age of first use and less physiological dependency (Westermeyer *et al.* 1996). Even so, the problems experienced by people with learning disabilities are similar to those experienced by the general population, including in the psychosocial, biomedical, family, legal and occupational domains (Krishef 1986). In other words, less use is required, compared to the general population, to precipitate the typical problems associated with alcohol/drug use (Westermeyer *et al.* 1996). Furthermore, while there is a lower prevalence of alcohol use, it has been found that among those who do use alcohol, the ratio of 'misusers' to users is almost equal, suggesting that alcohol use by people with learning disabilities is associated with a higher level of potential problematic use (McGillicuddy and Blane 1999). With regard to drugs, use of aerosol and solvent inhalants, LSD, cannabis, amphetamine, tobacco and cocaine has been found in samples of people who have learning disabilities, with relatively few reporting opiate use (e.g. Gress and Boss 1996; Westermeyer *et al.* 1988). There are also several sub-groups within this population (not mutually exclusive and often not recognized as having a learning disability) who have relatively high rates of alcohol/drug problems. These include offenders (McGillivary and Moore 2001), offenders who also have mental health problems (Kilmecki *et al.* 1994) and people with borderline and mild learning disabilities (Lottman 1993). It is unclear which type of agency should serve them: traditionally they fall between learning disability, drug and alcohol and mental health services (Sturmey *et al.* 2004).

People with learning disabilities who have alcohol/drug problems may be particularly vulnerable (Lindsay *et al.* 1991). One study found victimization, including robbery and physical and sexual assault perpetrated in the context of alcohol/drug use, in virtually all 40 participants who had alcohol/drug problems (Westermeyer *et al.* 1996).

Models that guide treatment

Because there are no empirically validated models and no best practice guidelines in this area (Christian and Poling 1997), the crucial treatment issue is how to best use existing 'mainstream' treatments with people with learning disabilities who have alcohol/drug problems (McMurran and Lismore 1993). These treatments, largely informed by learning and cognitive-behavioural models, include motivational interviewing, education, controlled drinking strategies, skills training, relapse prevention and self-help groups (see 'Treatment' section).

There has been little debate in either the learning disability or the alcohol and drug fields regarding best models of service delivery for clients who have co-existing learning disability and alcohol/drug problems. The major question is whether the best way to deliver services is to ensure good links between learning disability and alcohol and drug services (e.g. with good cross-referral pathways etc.), or whether there should be a joint service delivered by one team providing concurrent learning disability and alcohol and drug care. For reasons such as good continuity and co-ordination of care and provision of specialized assessment and treatment, the model of joint service delivery seems most beneficial. Whichever service configuration is established, at a minimum each service needs at least one person with specialist knowledge and skills in co-existing learning disability and alcohol/drug problems and all therapists (from both learning disability and alcohol/drug services) should have some training in both aspects (see 'Therapist variables' section).

CONTEXT OF THERAPY

Therapist variables

Therapists need to receive specialist training in learning disability, associated lifestyles, alcohol/drug issues and treatment (Lottman 1993). They need to have a good awareness of: (i) relatively common characteristics in this population which may increase vulnerability to the harmful effects of alcohol/drugs (e.g. medical problems such as cerebral palsy, epilepsy and cardiovascular, respiratory tract and gastrointestinal problems); (ii) potentially problematic interactions between medications and alcohol/illicit drugs (Christian and Poling 1997; Degenhardt 2000); (iii) various concomitant disorders or syndromes associated with learning disability (Krishef 1986) that may influence or interact with problematic alcohol/drug use (e.g. autistic spectrum disorder or foetal alcohol spectrum disorder); (iv) possible low tolerance to alcohol, including marked changes in behaviour, mood or personality or having amnesic episodes (blackouts) after only a few units (McCusker et al. 1993; Westermeyer et al. 1996); and (v) the importance of individually-based treatment modifications (see 'Treatment' section).

Client variables

It is suggested that people with learning disabilities use alcohol/drugs prob-lematically for the same range of reasons as do others: isolation and desire for social acceptance (Wenc 1981); low self-esteem (Moore and Polsgrove 1991); poor refusal skills; over-compliance and unassertiveness; susceptibility to peer pressure (Lindsay and Allen 1992; McGillicuddy and Blane 1999); poor knowledge (Lindsay *et al.* 1991); lack of social skills (Small 1981); and mental health problems (Kilmecki *et al.* 1994). In addition, the literature on a broader range of disabilities suggests alcohol/drug use may represent a form of managing negative feelings associated with having a disability and being part of an oppressed minority (Hepner *et al.* 1980) and a form of symptom management (Cosden 2001).

Because alcohol/drug problems are strongly associated with accessibility and availability, it is expected that, with increasing community access and integration, alcohol/drug problems will become more common in people with learning disabilities (Lottman 1993), and studies have found that people with learning disabilities who have alcohol/drug problems are more likely to have independent or group living arrangements (Krishef and DiNitto 1981; Rimmer *et al.* 1995). Alcohol and drug problems have also been found to be a prominent feature in younger age groups with associated risky behaviours (e.g. Pack *et al.* 1998), and in people with family members with alcohol/drug problems (Westermeyer *et al.* 1988). On the other hand, staff supervision and limited access to money represent poten-tial protective influences against alcohol/drug problems (Gress and Boss 1996).

People with learning disabilities are just as, if not more, likely to experience mental health problems as the general population (see Prosser 1999). Given the high prevalence of co-existing mental health problems and alcohol/drug problems in the general population (Hall and Farrell 1997), assessment (and treatment) of people with learning disabilities who have alcohol/drug problems should always include mental health issues (see 'Key Resources' section). A further consideration is that people with learning disabilities often can present with stress-related problems, sometimes manifesting as bizarre behaviour, which can be mistaken for major mental health problems instead (Sovner 1986). These issues highlight the need for comprehensive and specialized assessment.

Not only do people with learning disabilities experience a number of nega-tive social factors and life events (e.g. little integration with wider society, fewer social supports, family breakdown, institutionalization and stigmatiza-tion), they are also very vulnerable to the impact of such factors because of their reduced ability to conceptualize and express their feelings (Moss and Lee 2001). For example, inability to share grief has been linked to affective psychosis in this population (McLoughlin and Blate 1987). Negative social factors and life events have been associated with alcohol/drug problems in the general population (Tatossian *et al.* 1983).

ASSESSMENT OF CO-EXISTING LEARNING DISABILITIES AND DRUG AND ALCOHOL PROBLEMS

There is a risk that alcohol/drug problems will be missed in people with learning disabilities for a number of reasons: (i) there is a myth that people with learning disabilities do not have access to alcohol/drugs (Christian and Poling 1997); (ii) people with learning disabilities generally do not self-refer – usually this decision is taken by others supporting them (Nezu and Nezu 1994) who frequently are unable to decide whether a referral is appropriate (Moss and Patel 1993; Westermeyer *et al.* 1996); (iii) clients with learning disabilities cannot always articulate their problems (Fuller and Sabatino 1998); (iv) there is an increased likelihood of acquiescence to what it is believed the interviewer wants to hear, reduced attention span, poor time concepts and poor memory (Moss *et al.* 1997); (v) disability can be masked (Edgerton 1967); and (vi) crucial clinical signs or symptoms (e.g. aggression, forgetfulness, poor financial management) are sometimes dismissed as an inherent part of the learning disability (Reiss *et al.* 1982). If such obstacles are not minimized there is a danger of producing an inadequate assessment, resulting in delayed access to treatment. There are several ways of minimizing such obstacles (see below).

Comprehensive assessment

Assessment should be comprehensive, integrating information from a wide range of relevant sources and considering the broader social and ecological contexts (Moss 2001). Comprehensive assessments include multi-disciplinary team (MDT) assessment, clinical interview, case history, interview of care-givers, data recording including modified drink and drug diaries (if the person is able), interview schedules or questionnaires designed specifically for people with learning disabilities that indicate co-existing mental health or adjustment problems, and risk assessment. Further information on many aspects of assessment, consent, etc. are provided in the 'Key Resources' section at the end of the chapter.

Multi-disciplinary assessment

This might include the input of psychiatrist, social worker, clinical psychologist, nurse, occupational therapist and speech and language therapist. These all contribute to providing information about physical and psychological dependence; co-existing health, mental health or adjustment problems; social, interpersonal and intrapersonal factors influencing the alcohol/drug problem; the person's level of cognitive functioning, communication and comprehension; and the broader contexts of the problem including the social, economic and physical.

Clinical interview

This should include assessment of the person's pattern of alcohol/drug use, knowledge about and alternatives to alcohol/drug use (Lindsay *et al.* 1991), ambivalence and motivation to reduce alcohol/drug use (Velleman 2001) and fears about the implications of disclosing use. For example, people in institutional settings may not disclose the full extent of their problem in case it results in increased restrictions or staff observations (O'Neil 2000).

Ways of minimizing obstacles to interviewing people with learning disabilities include rapport building, use of single clause sentences, and frequent recapping and summarizing of what the client has said (Moss 2001; Prosser and Bromley 1999). Research has shown that people with learning disabilities can manage quite difficult questions provided they are structured appropriately (Moss *et al.* 1997). Furthermore, asking the client about their alcohol/drug use on a day-by-day basis following a recent memorable 'anchor event' (Prosser and Bromley 1999), as opposed to questioning them about their typical weekly consumption, may reduce cognitive demands as well as provide more valid information. For example, the client is first asked to think of an event which they can recall well which has occurred recently (e.g. a family visit or birthday) and are then asked about their consumption of alcohol/drugs on each of the days since that event.

The Psychiatric Assessment Schedules for Adults with Developmental Disability (PAS-ADD 10; Moss *et al.* 1997), a semi-structured interview schedule designed to detect mental disorders in people with learning disabilities, contains an alcohol screen (the Alcohol Use Disorders Identification Test or AUDIT) that is designed to identify excessive or harmful alcohol use (Bohn *et al.* 1995). The PAS-ADD 10 has good reliability and validity and is for trained users only.

Case history

It is important to include both general components (including family, psychological, health, occupational, social, psychiatric and forensic) and a history of alcohol/drug use and problems (evolution, current use, effects and physical components) within a case history. Such a history can be collated from information provided by the client and, with the client's consent, caregivers and case files.

Caregivers

Information from collateral sources such as caregivers (with prior informed consent from the client) about their concerns and the pattern, nature and effects of alcohol/drug use is important. Ideally the caregiver should have regular contact with the client and have known the client for more than six months.

Data recording

A period of data recording by the client and/or caregivers regarding issues such as frequency of alcohol/drug use, quantity consumed, money spent or mood charting can be extremely helpful. The client's ability (and motivation) to self-monitor needs to be assessed, because many people with learning disabilities struggle to self-monitor due to cognitive and communication limitations. For such reasons, adapted versions of drink and drug diaries and mood chartings (e.g. pictorial versions) may be required (e.g. Benson 1996).

Schedules and questionnaires

Assessment schedules specifically designed for use with people with learning disabilities should be used to assist with the identification of any co-existing adjustment or mental health problems. There are several, including the Psychiatric Assessment Schedules for Adults with Developmental Disability (PAS-ADD 10; Moss *et al.* 1997) and the PAS-ADD Checklist–Revised (Moss *et al.* 1998).

Using instruments designed for the general population and not adapted for this population can result in unreliable and invalid data for various reasons, including language comprehension problems and difficulties understanding graded rating scales or multiple choice. However, instruments designed for use with the general population have been used with people with learning disabilities, even though the reliability and validity of such instruments with this population has not been empirically established. Examples include the Symptom Checklist 90–Revised (SCL-90-R; Derogatis 1994) used by Kellett *et al.* (1999) and the Zung Self-Rating Anxiety Scale (Zung 1971) adapted by Lindsay and Michie (1988).

Risk assessment

This may be indicated in many cases and the results should be incorporated into formulation and intervention planning.

Formulation

All treatment plans need a formulation on which treatment recommendations are based – one which describes and hypothesizes causal pathways related to the person's alcohol/drug problems and how to alter them. Often alcohol/drug problems are multi-faceted and the treatment recommendations may not all be directly related to the alcohol/drug use. It is important to feed back and explain to the client and caregivers the assessment, formulation and treatment recommendations in a format that is understandable.

TREATMENT OF CO-EXISTING LEARNING DISABILITIES AND DRUG AND ALCOHOL PROBLEMS

Treatment considerations

Many people with learning disabilities live with, or are supported by, caregivers (professional or relatives). Often treatments for people with learning disabilities are dependent on the support of caregivers (e.g. transport, support in attending and implementing treatments). Therefore the clinician needs to engage the caregivers as well as the client. If the same clinician sees the client and the caregiver this may complicate treatment, jeopardize confidentiality and trust and be confusing for the client (Hurley 1989). An alternative approach is for someone to work with the client and someone else from the team to work with the caregivers (Hollins 2001), either for routine meetings or more in-depth work if indicated (see 'Treatment' section). However, this is only one view and many methods of family work require the client and caregivers to be seen together for various reasons, including reduction of the potential for splitting, secrets and alliances.

People with learning disabilities are a heterogeneous group and the level and type of limitations vary widely. Awareness of the client's specific limitations and strengths will allow treatment modifications based on their needs, and will also more accurately inform decisions about modality of treatment (e.g. group or individual). Modifying treatment for people with learning disabilities requires clinician flexibility with regard to technique implementation and adherence to model-specific principles (Hurley 1989).

There are many ways in which to modify treatments when working with people with learning disabilities. These strategies can be used individually or in group formats and include: adapting the pace of treatment; simplifying language; avoiding euphemisms and abstract concepts; paraphrasing; encouraging the client regularly to feed back their understanding of treatment material; defining unfamiliar words; presenting treatment material in several different modalities including visual (e.g. video, photographs) and active (e.g. role-play) modalities; providing concrete and individualized examples; modelling; and simple rule teaching (Cosden 2001; Orlando and Bartel 1989).

When working with people with learning disabilities, the clinician must consider the same relationship issues as when working with other groups. However, the clinician needs to be aware that the relationship histories of people with learning disabilities are often characterized by inequality, rejection, loss and exploitation. Often the person has effectively learned to placate or conform to what they believe the other wants. Also, the relationship can be complicated by the nature of the client's disability and associated dependence, which can evoke several reactions in the clinician including rescue wishes, overprotection and fear of setting limits (Hurley 1989).

Being aware that these feelings can manifest in the client–clinician relationship, demonstrating a respectful and non-judgmental attitude and using supervision will help the clinician to manage these aspects of treatment. The clinician may need to allow extra time to establish the therapeutic alliance (a good alliance improves outcome; Mueser and Kavanagh 2004) before efforts can be made to change.

As with other clients, often skills learnt in the treatment setting may not generalize to other settings. In many cases there is a need to address the primary environments for generalization of skill acquisition and this can be done either *in vivo* with the client or indirectly by training caregivers, either to teach the client skills or to prompt the client to practise and use the skills learnt in treatment settings in their home and other settings.

Co-ordinated multi-disciplinary multi-modal treatment

Recommendations from assessment are likely to include several different interventions due to the multi-faceted nature of the client's alcohol/drug problem. If there is going to be more than one clinician involved in the case, it is essential to have one acting as case manager. The case manager should co-ordinate regular meetings of all clinicians involved in order to monitor the client's progress and situation and the effectiveness of treatments, and collate any new information that needs to be incorporated into the formulation and treatment plan.

Individual alcohol/drug treatment with the client

While the treatments reviewed in the following section are discussed in the learning disability literature, they have very little, if any, evidence base in terms of delivery to people with learning disabilities with co-existing alcohol/drug problems. Also, most of the literature is based on alcohol rather than drug problems, and detoxification for people with learning disabilities is hardly discussed in the literature.

As outlined above, treatments discussed in the learning disability literature cover the key components of motivational interviewing, education, controlled drinking strategies, skills training, relapse prevention and self-help groups (all described elsewhere in this book). A simplified form of motivational interviewing has been used (McMurran and Lismore 1993), whereby two separate lists are created from suggestions elicited from the client about the good effects of drinking (e.g. it helps you to talk to other people, it's something to do) and the bad effects (e.g. it's expensive and makes you feel ill). These lists are then reviewed with the client with reference to more moderated drinking. Alcohol education groups have been conducted with people with learning disabilities, and have included discussions of safe limits and the symptoms of alcohol use (Lindsay *et al.* 1991). Education about topics such as the adverse effects of mixing medication and alcohol, and the use of alcohol/illicit drugs to manage symptoms (and alternative strategies for symptom management), may be indicated.

During controlled drinking and other skills training activities, the client can be encouraged to generate their own strategies by simple questions that are directly related to their experience and current life situation. It is important to be specific when discussing what strategies the client could use. For example, 'drink cola or orange juice' and 'go to the cinema' are specific, compared to 'just stop' or 'do something else instead' (McMurran and Lismore 1993). *In vivo* sessions in the pub have been used (McCusker *et al.* 1993) to increase generalization of skill.

Learning how to resist social pressure to drink is considered an important aspect of treatment for people with learning disabilities (McCusker *et al.* 1993). Such skills have been taught using various strategies including role-play and *in vivo* sessions in the pub. However, research has also found that people with learning disabilities are more likely to drink at home (Westermeyer *et al.* 1988). Therefore, other skills or provision of alternative activities may also be indicated. One such skill is relaxation, considered a fundamental coping skill in people trying to avoid excessive alcohol use (Parks *et al.* 2004) and incorporated into some alcohol services for people with learning disabilities (Small 1981). Behavioural relaxation is a particular relaxation technique that has been found to be effective for people with learning disabilities (e.g. Lindsay and Baty 1986) because it is a simple procedure that is not dependent on conceptual understanding. Clients are encouraged to adopt relaxed breathing and a relaxed posture in areas of their body by methods such as demonstration, imitation and, if required, manual guidance.

Relapse prevention is vital. This may involve identifying personal warning signs of relapse (e.g. feeling bored or sad) and specific skills training such as avoidance of high-risk situations (Paxon 1995). Disulfiram (Antabuse) has been suggested as an effective method of preventing relapse in people with learning disabilities due to immediate adverse consequences (Degenhardt 2000). However, disulfiram is also reported to have greater side-effects in the learning disabilities population (Westermeyer *et al.* 1996).

Treatment must also account for the potential of alcohol/drug problems to be persistent (Wenc 1981). The difficulty of maintenance of therapeutic gain will need to be considered carefully when working with people with learning disabilities and will be enhanced by long-term planning, support and after-care to the client and, if required, the caregivers.

It has been suggested that people with learning disabilities could benefit from the social aspects of self-help groups and should be supported to attend (Wenc 1981). However, it is unclear how effective such groups are for people with learning disabilities. It is reported that when people with learning disabilities have attended self-help groups, group members have felt 'uncomfortable', and groups specifically for people with learning disabilities are an alternative (Small 1981).

Individual non-alcohol/drugs treatment

A number of factors have been identified as underlying or compounding alcohol/drug problems in people with learning disabilities (see the 'Introduction' and 'Client variables' sections). This section will briefly review issues related to mental health, disability and social skills. The idea is that, for some individuals, addressing these factors will indirectly reduce alcohol/drug use.

Co-existing mental health problems and learning disability

Effective psychological treatments for people with learning disabilities who have co-existing mental health and alcohol/drug problems should be guided by what we know already about treatments for people with learning disabilities with co-existing mental health problems. For information regarding treatment approaches in this area, suggested reading is listed in the 'Key Resources' section at the end of this chapter.

Disability issues

It is suggested that people with other disabilities use drugs/alcohol to reduce negative feelings associated with their disability (Hepner et al. 1980) and/or for symptom management (Cosden 2001). People with learning disabilities are usually aware that they belong to a devalued group and have multiple experiences that are isolating and impact on self-worth (Hurley 1989). Directly addressing the person's experience of their disability and helping them to gain a better understanding of their abilities is beneficial (Bicknell 1983). Issues regarding disability can be addressed in psychotherapy conducted by a therapist with experience in this area. Helping the client with alternative means for symptom management requires specialized assessment and treatment.

Social skills

Social skills deficit is common in people with learning disabilities (Fuller and Sabatino 1998). Therefore people with learning disabilities may have fewer resources to draw upon when their alcohol/drug use becomes problematic (Moore and Polsgrove 1991) or in social or stressful situations once rehabilitated (Degenhardt 2000). The aim of social skills training is to increase the person's resources for dealing with stressors associated with everyday life and interpersonal situations, and thereby reduce the possibility that they will return to substance misuse (Degenhardt 2000).

Individual support for pragmatic daily living

The client may need support to manage day-to-day stressors that may be compounding the alcohol/drug problem. For example, the client may be struggling financially, residentially or with managing their medication, childcare and domiciliary responsibilities. A few sessions or long-term support may be indicated.

Indirect work with caregivers

As discussed above, when intervening with people with learning disabilities it is quite common for one clinician to work with the client, and for another to work with the caregivers in order to facilitate their engagement. However, in some cases it may also be recommended that the caregiver be offered some kind of intervention, either with or without the client. For example, caregivers may need support to help them gain a better understanding of the client and their needs, they may need training about alcohol/drug problems and the relapse process, and they may require advice over strategies that they can implement to support the client (and more successfully manage the alcohol/drug problem) or for relapse prevention and management (they can be taught to recognize and act upon signs of relapse early in the process).

Co-existing learning disability and alcohol/drug problems are associated with family conflict and alienation from the family (Westermeyer et al. 1988). Family therapy has been used in the general population with alcohol/drug problems (Vetere and Henley 2001) and in the learning disabilities field (Vetere 1993). Such therapy helps to maintain family support and can address complex relationship issues within the family that may arise as the client changes their alcohol/drug-related behaviour (Vetere and Henley 2001).

Addressing the broader social context

Alternative activities should be established as a replacement for alcohol/drug use (Lindsay and Allen 1992). This is particularly important when it is considered that people with learning disabilities often have little meaningful occupation, and are often socially isolated with poor employment possibilities (Cosden 2001). Vocational, social and educational opportunities should be considered. These opportunities should build on the client's strengths, interests and abilities and be in addition to more formal treatment. In a multi-disciplinary team, identification of such opportunities might be undertaken by the occupational therapist.

Ending treatment

The ending of treatment will require sensitive planning, preparation and time. Given the typical relationship history and temporary nature of the relationships that people with learning disabilities can experience, talking with the client about the process of ending – reviewing what has been achieved and helping them to understand their feelings – is crucial.

CASE STUDY

Mr A was a 22-year-old unemployed man with mild learning disabilities and a medical disorder who was living with his family. He was referred to the learning disability team because of concerns regarding multiple failed employment placements, increased problems with a medical disorder and physical assault against his family.

Assessment

He was seen by the psychiatrist and nurse regarding possible physical and mental health problems. Initial assessments revealed no apparent symptoms indicative of mental health problems. However, Mr A was using alcohol excessively and the assessment therefore incorporated this.

Mr A was asked about his alcohol use on each day in the previous week. To help with recall and to keep him focused, an 'anchor event' (Prosser and Bromley 1999) was first identified that he could remember well (he had visited his aunt a week ago). This event was then referred to during the interview when he was asked about his alcohol/drug use. He reported drinking strong lager on two to three nights per week (about 90 to 96 units per week) when out with his peer group. Alcohol use was associated with physical assault (family and public), property damage, several emergency hospital admissions associated with his medical disorder, peer group financial exploitation, peer group provocation and involvement with the police because of anti-social behaviour when intoxicated. No charges had ever been pressed. He used cannabis occasionally and denied any other drug use.

Mr A had little knowledge about alcohol, did not see his alcohol use as a problem, was not willing to abstain and wanted to move out of the family home and get a job. His medical disorder required daily monitoring and was managed relatively well, but with no daytime occupation and structure to his day, along with alcohol contraindications, he was struggling with managing his medical disorder effectively.

He had difficulties describing his experiences. Therefore, the team had to consider other ways to collect information in order to get a fuller picture of his alcohol use. Thus, further assessments were conducted with his parents, including behavioural recordings over a two-week period.

Interviews with the parents revealed that they did not understand his behaviour. They did not fully recognize the limitations associated with his learning disability, and also had difficulty seeing Mr A as an independent man who was at the stage where he wanted to develop his own life. Furthermore, they felt stressed and helpless about how to manage the situation, and were ambivalent about continuing their caring role.

Formulation

Mr A and his parents struggled with accepting his disability, leading to unrealistic hopes and expectations (e.g. inappropriate employment placements). Such hopes and expectations were associated for Mr A and his parents with many unresolved feelings, including loss, anger, anxiety and low self-worth. Mr A was also experiencing life stage and emotional difficulties akin to adolescence. His alcohol use was associated with attempts to identify with his peer group. Unresolved feelings about his disability manifested in his aggressive behaviour towards his family when intoxicated, and this further compounded the emotional climate in the family. Mr A had little insight into or knowledge about his alcohol use and consequences. He had little external or parental containment and few skills to manage his feelings. His learning disability affected his proficiency in making decisions, including with regard to risk behaviours and his peer group. He was susceptible to peer pressure and exploitation and had few social skills for effective peer negotiation.

It was hypothesized that interventions to improve his knowledge, train him in social and anger management skills, explore his motivation to change his drinking behaviour, provide emotional and practical support for Mr A and his family, allow him access to alternative relationships and provide meaningful occupational and recreational opportunities would help alleviate the difficulties. Furthermore, a referral to the alcohol service would provide specialized assessment, advice and treatment around issues such as alcohol dependence. Also, specialist advice regarding his medical disorder was indicated.

Treatment

The alcohol service identified no symptoms of dependence and hence little likelihood of withdrawal symptoms. Mr A and his family were offered support groups, which Mr A declined and the family did not attend.

The nurse from the learning disability team provided support to Mr A for his communication and to help with his understanding during his meetings with the specialist alcohol and medical disorder services. The nurse also liaised between the learning disability team and these services. As well as onward referral to the alcohol and specialist medical disorder services, the learning disability team also offered a number of interventions with advice available from the alcohol service when needed.

Basic individual modified alcohol and social skills education was offered to Mr A by his nurse. To facilitate Mr A's understanding, the education was tailored to his communication needs and incorporated explicitly the particular consequences for him. Mr A had developed a trusting relationship with his nurse and he agreed to the intervention and engaged well. He attended all 12 sessions.

Exploration of Mr A's motivation to change his drinking behaviour was also undertaken by the nurse. Mr A's difficulty describing his experience was highlighted when his motivation for change was explored. For example, when asked about the 'good' and 'bad' aspects of his alcohol use he could only say that he liked being 'wasted' and alcohol made him 'a bad person'.

With respect to the emotional and broader family issues, Mr A was seen by a psychologist. He was assessed as suitable for a psychotherapy group for young people with a learning disability, with the aim of helping him deal with some of the emotional problems he was experiencing. While anger management was suggested, he demonstrated no motivation, insight or recognition of this as a problem. Mr A's parents were seen by another psychologist to enhance their understanding of his behaviour, disability and emotional needs.

The police offered to liaise with the family and also advise on action to take in the event of Mr A committing an offence against them or their property. Social services organized respite care to ease the immediate anxiety and tension in the family. Following family discussions, longer-term plans were made for alternative accommodation. Support for Mr A, and his parents, in the transition from home to more independent living was provided by a social worker and the nurse.

An occupational therapy assessment identified Mr A's residential and independent living needs. This assessment also identified Mr A's occupational, social and recreational interests and needs (as alternatives to his alcohol and peer group). This assessment also recommended referral to a supported employment scheme.

Mr A's case was subject to ongoing multi-disciplinary review and monitoring. The nurse was the co-ordinating case worker.

Outcome

Mr A responded well to the specialist advice and education regarding his alcohol use and medical disorder. He also responded well to the periodic respite care. However, he continued to use alcohol problematically and to mix with his peer group when back at home. He had subsequent involvement with the police, including arrest after assaulting his family, and several hospital admissions for medical complications after drinking.

Mr A's parents demonstrated a more realistic understanding of Mr A and his needs, and began to place limits on and consequences to his behaviour. Mr A was eventually found a residential placement with 24-hour support. Ground rules were set and negotiated. He was able to contract with the staff group safe limits and rules around his alcohol use. He developed good relationships with the staff and had a full weekly schedule of activities as alternatives to alcohol use. With support, he started exploring appropriate employment opportunities. Mr A demonstrated increased recognition of and willingness to address his difficulties with anger. There were no incidents of aggression and no alcohol problems, although the staff group undertook training on relapse prevention and management, and a plan was devised on action to take if relapse occurred.

In summary, this case highlights the need for a co-ordinated approach to assessment and treatment, and good links between learning disability services and caregivers, related services and agencies. These links are particularly important when the person will only engage to a certain degree and is at the pre-contemplation stage (Prochaska and DiClemente 1983; see also Chapter 3 in this volume) with regard to change. Alcohol education and motivational techniques were not a 'stand alone' treatment in this case. Addressing the broader context along with the emotional issues, both directly and with caregivers, resulted in a significant reduction in drinking and associated problems.

CONCLUSION

Research regarding learning disabilities and alcohol/drug problems is very limited; what research has been conducted has been based on small and restricted samples, probably weighted to those populations with borderline to mild learning disabilities. There are many research questions. Further research is needed to obtain accurate prevalence data on alcohol/drug use and problems in the learning disability population, and risk and protective factors need to be identified. Also, research needs to inform best practice guidelines for assessment, treatment and service configuration.

A major component of current social and health care policy (e.g. the UK government White Paper *Valuing People: A New Strategy For Learning*

Disability for the 21st Century; Department of Health 2001) is reduction in the health inequalities experienced by people with learning disabilities and increased equity with regard to access to mainstream health services. Methods outlined to facilitate such aims include having identified professionals assist people with learning disabilities to access services, and developing mainstream services so that they have the necessary capacity and skills. As 'mainstreaming' is emphasized, it is likely that people with learning disabilities will be increasingly exposed to alcohol/drugs, and thus that use (and hence problems) will rise. A key question is: what is currently being done in practice with respect to people with a learning disability who also have alcohol/drug problems, and what will need to be done as numbers rise? Research is needed to look at referral routes, care pathways, accessibility and utility of specialized alcohol/drug services for people with learning disabilities, the support of such services by specialist learning disability services and what, if any, the obstacles may be (Lottman 1993).

KEY RESOURCES

Interviewing people with learning disabilities

Prosser, H. and Bromley, J., 'Interviewing people with intellectual disabilities', in Emerson, E., Hatton, C., Bromley, J. and Caine, A., eds, *Clinical Psychology and People with Intellectual Disabilities*, pp. 99–113. Chichester: Wiley, 1999.

Assessment tools

Benson, B., 'Psychotherapy tools: A daily mood check form for use in outpatient services', *The Habilitative Mental Healthcare Newsletter*, *15*, 91–6, 1996.

Kellett, S. C., Baeil, N., Newman, D. W. and Mosley, E., 'Indexing psychological distress in people with an intellectual disability: Use of the Symptom Checklist-90-R', *Journal of Applied Research in Intellectual Disabilities*, *12*, 323–34, 1999.

Lindsay, W. R. and Michie, A. M., 'Adaptation of the Zung Self-rating Anxiety Rating Scale for people with a mental handicap', *Journal of Mental Deficiency Research*, *32*, 485–90, 1988.

Moss, S., Ibbotson, B., Prosser, H., Goldberg, D., Patel, P. and Simpson, N., 'Validity of the PAS-ADD for detecting psychiatric symptoms in adults with learning disability', *Social Psychiatry and Psychiatric Epidemiology*, *32*, 344–54, 1997.

Moss, S., Prosser, H., Costello, H., Simpson, N., Patel, P., Rowe, S. *et al.*, 'Reliability and validity of the PAS-ADD checklist for detecting psychiatric disorders in adults with intellectual disorders', *Journal of Intellectual Disability Research*, *42*, 172–83, 1998.

Consent issues

Department of Health, *Seeking Consent: Working with People with Learning Disabilities*. London: Department of Health, 2001. Available at http://www. dh.gov.uk/publicationsand statistics/publications/publicationspolicyandguidance/ publicationspolicyandguidancearticle/fs/en?content_id=4007861&chk=a3qncs (accessed 15 January 2005).

Mental health and learning disability

Bouras, N., *Psychiatric and Behavioural Disorders in Developmental Disabilities and Mental Retardation*. Cambridge: Cambridge University Press, 2001.

Bouras, N., Murray, B., Joyce, T., Kon, Y. and Holt, G., *Mental Health in Learning Disabilities: A Training Pack for Staff Working with People who have a Dual Diagnosis of Mental Health Needs and Learning Disabilities*. Brighton: Pavilion, 1997.

Dosen, A. and Day, K., *Treating Mental Illness and Behavioural Disorders in Children and Adults with Mental Retardation*. Washington: American Psychiatric Publishing, 2001.

Foundation for People with Learning Disabilities, *Count Us In. The Report of the Committee of Inquiry into Meeting the Mental Health Needs of Young People with Learning Disabilities*. London: The Mental Health Foundation, 2002.

Holt, G., Gratsa, A., Bouras, N., Joyce, T., Spiller, M. J. and Hardy, S., *Guide to Mental Health for Families and Carers of People with Intellectual Disabilities*. London: Jessica Kingsley Publishers, 2005.

Health policy

Department of Health, *Valuing People – A New Strategy for Learning Disability for the 21st Century*. London: Department of Health, 2001. Available at http// www.archive.official-documents.co.uk/document/cm50/5086/5086.pdf (accessed 15 January 2005).

Websites

British Institute of Learning Disabilities, *BILD – British Institute of Learning and Disabilities*. Kidderminster: British Institute of Learning Disabilities, 2005. Available at http://www.bild.org.uk (accessed 15 January 2005).

Foundation for People with Learning Disabilities, *Foundation for People with Learning Disabilities*. London: Mental Health Foundation, 2005. Available at http://www. fpld.org.uk (accessed 15 August 2005).

Mencap, *Mencap – Understanding Learning Disabilities*. London: Mencap, 2004. Available at http://www.mencap.org.uk (accessed 15 January 2005).

National Society for Epilepsy, *E-Epilepsy*. Chalfont St. Peter: National Society for Epilepsy, 2005. Available at http://www.e-epilepsy.org.uk (accessed 15 January 2005).

PAS-ADD Websites

Information about the Psychiatric Assessment Schedules for Adults with Developmental Disability (PAS-ADD; Moss *et al.* 1997, 1998), training and purchasing also available, at http://www.pasadd.co.uk (accessed 15 January 2005). Purchase the PAS-ADD Checklist–Revised from Pavilion Publishing. available at http://www.pavpub.com/pavpub/trainingmaterials/showfull.asp?section=1& subsection=4&product=299 (accessed 16 January 2005).

REFERENCES

Benson, B., 'Psychotherapy tools: A daily mood check form for use in outpatient services', *The Habilitative Mental Healthcare Newsletter*, *15*, 91–6, 1996.

Bicknell, J., 'The psychopathology of handicap', *British Journal of Medical Psychology*, *56*, 167–78, 1983.

Bohn, M. J., Babor, T. F. and Kranzker, H. R., 'The Alcohol Use Disorder Identification Test (AUDIT): Validation of a screening instrument for use in medical settings', *Journal of Studies on Alcohol*, *56*, 423–32, 1995.

Christian, L. and Poling, A., 'Drug abuse in persons with mental retardation: A review', *American Journal on Mental Retardation*, *102*, 126–36, 1997.

Cosden, M., 'Risk and resilience for substance abuse among adolescents and adults with learning disabilities', *Journal of Learning Disabilities*, *34*, 352–9, 2001.

Degenhardt, L., 'Intervention for people with alcohol use disorders and an intellectual disability: A review of the literature', *Journal of Intellectual and Developmental Disability*, *25*, 135–46, 2000.

Department of Health, *Valuing People: A New Strategy for Learning Disability for the 21st Century*. London: Department of Health, 2001. Available at http://www.archive.official-documents.co.uk/document/cm50/5086.pdf (accessed 15th January 2005).

Derogatis, L. R., *SCL-90-R: Administration, scoring, and procedures manual*, 3rd ed. Minneapolis, MN: Derogatis, 1994.

Edgerton, R. B., *The Cloak of Competence*. Berkeley: University of California Press, 1967.

Fuller, C. G. and Sabatino, C. A., 'Diagnosis and treatment considerations with comorbid developmentally disabled populations', *Journal of Clinical Psychology*, *54*, 1–10, 1998.

Gress, J. R. and Boss, M. S., 'Substance abuse differences among students receiving special education school services', *Child Psychiatry and Human Development*, *26*, 235–46, 1996.

Hall, W. and Farrell, M., 'Co-morbidity of mental disorders and substance misusers', *British Journal of Psychiatry*, *171*, 484–5, 1997.

Hepner, R., Krishbaum, H. and Landes, D., 'Counselling substance abusers with additional disabilities: The centre for independent living', *Alcohol Health and Research World*, *5*, 11–15, 1980.

Hollins, S., 'Psychotherapeutic methods', in Dosen, A. and Day, K., eds, *Treating Mental Illness and Behavioural Disorders in Children and Adults with Mental Retardation*, pp. 27–44. Washington: American Psychiatric Publishing, 2001.

Hurley, A. D., 'Individual psychotherapy with mentally retarded individuals: A review and call for research', *Research in Developmental Disabilities*, *10*, 261–75, 1989.

Kellett, S. C., Baeil, N., Newman, D. W. and Mosley, E., 'Indexing psychological distress in people with an intellectual disability: Use of the Symptom Checklist-90-R', *Journal of Applied Research in Intellectual Disabilities*, *12*, 323–34, 1999.

Kilmecki, M. R., Jenkinson, J. and Wilson, L., 'A study of recidivism among offenders with an intellectual disability', *Australia and New Zealand Journal of Developmental Disabilities*, *19*, 209–19, 1994.

Krishef, C. H., 'Do the mentally retarded drink? A study of their alcohol usage', *Journal of Alcohol and Drug Education*, *31*, 64–70, 1986.

Krishef, C. H. and DiNitto, D. M., 'Alcohol abuse among mentally retarded individuals', *Mental Retardation*, *19*, 151–5, 1981.

Lindsay, W. R. and Allen, R., 'The art of positive drinking', *Nursing Times*, *88*, 46–8, 1992.

Lindsay, W. R., Allen, R., Walker, P., Lawrenson, H. and Smith, A. H. W., 'An alcohol education service for people with learning difficulties', *Mental Handicap*, *19*, 96–100, 1991.

Lindsay, W. R. and Baty, F., 'Abbreviated progressive relaxation', *Mental Handicap*, *14*, 121–6, 1986.

Lindsay, W. R. and Michie, A. M., 'Adaptation of the Zung Self-rating Anxiety Rating Scale for people with a mental handicap', *Journal of Mental Deficiency Research*, *32*, 485–90, 1988.

Lottman, T. J., 'Access to generic substance abuse services for persons with mental retardation', *Journal of Alcohol and Drug Education*, *39*, 41–55, 1993.

McCusker, C. G., Clare, I. C. H., Cullen, C. and Reep, J., 'Alcohol related knowledge and attitudes in people with a mild learning disability: The effects of a "sensible drinking" group', *Journal of Community and Applied Social Psychology*, *3*, 29–40, 1993.

McGillicuddy, N. B. and Blane, H. T., 'Substance use in individuals with mental retardation', *Addictive Behaviours*, *24*, 869–78, 1999.

McGillivary, J. and Moore, M. R., 'Substance abuse by offenders with mild intellectual disability', *Journal of Intellectual and Developmental Disability*, *26*, 297–310, 2001.

McLoughlin, I. J. and Blate, M. S., 'A case of affective psychosis following bereavement in a mentally handicapped woman', *British Journal of Psychiatry*, *151*, 552–4, 1987.

McMurran, M. and Lismore, K., 'Using video-tapes in alcohol interventions for people with learning disabilities: An exploratory study', *Mental Handicap*, *21*, 29–31, 1993.

Moore, D. and Polsgrove, L., 'Disabilities, developmental handicaps and substance misuse: A review', *The International Journal of the Addictions*, *26*, 65–90, 1991.

Moss, S., 'Assessment conceptual issues', in Bouras, N., ed., *Psychiatric and Behavioural Disorders in Developmental Disabilities and Mental Retardation*, pp. 18–38. Cambridge: Cambridge University Press, 2001.

Moss, S., Ibbotson, B., Prosser, H., Goldberg, D., Patel, P. and Simpson, N., 'Validity of the PAS-ADD for detecting psychiatric symptoms in adults with learning disability', *Social Psychiatry and Psychiatric Epidemiology*, *32*, 344–54, 1997.

Moss, S. and Lee, P., 'Mental health', in Thompson J. and Pickering, S., eds, *Meeting the Health Needs of People who have a Learning Disability*, pp. 235–59. London: Harcourt Brace, 2001.

Moss, S. and Patel, P., 'The prevalence of mental illness in people with intellectual disability over 50 years of age, and the diagnostic importance of information from carers', *The Irish Journal of Psychology, 14*, 110–29, 1993.

Moss, S., Prosser, H., Costello, H., Simpson, N., Patel, P., Rowe, S. *et al.*, 'Reliability and validity of the PAS-ADD checklist for detecting psychiatric disorders in adults with intellectual disorders', *Journal of Intellectual Disability Research, 42*, 172–83, 1998.

Mueser, K. T. and Kavanagh, D., 'Treating comorbidity of alcohol problems and psychiatric disorder', in Heather, N. and Stockwell, T., eds, *The Essential Handbook of Treatment and Prevention of Alcohol Problems*, pp. 139–60. Chichester: Wiley, 2004.

Nezu, C. M. and Nezu, A. M., 'Outpatient psychotherapy for adults with mental retardation and concomitant psychopathology: Research and clinical imperatives', *Journal of Consulting and Clinical Psychology, 62*, 34–42, 1994.

O'Neil, H., *Managing Anger*. London: Whurr Publishers, 2000.

Orlando, J. E. and Bartel, N. R., 'Cognitive strategy training: An intervention model for parents of children with learning disabilities', *Reading, Writing and Learning Disabilities, 5*, 327–44, 1989.

Pack, R. P., Wallander, J. L. and Browne, D., 'Health risk behaviours of African American adolescents with mild mental retardation: Prevalence depends on measurement method', *American Journal of Mental Retardation, 102*, 409–20, 1998.

Parks, G. A., Marlatt, G. A. and Anderson, B. K., 'Cognitive-behavioural alcohol treatment', in Heather, N. and Stockwell, T., eds, *The Essential Handbook of Treatment and Prevention of Alcohol Problems*, pp. 69–86. Chichester: Wiley, 2004.

Paxon, J. E., 'Relapse prevention for individuals with developmental disabilities, borderline intellectual functioning or illiteracy', *Journal of Psychoactive Drugs, 27*, 167–72, 1995.

Prochaska, J. O. and DiClemente, C. C., 'Transtheoretical therapy: Toward a more integrative model of change', *Psychotherapy: Theory, Research and Practice, 19*, 276–88, 1983.

Professional Affairs Board of the British Psychological Society, *Learning Disability: Definitions and Contexts*. Leicester: British Psychological Society, 2001.

Prosser, H., 'An invisible morbidity?' *The Psychologist, 12*, 234–7, 1999.

Prosser, H. and Bromley, J., 'Interviewing people with intellectual disabilities', in Emerson, E. Hatton, C. Bromley, J. and Caine, A., eds, *Clinical Psychology and People with Intellectual Disabilities*, pp. 99–113. Chichester: Wiley, 1999.

Reiss, S., Levitan, G. W. and Szyszko, J., 'Emotional disturbance and mental retardation: Diagnostic overshadowing', *American Journal of Mental Deficiency, 86*, 567–74, 1982.

Rimmer, J. H., Braddock, D. and Marks, B., 'Health characteristics and behaviours of adults with mental retardation residing in three living arrangements', *Research in Developmental Disabilities, 16*, 489–99, 1995.

Small, J., 'Emotions anonymous: Counselling the mentally retarded substance abuser', *Alcohol Health Research World, 5*, 46, 1981.

Sovner, R., 'Limiting factors in the use of DSM-III criteria with mentally ill/retarded persons', *Psychopharmacology Bulletin, 22*, 1055–9, 1986.

Sturmey, P., Taylor, J. and Lindsay, W. R., 'Research and development', in Lindsay, W. R., Taylor, J. and Sturmey, P., eds, *Offenders with Learning Disabilities*, pp. 327–51. Chichester: Wiley, 2004.

Tatossian, A., Charpy, J. P., Remy, M., Prinquey, D. and Poinso, Y., 'Events in the lives of 120 chronic alcoholics: Preliminary study', *Annals Medico-Psychologiques, 141,* 824–41, 1983.

Velleman, R., *Counselling for Alcohol Problems*, 2nd ed. London: Sage, 2001.

Vetere, A., 'Using family therapy in services for people with learning disabilities', in Carpenter, S. and Treacher, A., eds, *Using Family Therapy in the 90's*, pp. 111–30. Oxford: Blackwell, 1993.

Vetere, A. and Henley, M., 'Integrating couples and family therapy into a community alcohol service: A pantheoretical approach', *The Association for Family Therapy and Systemic Practice, 23,* 85–101, 2001.

Wenc, F., 'The developmentally disabled substance abuser', *Alcohol Health and Research World, 5,* 42–6, 1981.

Westermeyer, J., Kemp, K. and Nugent, S., 'Substance disorder among persons with mild mental retardation. A comparative study', *American Journal on Addictions, 5,* 23–31, 1996.

Westermeyer, J., Phaobtang, T. and Neider, J., 'Substance use and abuse among mentally retarded persons: A comparison of patients and a survey population', *American Journal of Drug and Alcohol Abuse, 14,* 109–23, 1988.

Zung, W. K., 'A rating instrument for anxiety disorders', *Psychosomatics, 12,* 371–9, 1971.

Chapter 18

Training in co-existing mental health and drug and alcohol problems

High priority in policy requires resources

Ilana Crome and Roger Bloor

KEY POINTS

1 Since co-existing mental health and drug and alcohol problems affect so many areas of health and social care, a very wide range of health and social care professionals need training and education in how to deal with them.

2 There are many obstacles preventing health and social care practitioners from accessing training.

3 There are many different terms applied to this problem area: in each local area, agencies should consider how they use terms operationally to identify practitioner roles and service components and capacity, and how to ensure that such terms are not used to exclude people from getting the help they need.

4 The issue of co-existing mental health and drug and alcohol problems is a large one: prevalence data are provided, demonstrating the need to assess, treat and manage this group. This evidence of need, however, does not translate into practice, either in initial training, regular supervision or in later service provision.

5 Models for training have been described, and some have been evaluated, but their implementation is not widespread. The reasons for this are discussed; various training models are outlined, as are the results of evaluation of training.

6 On the basis of models and evaluations, it is concluded that the content of a training programme on co-existing problems needs to be both extensive and specific.

7 The UK experience is provided as a case example.

INTRODUCTION: TRAINING – WHO NEEDS IT?

Training objectives: extent of the problems

It is increasingly well documented that excessive use of substances such as tobacco, alcohol and other drugs results in multiple social, physical and psychological complications, which cluster together. Clients present to a whole range of health care professionals within accident and emergency departments, and paediatric, geriatric, general medical and surgical, general psychiatric, primary care and, of course, specialist mental health and addiction services. Thus, the range of practitioners who may potentially be involved in the care of people with alcohol and drug problems who may also have multiple co-existing disorders is broad and not limited only to specialists in addiction and mental health.

Barriers to training?

In order to understand how to implement a training programme success-fully, it is worth reflecting on the many obstacles to facilitating change: the complexity of providing teaching on health issues with wide psychosocial implications within the traditional medical, nursing or psychology curricula; persisting stigma related to both those with mental health problems and those with alcohol and drug problems (Crisp *et al.* 2000; Crome and Day 1999; Glass 1987; *The Lancet* 2001); increasing pressures within the United Kingdom on National Health Service (NHS) addiction treatment services; a lack of competent practitioners who have the time to provide training; and a diversity of opinion about what priority drug and alcohol problems have in the hierarchy of those issues in which students training in health care should be proficient. The shortage of clinicians trained in the management of co-existing mental health and substance use disorders is seen as one of the major barriers to provision of adequate treatment systems. The lack of adequate training for staff is seen as a barrier to the implementation of services (Drake *et al.* 2001; Power and Demartino 2004) with consequent negative effects on treatment outcome (Department of Health 2002).

A study of the training needs of UK health care professionals (Mears *et al.* 2001) asked for views on the best approaches for delivering training in the area of 'dual diagnosis'. A total of 272 responses were reported, and the three characteristics considered most important in relation to training were that it needs to be multidisciplinary/cross-training, regular and expert-led. The training was reported to be needed at the undergraduate, pre-registration, continuous professional development and postgraduate levels. The need for mental heath training for community agency staff, to be delivered on a multi-agency basis, was supported in a focus group study of the mental health training needs of a variety of community agencies (Secker and Hill 2002).

Training has to be the way forward, but what is the route?

In fairness, however, the most recent UK General Medical Council guidance on *Tomorrow's Doctors* does, for the first time, make specific mention, albeit once, of drug and alcohol problems (General Medical Council 2002). In its broadest sense, education is acknowledged as one channel that might begin to ameliorate this lack of professional engagement, since training in effective and cost-effective interventions can enhance knowledge, competence and skills, and thereby encourage change. Empowering students to drive change is another such channel (Crome and Shaikh 2004), although previous studies have demonstrated the parlous state of undergraduate addiction training, which has been given less undergraduate curricular time over the years.

Moreover, most assessment tools and many interventions for drug, alcohol and smoking problems can, and should, be effectively delivered by generalists (Heather 1996). A review of the priority actions needed to improve the care of persons with co-existing mental health and drug and alcohol problems concluded that there was a need to expand training programmes to ensure a high level of competence in health care professionals providing integrated services. The success of such training courses was seen to be dependent on the provision of programmes to train educators and the development of tools to facilitate training (O'Brien *et al.* 2004).

Establishing the need for training

The UK Royal Colleges of General Practitioners and Psychiatrists and the National Treatment Agency for Substance Misuse recognize the dearth of training opportunities and standards for qualified practitioners in the field (Royal College of Psychiatrists and Royal College of General Practitioners 2005). Not only is there some evidence in the literature, but it is abundantly clear in the frontline clinical situation that clinicians and social and health care professionals at all levels feel incompetent to deal with an intrinsically complex group of clients.

Despite the fact that working with people who have co-existing mental health and drug and alcohol problems is now part of routine work in any field of mental health or social care, and in criminal justice services and drug services (Banerjee *et al.* 2002), repeated reviews of medical and nursing curricula at both undergraduate and postgraduate levels in the UK, the USA and Australia have shown that drug and alcohol education has, at best, a very small presence (Happell *et al.* 2002), and findings are similar for other professions (e.g. Crome and Shaikh 2004). Indeed, most clients have not been asked about substance use disorders by admitting psychiatrists (Barnaby *et al.* 2003; Farrell and David 1988).

Models for training have been described (see below), but their implementation is not widespread. There is an urgent need for action to ensure that training is available for all staff working with people who have co-existing mental health and drug and alcohol problems (Gournay *et al.* 1997).

TRAINING MODELS

A number of organizations have developed standards for training in the management of co-existing mental health and drug and alcohol problems. These include the UK National Treatment Agency (NTA) for Substance Misuse, the American Psychiatric Association, the UK Department of Health, the UK Royal College of Psychiatrists and the UK Royal College of General Practitioners. The need to develop training resources has been highlighted in a number of studies (American Psychiatric Association 1996; Brems *et al.* 2002; McNamara 2003; Morris and Stuart 2002; Pulice *et al.* 1994).

National Treatment Agency, UK

The UK NTA defines key training elements for teams engaging with people who have co-existing mental health and drug and alcohol problems (National Treatment Agency 2002: 174–5):

- Drug and alcohol and mental health service staff need to be adequately trained to assess co-existing mental health problems.
- All staff need to have training in risk assessment.
- All services providing care and management to those with co-existing mental health and drug and alcohol problems need to have a lead medical officer with experience in the treatment of drug and alcohol problems and psychiatry.
- All staff in general psychiatric services should have some training in drug and alcohol problems.

The essential components of a training programme in this area, as recommended by the NTA, are outlined in Table 18.1.

Department of Health, UK

The UK Department of Health has published good practice guidelines for training staff in the management of people with combined mental health and alcohol and drug problems (Department of Health 2002). These guidelines suggest that an integrated training strategy should contain three main strands: interagency collaboration and information exchange through interagency training; theoretical and skills-based training; and practice development and

Table 18.1 Essential components of a training programme for co-existing mental health and drug and alcohol problems recommended by the UK National Treatment Agency for Substance Misuse (2002)

- Training and ongoing professional development is important in ensuring that staff are adequately trained to work with clients with co-existing mental health and drug and alcohol problems.
- Each local area should develop a training strategy to identify the training needs of all staff and professional groups working in statutory and non-statutory organizations.
- Mental health services should appoint staff who have formal training in co-existing mental health and drug and alcohol problems, or ensure that staff have access to substance misuse training once they are in post.
- Mental health services should have a substance misuse training strategy that pertains to all staff and professional groups and which is monitored and evaluated.
- For staff working within substance misuse services, training should be provided which includes the recognition and care of service users with mental illness and collaborative working with mental health services.

supervision. Within these three areas a number of key training needs were identified, as outlined in Table 18.2.

The process of developing a training strategy will, however, need to address local training needs on an interagency basis and will evolve from a detailed training needs analysis using these key elements as a framework for interagency discussion.

American Psychiatric Association, USA

The American Psychiatric Association's position statement on the need for improved training for the treatment of clients with co-existing mental health and drug and alcohol problems (American Psychiatric Association 1993) recommended that psychiatrists in training receive specific education in the assessment and management of co-existing mental health and drug and alcohol problems, and that psychiatric programmes in hospitals and other centres implement training in this field for psychiatrists and other health professionals.

A recent review of service models for clients with co-existing mental health and drug and alcohol problems within the USA (Drake *et al.* 2004) identified the key basic competencies for clinicians with a mental health background, related to dealing with these co-existing problems, as being: knowledge of alcohol and drug use and problems and how substances affect mental health; assessment of drug and alcohol use; motivational counselling for clients who are not ready to pursue abstinence; and counselling for drug and alcohol

Table 18.2 Key training needs in co-existing mental health and drug and alcohol problems, as identified by the UK Department of Health (2002)

Key elements for interagency training

- Increase awareness of mental health issues and therapeutic responses
- Increase awareness of drug-related issues and therapeutic responses
- Increase awareness of the relationship between substance misuse and mental health problems
- Challenge negative attitudes and prejudices around both mental health problems and substance misuse
- Increase staff confidence and reduce fear and anxiety in relation to working with people with complex needs
- Implement joint/shared training on assessment and referral
- Increase knowledge of other relevant services and referral criteria
- Increase knowledge of cross-cultural and gender issues
- Access users' views
- Increase knowledge of scope and limitations of compulsory powers under mental health legislation

Key elements for theoretical and skills-based training

- Increase knowledge of co-existing mental health and drug and alcohol problems
- Increase drug and alcohol awareness
- Improve assessment skills for substance misuse
- Improve assessment skills for mental health problems
- Improve risk assessment and management skills
- Increase knowledge of the management of substance misuse problems
- Increase knowledge of the management of mental health problems
- Improve engagement skills
- Improve care coordination
- Teach motivational enhancement strategies, including motivational interviewing
- Improve relapse prevention for substance misuse
- Improve early warning sign monitoring and relapse prevention for mental health problems
- Increase knowledge of mental health legislation

Key strategy elements for practice development and supervision

- Ensure that staff are supported in the implementation of the practices resulting from the training
- Ensure that staff are supported in their practice through development of supervision systems
- Encourage specialist services for co-existing mental health and drug and alcohol problems to provide supervision for generic services
- Establish peer supervision networks during the training sessions
- Establish management-level support for supervision, ensuring that time is allocated for reflection on practice
- Utilize individuals or peer supervision groups to identify communication issues to feed back into the service planning groups

problems for clients who are ready to work on attaining abstinence or preventing relapses.

Postgraduate psychiatry training

Postgraduate psychiatry training often fails to address the needs of clients with both mental health and drug and alcohol problems. A model integrating such training within general psychiatry training has been proposed (Renner 2004) with the following guidelines:

- Effective training should address knowledge, attitudes and skills necessary to provide comprehensive care to this client group.
- All training activities should be multi-dimensional and include didactic lectures backed by handouts and presentations, case discussions, critical literature reviews and reading assignments.
- The training should be coordinated with the general psychiatry curriculum and should reflect the trainees' current needs in their clinical rotation.
- The training should be of a progressive nature over the years of training placements, and coordinated with the possibility of supervised application of new treatment skills. The training should enable exposure to the long-term treatment needs of clients.
- Trainers should be skilled, knowledgeable and involved in the treatment of the client group, and should provide positive role models for the trainees working with them.

Inter-professional models for training

COMPASS

The COMPASS programme (Graham *et al.* 2003) provides multidisciplinary team training as part of a Combined Psychosis and Substance Use Service (COMPASS; see Chapters 7 and 19 for further information). This model aims to provide support and training in the management of clients with co-existing mental health and drug and alcohol problems to primary and secondary mental health care teams. The key principle of the project is to ensure that mainstream services provide care for both the mental health and substance use elements of clients' needs. Where this is not possible, the project aims to ensure that the shared care approach is used by all involved.

COMPASS training consists of a two-stage package. The initial stage is a whole team-based approach, which aims to raise awareness of the issues involved in managing clients with co-existing mental health and drug and alcohol problems. The second stage is focused on two staff members, who are designated as having a lead role within the team for these issues, and who will act as designated liaison personnel with other services. The package offers skills-based training and awareness-raising sessions to ensure that staff within mental health services are able to work effectively with drug and alcohol problems and that staff in addiction services have raised awareness of mental heath problems. The overall aim of the COMPASS programme is to improve access to services, and movement between services where appropriate, for this client group.

The St. Luke's/Roosevelt Hospital Centre Dual Diagnosis Training Curriculum

The St. Luke's/Roosevelt Hospital Centre Dual Diagnosis Training Curriculum (O'Neil 1993) is an integrated, inter-professional training course developed and implemented in a multidisciplinary department of addiction and psychiatry within a large urban hospital. The curriculum was designed to deliver a range of modules covering theoretical models, diagnosis and treatment.

Using a biopsychosocial model, the course addresses general concepts, diagnosis and differential diagnosis, working in a variety of settings, treatments (both long- and short-term) and adolescent populations, with a variety of pharmacology, family, HIV/AIDS, parental substance misuse and finally counter-transference issues. The course design emphasizes the importance of multiple teaching methods when working with a diverse participant group. Methods include didactic lectures, role-playing sessions, experiential exercises, case presentations and discussions.

The goals of the training are defined as enhancing knowledge, reducing attitudinal barriers and improving clinical skills across a range of professionals. A detailed description of the educational objectives and lecture content is available (O'Neil 1993), together with advice on training design and implementation.

SETTING THE SCENE: CONTENT OF A TRAINING PROGRAMME

From all of the above, there seems to be a consensus that, in essence, training in dealing with co-existing mental health and alcohol and drug problems should equip the student to:

Appreciate the range of definitions of co-existing conditions

It is important that training courses emphasize the need to be clear that the term 'dual diagnosis' when used in this area is not a diagnosis in itself;

instead it simply describes the fact that an individual has both a mental health disorder and an alcohol and/or drug problem. Any 'diagnosis' will involve the identification of the nature of each of these problems.

Be conscious of the fact that *all* substances (tobacco, non-compliance with prescribed medications and over-the-counter medications, illicit drugs and alcohol) should be included in the definition

Coverage of a range of substances and disorders is needed within a course curriculum to demonstrate the multiple clinical (physical and psychological) difficulties experienced by a population with both serious mental disorders and alcohol and drug problems. This is a mixed group of clients with complex needs, on a continuum of severity for many diverse problems, including substance use (tobacco, alcohol, opioids, hallucinogens, sedative-hypnotic drugs, cannabis, stimulants and volatile solvents), misuse of over-the-counter medications, mental health problems, non-compliance with prescribed medication and social needs.

Understand that the high prevalence of co-existing problems has implications for service delivery

When providing any training in this area it is necessary to draw students' attention to the fact that the majority of studies are USA-based. In a review undertaken in 2001, only 10 per cent were based in the UK (Crawford and Crome 2001). Recent prevalence studies are described in Chapter 1. Frisher *et al.* (2004) have shown that the active early recognition of co-existing mental health and drug and alcohol problems may lead to better outcomes. Clients with co-existing mental health and drug and alcohol problems who had contact with secondary care psychiatric services had fewer accident and emergency department visits (Frisher *et al.* 2004). This at least suggests the potential of active engagement to reduce the need for crisis care.

Training courses should address the importance of primary care services in treating individuals with co-existing mental health and drug and alcohol problems. In a recent study using the General Practice Research Database (GPRD; Frischer *et al.* 2004), the annual period prevalence of co-existing conditions increased in England and Wales by 62 per cent (24,226 to 39,296) over the study period 1993–1998. The rates of drug and alcohol problems co-existing with psychoses overall, schizophrenia and paranoia increased by 147 per cent, 128 per cent and 144 per cent respectively. In 1998, 11 potentially chronic cases of co-existing mental health and drug and alcohol problems were likely to be encountered in a typical general practice during the year. If the rates for the period 1993–1998 are extrapolated, it is estimated that this number would have doubled by 2004. This has major implications for general practitioners' workload, as primary care resources in mental health are already thinly spread and general practitioners are not trained to deal effectively with co-existing issues (Frisher *et al.* 2004).

Be aware of, administer, and access where necessary, the range of effective psychosocial and pharmacological interventions

There is emerging evidence for the value of behavioural treatments in the management of individuals with co-existing mood and substance use disorders. There is a need for training courses to develop the skills of health care professionals in these techniques (Carroll 2004).

The British Association for Psychopharmacology has published evidence-based guidelines for the pharmacological management of substance misuse, addiction and comorbidity. This is a 'must-read' for all those interested in the strength of the developing evidence base in this complex area (Lingford-Hughes *et al.* 2004).

Be aware of the roles and responsibilities of key service providers

In any training programme on this topic it is important to outline for students the nature and extent of problems, putting together the best available evidence nationally, and locally if possible. Each health service area will have, or should have, some relevant data on which to draw. A rough, 'ball-park' figure is that 30–50 per cent of people with drug or alcohol problems have some kind of mental health problem, and 30–50 per cent of mental health clients have a problem with drugs or alcohol. In general, the variation depends on the setting in which the study was undertaken (Weaver *et al.* 2003). As described earlier, the findings of Frisher *et al.* (2004) point to the need to re-evaluate the workload and training needs of staff, and the extent and range of service provision for people with co-existing problems in primary care. For example, the Scottish Executive Plan to tackle co-existing problems was formulated around care pathways and tiered service provision (Scottish Executive 2003).

Recognize that people with co-existing mental health and drug and alcohol problems are a highly vulnerable group, who often fail to receive appropriate care

Training courses often concentrate on working-age adults or young people. It is important for trainers to demonstrate that the needs of older people often do not feature at all in service planning for co-existing problems, although they constitute about 15 per cent of the population of any developed country, and have a high prevalence of mental health and physical problems. This is quite apart from the combination of alcohol and medications (both prescribed and over-the-counter) which they may be taking (compliantly or non-compliantly) and which may interact with each other.

Descriptions of client populations attending treatment programmes can be used in training courses to discuss issues of vulnerability. Individuals attending a clinic in New York were characterized as having common psychosocial factors such as homelessness, fragmented family structure, poor social supports, concurrent medical problems, poor nutrition and poor hygiene (Kastan 1993).

The core content of a training programme incorporating the recommendations made in the reviews above is outlined in Table 18.3.

EVALUATION OF TRAINING

Although so far in this chapter we have drawn attention to the lack of training in this area, some training *has* been delivered, and looking at evaluations of it demonstrates how to make improvements. Evaluation of the effectiveness of training can be focused on a series of outcomes, including change in the behaviour of health professionals in areas such as general patient management, prescribing practices, treatment of specific conditions, diagnostic and assessment accuracy and general measures of clinical effectiveness.

In a systematic review of 102 studies of the effectiveness of different types of intervention in improving health professionals' performance and health outcomes, no single intervention method was identified as improving the quality of health care. A wide range of interventions was shown to be effective if used appropriately, leading to important improvements in professional practice and client outcomes (Oxman *et al.* 1995). Three general areas can be identified for the evaluation of training in the treatment of clients with co-existing mental health and drug and alcohol problems: client assessment, client outcomes and clinician effectiveness.

Client assessment

Diagnostic accuracy and adequacy of assessment in this field have been shown to be a significant variable in previous research (Todd *et al.* 2004). Evaluations of the effect of training courses on assessment techniques and diagnostic accuracy have shown that the use of trained volunteers, otherwise known as 'standardized clients', as part of evaluation of training outcomes enables assessment of trainees' assessment competence (Murphy *et al.* 1995). The use of Objective Structured Clinical Examinations (OSCEs) using standardized clients has been shown to be an effective evaluation method. Measurement of the effect of training on knowledge and skills in the

Table 18.3 The core content of a training programme incorporating the recommendations made in various reviews

- Conceptual and theoretical issues: classificatory systems for drug and alcohol problems and for psychiatric disorders
- Effects of, intoxication with, withdrawal from and complications of substance use
- Psychiatric conditions
- Potential relationships between substance use, harmful use and dependence and psychological problems and psychiatric disorders
- Epidemiology of international, national and local comorbidity, including methodological problems
- Lifespan aspects: neonatal, children, adolescents and older people
- Screening and assessment protocols
- The effectiveness and cost-effectiveness of pharmacological and psychosocial interventions at the specialist, generalist or primary care level
- Psychological and pharmacological interventions for alcohol and drug problems
- Psychological and pharmacological interventions for psychiatric disorders
- Organizational issues: service delivery models, governance and evaluation
- Legislative framework including (in the UK) Misuse of Drugs Legislation, the Misuse of Drugs Act, the Mental Health Act and similar legislation in other countries
- Ethical issues
- Critical analysis of the evidence for what works and gaps in understanding
- Training needs: information sources and materials
- National policies for mental health and for addiction as well as for their co-existence, with development and implementation strategy

assessment of alcohol and other drug disorders in adolescent clients by paediatric residents was studied using OSCEs before and after training. Evaluation of videotapes of OSCEs showed significant improvements in the use of specific screening techniques and interviewing skills in residents who had completed training when compared with a control group (Kokotailo *et al.* 1995).

Client outcomes

There have been no studies directly evaluating the effects of training on client-related outcomes, although indirect evidence may be obtained from considering evaluations of integrated treatment programmes (Drake *et al.* 1997; Mueser *et al.* 1997). Evaluation of the effectiveness of training in terms of client outcomes may be centred on topics such as housing, days hospitalized and degree of progress towards recovery. Further longer-term research with larger numbers of clients is required in order to produce valid and reliable indicators of client outcomes related to staff training.

Clinician effectiveness

There are no simple systems for ensuring that training produces an improvement in clinical effectiveness, but the wide range of interventions available can lead to important improvements in professional practice and client outcomes (Oxman *et al.* 1995). Much of the relevant research on evaluation of clinician effectiveness following training has been in the area of drug and alcohol problems rather than in the area of comorbidity and has been hampered by short-term evaluations, which often lack a robust methodology.

Motivational interviewing

Baer and colleagues (2004) studied the impact of workshop training in motivational interviewing on clinicians working in an addiction environment, or in an allied field where drug and alcohol problems are common. They explored concerns from earlier research that clinician improvement following motivational interviewing training was not maintained. This study found that some skills were shown to improve and some clinicians showed continued improvement at follow-up. The study highlighted the need for additional research on the use of standardized clients and alternative techniques to assess the outcomes of training.

Distance learning

The use of televised distance learning techniques to train staff from a substance misuse facility in the application of motivational interviewing techniques was reported to result in significant knowledge gains but little enhancement of skills (Shafer *et al.* 2004).

Lecture format

The effectiveness of a simple lecture format for delivery of an educational session on drug and alcohol problems were assessed by a questionnaire administered to motivated health care professionals and to a control group. The workshop participants showed significant knowledge gain and belief changes, whereas the two control groups showed no change in knowledge or beliefs. After six months knowledge gains decreased, but were still higher than pre-test scores (Erickson *et al.* 2003).

Curricular changes

Simple educational techniques such as introducing curricular changes can be shown to have positive effects on the attitudes of medical students towards addiction clients (Matthews et al. 2002). The replacement of one week of a six-week psychiatry clerkship with an attachment to a drug and alcohol problem treatment site increased regard for clients with alcoholism without adversely affecting measures of attitudes toward, and knowledge about, psychiatric clients (Christison and Haviland 2003).

Training of social workers in the management of addiction has been shown to have a positive effect on the perception of confidence in treating clients with substance misuse problems. Those social workers who completed an intensive training scheme were shown to take on an increased caseload of clients with alcohol and drug problems, compared with social workers who had not undergone training (Amodeo and Fassler 2000).

The evidence from these evaluations is that improvements in knowledge, skills and attitude gained from training are lost if there is not adequate support, supervision and opportunity to put the training into practice. An essential step towards maximizing the gains of a training course is to ensure that the training is seen as one element of a longer-term support and supervision system for practitioners (Department of Health 2002).

CONCLUSION

The UK experience: how to get it going

Although awareness of co-existing mental health and drug and alcohol problems dates back many years, it was not until 1996 that the UK Department of Health established a working party to look at ways in which substance misuse and mental health issues might be addressed. This was based on a growing acceptance of the high prevalence of drug and alcohol problems and their impact on the health and well-being of the community and, more recently, the growing concern around public/community safety.

In 2001 funding was made available for a number of initiatives: the development of a training manual (Banerjee et al. 2002), a comprehensive literature review (Crawford and Crome 2001) and a training needs analysis (Mears et al. 2001). The literature review drew upon 1,100 abstracts dating from 1991 onwards: 200 were summarized, analyzed and synthesized into topic areas – epidemiology; assessment and screening tests; professional education; substance-specific research; specific co-existing psychiatric conditions; childhood, women, violence and suicide; and treatment. The literature review (Crawford and Crome 2001) and training manual (Banerjee et al. 2002) were published and both were circulated nationally to a wide range of clinicians and statutory and voluntary services.

Thus, over the last eight years the Department of Health, working strategically with the Royal Colleges of Psychiatrists and General Practitioners, the College Research Unit of the Royal College of Psychiatrists and the NTA for Substance Misuse, and taking into account the National Service Frameworks for Adult Mental Illness, has developed the Department of Health good practice guidelines. Part of the plan was to fund relevant research: the Drug Misuse Research Initiative, funded by the policy arm of the Department of Health (Frisher *et al.* 2004; Macleod *et al.* 2004a, 2004b; Weaver *et al.* 2003). The Department of Health has been working with the NTA to produce a range of teaching materials, setting standards and implementing policy.

Training should not be an isolated optional extra. It is integrally related to clinical excellence, determination of key research questions and the appropriate implementation of models of service delivery in order to meet new needs presented by changing situations.

Training is therefore necessary for all levels of staff, in all the disciplines and professions that provide support to people and their families, often at very distressing times. There are still questions regarding whether interdisciplinary training is best, and it is probably true that, as in the clinical situation, one option may be preferable at one time, whereas another is appropriate at another time. The question is: What works best for whom, when? We are only at the very beginning of being able to answer that question. This book is a valuable contribution.

KEY RESOURCES

Anderson, T., McNelis, D. and Riggs, P., *Co-occurring Substance Use and Mental Health Disorders in Adolescents: Integrating Approaches for Assessment and Treatment of the Individual Young Person*. Philadelphia: Drexel University College of Medicine, 2004. Available at http://www.ireta.org/store/customer/home.php accessed 29 June 2005).

Banerjee, S., Clancy, C. and Crome, I., *Co-existing Problems of Mental Disorder and Substance Misuse (Dual Diagnosis)*. London: Royal College of Psychiatrists Research Unit, 2002.

Centre for Mental Health Services (CMHS), *Evidence-Based Practices: Shaping Mental Health Services Toward Recovery. Co-Occurring Disorders: Integrated Dual Disorders Treatment*. Rockville: The Substance Abuse and Mental Health Services Administration (SAMHSA), 2003. Available at http://www.mentalhealth.org/cmhs/communitysupport/toolkits/cooccurring/default.asp

Co-occurring Collaborative of Southern Maine, *Co-occurring Collaborative of Southern Maine: Bridging Mental Health and Substance Abuse Services*. Maine, 2004. Available at http://www.ccsme.org/index.htm (accessed 28 June 2005).

Hughes, L., *Pan London Dual Diagnosis Dissemination Project DD3T Trainers' Manual*. London: Development Centre for Mental Health, 2002. Available at http://www.londondevelopmentcentre.org/index.php?topic=77 (accessed 4 July 2005).

Mid-America Addiction Technology Transfer Center, *A Collaborative Response: Addressing the Needs of Consumers with Co-occurring Substance Use and Mental Disorders – Participant Guide. Training Curricula and Training on Co-occurring Disorders.* Maine: Co-occurring Collaborative of Southern Maine, 2004. Available at http://www.mattc.org (accessed 28 June 2005).

Minkoff, K. and Cline, C., *Co-Occurring Disorders Educational Competency Assessment Tool (CODECAT).* Albuquerque: ZiaLogic, 2001. Available at http://www.zialogic.org/toolkits.htm (accessed 29 June 2005).

National Treatment Agency, *Competency-based Training Modules.* (Undated.) Available at http://www.nta.nhs.uk/programme/competency.htm (accessed 29 June 2005).

Northeastern States ATTC of New York State, *An Eco-systemic Addiction and Mental Health Treatment Model: A Training Module.* New York: Northeastern States ATTC, 1999. Available at http://www.ireta.org/store/customer/home.php?cat=1 (accessed 29 June 2005).

Northeastern States ATTC of New York State, *Training for Professionals Working with MICA Offenders: Cross Training for Staff in Law Enforcement, Mental Health, and Substance Abuse Settings.* New York: Northeastern States ATTC, 1998. Available at http://www.ireta.org/store/customer/home.php?cat=1 (accessed 29 June 2005).

Northeastern States ATTC of New York State, *Train-the-Trainer on Mentally Ill Substance Abusers Consortium Curriculum.* New York: Northeastern States ATTC, 2001. Available at http://www.ireta.org/store/customer/home.php?cat=1 (accessed 29 June 2005).

Pepper, B. and Hendrickson, E. L., *Developing a Cross Training Project for Substance Abuse, Mental Health and Criminal Justice Professionals Working with Offenders with Co-Existing Disorders (Substance Abuse/Mental Illness).* 1998. Available at http://www.toad.net/~arcturus/dd/ddhome.htm (accessed 28 June 2005).

Tennessee Department of Health Bureau of Alcohol and Drug Abuse Services, *Co-occurring Disorders Training Guide, Participant Manual.* Tennessee: Tennessee Department of Health, 2000. Available at http://www2.state.tn.us/health/a&d/trainmanual.pdf

Video training resource

MIND, *Pillar to Post*, London: Mind Publications. Available at http://mindin croyden.org.uk or tel +44 (0) 20 8221 9666.

REFERENCES

American Psychiatric Association, *The Need for Improved Training for Treatment of Patients with Combined Substance Use and other Psychiatric Disorders.* Washington: APA, 1993. Available at http://www.psych.org/edu/other_res/lib_archives/archives/199306.pdf (accessed 13 September 2005).

American Psychiatric Association, 'Position statement on training needs in addiction psychiatry', *American Journal of Psychiatry, 153*, 852–3, 1996.

Amodeo, M. and Fassler, I., 'Social workers and substance-abusing clients: Caseload composition and competency self-ratings', *American Journal of Drug and Alcohol Abuse*, *26*, 629–41, 2000.

Baer, J. S., Rosengren, D. B., Dunn, C. W., Wells, E. A., Ogle, R. L. and Hartzler, B., 'An evaluation of workshop training in motivational interviewing for addiction and mental health clinicians', *Drug and Alcohol Dependence*, *73*, 99–106, 2004.

Banerjee, S., Clancy, C. and Crome, I., *Co-existing Problems of Mental Disorder and Substance Misuse (Dual Diagnosis)*. London: Royal College of Psychiatrists Research Unit, 2002.

Barnaby, B., Drummond, C., McCloud, A., Burns, T. and Omu, N., 'Substance misuse in psychiatric inpatients: Comparison of a screening questionnaire survey with case notes', *British Medical Journal*, *327*, 783–4, 2003.

Brems, C., Johnson, M. E., Bowers, L., Lauver, B. and Mongeau, V. A., 'Comorbidity training needs at a state psychiatric hospital', *Administration and Policy in Mental Health*, *30*, 109–20, 2002.

Carroll, K. M., 'Behavioral therapies for co-occurring substance use and mood disorders', *Biological Psychiatry*, *56*, 778–84, 2004.

Christison, G. W. and Haviland, M. G., 'Requiring a one-week addiction treatment experience in a six-week psychiatry clerkship: Effects on attitudes toward substance-abusing patients', *Teaching and Learning in Medicine*, *15*, 93–7, 2003.

Crawford, V. and Crome, I., *Co-existing Problems of Mental Health and Substance Misuse (Dual Diagnosis): A Review of Relevant Literature*. London: Royal College of Psychiatry Research Unit, 2001.

Crisp, A. H., Gelder, M. G. and Rix, S., 'Stigmatisation of people with mental illnesses', *British Journal of Psychiatry*, *177*, 4–7, 2000.

Crome, I. B. and Day, E., 'Substance misuse and dependence: Older people deserve better services', *Reviews in Clinical Gerontology*, *9*, 327–42, 1999.

Crome, I. B. and Shaikh, N., 'Undergraduate medical education in substance misuse in Britain III: Can medical students drive change?' *Drugs: Education, Prevention and Policy*, *11*, 483–503, 2004.

Department of Health, *Mental Health Policy Implementation Guide: Dual Diagnosis Good Practice Guide*. London: Department of Health, 2002.

Drake, R. E., Essock, S. M., Shaner, A., Carey, K. B., Minkoff, K., Kola, L. *et al.*, 'Implementing dual diagnosis services for clients with severe mental illness', *Psychiatric Services*, *52*, 469–76, 2001.

Drake, R. E., Morse, G., Brunette, M. F. and Torrey, W. C., 'Evolving U.S. service model for patients with severe mental illness and co-occurring substance use disorder', *Acta Neuropsychiatrica*, *16*, 36–40, 2004.

Drake, R. E., Yovetich, N. A., Bebout, R. R., Harris, M. and McHugo, G. J., 'Integrated treatment for dually diagnosed homeless adults', *Journal of Nervous and Mental Diseases*, *185*, 298–305, 1997.

Erickson, C. K., Wilcox, R. E., Miller, G. W., Littlefield, J. H. and Lawson, K. A., 'Effectiveness of addiction science presentations to treatment professionals, using a modified Solomon study design', *Journal of Drug Education*, *33*, 197–216, 2003.

Farrell, M. P. and David, A. S., 'Do psychiatric registrars take a proper drinking history?' *British Medical Journal (Clinical Research Edition)*, *296*, 395–6, 1988.

Frisher, M., Collins, J., Millson, D., Crome, I. and Croft, P., 'Prevalence of comorbid psychiatric illness and substance abuse in primary care in England and Wales between 1993–1998', *Journal of Epidemiology and Community Health*, *58*, 1034–41, 2004.

General Medical Council, *Tomorrow's Doctors: Recommendations on Undergraduate Medical Education*. London: General Medical Council, 2002.

Glass, I. B., 'Undergraduate training in substance abuse in the UK', *British Journal of Addiction*, *84*, 197–202, 1987.

Gournay, K., Sandford, T., Johnson, S. and Thornicroft, G., 'Dual diagnosis of severe mental health problems and substance abuse/dependence: A major priority for mental health nursing', *Journal of Psychiatric Mental Health Nursing*, *4*, 89–95, 1997.

Graham, H., Copello, A., Birchwood, M., Orford, J., McGovern, D., Georgiou, G. and Godfrey, E., 'Coexisting severe mental health and substance use problems: Developing integrated services in the UK', *Psychiatric Bulletin*, *27*, 183–6, 2003.

Happell, B., Carta, B. and Pinikahana, J., 'Nurses' knowledge, attitudes and beliefs regarding substance use: A questionnaire survey', *Nursing and Health Science*, *4*, 193–200, 2002.

Heather, N., 'The public health and brief interventions for excessive alcohol consumption: The British experience', *Addictive Behaviour*, *21*, 857–68, 1996.

Kastan, J., 'Program development – organizing clinical innovations', in Solomon, J., Zimberg, S. and Shollar, E., eds, *Dual Diagnosis: Evaluation, Treatment, Training and Program Development*, pp. 253–70. New York: Plenum Medical Book Company, 1993.

Kokotailo, P. K., Langhough, R., Neary, E. J., Matson, S. C. and Fleming, M. F., 'Improving pediatric residents' alcohol and other drug use clinical skills: Use of an experiential curriculum', *Pediatrics*, *96*, 99–104, 1995.

Lingford-Hughes, A., Welch, S. and Nutt, D., 'Evidence-based guidelines for the pharmacological management of substance misuse, addiction and comorbidity: Recommendations from the British Association for Psychopharmacology', *Journal of Psychopharmacology*, *18*, 293–335, 2004.

Macleod, J., Oakes, R., Copello, A., Crome, I., Egger, M., Hickman, M. *et al.*, 'Psychological and social sequelae of cannabis and other illicit drug use by young people: A systematic review of longitudinal, general population studies', *The Lancet*, *363*, 1579–88, 2004a.

Macleod, J., Oakes, R., Oppenkowski, T., Stokes-Lampard, H., Copello, A., Crome, I. *et al.*, 'How strong is the evidence that illicit drug use by young people is an important cause of psychological and social harm? Methodological and policy implications of a systematic review of longitudinal, general population studies', *Drug Education, Prevention and Policy*, *11*, 281–97, 2004b.

Matthews, J., Kadish, W., Barrett, S. V., Mazor, K., Field, D. and Jonassen, J., 'The impact of a brief interclerkship about substance abuse on medical students' skills', *Academic Medicine*, *77*, 419–26, 2002.

McNamara, K., 'Treatment of patients with dual diagnosis', *Australian and New Zealand Journal of Psychiatry*, *37*, 240, 2003.

Mears, A., Clancy, C., Banerjee, S., Crome, I. and Agbo-Quaye, S., *Co-existing Problems of Mental Disorder and Substance Misuse (Dual Diagnosis): A Training Needs Analysis*. London: Royal College of Psychiatrists, 2001.

Morris, J. A. and Stuart, G. W., 'Training and education needs of consumers, families, and front-line staff in behavioral health practice', *Administration and Policy in Mental Health*, 29, 377–402, 2002.

Mueser, K., Drake, R. and Miles, K., 'Treatment of drug dependent individuals with comorbid mental disorders', *NIDA Research Monograph*, 172, 86–109, 1997.

Murphy, S. A., Scott, C. S. and Mandel, L. S., 'Evaluating students' substance abuse assessment skills', *Journal of Substance Abuse*, 7, 357–64, 1995.

National Treatment Agency, *Models of Care for the Treatment of Drug Misusers*. London: National Treatment Agency, 2002.

O'Brien, C. P., Charney, D. S., Lewis, L., Cornish, J. W., Post, R. M., Woody, G. E. et al., 'Priority actions to improve the care of persons with co-occurring substance abuse and other mental disorders: A call to action', *Biological Psychiatry*, 56, 703–13, 2004.

O'Neil, M., 'Dual diagnosis training – an integrated curriculum – design and implementation', in Solomon, J., Zimberg, S. and Shollar, E., eds, *Dual Diagnosis: Evaluation, Treatment, Training and Program Development*, pp. 271–85. New York: Plenum Medical Book Company, 1993.

Oxman, A. D., Thomson, M. A., Davis, D. A. and Haynes, R. B., 'No magic bullets: A systematic review of 102 trials of interventions to improve professional practice', *Canadian Medical Association Journal*, 153, 1423–31, 1995.

Power, K. and Demartino, R., 'Co-occurring disorders and achieving recovery: The substance abuse and mental health services administration perspective', *Biological Psychiatry*, 56, 721–2, 2004.

Pulice, R. T., Lyman, S. R. and McCormick, L. L., 'A study of provider perceptions of individuals with dual disorders', *Journal of Mental Health Administration*, 21, 92–9, 1994.

Renner, J. A., Jr., 'How to train residents to identify and treat dual diagnosis patients', *Biological Psychiatry*, 56, 810–6, 2004.

Royal College of Psychiatrists and Royal College of General Practitioners, *Roles and Responsibilities of Doctors in the Provision of Treatment for Substance Misusers*. London: Royal College of Psychiatrists/Royal College of General Practitioners, 2005. Available at http://www.rcpsych.ac.uk/publications/cr/cr131.htm (accessed 13 September 2005).

Scottish Executive, *Mind the Gap: Meeting the Needs of People with Co-occurring Substance Misuse and Mental Health Problems*. Edinburgh: Scottish Executive, 2003. Available at http://www.scotland.gov.uk/resource/doc/47063/0013752.pdf (accessed 13 September 2005).

Secker, J. and Hill, K., 'Mental health training and development needs of community agency staff', *Health and Social Care in the Community*, 10, 323–30, 2002.

Shafer, M. S., Rhode, R. and Chong, J., 'Using distance education to promote the transfer of motivational interviewing skills among behavioral health professionals', *Journal of Substance Abuse Treatment*, 26, 141–8, 2004.

The Lancet, 'Editorial: Reducing the stigma of mental illness', *The Lancet*, 357, 1055, 2001.

Todd, J., Green, G., Harrison, M., Ikuesan, B. A., Self, C., Baldacchino, A. and Sherwood, S., 'Defining dual diagnosis of mental illness and substance misuse: Some methodological issues', *Journal of Psychiatric Mental Health Nursing*, 11, 48–54, 2004.

Weaver, T., Madden, P., Charles, V., Stimson, G., Renton, A., Tyrer, P. *et al.*, 'Comorbidity of substance misuse and mental illness in community mental health and substance misuse services', *British Journal of Psychiatry*, *183*, 304–13, 2003.

Chapter 19

Clinical team supervision for practitioners treating co-existing mental health and drug and alcohol problems

Alex Copello and Derek Tobin

KEY POINTS

1   Skill acquisition in delivering psychosocial treatments requires more than one-off training: it also requires ongoing clinical supervision.
2   Team supervision is necessary when attempting to integrate substance misuse intervention within assertive outreach mental health teams.
3   A model of supervision utilized within the COMPASS programme is described and case examples are provided which demonstrate its utility.

INTRODUCTION

Working with clients who experience combined and often complex problems with mental health and drug and alcohol misuse poses a number of significant challenges, as has been amply illustrated in the preceding chapters. How to develop an effective response to these problems and maintain this response over time is a challenge for those delivering psychosocial treatment (albeit not a challenge restricted to this area of work). We know from the research evidence that training by itself is not enough to develop and maintain good and effective practice (e.g. Beck 1986; Miller and Mount 2001; Milne *et al.* 2000). Evidence from the experience of the United Kingdom Alcohol Treatment Trial (UKATT Research Team 2005), for example, showed that supervision after initial training was critical in the acquisition and maintenance of competence in delivering psychosocial interventions (Tober *et al.* 2005). Within this trial, supervision not only ensured that therapists adhered to the treatment protocols, it also underpinned their understanding of the treatment and its purpose. As we aim to illustrate in this chapter, ongoing clinical supervision plays a central role in the competent delivery of interventions for people with co-existing mental health and substance misuse problems.

There is a lack of consensus in the literature as to what constitutes clinical supervision. A useful definition has been articulated by Kavanagh and colleagues (Kavanagh *et al.* 2002; Spence *et al.* 2001), who propose that supervision involves a working alliance between practitioners, aiming to enhance clinical practice, meet the goals of the employing organization and ensure compliance with ethical and professional standards, while providing personal support in relation to professional practice. A related important aspect of supervision is to ensure that clients are safe and protected from poor or indeed harmful practice. Several authors have written extensively about models of supervision (e.g. Dryden and Thorne 2004; Hawkins and Shohet 2000). Most of the models discussed are based on individual supervision. In this chapter we focus on our experience of delivering cognitive behavioural integrated treatment (C-BIT; Graham *et al.* 2004; see also Chapter 7 in this volume on the consultation-liaison service model) in services for people with severe mental health problems who also misuse substances, and we describe the supervision model that we use, based on a team supervision approach in assertive outreach teams. We conclude with two case examples that illustrate the work to be done during team supervision sessions. The Combined Psychosis and Substance Misuse (COMPASS) programme has two main arms: intensive input to and training in assertive outreach teams, and the development of a consultation-liaison service (see Chapter 7). This chapter is based on the former – that is, the supervision that followed training of mental health staff within assertive outreach teams.

Clearly, any supervision needs to build on a platform of good training. In our work with those experiencing co-existing mental health and drug and alcohol problems, we started with a training programme implemented across a range of assertive outreach teams. Ongoing *in situ* training/modelling, co-working and supervision are an in-built part of the training package. Once teams are trained, they are allocated a member of our specialist COMPASS team (Graham *et al.* 2003) who works alongside team members two days per week on a long-term basis. The role of this clinician with specialist skills is to facilitate further implementation of the new integrated treatment approach into the team's routine working practice. This person serves as a 'product champion', who models the approach within the team setting, develops integrated treatment/care plans and co-works with clients alongside the team and keyworkers. In addition, his/her role is to provide specialist team supervision sessions approximately every six weeks. The aim of these sessions is to facilitate the process whereby the team develops expertise using the new treatment approach, thinking through a particular client's current problems in light of his/her case formulation and then refining treatment plans.

We start with a brief outline of the C-BIT approach to provide the necessary context for our more detailed discussion about supervision. For a more detailed description of the C-BIT approach, the reader is referred to Graham *et al.* (2004).

COGNITIVE BEHAVIOURAL INTEGRATED TREATMENT (C-BIT)

The overall objective of C-BIT is to help clients who experience severe mental health problems to negotiate and maintain behaviour change related to the use of alcohol and/or drugs. Clinicians are encouraged to use a number of strategies in order to develop alternatives to alcohol and drug misuse, and to recognize the relationship between substance use and mental health difficulties.

C-BIT is based on a harm reduction approach (Heather *et al.* 1993; Marlatt 1998). Any positive change is encouraged, including a reduction in the amount or types of substances used, a change in the way the substance is used or even abstinence. Abstinence is not seen as the only possible goal. The overall aim of C-BIT is to help clients achieve their self-identified goals within their spiritual and cultural frame of reference, through:

* working collaboratively to identify, challenge and undermine unrealistic beliefs about drugs or alcohol that maintain problematic use and replace them with more adaptive beliefs that will lead to and strengthen behavioural change;
* facilitating an understanding of the relationship between substance use and mental health problems; and
* teaching specific skills for controlling and self-managing substance use and the early warning signs of psychosis, and developing social support for alternative lifestyles.

The C-BIT approach is structured but flexible. It consists of an assessment phase (screening and assessment) and four treatment phases (engagement and building motivation to change, negotiating some behaviour change, early relapse prevention and relapse management). There are two additional treatment components (skills building and working with families and social network members) that are designed to be used in parallel with the four treatment phases where appropriate.

Those delivering the C-BIT intervention therefore need to be able to make detailed assessments of the particular client they are working with. The assessment guides the particular focus of the intervention and the specific strategies to be used at a particular point with each client.

In our services, we have developed and used the C-BIT approach in order to train a range of professionals working within assertive outreach teams. Those trained attend a workshop over six half days, followed by joint working and team supervision. Trainees attending the workshop are provided with a C-BIT treatment manual prior to the training event. Training involves both didactic presentations and skills development and practice. Within our work in Birmingham (UK), the overriding aim has been to create mental health teams capable of addressing substance use problems, while maintaining awareness of the unique needs of those with severe mental health problems.

This has involved a significant shift in the treatment philosophy of those mental health teams, to allow them to embrace the concept of integrated treatment. As we have argued elsewhere (Copello *et al.* 2001), teams working with people with combined severe mental health and substance misuse problems need to be seen as a unit for the purposes of training and evaluation, and therefore all clinicians on the team need to be trained and take part in on-going team supervision. Training each mental health team together as a unit has, in our experience, been central to facilitating a change in the teams' approach. This training method provides the clinicians within each team with an opportunity to be exposed at the same time to the issues and to work through, as a team, any difficulties anticipated in implementing the treatment approach.

We found that, following training, teams have benefited from receiving team supervision. The aim of supervision sessions has been to facilitate a process whereby the team can use the treatment approach to think through a particular client's current problems or review his/her overall case. The end result is typically a reformulation of the client's difficulties and a more focused treatment plan that addresses alcohol and drug use and the mental health problems, as well as the interactions between the two. In addition to the benefits already mentioned, team supervision also provides a cost-effective method compared to individualized supervision sessions.

SUPERVISION BASED ON C-BIT APPROACH

> The overriding goal of supervision is to assist those supervised to think and communicate as effective helpers and, in so doing to become their own internal supervisors.
>
> (Nelson-Jones 2003: 181)

The above principle can also be applied to team supervision. Team supervision has the added advantage of providing a forum for clinicians from different professional backgrounds to discuss cases at length and to share skills and knowledge. Team supervision needs to address three levels of need (Hawkins and Shohet 2000), including the task in hand, the individuals within the group and group maintenance activities (e.g. issues of inclusion/exclusion, authority, competitiveness etc.).

As we stated above, the overall aim of the C-BIT approach is to enhance the confidence and skills of all team members in the delivery of interventions for clients with co-existing mental health and drug and alcohol problems based on a philosophy of integrated treatment. To achieve effective team supervision it is essential that all team members are involved. Assertive outreach

teams provide intensive community support to people with severe and enduring mental health problems. The C-BIT approach is designed specifically to
address the needs of this client group. The following sections outline setting
up and implementing team supervision within these teams.

Getting team involvement

Early on in the development of our services, we conducted both a prevalence
study (Graham *et al.* 2001) and a staff training and support needs survey
(Maslin *et al.* 2001) with staff working in mental health and substance misuse
services in north Birmingham. Results indicated a prevalence of problematic
substance use of over 50 per cent among clients in a proportion of teams
within mental health services. Staff within these teams felt that it was within
their remit to work with clients with co-existing problems. However, they felt
that they did not have the skills, knowledge, training and supervision to work
effectively with the client group. As a result of these findings, and based on
the available treatment evidence, the C-BIT model was developed in order to
address the areas of need identified by staff working within teams. We are
currently completing a study (Graham *et al.* 2006) that sought to evaluate
the training and implementation of the C-BIT approach within assertive
outreach teams.

Teams were provided with training and supervision to deliver C-BIT using
a quasi-experimental time lag design. The aim of the supervision sessions
was to encourage staff to think through specific clients based on their case
formulation and refine treatment plans based on the C-BIT approach. Staff
members were encouraged to discuss individual cases and agree treatment
plans as a team during regular supervision sessions. Given that the teams
identified this area of work as important, yet mostly felt that team members
were lacking in the necessary skills to deliver appropriate intervention, there
was positive acceptance of the C-BIT approach, which offered evidence-
based interventions that could be integrated into clinical practice. As
described, team supervision was implemented within the teams and facilitated by a COMPASS programme clinician. Finally, organizational support –
crucial for development, commitment and ability to practise (Cartwright
1980) – was achieved through the involvement of key managers both within
the organization as a whole and the individual teams.

Team approach and involvement

Assertive outreach teams adopt a team approach to working with clients.
Frequently, different members of the team will visit the same client. Therefore,
team supervision has an important role in ensuring that all team members are
aware of individual treatment plans and thus all team members can agree to
work to agreed plans with individual clients. Ensuring that all members of

each team were trained meant that clients in the study could receive a consistent approach from all staff. Moreover, issues regarding mental health and problematic substance use could be pre-planned and strategies to address these could be implemented at each visit. The experience of the supervisors was that the effectiveness of team supervision is enhanced if all team members are involved and all feel supported to contribute to the session. Although staff showed improvement in confidence and skills immediately after training (Graham 2004), ongoing team supervision facilitated the development of staff skills in the delivery of C-BIT and encouraged independent use of the manual and maintenance of C-BIT practice.

The following section will focus on the implementation of team supervision within assertive outreach teams trained to use C-BIT. First, the roles of clinician and supervisor will be described and the structure of sessions outlined. Detailed guidance on how to facilitate supervision sessions and strategies to deal with conflict is provided. Finally, the importance of evaluating the effectiveness of team supervision sessions is discussed.

The role of individual clinicians delivering the intervention

The role of individual clinicians is to use the C-BIT approach with clients with co-existing mental health and drug and alcohol problems. In order to achieve this, clinicians need to plan sessions with each client and identify the most appropriate interventions to use based on the client's stage of change (Prochaska *et al.* 1992). Clinicians are therefore expected to carry out a comprehensive assessment with clients and to develop a formulation to guide treatment planning and implementation (outlined in Chapter 7). Through this process clinicians can identify issues that they would like to bring to team supervision for discussion within the team, and the plan can be agreed as a team. This supports both individual clinicians and the team as a whole as they focus their interventions based on the needs of individual clients.

The role of the supervisor

Supervisors are members of the COMPASS team fulfilling the following criteria: a professional qualification (e.g. nursing, psychology, occupational therapy), at least two years of experience in either mental health or substance misuse work or preferably in both, having received training in C-BIT (Graham *et al.* 2004) and practised under supervision, and having access to regular team meetings with other supervisors through the COMPASS team regular meetings. The role of the supervisor is to arrange supervision sessions with the team and to ensure that they are held on a regular basis. It is important that the supervision sessions are built into the work of the team and are seen as an essential part of clinical practice. The supervisor should pre-plan with the team the content of the supervision session, described later in the chapter.

During the supervision session the supervisor needs to facilitate the discussion and encourage all team members to participate. The supervisor should aim to keep the discussion focused and encourage the team to work towards an agreed plan and to agree on who will implement areas identified. Within this process, the supervisor should also agree some ground rules with the team including:

* all available team members will attend supervision;
* everyone should feel able to express their opinion and be respected; and
* differences of opinion should be acknowledged and worked through to enhance the overall outcome of the supervision session.

Supervision sessions

Structure

In order to keep sessions focused, it is important to facilitate sessions within an agreed structure. The structure used in C-BIT supervision sessions is based on a treatment planning template (Table 19.1). This assists the team in identifying some of the key components that need to be addressed when working towards an agreed plan. It also helps the team identify interventions most appropriate to the client's needs, based on current presentation.

Within the supervision sessions, team members should be encouraged by the supervisor to discuss any difficulties they may experience implementing C-BIT within their clinical practice. This encourages the team to work through difficulties together and to support each other in this area of work.

Facilitating team supervision sessions

When facilitating the session, the supervisor needs to be clear about the rationale for team supervision and understand its aims and objectives. The

Table 19.1 Treatment planning template used in C-BIT supervision sessions

1 Identify the client's stage of change: e.g. is the client in the precontemplation, contemplation or action phase of change (Prochaska *et al.* 1992)?
2 Identify the phase of engagement the client is in (i.e. engagement, negotiating behaviour change, early relapse prevention, relapse prevention management; Graham *et al.* 2004; Mueser *et al.* 1998).
3 What is the function of the client's current substance use?
4 What are the client's current substance-related beliefs?
5 What are the client's goals for treatment; what are the team's goals of intervention?
6 What are the agreed interventions and who will implement them?

key tasks of the supervisor are to facilitate the development of team members' skills and to integrate the delivery of interventions for clients with co-existing mental health and drug and alcohol problems within the team. The supervisor therefore has an important role to play in ensuring that the sessions are effective and that team members find them beneficial.

Prior to the team session, the supervisor should agree with the team a case to be discussed. Before the session, the case is then discussed between the case's care co-ordinator and the supervisor. The care co-ordinator should then have the opportunity to prepare a brief summary of the case, which will include background, current circumstances, the links between the person's mental health and problematic substance use and a formulation of the case (Beck *et al.* 1993).

Following an introduction by the supervisor, the session starts with an outline of the case to be discussed, presented by the care co-ordinator. The discussion is then opened up to the team. To facilitate this process the supervisor refers to the treatment planning template (Table 19.1) to structure the session. It is important at the early stages of the supervision to encourage the team to identify the client's stage of change and engagement. This helps the team to ensure that the plan they develop through the session will include interventions best placed to meet the needs of the client. Facilitating an open discussion, the supervisor guides the team to reach an agreement on these points, as well as encouraging discussion around the evidence and rationale for their decisions.

The supervisor aims to engage the team to consider the function of the client's alcohol and drug use and to identify the client's substance-related beliefs. This encourages the team to develop an understanding of the client's substance use and the part it plays in the context of the client's life. Facilitating discussion around the client's substance-related beliefs is important in getting the team to understand the cognitions that may maintain a problematic cycle of substance use (e.g. 'I can't socialize without alcohol'). Part of treatment planning may include strategies to help the client to re-evaluate these beliefs in order to enhance the process of change.

Identifying goals for treatment

The supervisor should direct the team to identify clearly both the team's goals for the interventions that will be provided, and the client's goals for treatment. Client goals should be discussed with the client prior to the supervision session. This is important in terms of treatment planning and also in identifying any differences that might arise between the team and the client. For example, a client may be at the precontemplation stage of change regarding their substance use and may not view their use as problematic. The team might work towards engaging the client in discussing their substance use and build on motivation towards change. It is important that the supervisor encourages team awareness of these issues and facilitates a discussion addressing how the team can work with the client in addressing any differences, preferably avoiding or at least minimizing a negative effect on the client's engagement and involvement in the treatment process.

Treatment planning

The final stage of supervision involves agreeing a treatment plan based on the team discussion. An important task for the supervisor is to ensure that the client's views are considered in the formulation of the treatment plan. The supervisor needs to guide the team in order to enable team members to be clear on the aims and objectives of the plan. With regard to intervention, team members should be encouraged to identify who will take responsibility for different areas identified. This is important, as treatment plans should have a focus not only on problematic substance use but also on areas including social networks, occupational/recreational activities, harm reduction steps, mental health interventions and other interventions based on the client's needs.

In summary, the overall aim of the supervision session is to facilitate a process by which team members agree a plan that can be implemented and reviewed by the team at a later pre-defined time. However, there may be occasions when the outcome of the supervision session will require further assessment or discussion with the client, thus ensuring as effective a plan as possible based on a formulation of the case. The supervisor should encourage the team to see this as a positive outcome, as it is very unlikely that a treatment plan can be identified if there is not enough available information to base it on. This also helps the team to focus on working in a structured way with clients and enhances the philosophy of integrated treatment.

Addressing conflict

The structure outlined so far allows the supervisor to focus the sessions with the team and to bring them to a clear conclusion with an agreed treatment plan. This format does not, however, guarantee that conflict or disagreement will not occur within the supervision sessions. The supervisor needs to be aware of this and identify strategies that will enable conflict to be addressed should it arise. Conflict may occur within team supervision sessions for a number of reasons, including differences of opinion among team members regarding interventions, opposing perceptions of the client's substance use, frustration due to ongoing difficulties with engaging the client and frustration with ongoing problematic substance use with little change over time. In addition, different professionals within the team may have different approaches to addressing particular issues with the client.

From the supervisor's perspective, conflict within a supervision session should not necessarily be viewed as a negative occurrence. Differences in opinion and approaches can enhance the session and lead to a more comprehensive discussion, which the supervisor should aim to facilitate. Conversely, conflict may increase the likelihood that a constructive outcome will not be reached, and the supervisor needs to address such situations. All team members should have the opportunity to express their views, to be listened to and to give a rationale for their views. The supervisor should encourage opposing views to be expressed in a constructive and respectful way. The supervisor is trained to understand and acknowledge the validity of different points of view, while seeking a compromise position which can be reviewed at the next session. It is useful for the supervisor to provide brief summaries of the discussion as it progresses, ensuring that everyone is clear on what has been said or suggested. The supervisor should remain objective and aim to keep the session focused. Once it is clear that a particular issue has been sufficiently discussed, the supervisor should encourage the team to make a decision. If there is a difference in opinion at the end of the session, the supervisor should encourage the team to acknowledge this but guide them to agree a plan that can be discussed with the client and reviewed. There are cases where the supervisor can be challenged by the team or team members or some of the supervisees may be displaying disengaged behaviours. It is important to explore the thoughts that may be giving rise to these behaviours: 'This intervention is not going to work'; 'I know best'; or 'I am already doing what you suggest.' Such thoughts should be explored before further progress can be made. Some of these issues will be addressed further in the case examples later in the chapter.

Rating sessions

In order to monitor the effectiveness of team supervision it is important to have a method to evaluate supervision sessions. During our evaluation of C-BIT (Graham *et al.* 2006) we used a three-point scale to monitor the components of C-BIT used during supervision sessions. An independent non-participant observer rated on a three-point scale the extent to which each of the assessment phase, four main treatment components (engagement, education, motivation, relapse prevention) and two additional components (skills building, family/network strategies) of the approach were being utilized in the case discussion during the team supervision session. The ratings were 1 ('No attempt made to deliver the component'), 2 ('The component is delivered in an incomplete manner/is not matched to the client's needs') and 3 ('Comprehensive attempts are made at delivering the component'; 'gold standard'). All of these components may not be applicable in every session. However they are useful in identifying the interventions utilized and identifying areas that clinicians may need to focus on, within an agreed treatment plan.

One aim of team supervision is to encourage the team to agree on a treatment plan that team members feel they can implement in a consistent and focused way in collaboration with individual clients. It is helpful to get feedback from the team at the end of supervision sessions to enable team members to express their views and resolve any outstanding issues. As far as possible, team supervision sessions should end on a positive note. In addition, as part of future developments, we are starting to discuss with the teams the use of video recording of client sessions for supervision purposes in order to explore and discuss practice. This method of supervision is increasingly used in addiction treatment and was successfully implemented in the United Kingdom Alcohol Treatment Trial (Tober *et al.* 2005; UKATT Research Team 2005).

CASE STUDIES

The remainder of this chapter will focus on two case studies. Names and details of the clients discussed have been changed to maintain confidentiality. The team supervision session for each case is outlined and followed by the treatment plan agreed by team members at the close of the session. These cases have been chosen to illustrate some of the issues described and discussed in previous sections of this chapter.

Paul

Paul was a 48-year-old man with a mental health diagnosis of schizophrenia. He also had a long history of problematic alcohol use. He was divorced and had two grown-up sons with whom he had little contact. Paul lived alone in a council flat. He spent a lot of time caring for his elderly father and this had started to put him under a lot of strain. More recently, Paul had started to experience frequent lapses in his alcohol use leading to a binge pattern of use. Although Paul had achieved periods of abstinence in the past he did not view this as a positive achievement: 'I am less sociable without alcohol and spend most of my time alone.' Paul always felt very guilty following periods of alcohol use and believed that he lets himself, his family and the team down when he drank.

Prior to the team arranging the supervision session, Paul's alcohol use had become problematic and it was difficult for the team to engage him as he was spending most of his time out. The purpose of supervision was to help the team to agree a treatment plan in order to re-engage Paul, to assist him with his presenting difficulties and to build on his motivation to address his problematic alcohol use.

Following a brief presentation at the start of supervision the team was encouraged to identify the triggers for Paul's most recent lapse. Four triggers were identified: the stress of looking after his elderly father, his son being given a prison sentence, pressure from his family to maintain his caring role and feelings of social isolation. Identifying these triggers helped to identify the start of a chain of events that led to a problematic cycle of use. Discussion of Paul's case focused around the treatment planning template with an open discussion among the team. The agreed treatment plan is outlined in Table 19.2.

Debbie

Debbie was a 28-year-old woman with a diagnosis of bipolar affective disorder. Debbie had a long history of problematic crack cocaine use, which led to a chaotic lifestyle and resulted in Debbie working in prostitution to fund her use. Debbie had a rather strained relationship with her family and her social network consisted mainly of other users. Although Debbie had a flat, she tended to spend most of her time at various friends' houses, which contributed to difficulties with treatment engagement. Debbie had one child who was taken into local authority care and subsequently adopted.

Due to Debbie's lifestyle, there were periods when the team did not know where she was and she did not contact them. She usually made contact while in a crisis – after having been arrested, for example, or when she had no money or nowhere to live as her own flat was being used as a crack house. Debbie had a good relationship with some members of the team but viewed other team members as 'not being supportive'.

The aim of the supervision session was to facilitate a team discussion about Debbie's case and to agree a treatment plan that would enhance Debbie's engagement with the team in order to help Debbie address her crack cocaine use. During supervision it became clear that some members of the team felt angry about working with Debbie due to her somewhat chaotic presentation and frequent crises. They felt that Debbie took up a disproportionate amount of the team's time. Most team members believed that this was a result of her problematic crack cocaine use and not of her mental health problems. While it was important that everyone had the opportunity to contribute to the session, the supervisor's aim was to keep the session focused towards a positive outcome. Once issues raised had been discussed, and despite the differences in opinion, the supervisor facilitated a discussion towards an agreed treatment plan. The focus was on aiming to meet the needs of the client and enabling the team to work in a consistent and constructive way, which enhanced engagement in both mental health and substance use issues. At the end of this session the team agreed a treatment plan as outlined in Table 19.3. Although there were differences in opinion, the team still agreed a plan that would be reviewed at the next session.

In both of the cases outlined, the process followed enabled the team to agree treatment plans which were felt to be realistic. Despite disagreement among the team in Debbie's case, the supervisor managed to facilitate a

Table 19.2 Paul's treatment plan

Stage of change	Stage of engagement	Function of use	Beliefs	Goals	Interventions
Contemplation	Negotiating behaviour change	To feel sociable with friends To cope with stress and worries To feel good	'Alcohol makes me feel good' 'Alcohol eases my pain' 'I can't be sociable without alcohol'	*Client* To reduce alcohol use To build bridges with family To be able to socialize without alcohol To cope with problems without alcohol *Team* To increase engagement To support Paul To reduce alcohol use and achieve abstinence To build a rapport with Paul's family To identify Paul's social and recreational needs	Identify and agree achievable harm reduction goals with Paul (care co-ordinator) Identify activities of interest to enhance Paul's social contact (team) Liaise with family members and include them in interventions with Paul's agreement (care co-ordinator and Paul) Set some behavioural experiments with Paul to enhance process of change (care co-ordinator) Support Paul to make contact with his son via a letter (care co-ordinator)

Table 19.3 Debbie's treatment plan

Stage of change	Stage of engagement	Function of use	Beliefs	Goals	Interventions
Precontemplation	Engagement	To feel good To cope with problems in life To be part of a social network To occupy time	'Crack is the only thing that makes me feel good' 'Crack makes me forget my problems' 'Everyone I know uses' 'If I stop using crack I will not be able to cope with all the stress in my life'	Client To get stable accommodation To sort out finances To 'sort my head out' Team To establish more regular engagement with Debbie To build Debbie's motivation to make changes in her crack use To support Debbie to gain stable accommodation To support Debbie addressing stressful events in her life	Apply for appropriate accommodation (care co-ordinator) Arrange two planned visits per week (team) Plan sessions to discuss Debbie's issues and aim to re-evaluate positive substance-related beliefs (care co-ordinator) Build motivation to address crack cocaine use through analysis of advantages/disadvantages pros/cons of change (care co-ordinator)

constructive outcome. It is important that team members have the opportunity to express their views and to share ideas towards a comprehensive plan, particularly when cases are complex and challenging. Having a structure to work to, enabled the team to develop treatment plans that considered the client's stage of change and of engagement. In turn, this helped team members, through discussion and exploration of interventions best placed to meet the client's needs at that point in time. Given that the clients discussed were at the contemplation and precontemplation stages of change, the focus of interventions was to enhance engagement and build on motivation to change. Implementing these plans enabled the team to work towards realistic goals which could then be developed to address the clients' needs in terms of life experiences and, importantly, the relationship between these, their mental health and their problematic substance use.

CONCLUSION

We conclude that working with this complex client group requires a good level of training as a basic platform followed by ongoing regular supervision. We have argued in this chapter that when working with complex cases that have combined mental health and alcohol/drug problems, we need to use intervention strategies that integrate mental health and substance misuse treatment and are delivered by the same team. Supervision arrangements need to reflect this need and are a key component of these services. Based on our work, we believe that the whole team should receive regular team supervision sessions as described in this chapter. Taking a structured approach to the team supervision sessions is helpful for the supervisor and the team members. Supervision should be scheduled and become a regular component of the team's work, and should be considered an essential part of the service.

KEY RESOURCES

Graham, H. L., Copello, A., Birchwood, M. J., Mueser, K., Orford, J., McGovern, D. et al., *Cognitive-Behavioural Integrated Treatment (C-BIT): A Treatment Manual for Substance Misuse in People with Severe Mental Health Problems*. Chichester: John Wiley, 2004.

Hawkins, P., and Shohet, R., *Supervision in the Helping Professions*, 2nd ed. Maidenhead: Open University Press, 2000.

Walker, M. and Jacobs, M., *Supervision: Questions and Answers for Counsellors and Therapists*. London: Whurr, 2004.

REFERENCES

Beck, A. T., 'Cognitive therapy: A sign of retrogression or progress', *Behaviour Therapist*, 9, 2–3, 1986.

Beck, A. T., Wright, F. D., Newman, C. F. and Liese, B. S., *Cognitive Therapy of Substance Abuse*. New York: Guilford Press, 1993.

Cartwright, A., 'The attitudes of helping agents towards the alcoholic client: The influence of experience, support, training and self-esteem', *British Journal of Addiction*, 75, 413–31, 1980.

Copello, A., Graham, H. L. and Birchwood, M. J., 'Evaluating substance misuse interventions in psychosis: The limitations of the RCT with "patient" as the unit of analysis', *Journal of Mental Health*, 10, 585–7, 2001.

Dryden, W. and Thorne, B., *Training and Supervision for Counselling in Action*. London: Sage, 2004.

Graham, H. L., 'Implementing integrated treatment for co-existing substance use and severe mental health problems in assertive outreach teams: Training issues', *Drug and Alcohol Review*, 23, 463–70, 2004.

Graham, H. L., Copello, A., Birchwood, M. J., Mueser, K. T., Orford, J., McGovern, D. et al., *Cognitive-Behavioural Integrated Treatment (C-BIT): A Treatment Manual for Substance Misuse in People with Severe Mental Health Problems*. Chichester: John Wiley, 2004.

Graham, H. L., Copello, A., Birchwood, M. J., Orford, J., McGovern, D., Georgiou, G. and Godfrey, E., 'Co-existing severe mental health and substance use problems: Developing integrated services in the UK', *Psychiatric Bulletin*, 27, 183–6, 2003.

Graham, H. L., Copello, A., Birchwood, M. J., Orford, J., McGovern, D., Mueser, K. T. et al., 'A preliminary evaluation of integrated treatment for co-existing substance use and severe mental health problems: Impact on teams and service users', *Journal of Mental Health*, 15, 577–91, 2006.

Graham, H. L., Maslin, J., Copello, A., Birchwood, M. J., Mueser, K. T., McGovern, D. and Georgiou, G., 'Drug and alcohol problems amongst individuals with severe mental health problems in an inner city area of the UK', *Journal of Social Psychiatry and Psychiatric Epidemiology*, 36, 448–55, 2001.

Hawkins, P. and Shohet, R., *Supervision in the Helping Professions*, 2nd ed. Maidenhead: Open University Press, 2000.

Heather, N., Wodak, A., Nadelman, E. and O'Hare, P., *Psychoactive Drugs and Harm Reduction: From Faith to Science*. London: Whurr, 1993.

Kavanagh, D., Spence, S., Wilson, J. and Crow, N., 'Achieving effective supervision', *Drug and Alcohol Review*, 21, 247–52, 2002.

Marlatt, G. A., *Harm Reduction: Pragmatic Strategies for Managing High-Risk Behaviours*. New York: Guilford Press, 1998.

Maslin, J., Graham, H. L., Cawley, M., Copello, A., Birchwood, M. J., Georgiou, G. et al., 'Combined severe mental health and substance use problems: What are the training and support needs of a staff working with this client group?' *Journal of Mental Health*, 19, 131–40, 2001.

Miller, W. R. and Mount, K. A., 'A small study of training in motivational interviewing: Does one workshop change clinician and client behaviour?' *Behavioural and Cognitive Psychotherapy*, 29, 457–71, 2001.

Milne, D., Gorenski, O., Westerman, C., Leck, C. and Keegan, D., 'What does it take to transfer training?' *Psychiatric Rehabilitation Skills*, *4*, 259–81, 2000.

Mueser, K., Drake, R. and Noordsy, L., 'Integrated mental health and substance abuse treatment for severe psychiatric disorders', *Journal of Practical Psychiatry and Behavioural Health*, *4*, 129–39, 1998.

Nelson-Jones, R., *Theory and Practice of Counselling and Therapy*, 3rd ed. London: Sage, 2003.

Prochaska, J. O., DiClemente, C. C. and Norcross, J. C., 'In search of how people change: Applications to addictive behaviours', *American Psychologist*, *47*, 1102–14, 1992.

Spence, S., Wilson, J., Kavanagh, D., Strong, J. and Worrall, L., 'Clinical supervision in four mental health professions: A review of the evidence', *Behaviour Change*, *18*, 135–55, 2001.

Tober, G., Godfrey, E., Parrott, S., Copello, A., Farrin, A., Hodgson, R. *et al.*, 'Setting standards for training and competence: The UK Alcohol Treatment Trial', *Alcohol and Alcoholism*, *40*, 413–8, 2005.

UKATT Research Team, 'Effectiveness of treatment for alcohol problems: Findings of the randomised UK Alcohol Treatment Trial (UKATT)', *British Medical Journal*, *331*, 541–4, 2005.

Chapter 20

Where to from here?

Amanda Baker and Richard Velleman

We have provided practical chapters which are clinically relevant, which clinicians can pick up and use relatively quickly. In doing so, we have deliberately not emphasized theoretical issues. As the evidence base for most co-existing mental health and drug and alcohol problems is only just emerging, we recognize that many of the recommendations made in this book will require revision as further evidence is gathered. In this chapter we highlight some of the central and common themes that have emerged across the chapters of this book. The fact that there are common themes here is all the more remarkable, given that they have cropped up in relation to disparate clinical topics and from clinicians in various settings and different countries with very different health services. We also take the opportunity to discuss ideas for further research and clinical innovation.

COMMON THEMES

High prevalence necessitates an overall broad approach to co-existing problems

Several chapters have commented upon the high prevalence of co-existing mental health and drug and alcohol problems, and implications for practice. In Chapter 2, Richard Velleman pointed out that the range of practitioners who may potentially be involved in interventions with people with co-existing problems is necessarily broad and not limited only to specialists in drug and alcohol and mental health settings. One overall approach to co-existing problems which is likely to work well, discussed by Amanda Baker and colleagues in Chapter 1, is a stepped care model, with inexpensive, low-intensity interventions at initial stages and more intensive and expensive interventions reserved for those who do not respond sufficiently. Stepped care approaches were particularly recommended for the high prevalence disorders of anxiety and depression with co-existing drug and alcohol problems (Chapters 11 and 12) and in rural areas (Chapter 9).

One challenge will be training staff to adopt an optimistic and early approach to co-existing problems, with provision of ongoing screening and monitoring so that care can be stepped up or down in flexible and responsive ways. A common suggestion has been to intervene in mental health and drug and alcohol problems that may not meet formal diagnostic criteria for diagnosis. For example, in Chapter 15, Jennifer Coelho and colleagues recommended that clinicians should screen for sub-clinical eating disorder presentations in the hope that early detection and treatment may prevent the development of clinical conditions. Screening and brief interventions for hazardous drinking have been effective and it is likely that they may be helpful for some mental health symptoms as well.

A common overall approach: harm reduction focus, case formulation-based and integrated

Most chapters (e.g. Chapter 15 on eating disorders) have commented on the dearth of literature regarding effective treatment, noting that people with co-existing drug and alcohol problems have routinely been excluded from studies of mental health problems, that people with serious mental health problems have usually been excluded from studies of drug or alcohol problems, and that people with certain mental health problems (e.g. personality disorders, Chapter 16) have often been excluded from clinical research on either other mental health or drug and alcohol problems.

Clinical wisdom from various chapters suggests the following. First, it is often difficult to disentangle primary from secondary problems (e.g. Chapters 12 and 16). By the time a client is assessed it is often the case that mental disorder and drug and alcohol problems have been concurrent for many years, hence both mental health and drug and alcohol problems need to be addressed. Too great an emphasis on determining primary diagnosis can often be counter-productive and reinforces the system of constant cross-referral between services, something which so many people with co-existing problems experience as so unhelpful. In fact, the chapters in this book underline the importance of a good assessment and formulation, which teases out these often complex interrelationships and clarifies whether the problems are related or simply co-occurring. Even when the chronological sequence of progression can be identified, it may be misleading in implying cause or effect between different disorders (e.g. Chapter 14).

All chapters recommend an integrated approach, in which both mental health and drug and alcohol problems are treated by the same clinician, based on a case formulation. Such an approach is more respectful of the client, in that they are treated as a whole person with complex and interrelated issues.

By definition there are at least two problems to be dealt with, but the order in which they are tackled may vary. For co-existing anxiety and drug and alcohol problems (Chapter 11), where there is somewhat more evidence than for other co-existing problems, Andrew Baillie and Claudia Sannibale recommend that if the client can abstain from alcohol, then the alcohol problem should be treated first. They recommend an integrated approach to both problems if abstinence is not possible for the individual. In all cases, chapter authors recommend deciding on which problems to deal with first, or on whether to deal with problems concurrently, in collaboration with the client as opposed to via therapist edict. Where a team is involved in treatment, the treating team should aim to address all the presenting problems (e.g. Chapter 14). A harm reduction rather than abstinence-based approach, whereby any decision to change substance misuse is left up to the client (e.g. Chapter 13) and is placed within the context of other self-identified goals, which may involve practical or other issues, has generally been recommended (e.g. Chapters 7, 10 and 13).

Common intervention strategies

Therapist characteristics were universally identified across all chapters as vitally important to effective therapy. Respect for the client, empathy, optimism and a non-confrontational demeanor are regarded as essential foundations for intervention. Working with clients with co-existing problems is often difficult and attendance can be erratic. Engagement may need to be enhanced by not setting too many rules, flexibility regarding appointments and willingness to stay with clients over rocky periods. In particular, in the case of people with severe mental health problems (Chapters 13 and 14), people with learning disability (Chapter 17) and people who are homeless (Chapter 10), designated staff working across separate services are recommended to help, train and supervise staff within these separate services, and act as mediator (and advocate) for the client, to ensure that clients with co-existing problems can access the level and variety of help which is on offer to clients with only a single problem in each separate service.

Chapters in this book have also emphasized common processes in therapy. Some of these issues are so central that whole chapters have been devoted to them (e.g. Chapter 3 on motivational interviewing [MI], Chapter 4 on cognitive behaviour therapy [CBT], Chapter 5 on family work, Chapter 7 on consultation and liaison, Chapter 18 on training and Chapter 19 on supervision), but the same issues recur in many other chapters too. Common features have included an awareness of the stages of change, a formulation-driven approach, involvement of family and significant others, and the need for clinician training and supervision, which we discuss later in this chapter. MI and an emphasis on client determination of goals and speed of change have been employed in each chapter in preparation for change and throughout intervention, to enhance optimism and bolster change attempts. For the action stage, many of the chapters recommend CBT (see Chapter 4; also for co-existing drug and alcohol problems and anxiety, Chapter 11; depression, Chapter 12; or psychosis, Chapters 13 and 14) or dialectical behaviour therapy (DBT; for co-existing personality and substance use disorders, see Chapter 16). Some recommend a combination of strategies, linking ideas from both DBT (building up client commitment to therapy, building up the relationship between client and therapist) and CBT (the emphasis on clear tasks and steps, homework, providing structure, etc.). For example, the treatment described for co-existing eating and substance use disorders (Chapter 15) included schema-focused therapy and DBT, in addition to MI and CBT, within the possible context of an inpatient stay involving psycho-dynamic treatment. Whatever the therapy approaches used, all chapters recommend that both mental health and drug and alcohol problems be assessed and directly treated. While most chapters describe individual therapy, group interventions for co-existing mental health and drug and alcohol problems (Chapter 6) may be useful in many clinical settings.

Training and supervision

Many authors in this book argue that training should not be an isolated optional extra. As discussed in Chapters 2 and 18, it is clear that many mental health staff know little about drug and alcohol problems and vice versa. Training (at least at an awareness level) is vital for all levels of staff, and in all disciplines and professions. Staff must know enough to screen mental health and substance use domains, to know what services exist for people with co-existing problems, and at least know how to refer on to these services. In services which offer help to people with co-existing or multiple problems, higher levels of training are needed: without good training we cannot provide good clinical interventions.

In addition to training, good institutional support is essential for staff working with co-existing problems. Support may include memoranda of understanding that line managers support clinical work which addresses co-existing problems and the provision of resources for supervision. Supervision can take place at two levels: individual and team (as described in Chapter 19). The whole team offering services to people with co-existing problems should receive regular team supervision sessions, using a structured approach, scheduled as a regular and essential component of the team's work. Individuals also need high levels of supervision and support with often difficult cases. Individual supervision should focus on cases where clinicians are experiencing difficulties. Individual supervision needs to work at a number of levels: it needs to be formal, scheduled and regular; it should provide an opportunity for the clinician to develop and explore, in a number of ways including the development of skills and understanding, his or her therapeutic work; it should help the clinician to develop self-awareness, insofar as this affects the quality of the therapeutic work; issues and difficulties for the clinicians or clients can be explored in sessions; and the client and the agency are protected through this monitoring of the clinician's work. Effective support and supervision is based on trust. Clinicians must feel able to disclose things during supervision which they might not tell other people – for example, feelings of incompetence, mistakes made, annoyance with the organization or frustration with their manager. The supervisor needs to help the clinician focus on the issues, rather than skirt around the edges: instead of allowing the clinician to recount, at great length, the case history which the clinician has painstakingly extracted from the client, supervision needs to get the clinician to focus on the issues that this client has thrown up for him or her, via questions such as: 'What are you actually doing with this client?'; 'What are your plans?'; and 'What are the difficulties which have emerged for you in the sessions so far?' Or the supervisor might focus on the clinician's understanding of the problem as opposed to his or her goals; or focus on the clinician's feelings for the client and how these might interact with the work which is being attempted.

FUTURE RESEARCH

In terms of randomized controlled trials (RCTs), interventions for people with co-existing problems remain virtually a greenfield site. RCTs of interventions among people with co-existing mental and substance use disorders are urgently needed.

Meanwhile, while we await RCTs for co-existing problems, rather than routinely excluding people with co-existing problems from research trials, mental health and drug and alcohol use should be assessed among research participants and related to treatment outcome. Results would thus be more generalizable to clinical presentations in real-world settings. As stated below, interventions for smoking among people with mental health problems are also needed.

In addition to RCTs, more detailed process studies should be conducted, including studies taking qualitative approaches, examining in more detail people's progress through often multiple and long-running encounters with mental health and other helping services. Long-term outcomes could be monitored, yielding naturalistic longitudinal data with which to evaluate overall progress through services and people's abilities to cope with multiple problems.

In at least a proportion of people, mental health and co-existing drug and alcohol problems may be unrelated, with the co-occurrence simply representing the co-probability of two otherwise unrelated disorders. Regardless of the relationship between problems, and despite the common recommendation in this volume for integrated interventions, interventions for separate problems delivered by different clinicians, either sequentially or in parallel, may also be feasible for some co-existing problems. Comparisons of integrated versus single focus treatments will be of great interest.

Although smoking is increasingly recognized as problematic among many of the client groups described in this volume (e.g. among people with anorexia, psychoses and depression), smoking has not usually been included in the literature concerning co-existing mental health and drug and alcohol problems. By and large, treatment studies have focused on alcohol and the illicit drugs, while the very high prevalence of tobacco smoking has been ignored. This is of concern because smoking is associated not only with health problems, but also with significant impact on the financial circumstances and quality of life of people with mental health and/or drug and alcohol problems. While rates of smoking are declining in the general community, rates among people with mental health and drug and alcohol problems remain very high. The reasons for this and interventions to reduce these smoking rates should be the focus of future research.

CONCLUSION

How best could we measure whether this book has been of benefit to practitioners? Applying the concept of 'readiness to intervene', we will have done well if the reader's sense of the importance of intervening with co-existing problems, and confidence in doing so, is enhanced. We have not sought to provide a panacea for co-existing problems and although we have generally recommended an integrated approach, future research may lead us to revise this recommendation. More important is that clinicians feel enabled to screen and assess for mental health and drug and alcohol problems, and to address both areas within the context of an empathic, non-judgmental and collaborative intervention.

On a wider front, the fact is that co-existing substance and mental health problems are a 'Cinderella' area within both drug and alcohol and mental health services. This is increasingly difficult for services and policy-makers to countenance, as prevalence rates of such co-existing problems rise. A good place to end this book is with part of the consensus conference statement from a major meeting on co-existing problems held in the USA in November, 2003. Participants included 43 experts in psychiatry, psychology, addiction treatment, health care policy, primary care, adolescent health, epidemiology and advocacy, drawn from across the USA, and all of them approved the final version of their consensus statement. Its conclusions stated:

> The needs of persons with co-occurring mental and substance use disorders must be addressed immediately, and long-range planning should be undertaken to improve treatment, access to care, parity, and professional training. There was overwhelming consensus among the experts at

the conference that integrated treatment for co-occurring mental and substance use disorders must be recognized as the standard of care, particularly for non-responding or severely ill patients. This was perhaps the strongest statement made by the participants as a group. In addition, participants agreed on the following:

- Co-occurring mental and substance use disorders are highly prevalent
- The precise burden of co-occurring mental and substance use disorders is not known
- Persons with co-occurring mental and substance use disorders are as deserving of accessible, effective, simultaneous care as are those with other disabling, chronic illnesses
- Medication, psychosocial, and self-help modalities are available that show promise of effectiveness, but data to inform treatment are relatively scarce
- There is a severe shortage of trained clinicians and services. The different elements of the health care system, including legislative bodies, governmental agencies, health care educators, pharmaceutical industry, and health care professionals, have not taken adequate responsibility for the care of patients with co-occurring mental and substance use disorders.

(O'Brien *et al.* 2004: 707)

Our aspiration for this book is that practitioners will find the distilled research and experience contained within these chapters clinically useful, and that the more effective practice that will flow from this will serve to encourage policy-makers, service organizers and those responsible for professional training and continued professional development to provide the attention and longer-term planning that this population of people with co-existing mental health and drug and alcohol problems so clearly need and deserve.

REFERENCE

O'Brien, C., Charney, D., Lewis, L., Cornish, J. W., Post, R. M., Woody, G. E. *et al.*, 'Priority actions to improve the care of persons with co-occurring substance abuse and other mental disorders: A call to action', *Biological Psychiatry*, *56*, 703–13, 2004.

Index